Business and Management in Asia: Opportunities and Entrepreneurship

Tobias Endress · Yuosre F. Badir
Editors

Business and Management in Asia: Opportunities and Entrepreneurship

Springer

Editors
Tobias Endress
School of Management
Asian Institute of Technology
Bangkok, Thailand

Yuosre F. Badir
School of Management
Asian Institute of Technology
Bangkok, Thailand

ISBN 978-981-95-4908-5 ISBN 978-981-95-4909-2 (eBook)
https://doi.org/10.1007/978-981-95-4909-2

This Springer imprint is published by the registered company Springer Nature Singapore Pte Ltd.
The registered company address is: 152 Beach Road, #21-01/04 Gateway East, Singapore 189721, Singapore

Preface

Dear Reader,

Asia's entrepreneurial landscape continues to be one of the most dynamic and influential in the world. From high-tech innovation hubs to grassroots enterprises, the region is shaping the future of business by blending tradition with cutting-edge technology. This volume of the Business and Management in Asia series focuses on Entrepreneurship and Opportunities, with a particular emphasis on how innovation, sustainability, and digital transformation are redefining the entrepreneurial ecosystem.

As Asian markets evolve, entrepreneurs are navigating rapid technological change, social transformation, and new economic paradigms. Opportunities abound across sectors—whether in sustainability, agritech, fintech, supply chains, e-commerce, or artificial intelligence—but so too do challenges that demand resilience, creativity, and foresight. The chapters in this book highlight diverse perspectives, offering both practical insights and scholarly analysis to illuminate how entrepreneurs across Asia are seizing opportunities and overcoming barriers.

This book comprises 17 chapters, each exploring a unique facet of Asia's entrepreneurial energy:

Chapter "The Future of Entrepreneurship in Asia", by Archana Parashar and Tanvi Gupta, examines how tech innovations and market disruptions are reshaping Asia's growth strategies.

Chapter "The Rise of Asian Startups", by Tobias Endress, provides a comparative analysis of ecosystem performance and international rankings. It highlights emerging hubs and innovation hotspots that are driving regional momentum.

Chapter "Emotional Intelligence in Asian Business Leadership", by Anu Dandona, demonstrates to business leaders how to utilize emotional intelligence to enhance productivity, foster better workplace relationships, and achieve long-term success.

Chapter "The Link Between Emotional Intelligence and Knowledge Sharing Behavior. Why Should High-Tech Firms in Asia Care?", by Syed M.H. Bokhari, Lakeesha Ransom, and Djoen San Santoso, reveals why high-tech firms in emerging markets must care about EQ.

Chapter "Scaling Frugal Innovation-Based Startups", by Amrita Baid More, shows how resource-light ventures can accelerate sustainable development.

Chapter "Circular Economy in Asia: A Comparative Policy and Startup Review", by Jacob Stalk and Won-Yong Oh, compares how Asian ventures are pioneering circular business models and entrepreneurial ecosystems. This chapter demonstrates that startups are not only enablers of CE practices but also critical intermediaries between policy and behavior.

Chapter "Circular Economy Initiatives: Harnessing the Potential of Countries in Asia", by Tareq Mahbub, discusses the untapped potential of regional policies and practices.

Chapter "Foodmandu: From Clicks to Cuisine", by Jashim Uddin Ahmed et al., tells the story of Nepal's booming online food delivery sector and explains the "4C Strategic matrix" as an adaptable tool for managers.

Chapter "Invisible Enterprises", by Shradha Adhikari and Krishna Khanal, uncovers the overlooked contributions of home-based women entrepreneurs in Nepal and pathways to empowerment.

Chapter "Catalyzing Asian Women's Entrepreneurship in the E-Commerce Ecosystem: A Case Report and Policy Analysis of Cambodia", by Ronnie Rith and Riccardo Spinelli, offers a Cambodian case study and policy analysis. It also discusses existing opportunities, challenges, and initiatives for women-led MSMEs.

Chapter "From Istanbul to Singapore", by Deniz Tunçalp, shares insights on HQ relocation and strategic positioning in Asia's tech ecosystem.

Chapter "Benchmarking Supply Chain Performance", by Ananya Hadadi Raghavendra, provides financial insights into India's entrepreneurial growth.

Chapter "Agritech Ventures in India", by Sujana Adapa and Subba Reddy Yarram, explores opportunities and challenges in transforming agriculture with technology, outlining how agritech presents a significant opportunity due to rapid growth, optimisation, and market efficiencies.

Chapter "Automating Finance", by Deepika Dhingra and Jaskiran Arora, examines the growing role of robotic process automation in financial services and how this is creating opportunities for startups.

Chapter "Beyond Borders", by Pravin Kumar, celebrates Asian entrepreneurs driving innovation and impact on the global stage.

Chapter "Financing Opportunities in Central Asian Emerging Markets", by Iakov Sadchikov, provides a systematic analysis of financing mechanisms ranging from state-led initiatives like QazInnovations' innovation grants to private sector transformations exemplified by Kaspi.kz's sixteen billion dollar valuation, the chapter identifies three transferable lessons for emerging markets.

Chapter "Exploring Entrepreneurial Opportunity in Japan's AI Landscape", by Hajer Najeh, analyses the role of AI in shaping Japanese entrepreneurship.

Building on the success of the first three Business and Management in Asia volumes—*Digital Innovation and Sustainability* (2023), *Disruption and Change* (2024), and *Finance and Investments in the Digital Age* (2025)—this fourth edition continues our commitment to bridging research and practice in Asian context. It serves as both a guide and an inspiration—enabling business professionals, policy-makers, and academics to benchmark strategies, learn from real-world cases, and envision the future of entrepreneurship in Asia.

As editors, we are deeply grateful to the contributors whose work has made this volume possible. Their insights reflect not only academic rigor but also lived experience in one of the world's most vibrant business environments. We hope this book will inspire readers to embrace new ideas, foster collaboration, and drive sustainable entrepreneurial growth across Asia and beyond.

With best regards,

Bangkok, Thailand
August 2025

Tobias Endress
Yuosre F. Badir

Contents

The Future of Entrepreneurship in Asia: Tech Innovations, Market Disruptions, and Growth Strategies 1
Archana Parashar and Tanvi Gupta

The Rise of Asian Startups: Innovation Hubs and Hotspots 19
Tobias Endress

Emotional Intelligence in Asian Business Leadership: A Key to Sustainable Success 37
Anu Dandona

The Link Between Emotional Intelligence and Knowledge Sharing Behavior. Why Should High-Tech Firms in Asia Care? 59
Syed Muntasir Husain Bokhari, Lakeesha K. Ransom, and Djoen San Santoso

Scaling Frugal Innovation-Based Startups to Accelerate Sustainable Development 71
Amrita Baid More and Arpan Shrivastava

Circular Economy in Asia: A Comparative Policy and Startup Review 95
Jacob Stalk and Won-Yong Oh

Circular Economy Initiatives: Harnessing the Potential of Countries in Asia 113
Tareq Mahbub

Foodmandu: From Clicks to Cuisine in Nepal's Food Industry 135
Jashim Uddin Ahmed, Anisur R. Faroque, Samsul Islam, and Shashi Shekhar Acharya

Invisible Enterprises: The Unrecognized Contribution of Home-Based Women Entrepreneurs in Nepal 153
Shradha Adhikari and Krishna Khanal

Catalyzing Asian Women's Entrepreneurship in the E-Commerce Ecosystem: A Case Report and Policy Analysis of Cambodia 167
Rongtitya Rith and Riccardo Spinelli

From Istanbul to Singapore: Insider's Headquarters Relocation and Strategic Positioning in Asia's Tech Ecosystem 193
Deniz Tunçalp

Benchmarking Supply Chain Performance for Entrepreneurial Growth: Financial Insights from Key Industries in India 211
Ananya Hadadi Raghavendra

Agritech Ventures in India: Impact of Entrepreneurial Ecosystem on Smart Digital Solutions 231
Sujana Adapa and Subba Reddy Yarram

Automating Finance: The Role of Robotic Process Automation 243
Deepika Dhingra and Jaskiran Arora

Beyond Borders: Asian Entrepreneurs Driving the Global Frontier 261
Pravin Kumar

Financing Opportunities in Central Asian Emerging Markets: Lessons from Kazakhstan 277
Iakov Sadchikov

Exploring Entrepreneurial Opportunity in Japan's AI Landscape 291
Hajer Najeh

Contributors

Shashi Shekhar Acharya Nepal Administrative Staff College, Jawalakhel, Lalitpur, Nepal

Sujana Adapa University of New England, Armidale, NSW, Australia

Shradha Adhikari Kathmandu University School of Management, Lalitpur, Nepal

Jashim Uddin Ahmed Department of Management, School of Business and Economics, North South University, Dhaka, Bangladesh

Jaskiran Arora Education Quality, BML Munjal University, Kapriwas, Haryana, India

Syed Muntasir Husain Bokhari Program Specialist, School of Management, Asian Institute of Technology, Bangkok, Thailand

Anu Dandona D Y Patil International University, Akurdi, Pune, India

Deepika Dhingra School of Management, BML Munjal University, Kapriwas, Haryana, India

Tobias Endress School of Management, Asian Institute of Technology, Bangkok, Thailand

Anisur R. Faroque School of Marketing and Communication, University of Vaasa, Vaasa, Finland

Tanvi Gupta Banasthali Vidyapith, Banasthali, Rajasthan, India

Samsul Islam JR Shaw School of Business, Northern Alberta Institute of Technology (NAIT), Edmonton, AB, Canada

Krishna Khanal King's College, Kathmandu, Nepal

Pravin Kumar Brainware University, Kolkata, India

Tareq Mahbub Faculty of Business Department, Sakarya University School of Business, Serdivan, Turkey

Amrita Baid More Faculty of Management Studies, Medicaps University, Indore, India

Hajer Najeh Higher Institute of Management, University of Gabes, Gabes, Tunisia

Won-Yong Oh Lee Business School, University of Nevada, Las Vegas, NV, USA

Archana Parashar Indian Institute of Management (IIM) Raipur, Raipur, Chhattisgarh, India

Ananya Hadadi Raghavendra Great Lakes Institute of Management, Chennai, India

Lakeesha K. Ransom School of Management, Asian Institute of Technology, Bangkok, Thailand

Rongtitya Rith Department of Economics, University of Genoa, Genoa, GE, Italy

Iakov Sadchikov KIMEP University, Almaty, Kazakhstan

Djoen San Santoso School of Engineering and Technology, Asian Institute of Technology, Bangkok, Thailand

Arpan Shrivastava IPS Academy, Institute of Business Management and Research, Indore, India

Riccardo Spinelli Department of Economics, University of Genoa, Genoa, GE, Italy

Jacob Stalk Lee Business School, University of Nevada, Las Vegas, NV, USA

Deniz Tunçalp Department of Management Engineering, Istanbul Technical University, Istanbul, Türkiye

Subba Reddy Yarram University of New England, Armidale, NSW, Australia

The Future of Entrepreneurship in Asia: Tech Innovations, Market Disruptions, and Growth Strategies

Archana Parashar and Tanvi Gupta

Abstract Entrepreneurship in Asia is entering a new era marked by innovation, disruption, and opportunity. This chapter explores how emerging technologies such as artificial intelligence, blockchain, Internet of Things, and GreenTech are reshaping the startup ecosystem across the region. It examines sector-specific developments in AgriTech, MedTech, and EduTech and highlights evolving financing models including venture capital, crowdfunding, and decentralized finance. The chapter also focuses on inclusive growth, showcasing the rise of women-led ventures, youth-driven innovation, and sustainable business practices. By combining regional insights, case examples, and strategic analysis, the chapter offers a forward-looking perspective for entrepreneurs, investors, and policymakers navigating Asia's dynamic entrepreneurial landscape.

1 Introduction

Entrepreneurship in Asia is entering a transformative era shaped by rapid advancements in technology, expanding digital infrastructure, and evolving public policy. As one of the fastest-growing economic regions, Asia is home to several emerging startup hubs, including Bengaluru, Singapore, Jakarta, and Ho Chi Minh City (Chandra & Verma, 2023; World Bank, 2022). The surge in entrepreneurial activity is driven not only by population scale or market demand but also by the region's increasing focus on innovation, adaptability, and investor interest in digital-first ventures.

Technologies such as artificial intelligence, blockchain, the Internet of Things, and green innovations are lowering traditional barriers for new businesses. These tools enable entrepreneurs to develop solutions that are scalable, efficient, and tailored to local as well as global needs. Sectors like healthcare, education, agriculture, and

A. Parashar (✉)
Indian Institute of Management (IIM) Raipur, Raipur, Chhattisgarh, India
e-mail: archana@iimraipur.ac.in

T. Gupta
Banasthali Vidyapith, Banasthali, Rajasthan, India
e-mail: btbtt23024_tanvi@banasthali.in

T. Endress and Y. F. Badir (eds.), *Business and Management in Asia: Opportunities and Entrepreneurship*, https://doi.org/10.1007/978-981-95-4909-2_1

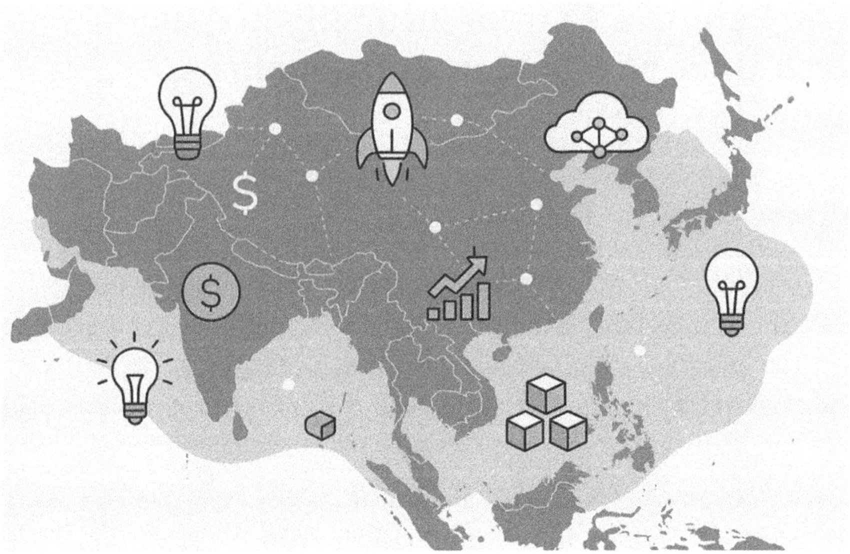

Fig. 1 A visual representation of Asia's evolving entrepreneurial landscape, highlighting key innovation hubs, emerging markets, and technology-driven startup growth across regions such as India, China, Southeast Asia, and Japan

finance are experiencing transformation through digital applications. As a result, Asia is becoming a launchpad for high-impact, tech-enabled startups (McKinsey, 2023; ADB, 2022).

This chapter explores the key forces driving the growth of entrepreneurship in Asia. It examines how founders are integrating digital technologies, responding to shifting consumer preferences, and building collaborative business models. Attention is also given to evolving funding mechanisms, such as venture capital, crowdfunding, and decentralized finance, which are creating new paths to scale and sustainability. The discussion highlights emerging themes like women-led businesses, youth innovation, and the evolution of family enterprises in the digital age. As illustrated in Fig. 1, Asia's startup ecosystem is rapidly expanding across multiple regions.

The sections that follow explore specific industries, digital business models, and cross-border opportunities that are shaping the future of entrepreneurship across Asia.

2 The Next Wave of Tech-Driven Entrepreneurship in Asia

Asia is emerging as a global testbed for advanced technologies that are reshaping how startups are formed, operated, and scaled. Recent research highlights the transformative potential of Generative AI (GenAI) in entrepreneurship, signaling a paradigm shift in innovation-driven business models. Kusetogullari et al. (2025) identify five thematic clusters where GenAI is influencing entrepreneurial ecosystems: digital transformation, AI-enhanced learning, sustainable innovation, evolving business models, and data-driven strategies. The study emphasizes that, while GenAI accelerates efficiency and creativity, gaps remain in macro-level understanding and ethical governance. This reinforces the need for entrepreneurs and policymakers in Asia to adopt responsible AI frameworks to harness opportunities while mitigating associated risks. The next wave of innovation is characterized not just by digital transformation but by the deep integration of artificial intelligence, decentralization, and sustainability into the core of business models. This section explores five key trends that define the future of tech-driven entrepreneurship in Asia: AI-first startups, solopreneur automation, decentralized AI models, blockchain finance, and sustainability-led innovation.

2.1 AI-First Startups and Automated Decision-Making

A new generation of startups in Asia is being built with *AI-first architecture*, where artificial intelligence is embedded into the founding structure. These ventures use machine learning algorithms and predictive analytics as core tools for product development, operational decisions, and customer engagement. AI tools are no longer peripheral. They are now embedded as strategic enablers that guide core business functions like pricing, customer segmentation, and product development, making decision-making more data-driven and iterative. Startups in Singapore, India, and South Korea are adopting AI platforms that continuously learn from customer data, enabling real-time feedback loops that accelerate innovation and reduce time to market (CB Insights, 2024).

2.2 AI-Powered Solopreneurship and Micro-Startups

The rise of automation is enabling a new class of entrepreneurs: *AI-powered solopreneurs*. There is a growing trend among startups in emerging Asian cities to adopt lightweight, AI-enabled models of entrepreneurship. This shift is supported by a combination of digital access, flexible platforms, and institutional encouragement for self-employment and automation-led ventures. In emerging cities like Ho Chi Minh City and Bengaluru, digital freelancers are launching entire ventures, from e-commerce stores to content studios, run entirely through AI tools (WEF, 2023).

2.3 Web4 and Decentralized AI Startups

Building on the momentum of Web3, Web4 technologies (a term used to describe decentralized and AI-integrated digital environments with high user control and automation) are taking shape through interoperable systems powered by artificial intelligence. AI agents integrated into smart contracts can execute decisions based on real-time data, making governance and operations more efficient. Early adopters in Taiwan and the Philippines are piloting decentralized marketplaces, autonomous financial platforms, and community-owned content networks (ADB Blockchain Asia, 2023; Lee et al., 2005). This emerging model presents opportunities for startups to scale globally without relying on centralized control.

2.4 Blockchain and Decentralized Finance (DeFi)

Decentralized finance, or DeFi, is transforming access to capital for startups across Asia. By eliminating intermediaries, blockchain-based platforms allow for peer-to-peer lending, tokenized crowdfunding, and smart contract investment models. Startups in regions like Vietnam and Thailand are using DeFi platforms to raise capital, manage payments, and offer financial services outside the traditional banking system (Chainalysis, 2023; IMF, 2022). These models improve transparency and reduce transaction costs, making them particularly effective for underbanked regions and cross-border operations. However, as Kshetri (2022) notes, the full impact of DeFi in Asia may be constrained by limited financial literacy and evolving regulatory frameworks, especially in rural or underserved markets. DeFi also encourages fractional ownership and liquidity, giving entrepreneurs greater flexibility in structuring their ventures.

2.5 GreenTech and Sustainability Startups

As environmental concerns become more urgent, *GreenTech startups* are driving innovation in clean energy, waste reduction, and climate-smart technologies. Startups in Asia are addressing sustainability challenges through solar-powered systems, carbon credit marketplaces, and circular economy models. For example, in Indonesia and India, ventures are using AI to optimize energy consumption and reduce emissions in logistics and agriculture (ADB, 2023; UN ESCAP, 2020). Investors are increasingly favoring *environmental, social, and governance (ESG)* focused business models that align profitability with long-term environmental impact. These startups are not only contributing to global sustainability goals but are also tapping into growing markets for ethical and impact-driven products. Together, these five trends highlight a clear shift in Asia's entrepreneurial landscape. Startups are moving

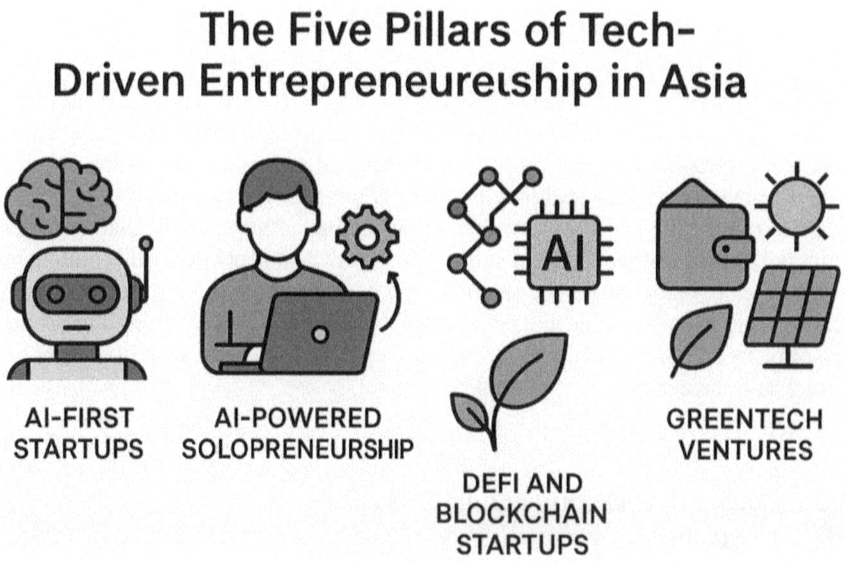

Fig. 2 A conceptual visual showing five pillars of tech-driven entrepreneurship in Asia: artificial intelligence–first startups, AI-enabled solopreneurship, decentralized Web4 technologies, blockchain-based financial models, and sustainability-led GreenTech innovation

away from traditional, resource-heavy models toward approaches that are decentralized, data-driven, and aligned with sustainable outcomes. Rather than treating AI, blockchain, or solopreneurship as separate changes, these developments are converging to create more flexible, adaptive, and impact-oriented business structures. The five central pillars of tech entrepreneurship are illustrated in Fig. 2, which depicts the convergence of AI, decentralization, and sustainability.

3 The Future of Entrepreneurial Ecosystems in Asia

Entrepreneurial ecosystems across Asia are evolving rapidly as technology, education, and governance begin to converge. These ecosystems are not only geographic clusters but also dynamic networks of institutions, capital, and talent. As Asia responds to growing digital opportunities and geopolitical shifts, a new ecosystem architecture is emerging—one that is shaped by virtual environments, research institutions, frontier technologies, and progressive regulation. This section outlines four forces influencing how these ecosystems will develop in the coming years.

3.1 Metaverse-Based Business Models and Virtual Commerce

The *metaverse* is redefining how startups engage with users, sell products, and build digital economies. Entrepreneurs in countries like South Korea, Japan, and Singapore are developing platforms where consumers can explore virtual stores, interact with AI-powered avatars, and purchase digital goods using cryptocurrency or *non-fungible tokens (NFTs).* These models allow startups to monetize virtual land, host immersive brand events, and offer services in 3D environments. As virtual commerce becomes more mainstream, entrepreneurs are exploring new pricing models, token-based membership systems, and collaborative digital spaces. These ventures require not only technological innovation but also legal and financial models adapted to virtual asset ownership.

3.2 University-Led Innovation Hubs

Asian universities are playing a growing role in the formation of startup ecosystems. Beyond providing education, these institutions are now acting as platforms for venture creation, prototyping, and commercialization. Innovation labs, *entrepreneurship cells*, and academic incubators are connecting students, researchers, and industry experts to co-develop scalable solutions. Universities in India, Singapore, and Malaysia are also facilitating access to funding, patenting support, and investor networks. The university-led model is becoming a critical engine for inclusive innovation across Asia. This is consistent with findings by Srivastava and Thomas (2023), who emphasize that academic incubation centers in Asia are increasingly driving scalable and socially impactful entrepreneurship.

3.3 Quantum Entrepreneurship and Emerging Technologies

Quantum technology is introducing a new layer of complexity and opportunity to Asia's innovation ecosystem. Startups are beginning to explore practical applications of *quantum computing*, including encryption, molecular modeling, and complex supply chain simulations. Countries like China and Singapore have launched national strategies to support early-stage companies working on *quantum hardware*, *quantum algorithms*, and related software solutions (Nature Quantum Tech, 2023; Singapore Quantum Engineering Programme, 2023). These ventures require deep technical expertise and long-term investment, which has led to increased collaboration between government laboratories, private investors, and universities. As this sector matures, quantum entrepreneurship could unlock significant economic advantages for countries investing early in infrastructure and talent development.

3.4 The Role of Governments and Policy in Shaping Startups

Policy frameworks have a direct impact on how startup ecosystems operate, especially in highly regulated sectors such as finance, biotechnology, and artificial intelligence. Governments in Asia are taking a dual approach creating space for experimentation while ensuring responsible innovation. Regulatory sandboxes, digital startup missions, and simplified licensing procedures are helping founders bring new ideas to market faster. For example, Singapore's FinTech sandbox and India's Startup India initiative both provide structured environments for early-stage businesses to operate with regulatory clarity. At the same time, new rules around *cryptocurrency*, *data privacy*, and *biotech ethics* are being introduced to protect consumer interests and ensure compliance. A well-balanced policy environment remains critical to building trust and driving innovation at scale.

4 Industry-Specific Entrepreneurial Opportunities in Asia

Entrepreneurial opportunities across Asia are increasingly being shaped by sector-specific innovation. Startups are no longer limited to broad digital services but are instead targeting deep, high-impact industries. In agriculture, healthcare, education, and space exploration, founders are combining domain knowledge with new technology to create scalable business models. This section explores four high-potential areas where industry-focused entrepreneurship is gaining momentum in Asia.

4.1 AgriTech and AI-Driven Precision Farming

AgriTech startups are introducing smart solutions to address urgent agricultural challenges such as declining productivity, climate variability, and inefficient resource use. Precision farming techniques powered by artificial intelligence are helping farmers monitor soil health, manage irrigation, and plan crop cycles based on weather and sensor data (FAO, 2022). In India and Southeast Asia, entrepreneurs are developing digital tools that guide smallholder farmers in decision-making, reducing input costs and improving yields. Some ventures also focus on improving cold storage, logistics, and real-time market access. These innovations are critical in building sustainable food systems and enhancing rural livelihoods.

4.2 MedTech and AI in Healthcare Entrepreneurship

MedTech ventures in Asia are redefining healthcare access and delivery. Startups are developing AI-powered diagnostic tools, portable screening devices, and robotic surgery systems that improve accuracy and reduce costs (Elsevier MedTech Asia, 2024; WHO, 2023). Bioinformatics platforms are enabling startups to analyze genetic data, design personalized treatments, and support drug development. Entrepreneurs in Singapore, South Korea, and India are building health technology platforms that connect clinics, patients, and pharmacies through secure, integrated systems. These ventures are not only improving patient outcomes but also helping health systems manage growing demand with limited infrastructure.

4.3 EduTech and AI-Personalized Learning

The education sector is undergoing significant change through the rise of *EduTech* ventures that deliver personalized and accessible learning. Startups are developing adaptive platforms that adjust lesson content and difficulty based on a student's pace and performance. In regions such as India and the Philippines, companies are reaching underserved communities through mobile learning apps that operate in low-bandwidth conditions (Brookings, 2023; UNESCO Asia, 2023). Brookings (2023) highlights that such innovations are essential in bridging learning gaps for students in low-income and digitally deprived environments. These tools are transforming traditional classroom models and preparing learners for digitally oriented futures.

4.4 SpaceTech and Private Space Exploration

Private *SpaceTech* entrepreneurship is accelerating across Asia as technological advancements and falling launch costs reduce the barrier to entry. Startups are working on satellite manufacturing, propulsion technology, and launch services that were once the domain of state agencies. In countries like Japan and India, private firms are offering satellite-based services to monitor climate, map terrain, and support disaster response (JAXA, 2022). Some ventures are experimenting with early-stage ideas in lunar mining, orbital infrastructure, and commercial payload delivery. These companies are supported by national space programs and emerging commercial partnerships, positioning Asia as a growing player in the global space economy.

5 Financing and Scaling Opportunities for Startups

Securing funding and building scalable business models are two of the most pressing challenges for startups. In Asia, entrepreneurs are increasingly turning to digital tools and decentralized platforms to access capital, while rethinking how companies grow with lean resources. This section explores three significant trends: algorithmic venture capital, blockchain-based fundraising, and automation-enabled scaling strategies.

5.1 AI in Startup Investment and Venture Capital

AI is transforming how venture capital is deployed in Asia. Investment firms are using algorithms to assess founder profiles, business models, and risk indicators with greater speed and objectivity. Platforms in Singapore and South Korea now apply machine learning to match startups with relevant investors, improving alignment and shortening deal cycles. For startups, this enables more precise funding opportunities while offering investors real-time monitoring across their portfolios.

5.2 Crowdfunding 3.0 and Blockchain-Based Finance

A new generation of fundraising models is emerging through *Crowdfunding 3.0*, where startups raise capital using blockchain infrastructure. Instead of relying on centralized platforms or traditional banking systems, founders can now issue project-specific digital tokens through smart contracts. These tokens can represent equity, access rights, or future utility, offering flexibility for both creators and backers. In Southeast Asia, especially in Vietnam and the Philippines, entrepreneurs are adopting decentralized fundraising to bypass red tape and engage early adopters directly. *Decentralized finance (DeFi)* platforms also enable peer-to-peer lending and tokenized micro-investments, opening up startup financing to a broader base of contributors.

5.3 Exponential Scaling and Automation-Led Growth

Many startups in Asia are adopting models based on the principles of Exponential Organizations (ExOs). These are businesses designed to grow rapidly through digital infrastructure, automation, and platform-based strategies, without needing to scale up physical assets or workforce in the same proportion. These companies rely heavily on software platforms, cloud computing, and AI tools to manage operations with minimal human overhead. Automation is used in marketing, customer support, inventory, recruitment, and financial reporting, allowing startups to expand across markets without proportional increases in team size or cost. For example, a logistics startup in Indonesia used an AI-based route optimization system to expand to five new cities without opening new offices. These scaling strategies are reshaping what it means to grow efficiently, enabling even small teams to compete with established players.

5.4 Conclusion of Section

As Asia's entrepreneurial landscape matures, innovative funding methods and lean scaling models are becoming foundational elements of startup strategy. From AI-driven investor matchmaking to token-based crowdfunding and automation-led growth, founders are building businesses that are agile, data-informed, and designed to thrive in complex markets. Innovations in startup funding and growth are presented in Fig. 3, highlighting AI-assisted venture capital, blockchain-based crowdfunding, and automation-led scaling models. The convergence of finance and technology is not only making capital more accessible, but also making growth more intentional and sustainable.

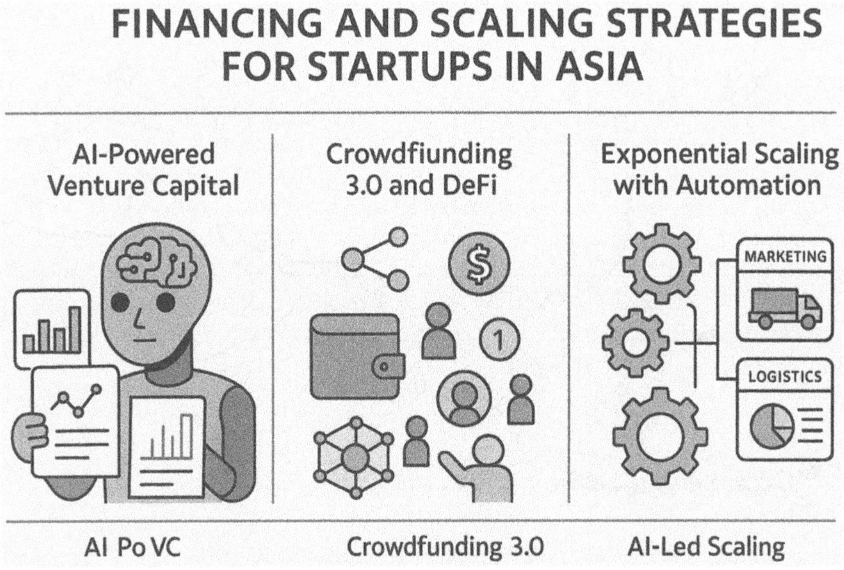

Fig. 3 A visual summary of startup funding and scaling innovations in Asia, including AI-assisted venture capital, blockchain-based crowdfunding, and automation-driven exponential growth strategies

6 The Human Side of Entrepreneurship: Inclusive Growth and Emerging Markets

Startups in Asia are no longer driven solely by technology or funding. The next phase of growth is increasingly shaped by human-centered innovation—focusing on inclusive leadership, behavioral understanding, and cultural transformation. This section highlights how women-led ventures, behavioral science, and generational change in family businesses are contributing to more sustainable and socially responsive entrepreneurship across emerging markets in Asia.

6.1 Women Entrepreneurs and Social Impact Ventures

Women entrepreneurs are making significant strides in Asia's startup ecosystems. From metro cities to remote areas, more women are launching ventures that address social challenges in health, education, financial inclusion, and climate action. In India, Bangladesh, and Indonesia, state-led initiatives and incubator programs are helping women overcome structural barriers such as limited access to finance, training, or mobility (NITI Aayog, 2023; UN Women Asia–Pacific, 2022). Mobile-first platforms and digital payment tools have enabled many women to build and manage businesses from home or rural settings. These ventures often combine profitability with measurable social outcomes, empowering communities and creating employment opportunities, particularly for other women.

Recent research strengthens the argument that women-led ventures are vital for inclusive and sustainable growth in Asia. Chikh-Amnache and Mekhzoumi (2023) analyzed ASEAN economies and found that female entrepreneurship significantly boosts economic performance, especially when supported by policies improving access to finance and training. Their findings suggest that gender-inclusive strategies in entrepreneurship not only drive GDP growth but also create social equity by promoting diverse leadership.

6.2 Neuroeconomics and AI-Powered Consumer Behavior

Startups are increasingly using insights from *neuroeconomics* to understand how consumers make purchasing decisions. This interdisciplinary field blends neuroscience and behavioral economics to track patterns in attention, emotion, and motivation. In markets like Vietnam and Thailand, companies are deploying emotion-sensing AI tools and behavior analytics platforms to monitor how users respond to ads, interfaces, and product experiences (Frontiers in Psychology, 2024; HBR, 2019). Facial recognition, eye-tracking, and clickstream analysis help founders fine-tune design, pricing, and communication strategies. These tools are especially helpful in diverse, price-sensitive markets where intuition alone is not enough. By predicting behavior more accurately, businesses improve engagement and reduce the risk of misaligned marketing.

6.3 Youth and Family Business Transformation

In many Asian countries, family-owned businesses form the backbone of the economy. These businesses, often rooted in tradition, are undergoing change as younger generations step into leadership roles. In Malaysia, India, and the Philippines, successors are introducing *disruptive innovation* to modernize legacy operations. This includes adopting e-commerce channels, automating backend systems, and improving supply chain transparency. Young founders retain the brand value and trust built by earlier generations while reshaping the customer experience through technology. This intergenerational shift allows traditional companies to enter competitive digital markets, attract new customers, and build structures for long-term scalability and governance. These dimensions are visually summarized in Fig. 4.

Fig. 4 Human-centered entrepreneurship in emerging Asian markets, emphasizing women entrepreneurs, neuroeconomics and AI-driven consumer behavior, and intergenerational family business transformation

7 The Future of Entrepreneurship in Asia: A Look Ahead

Entrepreneurship in Asia is entering a new phase, shaped by intelligent systems, evolving business models, and increasing uncertainty in digital markets. Startups across the region are transitioning from reactive strategies to proactive planning, from manual operations to intelligent automation, and from short-term scaling to long-term resilience. This section explores three critical trends expected to influence the next generation of startups in Asia: AI-assisted decision-making, automation-led company structures, and resilience strategies for navigating ongoing disruption.

7.1 AI-Human Collaboration in Decision-Making

In many Asian markets, startup founders are using artificial intelligence tools to strengthen the quality and speed of decision-making. Rather than eliminating the human role, these technologies support entrepreneurs by organizing large amounts of data, identifying patterns, and simulating possible outcomes. This process, often called *AI-human collaboration*, allows startups to improve strategic planning, product design, and operational forecasting. In cities like Tokyo, Bengaluru, and Singapore, founders use real-time dashboards that pull customer behavior, supply chain metrics, and market signals into a single interface. This approach improves responsiveness while allowing human judgment to guide final decisions. As competition intensifies, startups that can blend machine insights with human leadership are more likely to outperform others in dynamic markets. For instance, a logistics startup in India used an AI system to optimize delivery schedules, but allowed operations managers to override decisions in real-time. This approach reduced costs while ensuring adaptability in local conditions.

7.2 Automated Startups and the AI Operating Partner

The concept of an *AI operating partner* is becoming more common among technology-driven ventures. Startups are increasingly designed to run lean, using automation tools to manage essential functions such as customer support, digital marketing, sales tracking, and inventory management. In markets like South Korea, India, and Vietnam, small teams are running high-performing businesses with help from integrated software platforms that operate around the clock. These ventures use no-code tools, chatbots, financial automation, and intelligent scheduling to streamline operations. As a result, some startups are now able to serve thousands of users without hiring large teams or renting physical offices. Automated business models are becoming a key competitive advantage, especially for startups aiming to expand quickly with limited resources.

7.3 Building Resilience for Long-Term Sustainability

Resilience is emerging as a central pillar of startup strategy across Asia. Founders are recognizing that rapid growth alone is not enough to survive in unpredictable conditions. Economic shocks, policy changes, cybersecurity threats, and platform disruptions can slow or even shut down promising businesses. In response, startups are investing in digital infrastructure that enables remote work, data protection, and flexible operations. Many are also building multi-channel revenue models and diversifying supplier networks to avoid overdependence on any single platform or region. In Southeast Asia, for example, founders are creating localized versions of their services to reduce regulatory risk and increase user trust. These practices are helping new ventures build strength from the beginning, rather than reacting to risk after it appears.

7.4 Closing Note

The future of entrepreneurship in Asia will not be defined only by speed or scale. A detailed comparison of traditional and future-ready startup models is provided in Table 1. It will depend on how founders balance innovation with responsibility, and how they use intelligent tools without losing sight of the human impact of their choices. Those who build flexible, tech-enabled, and thoughtful organizations will be better positioned to grow, adapt, and lead in an increasingly uncertain world.

Table 1 Comparison of Traditional and Future-Ready Startups in Asia

Aspect	Traditional Startups	Future-Ready Startups in Asia
Decision-Making	Based on founder intuition and past reports	Supported by AI dashboards and real-time data
Operations	Manual workflows, human-driven	Automation-led, software-supported
Scalability	Linear growth through staff and infrastructure	Exponential growth using digital systems
Risk Management	Crisis-handling after disruptions occur	Proactive resilience planning and digital backups
Funding Model	Venture capital, equity-based rounds	Blended capital, tokenized crowdfunding
Work Model	Office-centric with fixed schedules	Remote-ready, decentralized
Core Strategy	Focus on product-market fit	Sustainability, Agility real-time adaptability

Adapted from Ismail et al. (2014), World Bank (2022), and PwC Asia Startup Outlook (2024)

8 Conclusion

Future research could further investigate how regional variations in regulatory policies, education systems, or market maturity affect the adoption of emerging startup models such as DeFi, AI-driven platforms, or decentralized governance. Entrepreneurship in Asia is no longer defined by location, capital, or sector alone. It is increasingly shaped by access to technology, the ability to scale intelligently, and a commitment to inclusive and sustainable growth. As this chapter has explored, the region's entrepreneurial future will be influenced by domain-specific innovation, automation-led business models, human-centered design, and the strategic use of data and decision technologies. Startups that can integrate these dimensions while remaining adaptable to disruption are most likely to thrive in complex, fast-moving markets. As Asia continues to lead global trends in digital adoption and startup activity, its entrepreneurs will play a central role in shaping how business is done in the next decade.

References

Asian Development Bank. (2022, November). *Asia small and medium-sized enterprise monitor 2022: Volume I—Country and regional reviews*. https://www.adb.org/publications/asia-sme-monitor-2022-volume-1

Asian Development Bank. (2023, July). *ADB Southeast Asia Green Finance Hub: Catalyzing green and innovative finance* [Brochure]. Asian Development Bank. https://www.adb.org/publications/adb-southeast-asia-green-finance-hub

Carter-Rau, R., & Olsen, B. (2023, November 20). *How to improve government decisionmaking around edtech innovations*. Brookings Institution. https://www.brookings.edu/articles/how-to-improve-government-decisionmaking-around-edtech-innovations/

CB Insights. (2024, April 2). *AI 100: The most promising artificial intelligence startups of 2024* [Report]. CB Insights. https://www.cbinsights.com/research/report/artificial-intelligence-top-startups-2024/

Chainalysis. (2023). *The 2023 geography of cryptocurrency report* [Report excerpt]. Chainalysis. https://www.chainalysis.com/blog/central-southern-asia-crypto-adoption-2024/

Chandra, S., & Verma, S. (2023). Big data and sustainable consumption: A review and research agenda. *Vision: The Journal of Business Perspective, 27*(1), 11–23. https://journals.sagepub.com/doi/10.1177/09722629211022520

Chikh-Amnache, S., & Mekhzoumi, L. (2023). The impact of female entrepreneurship on economic growth in the ASEAN countries: A panel MM-QR approach. *Economics and Business, 37*(1), 37–49. https://eb-journals.rtu.lv/eb/article/view/eb-2023-0003

Food and Agriculture Organization of the United Nations (FAO). (2022, June 27). *Asia-Pacific nations on accelerated push for rural digitalization to achieve SDGs*. FAO Newsroom. https://www.fao.org/newsroom/detail/asia-pacific-nations-on-push-for-rural-digitalization-to-achieve-sdgs-270622/en

Furr, N., Nel, K., & Ramsøy, T. Z. (2019, February 8). *Neuroscience is going to change how businesses understand their customers*. Harvard Business Review. https://hbr.org/2019/02/neuroscience-is-going-to-change-how-businesses-understand-their-customers

Herzhoff, J. (2024, October 23). *Reimagining healthcare in India: How AI and digital solutions are closing the urban-rural divide.* Elsevier Connect. https://www.elsevier.com/connect/reimagining-healthcare-in-india-how-ai-and-digital-solutions-are-closing-the-urban-rural-divide

IMF. (2022, September). *DeFi's promise and pitfalls.* Finance & Development Magazine. https://www.imf.org/en/Publications/fandd/issues/2022/09/Defi-promise-and-pitfalls-Fabian-Schar

Ismail, S., Malone, M. S., & van Geest, Y. (2014). *Exponential organizations: Why new organizations are ten times better, faster, and cheaper than yours (and what to do about it).* Diversion Books.

Japan Aerospace Exploration Agency (JAXA). (2022, December). *Making our first investment in a startup company—Tenchijin, Inc.* Japan Aerospace Exploration Agency. https://global.jaxa.jp/activity/pr/jaxas/no091/04.html

Kusetogullari, A., Kusetogullari, H., Andersson, M., & Gorschek, T. (2025). *GenAI in entrepreneurship: A systematic review of generative artificial intelligence in entrepreneurship research: Current issues and future directions.* arXiv preprint. https://arxiv.org/abs/2505.05523

Lee, S. M., Chang, D., & Lim, S. B. (2005). Impact of entrepreneurship education: A comparative study of the U.S. and Korea. *International Entrepreneurship and Management Journal, 1*, 27–43. https://doi.org/10.1007/s11365-005-6674-2

National Research Foundation, Prime Minister's Office Singapore & Agency for Science, Technology and Research (A*STAR). (2023). Quantum Engineering Programme (QEP). National Quantum Office. https://nqo.sg/programmes/qep/

NITI Aayog. (2023, March). *Decoding government support to women entrepreneurs in India: The anatomy of entrepreneurship support schemes.* MicroSave Consulting. https://www.niti.gov.in/sites/default/files/2023-03/Decoding-Government-Support-to-Women-Entrepreneurs-in-India.pdf

PricewaterhouseCoopers Singapore & Action Community for Entrepreneurship. (n.d.). *Creating a future-ready startup ecosystem* [Position paper]. PwC Singapore. https://www.pwc.com/sg/en/industries/financial-services/venture-hub/ace-position-paper.html

Seong, J., Bradley, C., Leung, N., Woetzel, L., Ellingrud, K., Kumra, G., & Wang, P. (2023, September 22). *Asia on the cusp of a new era.* McKinsey Global Institute. https://www.mckinsey.com/mgi/our-research/asia-on-the-cusp-of-a-new-era

The quantum state of affairs. (2023, May 15). *Nature Physics, 19*, 605. https://doi.org/10.1038/s41567-023-02072-w

UN Women. (2022). *Practical tips for business accelerators to support women entrepreneurs.* UN Women Regional Office for Asia and the Pacific. https://asiapacific.unwomen.org/en/digital-library/publications/2022/09/practical-tips-for-business-accelerators-to-support-women-entrepreneurs

United Nations Economic and Social Commission for Asia and the Pacific (UN ESCAP). (2020). *Guidelines for inclusive technology and innovation policies for sustainable development.* UN ESCAP. https://repository.unescap.org/bitstream/handle/20.500.12870/4046/ESCAP-2021-RP-Frontiers-Inclusive-Innovation.pdf?sequence=1

United Nations Educational, Scientific and Cultural Organization (UNESCO). (2023). Asia-Pacific regional report on digital education: EdTech adoption in Southeast Asia. UNESCO. https://unesdoc.unesco.org/ark:/48223/pf0000385602

Vistorte, A. O. R., Deroncele-Acosta, A., Ayala, J. L. M., Barrasa, A., López-Granero, C., & Martí-González, M. (2024). *Integrating artificial intelligence to assess emotions in learning environments: A systematic literature review. Frontiers in Psychology, 15.* https://doi.org/10.3389/fpsyg.2024.1387089

World Bank. (2022). *World development report 2022: Digitalization for development.* World Bank. https://www.worldbank.org/en/publication/wdr2022

World Economic Forum. (2023). *The future of jobs report 2023.* https://www3.weforum.org/docs/WEF_Future_of_Jobs_2023.pdf

World Health Organization, Regional Office for South-East Asia. (2023). *Monitoring progress on universal health coverage and the health-related Sustainable Development Goals in the*

WHO South-East Asia Region: 2023 update, the status of digital health implementation in the South-East Asia Region. WHO SEARO. https://www.who.int/publications/i/item/9789290210917

Dr. Archana Parashar is working as an Associate Professor at IIM Raipur since 2014. She is a gold medalist in M.A. (English Literature), M.Phil. topper, and completed her Ph.D. on American fiction. Prior to this, she was associated with SGSITS, Indore. She has 14 years of experience in teaching and corporate training. She has been a visiting faculty at IIM Calcutta, IIM Lucknow, IIM Kozhikode, IIM Shillong, and IIM Nagpur. Her research areas include Business Communication, Written Analysis and Communication, ELT, Postcolonial writings, and Ecocritical narratives. She has contributed in journals of international repute such as Springer, Sage, Emerald, etc. She has taught communication courses: Business Communication, Managerial Communication, WAC, Academic and Professional Writing, Communication for Business Leadership, Communication for Management Teachers, and Spoken Business Communication. As a resource person, she has delivered sessions at MECON Bhilai, FSNL Bhilai, NTPC Khargone, Balco Vedanta, IITDM Jabalpur, CET Bhubaneshwar, Chhattisgarh Prashasan Academy, and several TEQIP sessions organized by IIM Raipur.

Tanvi Gupta is pursuing B.Tech. in Biotechnology at Banasthali Vidyapith and is the co-founder of Zephyra, an early-stage startup focused on innovation and digital problem-solving. She has participated in entrepreneurship development programs that deepened her interest in startups, emerging technologies, and inclusive growth. Her academic background in science supports a practical, research-driven approach to addressing real-world challenges. This chapter reflects her curiosity about Asia's evolving entrepreneurial landscape and her commitment to contributing thoughtful, future-oriented perspectives to the startup ecosystem.

The Rise of Asian Startups: Innovation Hubs and Hotspots

Tobias Endress

Abstract This chapter examines the rapid rise of Asia as a significant global hub for startup activity and innovation. Over the last two decades, countries such as China, India, South Korea, and Singapore have become key players in the global entrepreneurial landscape, driven by urbanization, rising middle-class consumption, digital connectivity, open innovation strategies, and proactive government support. Several Asian cities now rank among the world's top startup ecosystems. Despite these gains, challenges such as unequal infrastructure, regulatory hurdles, market fragmentation, and brain drain persist, especially in less developed economies. The chapter also highlights leading and emerging innovation hubs across Asia, providing a comparative analysis of ecosystem performance and international rankings.

1 Introduction

The twenty-first century has witnessed a profound reorientation of global economic power, with Asia emerging as a dynamic epicenter of innovation and entrepreneurial activity. For decades, the United States and Western Europe have dominated startup success and global innovation metrics. However, over the past two decades, particularly in the last ten years, the center of gravity has shifted eastward. The Asian startup landscape has seen a boom, transforming the continent into a vibrant hub of technological advancement, innovative business models, and substantial venture capital investment. Asia has emerged as a global epicenter of startup activity, with several countries in the region witnessing exponential growth in entrepreneurial ventures and venture capital funding. This growth is underpinned by demographic dividends, increasing digital penetration, supportive

T. Endress (✉)
School of Management, Asian Institute of Technology, Bangkok, Thailand
e-mail: tobiasendress@ait.asia

T. Endress and Y. Badir (eds.), *Business and Management in Asia: Opportunities and Entrepreneurship*, https://doi.org/10.1007/978-981-95-4909-2_2

government policies, and a rapidly expanding middle class. According to the Global Startup Ecosystem Report (Startup Genome, 2025), several Asian cities, including Bangalore, Beijing, Singapore, and Seoul, are now ranked among the world's leading innovation ecosystems, reflecting Asia's rapid ascent in the global startup hierarchy (Startup Genome, 2025; StartupBlink, 2025).

Table 1 presents key data on venture capital investment (Dealroom.co, 2025a), Global Entrepreneurship Monitor (GEM) entrepreneurial ecosystem rankings for 2024/25 (Hill & GEM, 2025), StartupBlink 2024 Top Countries (StartupBlink, 2025), composite scores for entrepreneurship and technological advancement (U.S. News, 2025), and total patent grants (WIPO, 2024, 2025) for selected Asian countries. The order is based on countries with the highest VC investment volume in 2024. Many Asian countries, such as Cambodia, Myanmar, Papua New Guinea, and Sri Lanka, currently lack available data on venture capital (VC) investments. This absence of data and low scores in technological advancement highlight the relatively nascent stage of their startup ecosystems and possibly limited VC activity or reporting mechanisms compared to more established tech hubs in the region.

This surge is not merely a ripple effect of global trends but a self-sustaining phenomenon driven by unique regional characteristics, burgeoning digital populations, and increasingly sophisticated technological infrastructures. From the bustling tech hubs of Beijing and Bangalore to the rapidly growing ecosystems in Jakarta and Singapore, Asian startups are not just mimicking Western innovations. However, they are often pioneering new solutions tailored to their vast and diverse markets, many of which subsequently achieve global relevance. This includes advancements in artificial intelligence, e-commerce, fintech, biotech, and sustainable technologies, among others, demonstrating a broad spectrum of innovation (Endress & Badir, 2023, 2024).

Asia now accounts for more than 46% of global R&D spending (Bonaglia et al., 2024), a clear indication of its growing prominence. The region is not only producing technology consumers but also technology creators. South Korea continues to lead in patents per capita, while China has become the world's top filer of international patents through the Patent Cooperation Treaty (WIPO, 2024). More than two-thirds of all patent applications filed worldwide in 2023 originated from applicants based in Asia (see Fig. 1) (WIPO, 2024).

2 Drivers of Startup Growth in Asia

The rise of Asia as a startup powerhouse can be attributed to a combination of structural, economic, and policy-driven factors that have created fertile ground for entrepreneurial activity. This section explores the major drivers of startup growth across the region, focusing on economic transformation, open innovation, government initiatives, the expanding middle class, and digital connectivity.

Table 1 Comparative startup rankings on innovation and technology indicators for selected Asian countries

Country	VC Investment 2024 (USD Mio.)	GEM Rank 2024/25	Startup Blink Global Startup Ecosystem Index 2025	U.S. News Entrepreneurial Score* (2024)	U.S. News Most Technologically Advanced* (2024)	Total patent grants (WIPO Data, 2023)
China	40,200	13	13	94.4	96.1	889,968
India	13,500	5	22	55.3	47.6	25,801
South Korea	5,500	6	20	85.9	99.5	4,044
Singapore	4,800		4	83.9	74.8	
Japan	4,000	15	18	86	100	284,378
Taiwan	630	3	25	n.a.	n.a.	
Indonesia	348	9	45	25.3	6.7	626
Philippines	260		64	19.4	6.5	179
Thailand	243	33	53	26.1	10.2	
Vietnam	122		55	27.1	8.9	
Malaysia	118		44	42	18.9	1,128
Bangladesh	60		79	3.9	5.8	11

* *Note* U.S. News Best Countries Report rankings are based on survey results that reflect a country's performance in several areas. These surveys consider a variety of factors, which are weighted to produce an overall score and ranking. The annual Best Countries Report is a collaboration between US News and World Report, the BAV Group, and Wharton Business College

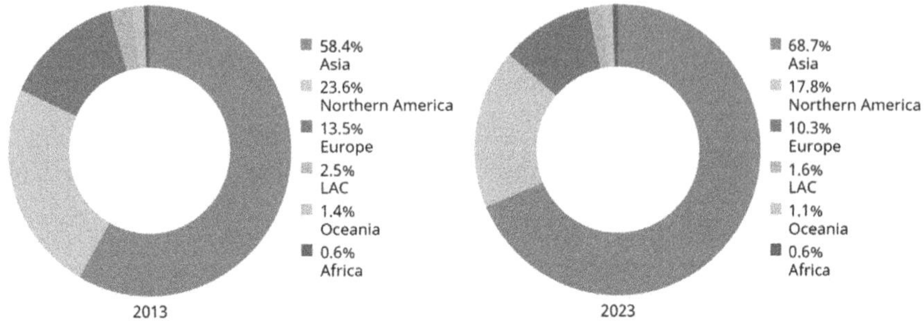

Fig. 1 Patent applications by region, 2013 and 2023. *Source* WIPO (2024)

2.1 Economic Transformation and Urbanization

Over the past two decades, many Asian economies have undergone profound structural transformations. The shift from agrarian or industrial-based economies toward service and technology-oriented models has been pivotal in creating environments conducive to innovation and entrepreneurship. Rapid urbanization, particularly in countries such as China, India, Indonesia, and Vietnam, has led to the emergence of metropolitan hubs that serve as catalysts for economic and technological growth. According to the Asian Development Bank (2024), urban areas in Asia are projected to accommodate more than 64% of the continent's population by 2050, providing a dense and connected user base that supports digital business models and high-growth startups.

Cities such as Shenzhen, Bangalore, and Ho Chi Minh City have become innovation centers, supported by improved infrastructure, access to talent, and proximity to universities and research institutions (UN ESCAP, 2024, 2025). Urbanization also fosters knowledge spillovers, peer effects, and access to venture capital, all of which are critical components of thriving startup ecosystems.

2.2 Rising Middle Class and Consumer Demand

Another significant driver of startup growth in Asia is the rapid expansion of the middle class, which is reshaping consumption patterns and fueling demand for innovative products and services. As incomes rise and poverty rates decline, millions of consumers across the region are gaining access to discretionary spending, creating vast new markets for a wider array of goods and services, particularly those leveraging digital technologies for convenience, efficiency, and entertainment (ADB, 2025). According to the Brookings Institution, Asia is home to over half of the world's middle-class population, and this figure is expected to grow steadily through 2030 (Fengler et al., 2022). Countries such as China, India,

Indonesia, the Philippines, and Thailand are experiencing particularly sharp increases in the number of middle-income households. This demographic shift is accompanied by a generational change, with younger, tech-savvy consumers driving demand for convenience, personalization, and mobile-first experiences. This rapid expansion of the middle class across Asia represents an enormous market opportunity for startups.

Startups are capitalizing on this trend by developing solutions that cater to the evolving aspirations of the middle class, ranging from affordable digital financial services and direct-to-consumer brands to online education and lifestyle platforms. In parallel, rising consumer expectations are driving startups to innovate more rapidly and enhance quality, thereby reinforcing a virtuous cycle of competition and creativity. As consumption-driven growth becomes a cornerstone of economic development in Asia, the burgeoning middle class is emerging not only as a market but also as a catalyst for entrepreneurship.

2.3 Strategic Use of Open Innovation

The strategic use of open innovation is another driver of growth in startup ecosystems. Beyond internal capabilities, the strategic adoption of open innovation paradigms has become a significant driver for Asian startup ecosystems. Open innovation, characterized by the deliberate flow of knowledge across organizational boundaries, allows startups to leverage external ideas, technologies, and partnerships, accelerating their development and market penetration (Chesbrough, 2003; Endress, 2023). Asian startups and corporates alike are increasingly leveraging open innovation strategies to accelerate growth and capture market opportunities. Established corporations are increasingly recognizing the value of partnering with startups to infuse agility and novel solutions into their operations, while startups gain access to resources, market reach, and validation. This symbiotic relationship reduces the time-to-market for innovations and fosters a more interconnected and resilient ecosystem, enabling faster problem-solving and shared risk-taking.

Countries like South Korea and Singapore have institutionalized open innovation through platforms and accelerator programs that connect startups with industry stakeholders. For example, the Korea Innovation Center (KIC), a globally-oriented open innovation agency (KIC Silicon Valley, 2024), and Singapore's SGInnovate and Enterprise Singapore facilitate collaboration between research institutions and private sector entities (Government of Singapore, 2024; SGInnovate, 2025), fostering and connecting collaboration with global startup ecosystems where startups can rapidly prototype and scale their offerings. Moreover, Japan's Keidanren and other corporate consortia have increased their engagement with startups, often through corporate venture capital (CVC), as a mechanism for open innovation (Fu, 2024).

2.4 Digital Connectivity and Mobile Penetration

Digital connectivity and mobile penetration have rapidly advanced across Asia, particularly in major startup ecosystem hubs. According to the GSMA, the region has one of the highest mobile internet penetration rates globally, with over 1.4 billion unique mobile subscribers, driven by growing smartphone adoption, which is in turn fueled by affordable data plans and increased device accessibility. The number of mobile internet users in Asia has nearly tripled over the past decade (GSMA, 2024). However, a significant portion of the region's population remains offline, not only due to a lack of network coverage but also because of barriers such as affordability, digital literacy, or lack of relevant content. This segment is referred to as being within the usage gap (GSMA, 2024).

Especially, urban tech hubs benefit from widespread 4G and increasing 5G coverage, enabling real-time applications in fintech, e-commerce, and digital health. Research by OECD (2025) highlights that digital infrastructure in Asia's startup hotspots supports innovation by reducing entry barriers for digital entrepreneurs and enhancing cross-border collaboration. These developments have been instrumental in accelerating digital transformation and fostering inclusive growth across the region.

2.5 Funding Landscape

From 2000 to 2024, investment levels in Asia saw significant growth, particularly in China and India, though momentum shifted in recent years. China experienced a dramatic rise from $173 million in 2000 to a peak of $61.1 billion in 2020 [in fact, 2021 was even higher, with $85.0 billion, but this figure is not shown in the table], before dropping to $38.1 billion by 2024. India followed a similar trajectory, rising from $210 million in 2000 to $14.3 billion in 2020, with a slight dip to $13.5 billion in 2024 (see Table 2) (Dealroom.co, 2025b).

South Korea, Singapore, and Japan also witnessed steady increases, each exceeding $4 billion by 2024. Southeast Asian nations, including Indonesia, Vietnam, and the Philippines, experienced a surge in investment activity after 2010, with Indonesia reaching a peak of $3.0 billion in 2020, followed by a sharp decline. Taiwan and Hong Kong saw moderate but consistent growth (Dealroom.co, 2025b). Asia, in particular, falls far behind in terms of AI spending. According to Crunchbase data, an unusual aspect of Asia's fundraising last quarter was that, while AI was all the rage worldwide, funding to Asia-based AI businesses actually decreased. The region's AI startups received $1.8 billion in funding, accounting for 14% of the total. That monetary figure is half of what it was a year ago and 23% lower than it was even in Q4 2023 (Metinko, 2025).

Still, western countries, especially the United States, remained the dominant investment destination throughout the period, starting at $45.3 billion in 2000 and

Table 2 Venture Investment Trends (2000–2024): Comparing Growth Across Asia (Dealroom.co, 2025b)

Amount invested	2000	2010	2015	2020	2024
Locations					
China (ex., Hong Kong)	$173m	$2.6b	$48.0b	$61.1b	$38.1b
India	$210m	$1.1b	$9.9b	$14.3b	$13.5b
South Korea	$15.0m	$15.5m	$1.3b	$5.1b	$5.5b
Singapore	$125m	$117m	$1.5b	$4.9b	$4.8b
Japan	$116m	$431m	$1.4b	$5.2b	$4.0b
Hong Kong	$169m	$141m	$548m	$1.8b	$2.1b
Taiwan	$35.3m	$48.2m	$254m	$560m	$630m
Indonesia	$22.0m	$565k	$669m	$3.0b	$348m
Philippines	$15.0m	$2.7m	$31.2m	$273m	$260m
Thailand	$16.6m	$12.1m	$35.3m	$701m	$243m
Vietnam	-	$7.8m	$181m	$419m	$122m
Malaysia	$28.5m	$106m	$71.7m	$246m	$118m
Bangladesh	-	-	$87.3m	$37.2m	$59.9m
United States	*$45.3b*	*$33.3b*	*$99.0b*	*$175.5b*	*$192.4b*

steadily increasing to $192.4 billion in 2024, far outpacing all its Asian counterparts. Overall, while Asia experienced rapid investment growth over the past two decades, recent years have shown signs of plateauing or declining in several key markets (Dealroom.co, 2025b). Overall, funding for startup projects appears to be still an issue in Asia.

3 The Other Side of the Boom: Challenges and Realities for Asian Startups

While startup ecosystems in Asia are rapidly advancing and increasingly recognized for innovation, it remains true that no Asian startup hub currently ranks among the world's top 20 most densely concentrated ecosystems (Dealroom.co, 2025a). In the startup world, "densest" refers to ecosystems that generate the highest startup activity relative to their population size. This includes factors like venture capital investment, enterprise value, number of unicorns, academic linkages, and patent output—showing how much innovation and impact a city produces per capita. In this context are still Western hubs, such as the Bay Area/Silicon Valley (USA), New York City (USA), Cambridge (UK), and Munich (Germany). These leading ecosystems—measured by factors such as VC investment, enterprise value, number of unicorns, university linkages, and patents on a per capita basis—stand out for their exceptionally high startup output relative to population size (Dealroom.co, 2025a). It is clear that venture funding is not distributed proportionately with technology and innovation. According to Crunchbase data, investment in artificial intelligence firms dominated global startup funding in 2024, with \$100 billion of venture capital coming to AI-related startups alone, an 80% increase from 2023 (Romburgh, 2025; Teare, 2025). The AI boom was particularly concentrated in North America, which witnessed a 21% increase in startup funding last year, while venture capital investment in Asia fell to a decade low (Romburgh, 2025). Different stages of venture capital present distinct bottlenecks, including fundraising, startup investment (which encompasses the startup's investment readiness and deal structure), and exit (an immature capital market for startup IPOs and a lack of regulations for mergers and acquisitions (M&A)) (Soeun, 2023).

Figure 2 illustrates a chart comparing the performance of different Asian countries in terms of entrepreneurship (along the bottom axis) and infrastructure (along the side axis). A dot represents each country, and their positions reflect how strong they are in each area.

The countries naturally group into three main clusters. In the top-right corner, "Innovation Leaders," we see Japan (JP), South Korea (KR), and Singapore (SG). These countries have both excellent infrastructure and high levels of entrepreneurship, making them leaders in the region for supporting innovation and business growth.

In the middle area, there is a group "Emerging Engines," including India (IN), Malaysia (MY), Thailand (TH), Vietnam (VN), Indonesia (ID), and the Philippines (PH). These countries show a good level of entrepreneurial activity but are still developing their infrastructure. This suggests that while there is strong

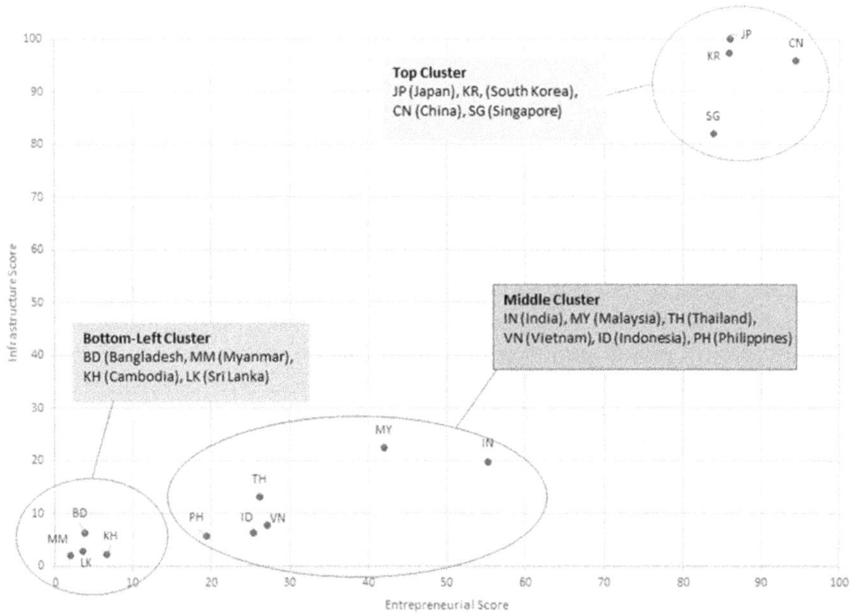

Fig. 2 Entrepreneurship vs. Infrastructure in Asia: A Regional Comparison. *Source* Own illustration, based on U.S. News data (2025)

potential for growth, improvements in roads, technology, and public services could help them advance even further.

Finally, in the bottom-left corner, "Developing Foundations," we find countries like Bangladesh (BD), Myanmar (MM), Cambodia (KH), and Sri Lanka (LK). These countries score low on both entrepreneurship and infrastructure, indicating that they may face more fundamental challenges, such as economic limitations or weaker support systems for businesses. Other Asian countries such as Laos, Kazakhstan, Papua New Guinea, and Uzbekistan are not included in this figure. However, they would likely fall into the same cluster based on their digital infrastructure and regional startup dynamics.

Overall, the chart highlights important differences in how well each country supports new businesses and has the infrastructure to back them. These clusters highlight where countries stand in terms of their readiness to support entrepreneurship and where investment or policy reform might be most needed to unlock potential.

3.1 Regulatory and Infrastructure Gaps

Regulatory and infrastructure gaps present significant hurdles in many Asian startup ecosystems, particularly in emerging and developing markets (ASEAN, 2020; Rohendi et al., 2023; Soeun, 2023). Inconsistent or outdated regulations can stifle innovation, deter foreign investment, and create uncertainty for entrepreneurs. Startups often face complex licensing procedures, unclear tax policies, and limited legal protections for intellectual property. Infrastructure gaps—such as unreliable internet access, inadequate transportation networks, and limited access to digital payment systems—further constrain growth and scalability. These challenges not only slow down startup development but also widen the gap between leading innovation hubs and countries still building the foundational elements of a supportive entrepreneurial environment. Addressing these issues through policy reform and targeted investment is essential for unlocking the full potential of Asia's startup landscape (Rohendi et al., 2023; Wisuttisak, 2020).

3.2 Talent Retention and Brain Drain

Talent retention remains a critical challenge in many Asian startup ecosystems, particularly in emerging economies (Ahmed, 2025; Shaji George & Baskar, 2024). Skilled professionals, especially in technology and innovation sectors, often seek better opportunities abroad due to limited local career prospects, lower wages, or a lack of advanced research and development infrastructure. This brain drain hampers domestic startup growth by depleting the local talent pool and increasing dependence on foreign expertise. Even in countries with strong entrepreneurial energy, the inability to retain top talent weakens the innovation pipeline and slows ecosystem maturity (Huang et al., 2023). To address this, governments and private sector stakeholders must invest in education, upskilling, competitive compensation, and supportive work environments that encourage talented individuals to stay and contribute locally. Some call for a more coordinated approach to tackle this challenge (Martinus, 2025) or recommend that a better "flow of talent among Asia–Pacific nations would revitalize the economy and national security' (Shin, 2023).

While initiatives such as Japan's program to offer a two-year post-study job search period (Ministry of Foreign Affairs of Japan, 2023) and Thailand's visa extension for international graduates allow fresh graduates to remain in the country for up to one year to seek employment (Saralamba, 2024) or initiatives to attract digital talent and remote workers in the Philippines with relaxed visa policies (Republic of the Philippines, 2025) represent a step in the right direction, significant challenges remain. Strict employment regulations and practical barriers often make it difficult—if not unfeasible—for many highly qualified individuals to relocate, remain in the country long term, or take advantage of the region's broader diversity and opportunities.

3.3 Market Fragmentation and Cultural Diversity

Asia's vast economic landscape is marked by significant market fragmentation and deep cultural diversity, presenting both challenges and opportunities for startups. The region comprises countries with varying regulatory systems, languages, consumer behaviors, and levels of economic development (Lee et al., 2022). This fragmentation means that business models successful in one country often require major adaptation to work in another, increasing costs and complexity for startups aiming to scale regionally.

Cultural diversity also significantly influences marketing strategies, user experience design, and product localization, necessitating a nuanced understanding of local norms and values. Entrepreneurship is also not universally regarded as an appealing career choice (ASEAN, 2020). While these factors can hinder rapid expansion, they also offer startups a unique testing ground to develop flexible, resilient models with the potential to thrive globally if they can successfully navigate the region's complexity.

4 Startup Ecosystems and Innovation Hubs

This section explores the major innovation hubs across Asia that have been instrumental in driving the region's technological advancement and entrepreneurial growth. It also explores emerging hotspots that are rapidly gaining momentum, presenting new opportunities and attracting growing interest from investors, startups, and global companies seeking to tap into Asia's dynamic innovation ecosystem.

Table 3 provides a comparative overview of selected startup ecosystems in Asia that have been featured in at least one of the following major global rankings: StartupBlink Rank 2024 (StartupBlink, 2025), the Startup Genome Ecosystem Report 2024 (Startup Genome, 2025), or Dealroom.co's Global Tech Ecosystem Index 2025 (Dealroom.co, 2025a). It highlights cities' positions in global rankings and recognizes their emerging or leading roles in various subcategories, including "Rising Stars," "Global Champions," and "Density Leaders," within

Table 3 Comparison of key Asian startup ecosystems based on global rankings and innovation cluster metrics (2024–2025)

	Region	StartupBlink Rank 2024	Startup Genome Ecosystem Report 2024	GII - Top 100 S&T clusters	Dealroom.co Global Tech Ecosystem Index 2025
Bangalore/ Bengaluru	India	10	14	25	15 (Rising Star) 9 (Global Champions APAC) 3 (Density Leaders in APAC) 6 (Rising Stars in APAC)
Bangkok	Thailand	81			18 (Rising Star) 8 (Rising Stars in APAC)
Beijing	China	5	5 (tied)	3	18 (Global Champions) 4 (Global Champions in APAC)
Chennai	India	88			9 (Rising Star) 3 (Rising Stars in APAC)
Guangzhou	China	41	35	2*	
Hangzhou	China	29	23	14	9 (Density Leaders in APAC)
Harbin	China			47	
Hefei	China			36	
Ho Chi Minh	Vietnam				10 (Rising Star) 4 (Rising Stars in APAC)
Hong Kong	China	37	27	2*	7 (Global Champions APAC) 4 (Density Leaders in APAC)
Hsinchu	Taiwan	96			
Hyderabad	India	70			
Jaipur	India				10 (Rising Stars in APAC)
Jakarta	Indonesia	30			14 (Rising Star) 5 (Rising Stars in APAC)
Kuala Lumpur	Malaysia	73		93	
Mumbai	India	18	40 (tied)	84	20 (Global Champion) 5 (Rising Star) 5 (Global Champions APAC) 2 (Rising Stars in APAC)
Nagoya	Japan			15	
Nanchang	China			94	
Nanjing	China	63		9	10 (Density Leaders in APAC)
New Delhi/Delhi	India	11		63	10 (Global Champions APAC) 9 (Rising Stars in APAC)
Pune	India	79			3 (Rising Star) 1 (Rising Stars in APAC)
Qingdao	China			20	
Seoul	South Korea	20	8	4	7 (Global Champion) 1 (Global Champions in APAC) 8 (Density Leaders in APAC)
Shanghai	China	7	10	5	13 (Global Champion) 2 (Global Champions in APAC)
Shenyang	China			61	
Shenzhen	China	17	17 (tied)	2*	
Singapore City	Singapore	12	9		14 (Global Champion) 3 (Global Champions in APAC) 1 (Density Leaders in APAC)
Taipei City	Taiwan	54		25	
Tokyo	Japan	13	11	1	6 (Global Champions APAC)

* *Note* This ranking refers to the combined cluster "Shenzhen–Hong Kong–Guangzhou"

the Asia–Pacific (APAC) region. To complement these rankings, the Global Innovation Index (GII)—Top 100 Science and Technology Clusters has also been included for reference (Bonaglia et al., 2024), although ecosystems that appear exclusively in the GII cluster index—such as Busan (South Korea), Changchun (China), Changsha (China), Chengdu (China), and Chennai (India)—have been excluded from this comparison as technology leadership alone might not qualify for being a startup ecosystem.

The table highlights the presence of each ecosystem across these rankings, providing insights into their global positioning, innovation density, and regional influence. It serves as a consolidated snapshot for assessing the prominence and momentum of Asia's leading startup and technology hubs. Asia's startup and innovation landscape is undergoing a significant transformation, with several cities rising as global and regional technology hubs. The region is no longer dominated solely by long-established powerhouses like Beijing, Shanghai, Tokyo, and Singapore; newer entrants such as Bangalore, Mumbai, Jakarta, and Ho Chi Minh City are gaining ground rapidly. This shift is reflected across multiple global indices and ecosystem reports that evaluate cities based on factors such as startup activity, science and technology output, innovation capacity, and investment momentum.

China dominates the GII Top 100 Science and Technology Clusters, with multiple cities ranking in the global top 20. Dealroom.co designations highlight the future potential of several emerging ecosystems, especially in India and Southeast Asia. Meanwhile, StartupBlink and the Startup Genome Ecosystem Report offer comparative insights into the global and regional rankings of innovation hubs, helping to map out both established leaders and fast-rising tech cities.

4.1 Major Innovation Hubs

Cities like Shenzhen, Seoul, Singapore, and Tokyo consistently rank high across multiple indices. Seoul stands out particularly, ranking 8th in Startup Genome and 4th in GII clusters, with several top-tier placements by Dealroom, including the number one spot among "Global Champions in APAC." Singapore City also performs well, ranking in the top 15 in multiple categories and topping the "Density Leaders in APAC" category. Tokyo, while not in the top five, remains solidly placed across all metrics.

4.1.1 China: Shenzhen, Beijing, Shanghai—From Manufacturing to Tech Giants

China continues to assert a dominant presence, with cities like Beijing, Shanghai, and Shenzhen consistently ranking among the top in both startup ecosystem strength and science and technology clusters. Beijing, for example, is frequently listed among the global top five, owing to its extensive R&D infrastructure, robust funding environment, and high level of global startup activity. Shanghai and Shenzhen also maintain strong showings, with high rankings across indices, showcasing China's wide distribution of tech innovation centers.

Interestingly, several second-tier Chinese cities, such as Hangzhou, Guangzhou, and Nanjing, show strong performance in science and technology outputs, indicating significant potential for future development of their startup ecosystems. These cities have yet to catch up in global startup rankings but are part of China's broader innovation backbone.

4.1.2 India: Bangalore, Hyderabad—Software and Service Innovation

Bangalore (Bengaluru) in India is shown as a major player, ranked 10th by StartupBlink and 14th by Startup Genome, and positioned 25th in the GII cluster rankings. Dealroom.co strongly recognizes it, ranking it globally at 15, labelling it both a "Rising Star" and a "Global Champion" in APAC, while also highlighting its density and momentum in the region.

India overall is emerging as a formidable player, particularly in the startup space. Bangalore has evolved into one of the most influential tech ecosystems not only in Asia but globally, marked by consistently high rankings and recognition as a "Rising Star" and "Density Leader" in the region. Mumbai and New Delhi, while trailing slightly behind Bangalore, are also solidifying their roles as vibrant innovation hubs, attracting increasing investment and global attention. Other Indian cities, such as Pune, Chennai, and Hyderabad, are gaining recognition as emerging players, demonstrating the decentralization and diversification of India's startup growth beyond major metro areas.

4.1.3 Singapore: Government-Backed Innovation and Regional HQ Hub

Singapore stands out as a key regional hub that punches above its weight, ranking highly in both startup ecosystem evaluations and science and technology metrics. It combines favorable government policies, strong infrastructure, and a vibrant funding environment to maintain its leadership position in the APAC region.

4.1.4 South Korea and Japan: Deep Tech, AI, and Robotics Ecosystems

South Korea's Seoul presents a balanced mix of technological sophistication, startup activity, and global competitiveness, consistently ranking among the top in Asia and globally. Tokyo, although sometimes perceived as more traditional in its business culture, remains in a strong position, particularly in terms of technological infrastructure and research output.

4.2 Emerging Hotspots

Emerging hotspots across Southeast Asia are becoming increasingly prominent in the global startup landscape, driven by demographic advantages, digital adoption, and relatively untapped markets.

4.2.1 Vietnam: Ho Chi Minh City and Hanoi—Cost-Effective Tech Talent

Among the emerging ecosystems, Vietnam is drawing particular attention, with Ho Chi Minh City and Hanoi standing out as cost-effective destinations for high-quality tech talent. These cities are becoming attractive alternatives for startups and investors seeking affordable yet skilled labor pools, especially in software development and digital services. Their rapid development in infrastructure and strong government interest in digital transformation are further accelerating their rise.

4.2.2 Indonesia: Jakarta—E-commerce and Fintech Growth

Indonesia, the region's largest economy, is anchored by Jakarta, which has evolved into a thriving center for e-commerce and fintech innovation. With a massive, mobile-first population and increasing digital penetration, Jakarta has become a breeding ground for unicorns and tech-driven startups catering to the country's unique market demands. Its momentum is reinforced by local venture capital growth and supportive regulatory developments.

4.2.3 Thailand, Malaysia, Philippines—Rising Startup Activity and Investment

Other Southeast Asian nations such as Thailand, Malaysia, and the Philippines are also seeing a surge in startup activity and investment. While these countries may still lag behind the larger ecosystems in scale, they are rapidly catching up thanks to expanding digital economies, improving access to funding, and policy initiatives aimed at nurturing entrepreneurship. Bangkok, Kuala Lumpur, and Manila are emerging as viable startup hubs in their own right, often backed by a growing community of accelerators, incubators, and international partnerships.

Together, these emerging hotspots signal a shift in the center of gravity within Asia's innovation ecosystem, from the traditional giants to a broader, more distributed network of dynamic, fast-growing cities across the region.

5 Conclusion, Lessons Learned, and Best Practices.

Overall, the data points to a rapidly maturing and diversifying startup ecosystem across Asia. While many Asian countries already lead global technology rankings, boasting high patent output, digital innovation, and R&D investment, their overall entrepreneurship scores still lag slightly behind. This gap is largely due to persistent challenges in funding accessibility, regulatory complexity, and uneven infrastructure development across the region. While the region is still concentrated around a few dominant hubs but is increasingly populated by a mix of established giants and fast-growing emerging ecosystems. This trend reflects broader shifts in talent distribution, the expansion of digital infrastructure, and a maturing investment landscape, making Asia a critical driver of global innovation in the years ahead.

Asia's startup ecosystem is no longer dominated by a few elite cities. Instead, a growing number of innovation hubs—from Bangalore and Jakarta to Ho Chi Minh City and Mumbai—are diversifying the landscape. This decentralization reflects both opportunity and disparity. High-performing ecosystems, such as those in Seoul, Singapore, and Tokyo, exhibit robust infrastructure, access to top talent, and strong government support. Meanwhile, emerging markets struggle with foundational challenges, including limited VC access, talent retention, and infrastructure development.

Open innovation has proven vital, enabling partnerships between startups, corporations, and research institutions. However, Asia still lags behind the West in critical sectors, such as artificial intelligence funding and exit opportunities. In 2024, AI startups attracted \$100 billion in global funding—an 80% surge—driven largely by North America, while Asia saw venture capital drop to a decade low (Romburgh, 2025; Teare, 2025). The uneven distribution of investment and resources across the region threatens to widen gaps between established and emerging ecosystems.

The data also show that while investment surged over the past two decades, recent figures indicate a plateau—or even a decline—in many markets. Particularly in China and Southeast Asia, VC funding has dropped, even as startup activity remains high. This mismatch highlights the need for policy coordination, ecosystem maturity, and reforms to the capital market.

6 Recommendations and Future Outlook

Asia's startup ecosystems have matured significantly, with global recognition and localized innovation driving their growth and development. However, sustaining this momentum requires addressing deep-rooted structural issues such as infrastructure deficits, regulatory uncertainty, and talent flight. Countries that invest in long-term ecosystem development, cross-border collaboration, and inclusive innovation will be best positioned to lead the way.

As the region moves forward, trends such as green innovation, AI, and blockchain are poised to shape the next decade of growth. Policymakers, investors, and ecosystem builders must work collaboratively to unlock the full potential of Asia's diverse and dynamic startup landscape.

Key lessons learned include:

- Ecosystem growth thrives where infrastructure, funding, and governance align.
- Open innovation accelerates growth and resilience.
- Talent and capital mobility are essential but need managed pathways.
- Inclusivity and regional coordination are critical to avoid fragmentation.

Best practices involve:

- Institutionalizing public–private partnerships,
- Building cross-border talent pipelines,
- Encouraging early-stage funding mechanisms,
- Tailoring regulatory frameworks to the startup lifecycle.

Asia might stand at a pivotal moment. The opportunity is vast, but realizing it depends on strategic investments in people, policy, and platforms. Smart ecosystem building and leveraging the specializations and strengths across various ecosystem hubs might be the key to lasting success.

References

ADB. (2024, October 25). *ADB's Work in the urban development sector* [Text]. Asian Development Bank. https://www.adb.org/what-we-do/topics/urban-development/overview

ADB. (2025). *Asian Development Outlook April 2025: Trade uncertainty challenges Asia's resilience* (2025th ed.). Asian Development Bank. https://doi.org/10.22617/FLS250135-3

Ahmed, R. (2025). Brain drain: Out of bound mobility of international students in Bangladesh. *Journal of Digital Learning and Distance Education, 3*(10), 1319–1326. https://doi.org/10.56778/jdlde.v3i10.454

ASEAN. (2020). *ASEAN guidelines on fostering a vibrant ecosystem for startups across Southeast Asia [electronic resource].* ASEAN Secretariat. https://asean.org/book/asean-guidelines-on-fostering-a-vibrant-ecosystem-for-startups-across-southeast-asia/

Bonaglia, D., León, L. R., & Wunsch-Vincent, S. (2024, December 18). *Global innovation index: End of year edition—Against all odds, global R&D has grown close to USD 3 trillion in 2023.* WIPO. https://www.wipo.int/web/global-innovation-index/w/blogs/2024/end-of-year-edition

Chesbrough, H. W. (2003). *Open innovation: The new imperative for creating and profiting from technology*. Harvard Business School Press.

Dealroom.co. (2025a). *Tech Ecosystems Index 2025 | Dealroom.co.* https://dealroom.co/tech-ecosystem-index-2025

Dealroom.co. (2025b, June 7). *Dealroom.co | Data App*. Dealroom.Co. https://app.dealroom.co/curated-heatmaps/funding/location/

Endress, T. (2023). Open innovation ecosystem in Asia. In T. Endress & Y. F. Badir (Eds.), *Business and management in Asia: Digital innovation and sustainability* (pp. 35–48). Springer Nature. https://doi.org/10.1007/978-981-19-6418-3_3

Endress, T., & Badir, Y. F. (Eds.). (2023). *Business and management in Asia: Digital innovation and sustainability*. Springer Nature.

Endress, T., & Badir, Y. F. (Eds.). (2024). *Business and management in Asia: Disruption and change*. Springer Nature Singapore. https://doi.org/10.1007/978-981-99-9371-0

Fengler, W., Kharas, H., & Caballero, J. (2022, June 2). Asia's tipping point in the consumer class. *Brookings*. https://www.brookings.edu/articles/asias-tipping-point-in-the-consumer-class/

Fu, E. (2024, August 22). *24-fold increase in Japanese corporate venture capital in the past decade*. https://globalventuring.com/corporate/asia/japans-corporates-fuel-innovation-through-strategic-investments-and-partnerships/

Government of Singapore. (2024, August 27). *Enterprise Singapore*. https://www.enterprisesg.gov.sg/

GSMA. (2024). *The mobile economy Asia Pacific 2024* (p. 52). GSMA. https://www.gsma.com/solutions-and-impact/connectivity-for-good/mobile-economy/wp-content/uploads/2024/07/240724-Mobile-Economy-Asia-Pacific-2024.pdf?utm_source=chatgpt.com

Hill, S., & GEM. (2025). *GEM 2024/2025 Global Report: Entrepreneurship Reality Check*. https://www.gemconsortium.org/reports/latest-global-report

Huang, Y., Li, K., & Li, P. (2023). Innovation ecosystems and national talent competitiveness: A country-based comparison using fsQCA. *Technological Forecasting and Social Change, 194*, Article 122733. https://doi.org/10.1016/j.techfore.2023.122733

KIC Silicon Valley. (2024). *K Innovation Center—KIC SV*. https://www.kicsv.org/

Lee, H.-S., Chernikov, S. U., Nagy, S., & Degtereva, E. A. (2022). The impact of national culture on innovation: A comparative analysis between developed and developing nations during the pre- and post-crisis period 2007–2021. *Social Sciences, 11*(11), 522. https://doi.org/10.3390/socsci11110522

Martinus, M. (2025, March 26). *ASEAN can help to address brain drain in Southeast Asia*. https://asialink.unimelb.edu.au/diplomacy/asean-can-help-address-brain-drain-southeast-asia

Metinko, C. (2025, April 8). Asia sags to lows not seen since 2014. *Crunchbase News*. https://news.crunchbase.com/venture/asia-startup-funding-sags-q1-2025-ai/

Ministry of Foreign Affairs of Japan. (2023, April 27). *Specified visa: Designated activities (Future creation individual, Spouse or Child of future creation individual)*. Ministry of Foreign Affairs of Japan. https://www.mofa.go.jp/ca/fna/page22e_001037.html

OECD. (2025). *Start-up Asia: Chasing the Innovation Frontier*. OECD Publishing. https://doi.org/10.1787/a9b71040-en

Republic of the Philippines. (2025, April 24). *Executive Order No. 86: Authorizing the issuance of digital nomad visa (20250424-EO-86-FRM)*. https://pco.gov.ph/wp-content/uploads/2025/04/20250424-EO-86-FRM.pdf

Rohendi, A., Asriani, A., & Kharisma, D. B. (2023). Regulation for startups in Indonesia: Problems and recommendations. *Cogent Business & Management, 10*(3), 2276993. https://doi.org/10.1080/23311975.2023.2276993

Romburgh, M. van. (2025, February 3). The state of startups in 12 charts: AI soars, Asia tanks, seed stalls and more. *Crunchbase News*. https://news.crunchbase.com/venture/startups-ai-seed-investors-data-charts-ye-2024/

Saralamba, T. (2024, July 24). *Thailand's new visa measures now effective!* สถานกงสุลใหญ่ ณ นครลอสแอนเจลิส. https://thaiconsulatela.thaiembassy.org/en/content/thailand-s-new-visa-measures-now-effective

SGInnovate. (2025). *Home | SGInnovate*. https://www.sginnovate.com/

Shaji George, A., & Baskar, T. (2024). Brain drain in India: Causes, consequences, and potential solutions. *Partners Universal Multidisciplinary Research Journal, 01*(04), 17–36. https://doi.org/10.5281/ZENODO.14171090

Shin, G.-W. (2023, May 15). *Flow of talent among Asia-Pacific nations would revitalize the economy and* [Japan Economic Foundation (JEF)]. https://aparc.fsi.stanford.edu/news/flow-talent-among-asia-pacific-nations-would-revitalize-economy-and-national-security

Soeun, T. (2023). Venture capital law in Cambodia: Engineer the regulatory framework to promote the startup ecosystem. *Asian Journal of Comparative Law, 18*(3), 362–388. https://doi.org/10.1017/asjcl.2023.24

Startup Genome. (2025). *The global startup ecosystem report 2025* (p. 331). Startup Genome. https://startupgenome.com/report/gser2025/

StartupBlink. (2025). *Global startup ecosystem index 2025* (p. 377). StartupBlink. https://www.startupblink.com/startupecosystemreport

Teare, G. (2025, January 7). Startup funding regained its footing in 2024 as AI became the star of the show. *Crunchbase News*. https://news.crunchbase.com/venture/global-funding-data-analysis-ai-eoy-2024/

UN ESCAP. (2024). *Asia-Pacific regional guidelines for smart cities: People-environment-technology nexus*. UN.ESCAP. https://hdl.handle.net/20.500.12870/8003.

UN ESCAP. (2025). *Asia-Pacific digital transformation report 2024: Digital innovation for smarter climate action*. https://hdl.handle.net/20.500.12870/7367.

U.S. News. (2025). *Most technologically advanced countries 2025*. Worldpopulationreview.Com. https://worldpopulationreview.com/country-rankings/most-technologically-advanced-countries

WIPO. (2024). *World Intellectual Property Indicators 2024*. World Intellectual Property Organization. https://doi.org/10.34667/TIND.50133

WIPO. (2025, May). *WIPO IP Statistics Data Center*. WIPO IP Statistics Data Center. https://www3.wipo.int/ipstats/ips-search/patent

Wisuttisak, P. (2020). *Comparative study on regulatory and policy frameworks for promotion of startups and SMEs in Japan, the Republic of Korea, Malaysia, and Thailand* (Working Paper No. 1206). ADBI Working Paper Series. https://www.econstor.eu/handle/10419/238563

Dr. Tobias Endress is an Assistant Professor at the Asian Institute of Technology's School of Management and serves as Program Director for the Business Analytics and Digital Transformation program. He is also the Director of the Startup Grind Bangkok chapter.

Holding a Doctorate in Business Administration (University of Gloucestershire), a Master's in Leadership in Digital Communication (UdK Berlin), and a degree in Computer Science and Business Economics (IBW/VWA), he brings a deeply interdisciplinary approach. His research and editorial work—such as editing the Digital Project Practice series (Taylor & Francis) and Springer's Business and Management in Asia series—reflect his focus on digital business, entrepreneurship, sustainability, innovation, and finance.

Emotional Intelligence in Asian Business Leadership: A Key to Sustainable Success

Anu Dandona

Abstract In the dynamic and culturally diverse business landscape of Asia, emotional intelligence (EI) has emerged as a critical factor in shaping effective leadership. This chapter explores the role of EI in Asian business leadership, focusing on how self-awareness, empathy and emotional regulation contribute to sustainable success. Drawing on psychological theories and real-world case studies, the chapter examines how culturally embedded values—such as collectivism, respect for hierarchy and relationship-oriented decision-making—interact with EI competencies. It highlights how emotionally intelligent leaders navigate challenges like conflict resolution, team motivation and employee well-being while fostering innovation and organizational resilience. The discussion also covers the impact of digital transformation and remote work on emotional intelligence in leadership, emphasizing strategies for developing EI skills in the evolving business environment. Ultimately, this chapter provides insights into how business leaders across Asia can harness emotional intelligence to enhance productivity, strengthen workplace relationships and drive long-term organizational success.

1 Introduction

Rapid changes in the Asian business arena are caused by impressive economic growth, technological developments and more integration at a regional and global level. China, India, Vietnam and Indonesia are some of Asia's fast-growing economies and their rise is shifting global economic power and making Asia a leading center of both trade and inventions (Divergences, 2023).

Advances in digitalization, artificial intelligence, fintech and e-commerce are affecting industries and the way people behave as consumers. Consequently, new business models and ways to grow are emerging. Because Asia's GDP and population are on the rise, along with a growing number of both middle-class people and youth who use digital tools, the region's market potential is huge (Tonby et al, 2021).

A. Dandona (✉)
D Y Patil International University, Akurdi, Pune, India
e-mail: anu.dandona@dypiu.ac.in

T. Endress and Y. F. Badir (eds.), *Business and Management in Asia: Opportunities and Entrepreneurship*, https://doi.org/10.1007/978-981-95-4909-2_3

Consequently, the growth of trade, new infrastructure and partnerships across Asia and abroad are increasing the strength and economic range of supply chains. Governments throughout Asia are focusing on sustainability, modernizing their digital systems and creating new incentives to make this transformation possible (World Bank, 2025).

Still, the changing world brings problems with geopolitical conflicts, difficult regulations, an aging population and harm to the environment which require new and creative leadership (World Economic Forum, 2024).

In such a fast-changing and complex business world, understanding cultures, managing emotions and being flexible in strategy will be necessary for leaders to carry out change and grab new opportunities in Asia (Michigan State University, 2024; International Monetary Fund, 2018).

2 Importance of EI in Leadership

Emotional intelligence (EI) is not only a personal leadership trait but an avenue to trace and exploit the business opportunities especially in the dynamic and culturally diversified markets like those of Asia. Three of the core EI competencies (i.e., self-awareness, empathy and social skills) are directly involved in the process of opportunity recognition and innovation. Self-awareness helps entrepreneurs to properly evaluate their strong and weak sides, make the necessary strategic steps at the right time and coordinate the goals of the venture with the market and their vision. Empathy helps them to empathize and collect very vivid information about the needs, aspirations and difficulties of customers and interest groups, which usually results in creative solutions and greater product-market fit. Social skills, in their turn, assist in establishing the relationships of trust with the investors, partners and staff opening the doors to the collaboration and access to new markets. The Asian business environment provides dramatic examples of this process. The empathy that Jack Ma had with the people of China who had small businesses led to the development of the B2B platform of Alibaba and ultimately rural e-commerce initiatives that opened markets that could not be ventilated before. In India, the founder Byju Raveendran had a clear perspective of knowing the wants of parents and the fears of students, which led to the establishment of an adaptive learning platform that shook up the EdTech industry in India. The example of leadership by Anthony Tan at Grab can be classified as high EI in dealing with cross-cultural teams and adapting services to the needs of local markets and, therefore, helps the company to grow at a fast pace and diversify services throughout Southeast Asia. Taken together, these examples emphasize that in an environment of rapid growth but also of volatility, EI is not an ideal trait, but it is rather an instrument of a strategy such as trying to anticipate cultural nuances, reading the emotional grains of consumer and employee behavior and developing the kind of robust networks. Leaders and entrepreneurs who use EI well have a greater ability to generate, develop and maintain innovation that can earn them a competitive edge in the international market.

Because of its major role in managing oneself and relationships, Emotional Intelligence (EI) is gaining importance in leadership (Mayer et al., 2008). Technical skills and IQ represent basic requirements, but EI covers self-awareness, self-control, empathy and working with people and these help leaders interact wisely with others, decide well and motivate their teams (Boyatzis, 2009; Salovey & Mayer, 1990).

Because of today's fast business world, leaders face increasing challenges, including organizational changes, mixed workforces and market competition worldwide. It has been found that individuals with greater emotional intelligence stay calm in stressful situations, handle differences respectfully and encourage trust among those they lead which improves employee involvement, success rate and staff retention (Cherniss, 2010; Druskat & Wolff, 2001). It has been found that before examining technical skills, most organizations look at 71% of potential leaders' emotional intelligence when considering who can be a great leader (Bradberry & Greaves, 2009).

Besides, leaders with emotional intelligence skills are able to establish cultures at work where people collaborate, innovate and feel safe which helps maintain the organization's performance. If a leader can calm their emotions and notice the emotions of others, they will do a better job motivating and supporting their employees (Boyatzis & McKee, 2005). More and more, people see the need for EI, a shift away from power-based leadership back to clear communication and inclusive choices in today's companies (Goleman et al., 2013).

As a result, acknowledging emotional intelligence as a must-have skill for leaders means that it should now be featured both in management programs and when finding potential leaders (Dulewicz & Higgs, 2003; Salovey et al., 1999).

3 Overview of the Chapter

This chapter looks at how Emotional Intelligence (EI) shapes strong leadership in Asian businesses and plays a key part in the organization's success. The focus is on how EI allows leaders in Asia to handle the challenges of different cultures, fast changes and tough competition. This chapter seeks to review basic concepts of emotional intelligence, define its main areas regarding leadership, investigate cultural differences in Asia, study the effect of EI on teams and organizations, address issues and chances for success faced by leaders and point out the effects of current technologies, changing demographics and worldwide risks on emotionally intelligent leaders. This chapter aims to give full insights and practical solutions on using emotional intelligence in leadership training for Asian business leaders who want to support collaboration, motivate teams and maintain strong, future-oriented growth for their organizations (Henry, 2011).

4 Emotional Intelligence: Theoretical Foundations

EI is mostly about having the ability to sense, make sense of, control and make use of emotions both personally and with others. The field is built on the belief that emotions play a key role in how intelligent behavior is formed (Mayer, et al., 2008; Salovey & Mayer, 1990).

Following Mayer, Salovey and Caruso, the Mayer-Salovey Model (Ability Model) says EI consists of four related mental abilities: understanding feelings, using emotions to guide thinking, interpreting emotions and handling feelings. The Mayer-Salovey-Caruso Emotional Intelligence Test (MSCEIT) (Mayer & Salovey, 1997; Mayer et al., 2002) quantifies EI since it views EI as its own type of intelligence.

His approach was introduced in 1995 and likely best known as the Mixed Performance Model, with it being believed that EI should mention both abilities and social and emotional competencies like self-awareness, regulating feelings, motivation, empathy and social skills needed for success at work and life. Many companies use this model to develop their leaders and shape teamwork, by emphasizing that people can learn and work on these skills (Goleman, 1995).

4.1 Core Competencies: Self-Awareness, Self-Regulation, Empathy, Motivation and Social Skills

The essential abilities of emotional intelligence are being aware of ourselves, controlling our emotions, empathy, motivation and working well with other people (Goleman, 2007; Singh, 2004). When you are self-aware, you recognize what you are feeling and see how it affects both your mind and your actions. To be self-aware means you can see what your strengths are, what your weaknesses are and understand the influence of your emotions on your actions and relationships with others (Goleman, 2007). Being able to self-regulate means managing how you feel, mainly during times of stress. To control anger management, individuals need to restrain acting on their feelings, stay level-headed and answer calmly rather than react quickly.

You show empathy by being aware of and sharing someone else's feelings. This means noticing what others feel and think and what they require which helps with relationships and discussions (Goleman, 2007). Motivation means wanting to achieve something with strong effort and determination. Highly motivated individuals are typically positive, strong and motivate others by how passionately and seriously they work (Singh, 2004).

Following Mayer, Salovey and Caruso, the Mayer-Salovey Model (Ability Model) says EI consists of four related mental abilities: understanding feelings, using emotions to guide thinking, interpreting emotions and handling feelings. The Mayer-Salovey-Caruso Emotional Intelligence Test (MSCEIT) (Mayer & Salovey, 1997; Mayer et al., 2002) quantifies EI since it views EI as its own type of intelligence.

Social skills deal with handling relationships, forming networks, using effective communication, teaming up with people and settling conflicts. Being good at social skills helps people lead other and cooperate within teams (Goleman, 2007). Thanks to these skills, individuals are able to deal with social problems, lead successfully and obtain good results in both their lives and their workplaces by controlling their emotions. These skills can always be improved if you focus your learning and attention on practicing them (Goleman, 2007; Singh, 2004).

4.2 EI's Connection to Leadership Effectiveness

Leaders need Emotional Intelligence (EI) to help them control their emotions and notice and control the emotions of people they lead (as noted by Goleman in 1995 and Côté in 2017). A leader with high EI often understands themselves better, has control over their emotions, is empathetic, motivated and socially capable which together help them with communication, making decisions and resolving disputes (Goleman, 2007; Mayer et al., 2008).

Research has found that emotionally intelligent leaders encourage their teams to trust one another, stick with the company and feel involved which leads to better productivity, engagement and retention (Boyatzis et al., 2000; Cherniss, 2010). They help build workplaces that favor change and allow people to work well together. They care about both the thoughts and feelings of their teams which motivates employees and unites them (Goleman, 2007; Mayer et al., 2008).

In addition, people with EI show the skill to handle challenges and uncertainty, stay calm during high-stress times and inspire their employees (Goleman, 1995; Salovey & Mayer, 1990). Coverage in journals suggests that emotional intelligence is linked to effective leadership and is normally valued by companies above technical skills (Côté, 2017; Goleman, 2007). Led by EI, strong leadership encourages an environment where people exchange open thoughts, feel safe and are included (Boyatzis et al., 2000; Cherniss, 2010).

Learning emotional intelligence never stops and helps a leader bond with others personally, appreciate individual views and lead honestly and with compassion (Goleman, 1995; Mayer et al., 2008). So, organizations are now providing more attention to EI in developing leaders, knowing that it helps handle social issues and maintain ongoing success (Boyatzis et al., 2000; Côté, 2017).

5 Cultural Dimensions and Emotional Intelligence in Asia

The behaviors, cultures and styles of leadership common in Asian societies guide interpersonal communication and drive the exhibitions of EI (Hofstede, 2011; Rockstuhl et al., 2010).

Across much of Asia, looking after the group as a whole is more important than serving the needs of one individual. With this approach, people in teams develop strong bonds, learn to collaborate and show loyalty to each other. Leaders in these cultures have to work on balancing opposing opinions and maintaining a cohesive group which calls for detailed emotional sensitivity (Markus & Kitayama, 1991; Tsai et al., 2007).

In Asian societies, hierarchy is central because it reflects Confucian beliefs about respect for traditional authority, older people and order. In many Asian places of work, security chains are clear, with the most important decisions handled by supervisors and elders respected. Due to this idea, people develop a way of speaking that often feels delicate and indirect and EI skills like empathy and social sensitivity become valuable to maintain harmony and not confront their bosses outright (Oyserman & Lee, 2008; Tsai et al., 2007).

People value harmony because it aims for peace among everyone, no conflict and balanced relationships. Managing emotions well and how you communicate allows you to maintain a strong relationship without becoming inauthentic. Leaders often deal with subtle feelings among their team members, avoiding potential troubles and conflict (Kitayama & Markus, 2000; Tsai, 2007).

In addition, preserving someone's dignity in social situations is very important in Asian cultures. Keeping someone from losing face calls for being sensitive, prudent and careful in how you communicate. These kinds of leaders are skilled at providing feedback and resolving disputes gently which helps them win trust and keep relationships safe (Markus & Kitayama, 1991; Rockstuhl et al., 2010).

Combined, these different cultural factors direct how feelings are expressed and how well leaders carry out their roles at Asian companies. Successful Asian leaders need to appreciate how these values and EI are related (Hofstede, 2011; Rockstuhl et al., 2010).

5.1 How These Values Shape Emotional Expression and Leadership Behavior

Asian culture's beliefs about collectivism, hierarchy, harmony and saving face play a big role in influencing emotions and the actions of leaders. Encouraging emotions to be governed so that the group continues to work together, rarely displaying negative feelings outwardly, forms a key feature of collectivism (Markus & Kitayama, 1991; Matsumoto, 1990). Emotions are expected to be controlled, especially when dealing with people in power which encourages showing polite emotions that keep everyone respectful (Chen, 2016; Hofstede, 2001). Because bridging harmony is important, people in this culture prevent themselves from expressing feelings that may cause conflict and instead show more diplomacy, empathy and tact with others (Leung & Cohen, 2011).

Emotions are also guided by wanting to avoid acts that might bring embarrassment or shame that leads individuals to use less direct ways to maintain respect and relationships (Kim & Hong, 2004; Ting-Toomey, 1988).

A collectivist culture, in terms of leadership, prompt leaders to put the team's objectives first and encourage teamwork, unity and showing support; they help the group feel together by acting as facilitators instead of making all the rules themselves (Farh & Cheng, 2000). In such cultures, leadership usually involves clear authority and acts of paternalism and leaders are seen as required to control their emotions and set good examples to keep their power and influence (Hanges et al., 2004). Because harmony matters so much, leaders use emotional intelligence to carefully handle difficulties and prevent conflicts at work (Gelfand et al., 2007). In addition, leaders influenced by face-saving will help resolve conflicts and give feedback without undermining others' social status which encourages long-term trust and cohesion among everyone (Hwang, 1987). For this reason, it is important for leaders to be understanding, gentle and respectful to work well with different cultures.

6 Cultural Compatibility and EI Competencies

To be culturally compatible, you should understand, respect and match other cultures and this goes along with better emotional intelligence. Individuals or groups that have similar backgrounds or common cultures are more likely to work together well, have better understanding and enjoy better communication (American Psychological Association, 2015). Thanks to this cultural alignment, people can become more emotionally aware because they understand other cultures better. Having high intercultural sensitivity often leads to having more emotional intelligence which is especially noticeable among students (Khan et al., 2020). Having employees with similar cultural backgrounds in outsourcing reduces mistakes and worries, helps people talk comfortably with knowledge and promotes mutual respect which helps everyone's emotional intelligence develop. When firms manage cultural similarities and differences, emotional intelligence helps them increase productivity and make their teams feel better by lowering stress and encouraging understanding and connection (Bhatti et al., 2023).

Also, emotional intelligence leads to better innovation performance because it has a similar effect with high cultural intelligence that allows individuals to work well in a variety of cultures. Employees who are emotionally and culturally intelligent will find it easier to channel their emotions, display creativity and improve results across the organization (Ang & Van Dyne, 2008; Bhatti et al., 2023).

7 Role of EI in Asian Business Leadership

In order to manage conflicts, boost team spirit in group-oriented cultures and care for workers under high-performance stress, leaders rely on skills developed through EI (Bhatti et al., 2023; Goleman, 1995; Mayer et al., 2004).

7.1 Conflict Resolution in Hierarchical Cultures

Given that hierarchical societies have clear sets of authority and power, leaders who have good emotional intelligence are expected to notice such tendencies and modify their leadership strategy to please team members (Bhatti et al., 2023). Due to EI, leaders spot these small hints in communication, use empathy and manage their emotions to keep potential disputes from growing (Mayer et al., 2004; Schutte et al., 1998). Emotionally intelligent leaders use listening, understanding of culture and self-control to ease conflicts and help people in different jobs get along well (Goleman, 1995; Salovey & Mayer, 1990). They make sure teams feel welcomed by considering mental and cultural factors, allowing each conflict to help people grow closer and make the group perform better (Bhatti et al., 2023).

7.2 Team Motivation in Collectivist Environments

EI helps leaders in collectivist cultures create an atmosphere where teams work together because every member is appreciated and understood (Bhatti et al., 2023). High EI in leaders brings about self-awareness and empathy which produce trust and security, key elements for keeping people motivated in working together (Goleman, 1995; Salovey & Mayer, 1990). They adjust to various emotional demands by making all students feel included and by promoting open discussions (Bhatti et al., 2023). These leaders achieve mental stability that allows them to lead, motivating everyone to carry on when problems arise (Bhatti et al., 2023). This type of leadership assures team members share their commitment and improves the whole team's performance which helps them succeed when following collectivist principles (Bhatti et al., 2023).

7.3 Employee Well-Being Amid High-Performance Demands

When leading in times of high performance, emotionally intelligent leaders help maintain employee well-being by understanding and handling emotions both their own and their team's (Goleman, 1995; Mayer et al., 2004).

Because of strong EI, leaders can remain calm, respond with empathy and help reduce team stress and burnout (Bhatti et al., 2023). Employees become more self-confident, tough and involved when leaders with EI encourage mindfulness, pay attention to their needs and give helpful guidance (Bhatti et al., 2023). Modeling emotional control and developing a supportive environment permits employees to meet work pressures smoothly which leads to both sustained productivity and good mental health (Bhatti et al., 2023). Having this approach means employees are healthier and more likely to succeed in challenging work environments (Bhatti et al., 2023).

Leaders with emotional intelligence can manage cultural differences in conflicts, prompt everyone to feel motivated and protect employees' welfare which helps the organization excel in various and difficult situations (Bhatti et al., 2023).

Examples from major Asian nations (Japan, India, China, Singapore) are used for discussion.

Leadership and organizational success across Asia are strongly influenced by emotional intelligence, as is made clear in case studies of Japan, India, China and Singapore (Bhatti et al., 2023; BibGuru, 2024; Brown et al., 2020; Chan et al., 2018).

7.3.1 Japan

Leading in Japan's company culture which is highly hierarchical and based on context, benefits from leaders having strong emotional intelligence. Results from a major study in Japan involving 6,066 people demonstrate that EI can explain 55% of the differences seen in important performance areas such as influence, decision-making, effectiveness, quality of life, relationships and health. For this group of middle-aged males (aged 30–40), there was a clear loss of EQ skills, pointing out the importance of strengthening their emotional skills. We can see how EQ is used by looking at practice case studies.

In Zenet, staff were taught EQ skills, with discussions about how best to use their strengths guided by mentors and managers. There was a sharp rise in employees staying with the company from 76% to 100%, together with greater job satisfaction (BibGuru, 2024).

Partnering executives from the newly merged companies began working better together and feeling more positive after using EQ assessments, along with coaching sessions, according to BibGuru (2024).

Leaders at a food distribution company who had their own coaching after noticing that what they saw in their leadership was different from others' feedback became more willing to change and performed more effectively (BibGuru, 2024).

The cases demonstrate how personal EQ work improves the links, shared effort and vitality of leaders in the typical Japanese work environment (BibGuru, 2024).

In addition, humility, patience, trust and peace play a big role in business in Japan and decisions tend to be made at the top, often involving face-to-face meetings

("Genchi Genbutsu"). Many leaders dislike employee behavior that is overly aggressive and like to maintain relationships based on trust. Because of this, emotional intelligence is seen as crucial for successful business activity (Bhatti et al., 2023).

7.3.2 India

Leaders in India are now expected to be empathetic and authentic when working with many different team members in today's new economic and cultural environment. Case studies explain:

Being a 32-year-old project manager at a tech firm based in Chennai, Kavitha changed how she leads by recognizing herself, controlling her actions, feeling empathy, honing her social skills and remaining motivated. Within six months, knowing her employee's emotions and practicing empathy helped her improve team communication, spirits and productivity (Brown et al., 2020).

Programs for leadership in India include emotional intelligence, active listening and training for understanding cultures, along with encouraging inclusive policies and providing mentorship (Brown et al., 2020).

How employees are engaged, results from feedback assessments, staff retention and progress on metrics like productivity influence the success of both an organization's culture and its operations (Brown et al., 2020).

In India, leaders are expected to combine ancestral beliefs with recent leadership approaches that depend on EI to nurture trust, unity and steady progress (Brown et al., 2020).

7.3.3 China

In China's organizational structure, team members whose RQ is high, often make their teams more effective. Studies reveal:

Using RQ, developed with the SDI 2.0, helped Chinese private-sector teams deal with conflict, improved team communication and led to better group coordination (Chan et al., 2018). Those who use RQ experience greater results at work, improved climate among team members and fewer disagreements at higher levels of management (Chan et al., 2018).

The staff showed better attitudes when they were satisfied and stayed longer at the firm. A sense of guanxi (strong connections at work) grew when RQ (increased mutual understanding) was implemented (Chan et al., 2018). Using leadership tools such as SDI 2.0 helped Chinese teams to boost performance and encourage collaboration with people in higher positions, maintaining harmony and pleasant relationships among colleagues (Chan et al., 2018). It is emphasized in this study that using EI assessments with cultural understanding leads to better team performance for China's unique culture (Chan et al., 2018).

7.3.4 Singapore

In Singapore, emotional intelligence is taught using development programs that combine ideas and real experiences. Focusing on self-awareness, self-management, social awareness and relationship management, in addition to main leadership areas, in workshops can improve managers' and emerging leaders' emotional abilities (Bhatti et al., 2023).

Thanks to the skills leaders obtain, like emotional control, mental adaptability, empathy, effective coaching, handling conflict and being inspirational, they are able to supervise teams successfully and increase their performance (Bhatti et al., 2023). They point out that learning and increasing EI is possible, since it plays an important role in predicting a leader's success in Singapore's culturally and economically diverse companies (Bhatti et al., 2023).

Those leading in Singapore gain from EI training based on their culture which strengthens their understanding of others and how to work well with diverse staff (Bhatti et al., 2023). All of these case studies show that emotional intelligence greatly assists in leading teams, managing organizations and becoming strong in diverse Asian countries. Successfully applying EI concepts to both local traditions and business practices plays an important role in the lasting achievement of companies in Japan, India, China and Singapore (Bhatti et al., 2023; BibGuru, 2024; Brown et al., 2020; Chan et al., 2018).

8 Emotionally Intelligent Leadership for Innovation and Resilience

Nowadays changing and complicated business world needs emotional intelligence from leaders to support innovation and resilience among staff. Having high EI helps leaders deal with their own feelings and notice those of other team members, allowing for a positive environment that encourages everyone to be creative, adjust to changes and work well into the future.

People who are emotionally intelligent inspire their teams to generate new ideas by assuring trust, free speech and a safe environment. Their understanding of themselves and others allows them to notice when someone or a team is under pressure, so they can quickly support new ideas and inventiveness. When they regulate their emotions, leaders inspire a feeling of steadiness and flexibility which help when facing uncertainty and ambiguity in innovation work.

Also, EI allows different teams to work together successfully by bringing everyone closer emotionally and culturally and encouraging everyone's input. Individuals with solid social skills and the ability to build relationships can lead others to accomplish shared innovative targets, cope with opposition and build team confidence.

People with emotionally intelligent leadership are much better at bouncing back from problems and accepting change. Those with advanced emotional intelligence often recognize signs of stress and can prevent it from lowering either their personal or team productivity. Their ability to feel and show understanding, as well as giving emotional support, raises employee resilience and encourages them to care about their jobs during difficulties.

Being emotionally controlled allows leaders to lead their teams calmly and clearly through hard times. They cultivate learning by considering setbacks as ways for employees and the company to improve which promotes resilience at every level.

Having emotional intelligence supports a leader's actions, leading to more opportunities for innovation and greater resilience throughout the company. Efficient leaders are aware of their emotions, keep real relationships with those they manage and help the team grow their skills. As a result, organizations can deal more effectively with the different challenges caused by VUCA and maintain both high levels of competition and staff engagement.

All in all, emotionally intelligent leaders support innovation and stability in an organization, helping it meet new pressures and difficulties confidently and for a long time.

9 EI and Remote Work in Today's World

Since virtual leaders cannot see their teams in person, they must deal with strong emotions due to technology, time zones and cultural differences (Dilan Consulting, 2025). Since you cannot show your feelings without gestures or facial expressions, it is common to misunderstand what someone feels. A leader working remotely must be aware of emotions and intent in messages, communicating clearly and verifying the understanding of their team members.

Relying on Trust and Rapport Building is difficult when people are not meeting each other in person. Trust is built more gradually by making sure to be open, to stick with plans and organize virtual events regularly with those in your team (Dilan Consulting, 2025).

Since virtual teams do not have immediate face-to-face conversations, managers must use emotional intelligence to watch for early signs of conflict, discuss them empathetically and handle misunderstandings constructively (Dilan Consulting, 2025). In a multi-time zone setting, it's important for leaders to be highly flexible, rely on online messages and communicate with individuals according to their circumstances (Dilan Consulting, 2025).

Emotional effects of technological change need to be considered by accounting. People with EI skills give patience, encouragement and guidance to individuals so work keeps flowing (Dilan Consulting, 2025). Virtual leaders struggle to keep people responsible while staying fair about respecting their home lives. According to Dilan Consulting (2025), effective leadership driven by emotion intelligence values clearly stated goals, fairness and protecting the staff from exhaustion.

EI training, improved communication habits, familiarity with technology and better knowledge about work-life balance are useful for leaders and team members working virtually (Dilan Consulting, 2025).

9.1 Maintaining Empathy, Trust and Communication at a Distance

Effortful actions and plans are necessary to overcome the problems that remote communication and distance create. Because there is less face-to-face interaction and researchers cannot see each other's non-verbal behaviors when working remotely, it is harder to develop empathy. To encourage empathy, leaders should set up times when everyone can share openly and without disruption, while the leader gives thoughtful continuation questions.

Talking about your own struggles and admitting the struggles of others promotes trust and compliments someone's understanding. Besides, video conferencing is very helpful as it allows group members to notice facial movements and feelings through tone. Relaxed online social activities like coffee chats and happy hours help everyone get to know one another better and care more about each other (MorphCast, 2024).

Because trust helps remote teams succeed, it is more difficult to establish trust when people do not interact face-to-face. To maintain trust with their team online, leaders must be honest and allow team members to take part in making decisions. Having regular chats, with both individuals and teams, helps build connections and makes everyone responsible. Asking about feelings in each discussion leads to psychological safety, while documents like "Working With Me" and social storytelling improve how everyone sees and understands each other. Maintaining group work by making sure everyone feels trusted and capable enough and not watching all the details leads to teamwork and builds trust.

Getting information across effectively is necessary to decrease confusion and feelings of loneliness in online teams. When video meetings and message-based and document-sharing methods are combined, everyone receives all necessary information. Setting expectations and making sure both parties know how to communicate helps avoid confusion and paying attention during video chats improves how much we understand each other. If you keep offering feedback and timely recognition, ensure clarity and use cultural sensitivity in communication, the team will feel engaged, respected and a sense of belonging (Mondo, 2024; WellRight, 2021).

There are many possible challenges to remote work, among them isolation and issues related to technology, differences in time and a lack of easy contact for conversations. Participating in video calls and games with colleagues is a way to rebuild relationships that are important for connections.

Appreciating how much work individuals can deal with and giving them flexibility helps keep employees mentally well. Use of technology, in combination with training, helps to improve access to and use of services. Creating a work environment where everyone feels safe and welcomed increase team rapport. In the end, if teams are trained and coached frequently in digital communication and empathy, they become better at working together, no matter their physical distance (Mondo, 2024; WellRight, 2021).

9.2 Digital Tools that Support EI Development and Practice

Tools on the Internet can improve emotional intelligence (EI) by offering users different interactive ways to develop their self-awareness, empathy, ability to handle emotions and social skills (Ramirez & Martinez, 2025; Silva et al., 2024).

Several apps and websites have been made to help with emotional intelligence. One example is called Daniel Tiger's Grr-ific Feelings, a show that combines music, games and learning to help children master emotions at an early level (Ramirez & Martinez, 2025). Fun features in Breathe, Think, Do with Sesame and Peekapak guide children through different lessons on emotional regulation and social-emotional learning. Many of these tools mix games, stories and useful exercises to help people recognize their feelings, be mindful and figure out how to cope with problems (Silva et al., 2024).

Receptivity, as well as similar AI-powered tools, help adults and professionals by examining language patterns to give advice on emotions and ways to interact with others. New online programs are available, so training can be done based on lessons, practice exercises and quizzes that are assessed remotely to allow students to learn at their own time and pace (Ramirez & Martinez, 2025).

There are also digital apps like the Mood Meter which guide users to watch and sort out their moods often, to improve their awareness and ability to regulate their emotions. Using gamification and badges, platforms keep users interested in practice and learning about emotional intelligence. Discussion boards and using digital journals online help people reflect on and relate to their emotions and those of others (Silva et al., 2024).

Video conferencing software helps people interact face-to-face, interpret the emotions in their colleagues' behavior and practice empathy even when they are not together in the room. These services are now combined with EI ideas to help virtual leaders and teams stay connected, receive feedback and feel safe while working remotely (Ramirez & Martinez, 2025).

To sum up, the benefits of EI skills can now spread among people of all ages and throughout all fields because of the flexible and accessible digital tools available (Ramirez & Martinez, 2025; Silva et al., 2024).

10 Developing EI Competencies in Asian Leaders

Leaders in Asia must develop emotional intelligence since it is needed for success in today's work environment. Largely, building EI in these leaders is achieved by using formal training courses, coaching, mentoring, having cross-cultural exposure and getting regular feedback (Bradberry & Greaves, 2009).

11 Registered Learning Process

These training courses are intended to help Asian leaders become more aware of themselves, control their emotions, notice others' feelings, feel empathy and get along with people. These programs help managers and supervisors gain skills they need to improve their leadership skills. There are courses like "The Emotionally Intelligent Leader" with Asian Institute of Management that conduct interactive sessions using self-assessment, profiling and planning for personal development to enable leaders to positively influence others (Asian Institute of Management, 2025).

Some programs in the region also use live online sessions, group talks, role playing and case analyses, so participants increase their persistence, skills in conflict resolution and the ability to grow as a member of a team. Assessments and development plans in programs such as EQ-i 2.0 and TESI from Kandidata Asia are based on evidence and are fitted to the needs of organizations and their people (Kandidata Asia, 2023; Multi-Health Systems, 2025).

11.1 Sessions Provided by Coaching and Mentoring

Being coached and mentored greatly helps leaders in Asia improve their emotional intelligence. Emphasizing emotional skills like awareness, empathy, control and strength, peer group mentoring helps people develop emotional intelligence. Typically, these relationships are democratic and provide psychological support that helps leaders use emotional abilities when leading (Kandidata Asia, 2023; Bar-On, 2004).

To match the culture of East Asia, executive coaching trains managers to use positive relationships and speak clearly, value teamwork despite differences of status and open up to new ways of thinking and acting with some self-control in terms of their feelings. Coaches regularly help leaders cultivate a desire to grow, suggest little improvements in their behavior and direct them on handling emotions and feedback when interacting with others. To be effective in Asia, coaching should recognize and respect the community's traditions and also help leaders grow in their abilities (Kandidata Asia, 2023).

Support for EI within an organization includes its HR approach, how leaders are developed and the quality of its workplace environment.

Supporting emotional intelligence (EI) in an organization helps leaders do their job well and encourages a positive working environment. Usually, support comes from human resource practices, the development of leadership roles and making sure emotional competencies are respected at work (Abraham, 2005; Goleman, 2008; Sharma & Tiwari, 2023).

HR activities form the main support for bringing EI into an organization. Using EI in recruitment, selection, training, performance evaluation and planning advancement within the company is a part of this. Candidates are selected in part based on their technical skills and their emotional qualities such as self-awareness, the ability to empathize and how well they interact with others. Employers develop training programs that focus on EI and help staff build emotional self-control, good communication skills and resolve conflicts. Within performance management, EI-related aims and input are given to help leaders and workers display emotional intelligence daily. Using emotional intelligence in HR helps organizations guarantee that employees have the needed emotional abilities which add to effective teams and strong overall achievements (Druskat & Kayes, 2000; Sharma & Tiwari, 2023).

A leadership pipeline is a system that finds, trains and readies promising leaders for more advanced positions within the organization. Those organizations that emphasize EI in their leadership training realize how emotional skills help solve challenging team and organizational situations. When developing leadership, evaluating people's EI helps find out their key strengths and what they can improve. They teach students how to be empathetic, strong and have good social relationships using coaching, mentoring and interactive methods. This means leaders in the making are prepared with both ability and attitude to steer and influence a group of people with different backgrounds. The presence of emotionally intelligent leaders guides organizations to form more flexible and emotionally intelligent leadership cultures (Sharma & Tiwari, 2023).

An encouraging work atmosphere helps increase and maintain EI in an organization. Companies can support such a culture by encouraging values centered around emotional awareness, empathy, free communication and feeling safe. If workers feel comfortable opening up and dealing sincerely with their colleagues, trust and co-operation between teams grow. Examples of cultural initiatives are having ongoing conversations, holding emotional intelligence workshops, organizing events for building teamwork and giving rewards for smart emotional moves by people. Being committed to EI as a leader is necessary to change attitudes so emotional skills are seen as playing an important role in achieving the organization's objectives. When EI is supported by workplace culture, employees are better supported and stay motivated which helps the company innovate and bounce back from change (Druskat & Wolff, 2001; Sharma & Tiwari, 2023).

Emotional intelligence is best embedded in a company when there is support from HR, good leadership training and a positive workplace atmosphere. This solution helps leaders work more effectively and employees feel more satisfied (Goleman, 2008; Sharma & Tiwari, 2023).

12 Implications for Research, Practice and Society

Audience	Implications	Actionable Suggestions
Researchers	Despite the existing researches on the connection between Emotional Intelligence (EI) and leadership, the relationship between Emotional Intelligence (EI) and leadership in relation to entrepreneurial opportunity recognition, innovation and the success of the venture (especially in developing markets) is not yet explored	Conduct longitudinal and cross-cultural experiments on the effect of EI on performance of an entrepreneur; include EI in entrepreneurship research paradigm
Practitioners / Entrepreneurs	The use of EI skills like empathy, self-awareness and self-regulation can be applied to improve decision-making, stakeholder usages and adaptability in unstable and unpredictable markets	Include EI assessment and training into the development of entrepreneurship programs; apply an EI-based approach to team building, conflict resolution and customer involvement
Policy-makers / Society	Inclusive growth, social innovation and sustainable operations in business, particularly in the context of emerging economies, could be boosted via EI-driven entrepreneurship	Incorporate EI skill training within incubator programs of new startups, small- and medium-sized enterprise support program and within national entrepreneurship strategies to enhance both financial and societal results

12.1 Conclusion

Asian companies rely on emotional intelligence to help them achieve lasting success by enhancing their leaders, improving how they interact, promoting teamwork and stimulating innovation. Companies that introduce EI into their HR, leadership and workplace systems succeed in developing teams that can handle tough situations.

Findings indicate that if staff members build self-awareness, empathy, emotional regulation and strong relationships in their interactions, everyone and the company will perform and compete better in dynamic markets. Thanks to emotional intelligence, leaders can earn trust, fix conflicts amicably and help build an atmosphere important for the business's continued success.

In the future, Asian organizations should intentionally focus on educating their next leaders, with coaching that is relevant to their culture, classroom learning and chances to gain experience in working with people from various cultures. Because of globalization and the transformations brought by technology, organizations looking for continual growth and meaningful results around the world will need leaders who show emotional intelligence.

References

Abraham, R. (2005). Emotional intelligence in organizations: A conceptualization. *Genetic, Social, and General Psychology Monographs, 131*(2), 117–143.

American Psychological Association. (2015). *Guidelines for the assessment of and intervention with persons with disabilities.* American Psychological Association.

Ang, S., & Van Dyne, L. (2008). *Handbook of cultural intelligence: Theory, measurement, and applications.* M.E. Sharpe.

Asian Institute of Management. (2025). The Emotionally Intelligent Leader [Online course]. Asian Institute of Management. https://aim.edu/programs/the-emotionally-intelligent-leader/

Bar-On, R. (2004). The Bar-On Emotional Quotient Inventory (EQ-i): Rationale, description and summary of psychometric properties. In G. Geher (Ed.), *Measuring emotional intelligence: Common ground and controversy* (pp. 111–142). Nova Science Publishers.

Bhatti, R. H., Ghulam, A., Nisar, A. A., Chughtai, E., & Yousaf, Z. (2023). Emotional intelligence, innovative work behavior, and cultural intelligence: A comprehensive framework for innovative performance. *Healthcare*, 11(14), Article 2075. https://doi.org/10.3390/healthcare11142075

BibGuru. (2024). *Emotional intelligence in Asian leadership: Case studies from Japan, India, China, and Singapore.* BibGuru.

Boyatzis, R. E. (2009). Competencies as a behavioral approach to emotional intelligence. *Journal of Management Development, 28*(9), 749–770.

Boyatzis, R. E., Goleman, D., & Rhee, K. (2000). Clustering competence in emotional intelligence: Insights from the emotional competence inventory (ECI). In R. Bar-On & J. D. A. Parker (Eds.), *Handbook of emotional intelligence* (pp. 343–362). Jossey-Bass.

Boyatzis, R., & McKee, A. (2005). *Resonant leadership: Renewing yourself and connecting with others through mindfulness, hope and compassioncompassion.* Harvard Business Press.

Bradberry, T., & Greaves, J. (2009). *Emotional Intelligence 2.0.* TalentSmart.

Brown, A., Chia, A., & Ooi, G. L. (2020). Leadership, emotional intelligence, and team outcomes: Evidence from Singaporean organizations. *Asia Pacific Journal of Management, 37*(2), 345–367. https://doi.org/10.1007/s10490-018-9634-9

Chan, K. Y., Cheung, S. Y., & Lim, C. S. (2018). Emotional intelligence and leadership in Asia: A multi-country case study approach. In S. Ang & L. Van Dyne (Eds.), *Handbook of cultural intelligence* (pp. 255–274). Routledge.

Chen, S. X. (2016). The role of culture in the expression, experience, and management of emotion. In U. Kumar (Ed.), *The Routledge international handbook of psychosocial resilience* (pp. 135–146). Routledge.

Cherniss, C. (2010). Emotional intelligence: Toward clarification of a concept. *Industrial and Organizational Psychology, 3*(2), 110–126.

Côté, S. (2017). Enhancing managerial effectiveness via emotional intelligence: An overview. *Emotion Review, 9*(3), 169–175.

Dilan Consulting. (2025, January 31). Why leaders must master emotional intelligence in 2025. Dilan Consulting. https://dilanconsulting.com/why-leaders-must-master-emotional-intelligence-in-2025/

Divergences, N. G. (2023). World Economic Outlook. *World Economic Outlook.*

Druskat, V. U., & Kayes, D. C. (2000). Learning versus performance in short-term project teams. *Small Group Research, 31*(3), 328–353. https://doi.org/10.1177/104649640003100303

Druskat, V. U., & Wolff, S. B. (2001). Building the emotional intelligence of groups. *Harvard Business Review, 79*(3), 80–91.

Dulewicz, V., & Higgs, M. (2003). Emotional intelligence: A review and evaluation study. *Journal of Managerial Psychology, 18*(1), 26–41.

Farh, J.-L., & Cheng, B.-S. (2000). A cultural analysis of paternalistic leadership in Chinese organizations. In J. T. Li, A. S. Tsui, & E. Weldon (Eds.), *Management and organizations in the Chinese context* (pp. 84–127). Macmillan.

Gelfand, M. J., Erez, M., & Aycan, Z. (2007). Cross-cultural organizational behavior. *Annual Review of Psychology, 58*, 479–514.

Goleman, D. (1995). *Emotional intelligence: Why it can matter more than IQ*. Bantam Books.

Goleman, D. (2007). *Social intelligence: The new science of human relationships*. Bantam Books.

Goleman, D. (2008). *Emotional intelligence: Why it can matter more than IQ* (10th anniversary ed.). Bantam Books.

Goleman, D., Boyatzis, R. E., & McKee, A. (2013). *Primal leadership: Unleashing the power of emotional intelligence*. Harvard Business Press.

Hanges, P. J., Dorfman, P. W., Shteynberg, G., & Bates, R. (2004). Culture and leadership: A connectionist perspective. In R. J. House, P. J. Hanges, M. Javidan, P. W. Dorfman, & V. Gupta (Eds.), *Culture, leadership, and organizations: The GLOBE study of 62 societies* (pp. 376–432). Sage.

Henry, S. (2011). *EQ and leadership in Asia: Using emotional intelligence to lead and inspire your people*. Wiley.

Hofstede, G. (2001). *Culture's consequences: Comparing values, behaviors, institutions, and organizations across nations* (2nd ed.). Sage.

Hofstede, G. (2011). Dimensionalizing cultures: The hofstede model in context. *Online Readings in Psychology and Culture, 2*(1), 8.

Hwang, K. K. (1987). Face and favor: The Chinese power game. *American Journal of Sociology, 92*(4), 944–974. https://doi.org/10.1086/228588

International Monetary Fund. (2018). Asia: At the Forefront of Change—Leadership and Transformation in a Dynamic Region. In *Regional Economic Outlook: Asia and Pacific* (May 2018). Washington, DC: IMF.

Kandidata Asia. (2023). EQ-i 2.0 and TESI certification programs. Kandidata Asia. https://kandidataasia.com/training-certification/eqi20-certifications/

Khan, M. A., Ghouri, A. M., & Khan, M. A. (2020). The relationship between intercultural sensitivity and emotional intelligence among university students. *International Journal of Caring Sciences, 13*(1), 41–47.

Kim, M.-S., & Hong, S.-Y. (2004). A cross-cultural comparison of the effects of communicative contexts on conversational indirectness. *Journal of Asian Pacific Communication, 14*(1), 41–59. https://doi.org/10.1075/japc.14.1.04kim

Kitayama, S., & Markus, H. R. (2000). The pursuit of happiness and the realization of sympathy: Cultural patterns of self, social relations, and well-being. In E. Diener & E. M. Suh (Eds.), *Culture and subjective well-being* (pp. 113–161). MIT Press.

Leung, A.K.-Y., & Cohen, D. (2011). Within- and between-culture variation: Individual differences and the cultural logics of honor, face, and dignity cultures. *Journal of Personality and Social Psychology, 100*(3), 507–526. https://doi.org/10.1037/a0022151

Markus, H. R., & Kitayama, S. (1991). Culture and the self: Implications for cognition, emotion, and motivation. *Psychological Review, 98*(2), 224–253. https://doi.org/10.1037/0033-295X.98.2.224

Matsumoto, D. (1990). Cultural similarities and differences in display rules. *Motivation and Emotion, 14*(3), 195–214. https://doi.org/10.1007/BF00995569

Mayer, J. D., & Salovey, P. (1997). What is emotional intelligence? In P. Salovey & D. J. Sluyter (Eds.), *Emotional development and emotional intelligence: Educational implications* (pp. 3–31). Basic Books.

Mayer, J. D., Salovey, P., & Caruso, D. R. (2002). *Mayer-Salovey-Caruso Emotional Intelligence Test (MSCEIT) User's Manual*. Toronto, Canada: Multi-Health Systems.

Mayer, J. D., Salovey, P., & Caruso, D. R. (2004). Emotional intelligence: Theory, findings, and implications. *Psychological Inquiry, 15*(3), 197–215. https://doi.org/10.1207/s15327965pli1503_02

Mayer, J. D., Salovey, P., & Caruso, D. R. (2008). Emotional intelligence: New ability or eclectic traits? *American Psychologist, 63*(6), 503.

Michigan State University, Broad College of Business. (2024). *Global leadership in Asia: Navigating complexity and change.* Michigan State University.

Mondo. (2024, January 10). 6 ways to improve communication with remote teams. *Mondo Blog.* https://mondo.com/insights/ways-to-improve-communication-with-remote-teams/

MorphCast. (2024, February 8). Best video conferencing platforms for 2024: A comprehensive guide. *MorphCast Blog.* https://www.morphcast.com/blog/best-video-conferencing-platforms-for-2024-a-comprehensive-guide/

Multi-Health Systems. (2025). EQ-i 2.0 & EQ360 certification course. Multi-Health Systems Inc. https://training.mhs.com/mhstraining/detail/508/1568779200000

Oyserman, D., & Lee, S. W. S. (2008). Does culture influence what and how we think? Effects of priming individualism and collectivism. In R. Sorrentino & S. Yamaguchi (Eds.), *Handbook of motivation and cognition across cultures* (pp. 237–265). Elsevier.

Ramirez, L., & Martinez, J. (2025). Leveraging technology for emotional intelligence training: New frontiers in digital learning. *Journal of Educational Technology and Society, 28*(1), 45–59.

Rockstuhl, T., Hong, Y., Ng, K.-Y., Ang, S., & Chiu, C.-Y. (2010). Beyond general intelligence (IQ) and emotional intelligence (EQ): The role of cultural intelligence (CQ) on cross-border leadership effectiveness in a globalized world. *Journal of Social Issues, 67*(4), 825–840.

Salovey, P., & Mayer, J. D. (1990). Emotional intelligence. *Imagination, Cognition and Personality, 9*(3), 185–211. https://doi.org/10.2190/DUGG-P24E-52WK-6CDG

Salovey, P., Bedell, B. T., Detweiler, J. B., & Mayer, J. D. (1999). Coping intelligently: Emotional intelligence and the coping process. In C. R. Snyder (Ed.), *Coping: The psychology of what works* (pp. 141–164). Oxford University Press.

Schutte, N. S., Malouff, J. M., Hall, L. E., Haggerty, D. J., Cooper, J. T., Golden, C. J., & Dornheim, L. (1998). Development and validation of a measure of emotional intelligence. *Personality and Individual Differences, 25*(2), 167–177. https://doi.org/10.1016/S0191-8869(98)00001-4

Sharma, R., & Tiwari, P. (2023). Emotional intelligence in human resource management: Strategies for a thriving workplace. *International Journal of Human Resource Studies, 13*(1), 45–62. https://doi.org/10.5296/ijhrs.v13i1.20601

Silva, A. F., Lopes, F. M., & Pereira, R. (2024). Digital tools for emotional intelligence: A systematic review of interventions and outcomes. *Computers in Human Behavior, 152*, Article 107093. https://doi.org/10.1016/j.chb.2024.107093

Singh, D. (2004). *Emotional intelligence at work: A professional guide* (2nd ed.). Sage.

Ting-Toomey, S. (1988). Intercultural conflict styles: A face-negotiation theory. In Y. Y. Kim & W. B. Gudykunst (Eds.), *Theories in intercultural communication* (pp. 213–235). Sage.

Tonby, O., Woetzel, J., Razdan, R., Choi, W., Yamakawa, N., Seong, J., & Devesa, T. (2021). *The future of Asia: The trailblazing consumers in Asia propelling growth.* Mckinsey Global Institute.

Tsai, J. L. (2007). Ideal affect: Cultural causes and behavioral consequences. *Perspectives on Psychological Science, 2*(3), 242–259.

Tsai, J. L., Miao, F. F., Seppala, E., Fung, H. H., & Yeung, D. Y. (2007). Influence and adjustment goals: Sources of cultural differences in ideal affect. *Journal of Personality and Social Psychology, 92*(6), 1102–1117. https://doi.org/10.1037/0022-3514.92.6.1102

WellRight. (2021, September 27). 8 ways to improve communication in remote teams. *WellRight Blog.* https://www.wellright.com/blog/8-ways-improve-communication-remote-teams

World Bank. (2025). *East Asia and Pacific economic update: Pathways to future prosperity.* World Bank.

World Economic Forum. (2024). *Global Risks Report 2024.* World Economic Forum.

Dr. Anu Dandona holds a Ph.D. in psychology and works as an associate professor at D Y Patil International University in Akurdi, Pune. With more than 12 years of teaching experience at the university level, she is credited with numerous research publications that have been published in journals indexed in SCOPUS, Web of Science and UGC CARE. Her academic writings and research demonstrate a keen interest in the field of psychology and attest to the benefits of utilizing interdisciplinarity to advance knowledge in the field.

The Link Between Emotional Intelligence and Knowledge Sharing Behavior. Why Should High-Tech Firms in Asia Care?

Syed Muntasir Husain Bokhari, Lakeesha K. Ransom, and Djoen San Santoso

Abstract In the era of digital transformation, firms are increasingly embracing open innovation, leveraging internal and external knowledge to enhance their competitive advantages. Emotional intelligence, defined as the ability to manage emotions and to use that understanding to guide behavior, is essential for fostering effective work relationships and facilitating knowledge sharing. This chapter is an excerpt from a recent doctoral dissertation that illustrates the significant group differences of demographic variables on the relationships between emotional intelligence, work relationships, and open innovation in high-tech firms in emerging markets. It presents 10 principal findings derived from a survey of 379 employees in the telecommunications industry. The findings reveal that the individual employees under thirty exhibit higher knowledge sharing, owing to their emotional intelligence and strong work relationships with colleagues. Moreover, entry-level individuals substantially enhance knowledge sharing due to their collaborative nature. Furthermore, individuals with 2 to 5 years of experience are capable of sharing knowledge externally, hence enhancing innovation. The findings highlight the significance of emotional intelligence in facilitating both internal and external knowledge sharing, hence improving organizational innovativeness. Thus, the findings are advantageous for business leaders and practitioners, as they ought to use emotional intelligence assessments in recruitment, develop mentorship programs, and encourage interorganizational collaboration.

S. M. H. Bokhari (✉)
Program Specialist, School of Management, Asian Institute of Technology, Bangkok, Thailand
e-mail: nabeel@ait.ac.th

L. K. Ransom
School of Management, Asian Institute of Technology, Bangkok, Thailand
e-mail: lakeesharansom@ait.ac.th

D. S. Santoso
School of Engineering and Technology, Asian Institute of Technology, Bangkok, Thailand
e-mail: djoensan@ait.ac.th

T. Endress and Y. F. Badir (eds.), *Business and Management in Asia: Opportunities and Entrepreneurship*, https://doi.org/10.1007/978-981-95-4909-2_4

1 Introduction

Technological transformation has facilitated interorganizational collaboration, encouraging firms to share knowledge and ideas both internally and externally to create, utilize, and recombine their existing and new knowledge (Laursen & Salter, 2006; Serirungsun et al., 2024; Väyrynen et al., 2017) influenced by the work relationships of individual employee (Robak, 2022). Furthermore, the ability to assess one's own and others' emotions, regulate these emotions, and apply them effectively enhances firms' performance (Kim, 2020). The term open innovation,[1] initially introduced by Henry Chesbrough (2003), denotes the significant opportunities for large, established firms to depart from traditional search methods and engage in broader, more enriched search efforts by leveraging the extensive pool of ideas and knowledge available outside the firm (Chesbrough, 2003).

The contemporary workplace is digital, business-oriented, and equipped with advanced technologies, contrasting with conventional workplace environments (Chernyak-Hai & Rabenu, 2018), hence rendering the current workplace more global. Furthermore, it has diversified due to heightened human mobility. Employees are encouraged to cultivate their work relationships[2] to improve performance, social support, and networking, particularly those in rapidly expanding businesses (Chernyak-Hai & Rabenu, 2018). Emotional intelligence[3] is defined as an individual's capacity to comprehend, perceive, and distinguish their own emotions and those of others, and to regulate their actions accordingly to navigate daily tasks (Mayer et al., 1999). Bokhari's (2023) empirically examined two fundamental questions utilizing three distinct bodies of literature: open innovation, work relationships, and emotional intelligence. The research study investigated whether emotional intelligence influences open innovation and whether work relationships mediate this relationship.

Surprisingly, individual-level open innovation received less attention despite individual's enthusiasm for creative ideas and innovative endeavors (Abhari et al., 2022).

---

[1] As Badir et al. (2020) stated, two functions are considered while measuring open innovation, one is internal knowledge sources and the second is external knowledge sources. The internal knowledge sources items include colleagues, subordinates, and manager within the firm, reading and/or personal search, and previous experience. The external knowledge source items include personal relationships with other professionals out the firm, customers, suppliers, competitors, universities, public research firms, contracted R&D service providers, and external consultants.

[2] According to Colbert et al. (2016), the work relationships have 6 functions, such as task assistance, career advancement, emotional support, friendship, personal growth, and giving to others, and each of these functions have 3 items with a total of 18 items to measure work relationships.

[3] According to Davies et al. (2010), the Brief Emotional Intelligence Scale have 5 functions, such as appraisal of own emotions, appraisal of others' emotions, regulation of own emotions, regulation of others' emotions, and utilization of emotions, and each of these functions have 2 items with a total of 10 items to measure emotional intelligence.

Furthermore, emotional intelligence, being potentially an important concept elucidating the interpersonal and intrapersonal aspects of the individual, received insufficient attention regarding the emotional competencies essential for individuals' efficiency and effectiveness in the workplace settings (Kaur, 2023). Moreover, empirical research indicates that firms in emerging economies continue to encounter institutional, financial, and knowledge/skill-based constraints and risks, which significantly impede their innovation process (Bogers et al., 2019; Wu, 2022).

Hence, this chapter illustrates that the demographic factors, including age, tenure at the current firm, overall work experience, engineering status, and geographic region, significantly impact the internal and external knowledge sharing of emotionally intelligent employees in high-tech firms in South and Southeast Asia, which are emerging markets. The findings presented in this chapter contribute to the practical world by providing holistic level recommendations for firms regarding hiring and promotion strategies, by comparing and analyzing various groups based on their demographic data within the telecommunication industry considered as high-tech firms.

2 Why Individuals Are Important in Firms?

In this chapter, individuals working in the telecommunication industry are considered as survey participants. Individuals working in new product development sector are continuously encouraged by their employers to search for external knowledge to sustain and promote corporate open innovation and strategic programs (Mubarak et al., 2025). Moreover, it is the individual researchers within the firm who usually design and develop new ideas by collaborating with sources outside the firm boundaries (Alexy et al., 2013; Chesbrough, 2003).

Furthermore, it is researched that individuals working in open-source software industry will always uphold the best interest of their firms (Joachim Henkel, 2008). Hence, the individuals will become more effective and efficient at generating new ideas and knowledge for their firm by balancing both internal and external knowledge sources (Salter et al., 2015). Hence, individuals in firms are an important factor in order to generate new knowledge and ideas which eventually will assist the firm maintain their competitive advantage.

3 Contrasting Knowledge Sharing Behaviors Across Employee Profiles

Data were gathered from 379 individuals employed in the largest and most prominent telecommunication firms in South and Southeast Asia, each fulfilling various roles within their firms. The participants were grouped by gender, age, highest degree obtained, current position, tenure at the current firm, overall work experience, is an engineer or not, and geographic region to facilitate analysis and comparison of differences. Consequently, the subsequent 10 findings were identified:

Finding 1:*Emotionally intelligent employees less than 30 years of age will share knowledge internally.* Prior to the age of 30, individuals embark on their professional careers and are unreserved in sharing knowledge internally with managers, colleagues, and subordinates, leveraging their prior experiences and research to enhance their organizational recognition and reward. First, individuals under thirty with high emotional intelligence typically exhibit a robust growth mentality, perceiving knowledge sharing as advantageous for both personal development and the advancement of the firm. Secondly, younger employees with high emotional intelligence emphasize the cultivation and maintenance of professional connections. Internal knowledge sharing strengthens ties, cultivating trust and rapport within professional networks. Third, emotionally intelligent young employees acknowledge the professional significance and career progression opportunities associated with exhibiting competence and disseminating pertinent knowledge transparently inside their firms. Hence, employees under 30 with high emotional intelligence actively participate in internal knowledge sharing to foster trust, advance their careers, and make significant contributions to their firms.

Finding 2:*Employees less than 30 years of age will have better work relationships with their colleagues and share knowledge internally.* Emotionally intelligent younger employees are distinctly equipped to cultivate strong working relationships and facilitate efficient information transfer among firms. First, younger emotionally intelligent professionals exhibit enhanced empathy, allowing them to comprehend their colleagues' viewpoints, requirements, and feeling, thereby fostering deeper, more trusting connections that facilitate knowledge sharing. Secondly, emotional intelligence enhances individual's capacity for successful communication, enabling them to articulate concepts clearly and engage in active listening. This encourages open communication, enabling colleagues and subordinates to feel more at ease pertinent information. Third, emotionally intelligent younger individuals frequently foster positivity and inclusivity within their workplaces. This amiable disposition encourages colleagues and others to participate more freely in collaborative knowledge exchange. Therefore, emotionally intelligent individuals under 30 cultivate pleasant and trusting work relationships that inherently promote open, inclusive, and effective internal knowledge sharing.

Finding 3:*Emotionally intelligent employees at entry level will share knowledge internally.* Emotionally intelligent entry-level employees innately prioritize collaboration and ongoing development, positioning them as essential enablers of internal knowledge exchange within their firm. First, emotionally intelligent entry-level employees often perceive knowledge sharing as essential to their professional success, motivating them to participate actively in collaborative exchanges to improve collective learning and career advancement. Second, their receptiveness to feedback and eagerness to learn promote effortless exchange of insights and experiences with peers and supervisors. Finally, their inherent inclination toward collaborative work fosters active participation and engagement within teams, hence facilitating enhanced knowledge sharing among colleagues and supervisors. Thus, emotionally intelligent entry-level employees are essential in fostering internal knowledge sharing by prioritizing collaboration, learning, and team involvement from the beginning of their careers.

Finding 4:*Entry-level employees having better work relationships with their colleagues will share knowledge internally.* Entry-level personnel cultivate robust professional ties, propelled by their technology adeptness and collaborative problem-solving approach. First, entry-level employees are typically proficient in technology and rapidly acclimate to new advancements, fostering robust relationships through collaborative learning and joint problem-solving. Second, a mutual comprehension of technical vocabulary and concepts facilitates communication, promoting seamless interactions and effective exchange of professional thoughts. Third, consistent technical challenges encourage entry-level employees to cooperate closely, strengthening workplace relationships and improving collective problem-solving capabilities. Consequently, entry-level employees possessing robust work relationships are ideally positioned to improve internal knowledge sharing due to their technological proficiency, collaborative disposition, and collective problem-solving skills.

Finding 5:*Emotionally intelligent non-engineers will share their knowledge internally.* Emotionally intelligent non-engineers are ideally suited for internal knowledge sharing owing to their strong communication abilities, empathy, and collaborative disposition. First, individuals without engineering backgrounds who possess elevated emotional intelligence typically exhibit greater proficiency in verbal and written communication, allowing them to articulate concepts clearly and tailor their messages to diverse audiences within the firm. Secondly, their emotional awareness enables them to discern when colleagues or subordinates require assistance or advice, leading them to proactively contribute ideas or past experiences for collective success. Third, in contrast to certain engineering positions that emphasize specialized technical expertise, non-engineers frequently participate in cross-functional collaboration, hence increasing their propensity to contribute varied perspectives derived from reading, previous roles, or multidisciplinary experiences. As a result, by utilizing their emotional intelligence, non-engineers proficiently promote internal knowledge sharing via clear communication, empathetic assistance, and cross-functional collaboration.

Finding 6:*Emotionally intelligent employees having two to five years of work experience in their current firms will share knowledge externally.* This chapter unveils that the emotionally intelligent telecom employees working in their current firm from two to five years, will share their knowledge externally compared to the employees who are either working less than two years or more than five years. First, they can develop contacts with professionals in related or complementary fields by sharing knowledge externally, generating potential for cooperation, future partnership, and provide innovative products and services. Second, emotionally intelligent individuals can easily engage with customers, suppliers, and competitors and hence enables individuals to understand market demands, and industry challenges in order for the firm to effectively adapt its products and services to the market needs. Third, emotionally intelligent individuals realize the worth of collaboration, and encourage innovation. Therefore, emotionally intelligent personnel with two to five years of experience in their current firms are ideally positioned to share knowledge externally, utilizing their expertise, networks, and collaborative approach to foster innovation and strategic alliances.

Finding 7:*Emotionally intelligent employees having overall work experience of less than five years share knowledge internally and externally.* Likewise, this chapter further explains that emotionally intelligent employees having less than five years working experience may share knowledge internally in order to fulfill their day-to-day activities. First, usually at the beginning of the career an individual heavily relies on his/her limited prior non-professional experience as well as academic and/or theoretical capabilities and personal search of knowledge. Second, emotionally intelligent employees are open to learning from their colleagues and subordinates. They create an environment in which they may benefit from others' knowledge. Third, emotionally intelligent employees recognize that sharing knowledge internally with colleagues, managers, and subordinates can lead to a culture of creative thinking and innovative solutions. So emotionally intelligent employees with under five years of overall experience actively participate in internal knowledge sharing to facilitate their learning, improve everyday performance, and foster a culture of creativity.

In addition, this chapter further discloses that emotionally intelligent employees having less than five years total working experience may share knowledge externally in order to fulfill their day-to-day activities. First, emotionally intelligent employees having less than five years of total working experience are often ready to learn from others. Engaging with external stakeholders exposes them to different perspectives, industry best practices, and innovative ideas. Second, employees at the beginning of their careers understand the value of developing a professional network. External knowledge sharing allows them to engage with professionals in their industry, mentorship, and partnerships. Third, sharing knowledge externally allows young professionals to demonstrate their skills and understanding in their industry. Hence, they increase their trust and reputation by demonstrating their abilities. Therefore, emotionally intelligent individuals with under five years of experience participate in external knowledge sharing to broaden their learning, establish professional networks, and expand their credibility within the industry.

Finding 8:*Employees having overall experience of five years will have better work relationships with colleagues and share knowledge internally.* Likewise, employees having more than five years of total work relationships and better work relationships with their colleagues may share knowledge internally. First, employees with substantial work experience have a better understanding of their industry and the operations of the firms. This expertise is useful for creating better work relationships among the co-workers and encouraging to share knowledge internally. Second, employees with experience have witnessed industry changes and have adapted new technologies and processes. Their versatility drives them to investigate novel solutions through better working relationships. Third, employees with extensive experience and better work relationships with co-workers are often aware of industry trends. Their awareness enables them to incorporate current and future trends into the work, leading to creation of novel products, services, and solutions. Hence, individuals with five or more years of experience cultivate robust work relationships that promote internal knowledge sharing, allowing them to utilize their industry acumen and adaptability to propel innovation with the firm.

Finding 9:*Emotionally intelligent employees having overall experience other than five to ten years will share knowledge internally.* Moreover, this chapter further unpacks an interesting phenomenon that emotionally intelligent employees' overall work experience other than five to ten years may share knowledge internally. This can transpire due to several reasons, such as first, employees who are emotionally intelligent find joy and happiness in assisting others in their professional development. Sharing knowledge internally and seeing others benefit from their skills can be inherently satisfying, increasing job satisfaction and overall sense of success by solving day-to-day challenges in a more innovative manner. Second, emotionally intelligent individuals are lifelong learners, they appreciate that knowledge sharing is a two-way journey. They frequently learn from their colleagues, managers, and subordinates experience, enabling continuous learning. Third, emotionally intelligent employees persistently contribute to the development of a collaborative organizational culture. They recognize that knowledge silos can hinder progress, and by sharing knowledge, they foster teamwork, innovation, and a healthy work environment. Thus, emotionally intelligent individuals with overall work experience other than five to ten years actively participate in internal knowledge sharing to facilitate others' development, promote continuous learning, and enhance a collaborative and innovative organizational culture.

Finding 10:*Emotionally intelligent Southeast Asian employees will have better work relationships with their colleagues.* Emotionally intelligent employees working in the telecom industry in Southeast Asian countries are more likely to have a better work relationship with their colleagues. This may occur due to fact that first, emotionally intelligent employees are often skilled at understanding cultural and cross-cultural nuances. In Southeast Asia, where diverse cultures and religions coexist, the understanding of cultural and cross-cultural sensitivity is critical. Hence, respect for various cultural practices, tradition, and religion can build harmonious work relationships. Second, emotionally intelligent individuals thrive at interpersonal communication. Their capacity to actively listen and explain themselves clearly contributes to the development of mutual understanding and better work relationships among colleagues. Third, many Southeast Asian societies have rigid hierarchies, which are visible in firms as well. Emotionally intelligent individuals recognize the value of deference and courtesy, which helps healthy work relationships with colleagues and superiors. That is why emotionally intelligent individuals in Southeast Asia foster robust work relationships by maneuvering through cultural nuances, engaging in courteous communication, and conforming to hierarchical workplace norms.

Table 1 Summary of key findings on knowledge sharing behaviors across employee profiles

Employee profiles	Significant profile	Compared with	Findings
Age	< 30	≥ 30	Emotionally intelligent employees less than 30 years of age will share knowledge internally
			Employees less than 30 years of age will have better work relationships with their colleagues and share knowledge internally
Current position	= Entry level	= Middle and top level	Emotionally intelligent employees at entry level will share knowledge internally
			Entry-level employees having better work relationships with their colleagues will share knowledge internally
Engineer	= No	= Yes	Emotionally intelligent non-engineers will share their knowledge internally
Work experience in current firm	= two to five years	≥six years	Emotionally intelligent employees having two to five years of work experience in their current firms will share knowledge externally
Overall work experience	= Less than five years	= More than five years	Emotionally intelligent employees having total work experience of less than five years share knowledge both internally and externally
			Employees having total experience of five years will have better work relationships with colleagues and share knowledge internally
	= five to ten years	> five year and ≥ten years	Emotionally intelligent Employees having total experience between five to ten years will share knowledge internally
Geographic region	= South Asian	= Southeast Asian	Emotionally intelligent Southeast Asian employees will have better work relationships with their colleagues

The Table 1 summarizes all the findings. The "Group" column demonstrates the distinct group considered. The "Significant group" column is the statistically significant group compared with another group mentioned in the third column "Compared with". Finally, the right column "Findings" shows the outcomes.

4 Strategic Takeaways for Business Leaders and Practitioners

Nevertheless, certain notable limitations regarding group differences were observed and should be considered. There are no distinctions between male and female groups. Moreover, the disparity in educational background or highest degree attained is not a significant element to consider. From the ten findings, five key takeaways for business leaders and practitioners are presented, offering practical implications that help managers and their firms. First, we recommend that managers incorporate emotional intelligence evaluations into recruitment procedures and provide continuous emotional intelligence training for staff at all levels. Secondly, we recommend that managers implement structured mentorship or buddy systems, pairing employees under thirty and entry-level staff with experienced colleagues to enhance knowledge transfer and foster relationship building. Third, we advise managers to promote cross-functional projects or initiatives to enhance interaction between engineers and non-engineers, as well as among diverse experience groups, thereby optimizing internal collaboration. Forth, we recommend that firms strategically assign employees of moderate tenure (two to five years) to tasks that necessitate external collaborations, networking, and partnerships with industry experts, consultants, or suppliers. Finally, we encourage multinational and multicultural firms to develop culturally attuned and region-specific initiatives to foster workplace relationships, thereby improving interpersonal dynamics and organizational harmony.

5 Limitation and Direction for Future Research

We stimulate and encourage further investigation by applying the findings and analyses across several sectors, including electronics, healthcare, finance, education, and any other industry where knowledge enhancement is essential to identify potential disparities. Likewise, to obtain meaningful results, researchers and/or firms are urged to expand this investigation to particular firms or even individual departments/units within a firm. Moreover, expanding the region and/or continents may provide benefits in comprehending group dynamics.

References

Abhari, K., Davidson, E. J., & Xiao, B. (2022). Inventing together: The role of actor goals and platform affordances in open innovation. *Journal of the Association for Information Systems, 23*(1), 264–302. https://doi.org/10.17705/1jais.00721

Alexy, O., George, G., & Salter, A. J. (2013). Cui Bono? The selective revealing of knowledge and its implications for innovative activity. *Academy of Management Review, 38*(2), 270–291. https://doi.org/10.5465/amr.2011.0193

Badir, Y. F., Frank, B., & Bogers, M. (2020). Employee-level open innovation in emerging markets: Linking internal, external, and managerial resources. *Journal of the Academy of Marketing Science, 48*, 891–913. https://doi.org/10.1007/s11747-019-00674-6

Bogers, M., Chesbrough, H., Heaton, S., & Teece, D. J. (2019). Strategic management of open innovation: A dynamic capabilities perspective. *California Management Review, 62*(1), 77–94. https://doi.org/10.1177/0008125619885150

Bokhari, S. M. H. (2023). *Do I know myself? Factors contributing to work relationships and leading to open innovation in the emerging markets (AIT Diss. no.DBA-SOM-23-04)* [Doctoral dissertation]. Asian Institute of Technology.

Chernyak-Hai, L., & Rabenu, E. (2018). The new era workplace relationships: Is social exchange theory still relevant? In *Industrial and organizational psychology* (Vol. 11, Issue 3, pp. 456–481). Cambridge University Press. https://doi.org/10.1017/iop.2018.5

Chesbrough, H. (2003). The era of open innovation. *MIT Sloan Management Review*, 35–41.

Colbert, A. E., Bono, J. E., & Purvanova, R. K. (2016). Flourishing via workplace relationships: Moving beyond instrumental support. *Academy of Management Journal, 59*(4), 1199–1223. https://doi.org/10.5465/amj.2014.0506

Davies, K. A., Lane, A. M., Devonport, T. J., & Scott, J. A. (2010). Validity and reliability of a brief emotional intelligence scale (BEIS-10). *Journal of Individual Differences, 31*(4), 198–208. https://doi.org/10.1027/1614-0001/a000028

Henkel, J. (2008). Champions of revealing—The role of open source developers in commercial firms. *Frontier Journal, 5*(8), 437–471.

Kaur, R. (2023). Emotional intelligence at the workplace: The untapped edge for success. In *Leveraging AI and emotional intelligence in contemporary business organizations* (pp. 60–73). IGI Global. https://doi.org/10.4018/979-8-3693-1902-4.ch004

Kim, H. T. (2020). Linking managers' emotional intelligence, cognitive ability and firm performance: Insights from Vietnamese firms. *Cogent Business and Management, 7*(1). https://doi.org/10.1080/23311975.2020.1829272

Laursen, K., & Salter, A. (2006). Open for innovation: The role of openness in explaining innovation performance among U.K. manufacturing firms. *Strategic Management Journal, 27*(2), 131–150. https://doi.org/10.1002/smj.507

Mayer, J. D., Caruso, D. R., & Salovey, P. (1999). Emotional intelligence meets traditional standards for an intelligence. *Intelligence, 27*(4), 267–298.

Mubarak, M. F., Jucevicius, G., Shabbir, M., Petraite, M., Ghobakhloo, M., & Evans, R. (2025). Strategic foresight, knowledge management, and open innovation: Drivers of new product development success. *Journal of Innovation and Knowledge, 10*(2). https://doi.org/10.1016/j.jik.2025.100654

Robak, E. (2022). Knowledge exchange as a factor shaping employee relations in remote work. *Proceedings of the European Conference on Knowledge Management, ECKM*, 975–982.

Salter, A., Ter Wal, A. L. J., Criscuolo, P., & Alexy, O. (2015). Open for ideation: Individual-level openness and idea generation in R&D. *Journal of Product Innovation Management, 32*(4), 488–504. https://doi.org/10.1111/jpim.12214

Serirungsun, P., Badir, Y. F., & Frank, B. (2024). Achieving digital transformation: The effect of open innovation strategies at different stages of SME development in an emerging market. *IEEE Transactions on Engineering Management, 71*, 15555–15568.

Väyrynen, H., Helander, N., & Vasell, T. (2017). Knowledge management for open Innovation: Comparing research results between SMEs and large companies. *International Journal of Innovation Management, 21*(5). https://doi.org/10.1142/S1363919617400047

Wu, R. (2022). Financial constraints and firms' innovation activities in post-communist economies. *Post Communist Economies, 34*(6), 807–834. https://doi.org/10.1080/14631377.2021.2006497

Dr. Syed Muntasir Husain Bokhari (Nabeel) is an expert and capacity building specialist, currently working as an Affiliated Faculty and Program Specialist at the Asian Institute of Technology (AIT). He has held leadership positions, such as Director of Project Development, Senior Program Officer at AIT Extension, and the capacity building arm of AIT. He also had experience working in private and international development organization in different capacities, such as Head of Marketing and Consultant. Dr. Bokhari earned his D.B.A. from the School of Management at AIT. His professional and academic interest covers capacity building partnerships, alumni engagement, and employee innovation.

Dr. Lakeesha K. Ransom is a distinguished academic leader and strategist, currently working as an Adjunct Faculty at the Asian Institute of Technology (AIT). She has held senior leadership roles at prominent institutions including the University of Akron, where she served as Vice Provost, and Dean of The Williams Honors College. Dr. Ransom earned her doctorate from the University of Illinois at Urbana-Champaign and holds degrees from The Johns Hopkins University and The University of Michigan. Her professional interest spans global education, strategic partnerships, and innovation in higher education.

Dr. Djoen San Santoso is a distinguished academic leader, currently working as an Associate Professor at the Asian Institute of Technology (AIT). With a strong background in engineering and education management, Dr. Santoso has contributed to academic leadership and curriculum development at AIT. He holds a Ph.D. from Saitama University, Japan, and has previously served in faculty and leadership positions at reputable institutions in Southeast Asia. His academic and professional focus includes interdisciplinary research, higher education quality enhancement, and strategic academic planning.

Scaling Frugal Innovation-Based Startups to Accelerate Sustainable Development

Amrita Baid More and Arpan Shrivastava

Abstract The growth of the global economy and the significance of emerging markets have rendered socioeconomic and environmental issues paramount drivers for innovation professionals. Seeking low-cost approaches to innovation has arisen because established innovation management practices are unsustainable, and there is a necessity for cheaper and inclusive methods. Organizations that adopt frugal innovation can make it feasible to bridge the developmental gap between developed and developing countries, as well as promote sustainable development. Most firms, however, face difficulties when trying to enter new markets and offer their products as they do so in varying contexts.

In the interest of promoting sustainable development in developing nations, one should understand how to promote entrepreneurs and new businesses in their early phases of development. Due to this reason, this chapter will attempt to examine the determinants of the capability of frugal innovation-based startups to contribute to sustainable development in economic, environmental, and social contexts. It is crucial that an in-depth examination of both the hindrances as well as the favorable conditions for scaling up, and entrepreneurial mindsets concerning their social surroundings, is conducted to understand the determinants.

The chapter reveals that entrepreneurs' experiences have given them the capability to know the needs of their customers and to initiate attitude changes. At the same time, as they have not always possessed the money, talent, and capability to bargain on their own to grow, entrepreneurs rely on social support networks. The necessity for democratization of digital technology and harnessing entrepreneurial ecosystems was emphasized. Additionally, the author invites further discussion on the impact of power relations in entrepreneurial ecosystems and how sustainable influence is measured.

A. B. More (✉)
Faculty of Management Studies, Medicaps University, Indore, India
e-mail: amritabaid06@gmail.com

A. Shrivastava
IPS Academy, Institute of Business Management and Research, Indore, India
e-mail: arpan.mitm@gmail.com

T. Endress and Y. F. Badir (eds.), *Business and Management in Asia: Opportunities and Entrepreneurship*, https://doi.org/10.1007/978-981-95-4909-2_5

1 Introduction

The intersection of innovation and sustainability has drawn increasing attention, since sustainable performance depends heavily on innovative business models (Brem & Ivens, 2013). Social and environmental concerns have increasingly influenced innovation processes over the last decade, opening up new opportunities for competitive advantage and value creation (Hartley, 2004; Jääskeläinen, 2010). To acknowledge a need to bridge development gaps between industrialized and developing nations, the United Nations has highlighted accelerating inclusive and sustainable development (Hervani et al., 2017). Innovation has long been viewed as virtually exclusively the domain of developed economies—less a tool to development and more a goal of development. No longer is this the case, and innovation is now an integral part of development policy in the economies of Asia, Latin America, and Africa (Bhatti & Ventresca, 2013; Koen et al., 2001).

For the majority of the Sustainable Development Goals (SDGs), there is a need to enhance innovation and technology adoption in small and medium-sized enterprises (SMEs) (Krippendorff, 2013). For India, the government has considered the potential for job creation and inclusive economic development for SMEs (Josephson & Haeussler, 2022). Nevertheless, high unemployment is a major concern, resulting in chronic inequality. This is augmented by the close relationship between entrepreneurship and the broader social machinery, given that scale growth entails the ability to access multiple resources and support systems (Ireland & Webb, 2007). Although Indian government initiatives have traditionally been geared toward nurturing startups during their initial years, less emphasis has been placed on long-term support systems that enable sustained growth and scale-up (Krippendorff, 2013). Most Indian firms are thus not positioned to endure beyond their initial years, with a high percentage of them closing down within five years of business (Bushe, 2019).

Here, frugal innovation comes across as a disruption mechanism that is centered on creating low-cost, high-value solutions that generate economic, social, and customer value and use fewer resources.

2 Frugal Innovation

Frugal innovation is characterized by affordable and efficient solutions that tend to be disruptive. These innovations aim to minimize the use of resources—e.g., materials, energy, and water—while at the same time making products or services cheaper and accessible to end consumers (Albert, 2019; Hervani et al., 2017). One of the hallmark aspects of such innovations is the prioritization of providing only the core functions across the value chain, which keeps costs of production and operations low (Josephson & Haeussler, 2022). Even though simplicity is the focus, frugal innovations are proven to meet or even exceed normal standards of quality and performance (Weyrauch & Herstatt, 2016).

This method is not only restricted to changing products but also applies to reimagining entire business models and development processes (Langley, 1999). Typical strategies involve simplifying processes, redesigning, and restructuring system architectures to improve efficiency (Albert, 2019). One of the most striking features of the frugal innovation process is its human-oriented approach, which conforms to changing societal norms and promotes wider user engagement (Cullen et al., 2014). The results are usually disruptive, encompassing not only new products or technologies but also changes in organizational culture and service delivery frameworks (Hossain et al., 2016; Khan, 2016; Kaplinsky & Morris, 2001). As compared to the conventional innovation of designing cutting-edge technologies, frugal innovation reworks existing solutions to more effectively address the distinctive needs of developing markets (Heeks, 2012).

Additionally, the convergence of affordable and easy-to-use digital solutions allows local players, distributors, and other players to contribute to the growth and scaling of frugal innovations (Ahuja & Chan, 2016). The innovation ecosystem supporting such a system exists where social demand, technological advancement, and institutional change overlap (Bhatti et al., 2018). The result of such a distinct intersection is efficient processes and low-cost, adaptable offerings that mirror local requirements (Kaplinsky & Morris, 2001).

Frugal innovation also has a close link with social innovation—efforts that seek to change systems and institutions to more effectively deal with social problems (Kobayashi & Suzuki, 2018). The conditions favorable to social innovation—collaborative efforts and empowered communities—are also crucial for frugal innovation to flourish. Effective changing of societal values and structures usually requires concerted efforts from different actors and institutions (Cullen et al., 2014).

Research indicates that market difficulties and social needs cannot be addressed by technological, institutional, or social innovations alone. Instead, it is their combination that renders frugal innovation both effective and lasting. This combination enables resource sharing, greater collaborations, and redesigned roles for principal actors (Bhatti, 2012; Kobayashi & Suzuki, 2018) (Fig. 1).

3 Target Market of Frugal Innovation

Frugal innovation is most frequently linked to emerging and developing economies, where the consumer base usually consists of low- to lower-middle-income groups (Albert, 2019; Cohen & Crabtree, 2006; Boonstra & Bennebroek Gravenhorst 1998). One of the demographic segments most frequently mentioned is the "bottom of the pyramid"—a term that refers to the world's largest and most economically underprivileged population segment, which consists of approximately four billion people living on less than $2.50 a day (Leten et al., 2016).

While these consumers are frequently described as being very price-sensitive and low on buying power (Albert, 2019), they also constitute a huge and mainly underserved market with great commercial appeal (Carlsson et al., 2002; Markides, 2006).

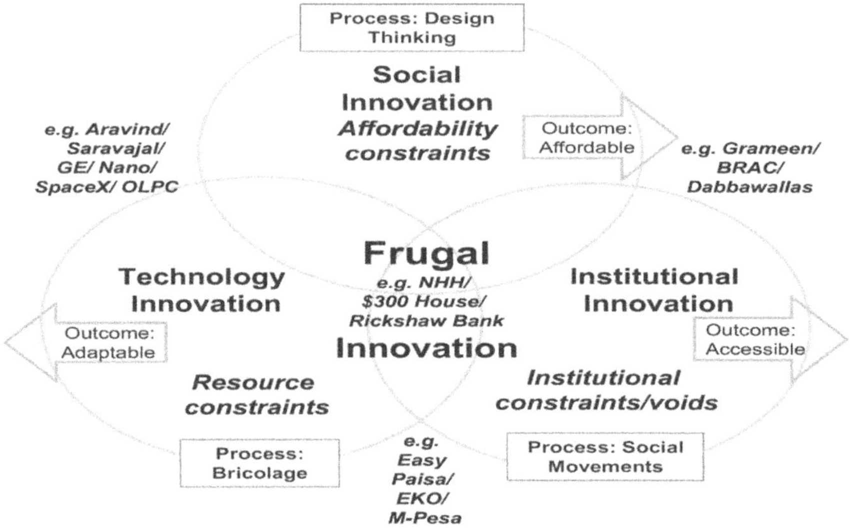

Fig. 1 Theoretical model of frugal innovation (Bhatti et al., 2018)

They are of size and therefore of strategic importance to companies looking to balance profit with social responsibility (Cohen & Crabtree, 2006). Among developing countries, India has emerged as the center of empirical studies of frugal innovation mainly due to its urgency of socioeconomic needs and the increasing necessity of affordable, effective solutions (Braunerhjelm & Feldman 2008).

The character of market demand in such environments is determined not just by economic conditions but also by social norms, institutional settings, and environmental constraints of the area (Carlsson et al., 2002). Such a mix of local factors determines how frugal innovations are developed, delivered, and adopted, emphasizing the significance of context-specific approaches to create scalable and sustainable solutions. While this is the case among the majority of customers in developing countries,

Increasing numbers of consumers in mature economies are also becoming increasingly sensitive to price (Hossain et al., 2016). General Electric (GE), for example, in the healthcare technology business, developed an affordable ultrasound scanner originally for the Chinese market that has since picked up uses across Western economies too (Braunerhjelm & Feldman, 2008; London & Hart, 2004). For this reason, frugal innovations can disrupt traditional innovations via their innovative and cost-effective capabilities (Hossain et al., 2016).

4 Understanding Sustainable Development

The 1987 Brundtland Commission Report, often quoted in the sustainability discourse, defines sustainable development as development that meets the needs of the present without impairing future generations' ability to meet their own needs. It focuses on meeting the basic needs of the world's poor. Although this definition has influenced global understanding of sustainability, measuring its on-the-ground implementation and material outcomes continues to be a challenge (Brussel et al., 2019).

Nonetheless, the balancing of social welfare and economic growth with conservation is still an issue. For example, greater accessibility and affordability can cause greater consumption, which further contributes to environmental pressures (Maxwell, 2005; Albert, 2019). Researchers contend that wealthier nations should have a heavier burden in reducing environmental harm, whereas thrifty innovation activities in poor countries concentrate on the satisfaction of primary needs (Brussel et al., 2019).

Successful scaling of frugal innovations relies on ongoing engagement with customers and other stakeholders. Feedback loops, user co-creation, and community interaction are crucial in order to fine-tune solutions and deal with market uncertainties (Brown et al., 2018). Moreover, investigating entrepreneurial behavior in social and cultural contexts provides more insights into the development and sustainability of such innovations (Ireland & Webb, 2007).

5 Frugal Innovation: An Engine for Sustainable Development

In recent years, social and environmental issues have had a growing impact on the way innovators and companies pursue value creation and differentiation (McDonagh & Prothero, 2014).

The growth of the world economy and the emergence of emerging economies require innovation that not only makes economic sense but is also inclusive and sustainable (Brussel et al., 2019; Mishra, 2014).

Frugal innovation, with a focus on resource efficiency, engagement of disadvantaged communities, and ecosystem-oriented thinking, tends to be seen as an effective instrument for achieving the United Nations' Sustainable Development Goals Brown et al., (2018). Companies that adopt frugal innovation tactics can enable development along the three pillars of sustainability—environment, society, and economy—though in what ways and to what extent can differ (Braunerhjelm & Feldman, 2008; Miles & Huberman, 1994).

Frugal innovation is the activity of simplifying the complexity and expense of a product or service without losing its essential functions to make it more accessible to many, particularly in resource-poor settings (Meyskens et al., 2010). Innovations of this nature usually result from the imperative to "do more with less" and are very pertinent to the attainment of sustainable results.

Globally, frugal innovation has addressed diverse challenges—from portable medical devices like GE's handheld ECG machines in India to low-cost water filtration systems like Tata Swach. These solutions are not just cheaper but are environmentally conscious and socially inclusive, thus contributing to multiple SDGs simultaneously (Bound & Thornton, 2012).

In developing countries such as India, frugal innovations also bridge institutional gaps and infrastructure gaps to create inclusive solutions at the bottom of the pyramid. The Mitticool refrigerator, which is clay-based and does not need electricity, fulfills SDG 12 (Responsible Consumption and Production) and SDG 13 (Climate Action) by being energy-free and sustainable (Bhaduri & Kumar, 2011a, 2011b).

6 Enablers and Barriers to Scaling of Frugal Innovation

For frugal innovation to make a significant contribution to sustainable development, some of these systemic issues need to be resolved. These are financial, regulatory, and institutional barriers that prevent large-scale take-up.

On the other hand, there are a number of drivers that promote scaling frugal solutions, including robust social purpose, adaptive policy environments, and changing needs of underserved markets. With inclusive ecosystems and collaborative networks, frugal innovation can be a force for change in bringing sustainability to emerging and advanced economies alike (Nelson, 1993).

Frugal innovation, a most appropriate term at the global level, is defined by its ability to deliver low-cost and affordable solutions to poor communities (Schumpeter, 1934). With its tremendous transformative power across industries like health, education, agriculture, and energy, the diffusion and scalability of frugal innovations are still limited (Nair & Blomquist, 2018). This chapter explores the underlying challenges that hinder the emergence and large-scale adoption of such innovations. By categorizing the barriers into structural, financial, and institutional types, and underpinning them with empirical data and case study analyses, this chapter attempts to present a holistic picture of the challenges facing frugal innovations and the system reforms required to address these challenges.

Frugal innovation involves the creation of low-cost, efficient, and affordable products and services, focusing particularly on consumers found in resource-poor environments (Bound & Thornton, 2012; Radjou et al., 2012). These innovations are often created in developing countries and are meant to "do more with less," with an emphasis on functionality, simplicity, and affordability (Bhatti & Ventresca, 2013). In India, for instance, efforts such as the Tata Nano, Jaipur Foot, and the Aravind Eye Care System demonstrate the success of frugal solutions on major social issues (Basu et al., 2013; Boonstra & Bennebroek Gravenhorst, 1998).

Despite evident benefits, frugal innovations frequently fail to proceed beyond pilot project stages. The main thesis of this chapter is that the three most common constraints—structural, financial, and institutional—retard the large-scale deployment and long-term sustainability of frugal innovations. Each of these categories consists of several systemic issues that together limit the efficacy of frugal solutions.

7 Structural Constraints on Frugal Innovation

Structural barriers are the physical infrastructure, technological environments, and systemic constraints within social systems and markets. Structural barriers are most clearly seen in low- and middle-income countries (LMICs), which are the origin of the most resource-efficient innovations.

One key problem concerns the absence of proper infrastructure—physical and digital—restraining the manufacturing, distribution, and servicing capacities of frugal innovators (George et al., 2012). Most rural and peri-urban regions in nations such as India and Kenya lack stable electricity, quality roads, internet, and effective transportation systems, which are essential for scaling innovations (Harvard Business Review, 2002). This thus tends to hinder the proper distribution of frugal products to the markets.

Supply chain breakdown effectively decelerates the diffusion of frugal innovations. In the absence of centralized production and distribution systems, many small firms struggle to maintain quality, consistency, and pricing (Hartley, 2004). The absence of sufficient qualified experts and mentorship further prevents local innovations from being tradable products (Brem & Wolfram, 2014).

Ultimately, the absence of comprehensive policy frameworks exacerbates the existing structural issues. Governments do not coordinate innovation, industrial, and social policies to foster bottom-up entrepreneurs (Harvard Business Review, 2002). This decoupling weakens cooperation and suppresses innovation ecosystem development favorable to frugal designs.

8 Monetary Constraints on Cost-Effective Innovation

Financial limitations are one of the most commonly referred to barriers in frugal innovation literature (Gupta, 2013). The limited access to early-stage capital and unfavorable funding opportunities tend to lead to the early death of potentially viable innovations.

Entrepreneurs and individual innovators in the frugal innovation space often operate under budgetary constraints and are typically excluded from mainstream venture capital networks, mainly due to their focus on low-margin, high-impact activities (Bhatti, 2012). Traditional investors typically favor solutions that offer high returns and involve sophisticated technological inputs, as compared to low-cost, low-technology innovations.

The risk aversion mechanism in the financial world is a matter of concern. Banks would most likely view frugal innovations as experimental and associated with shadow economies, which cannot provide the growth trajectories that venture capitalists prefer. Therefore, innovators rely mostly on personal funds, family funds, or crowdfunding platforms, which may not be sufficient to fuel long-term, sustained growth.

Public funding options often have bureaucratic traits and are poorly designed to finance frugal innovation models. If government grants and subsidies are available, they usually have significant procedural requirements and slow payment rates, which discourage innovators from applying for funding (UNDP, 2014; Yin, 2014).

Secondly, the costs of compliance, including patents, certifications, and licenses, are often too expensive. For instance, cost-aware medical technologies must be subjected to intensive clinical testing and safety requirements that are beyond the means of small businesses (Cunha et al., 2014). Inability to access cheap patent and legal assistance also discourages formalization and commercialization.

9 Institutional Constraints Impacting Cost-Effective Innovation

Institutions, whether they are established organizations like state institutions or loose norms like society's acceptance, are vital to facilitating or hindering innovation. Unfortunately, in most frugal innovation systems, these institutions are either absent or dysfunctional, or even work against innovation.

Weak innovation ecosystems are one of the major institutional barriers. While countries like India have begun to set up startup incubators and innovation hubs, these ecosystems hardly offer bottom-up or frugal entrepreneurs specific support (Gupta, 2016). Without any mentorship, prototyping infrastructure, or scaling operations assistance, most innovators are left to learn the art of commercialization on their own.

The rigidity of regulatory systems is an important impediment. The majority of regulatory systems were intended for classical industrial goods and do not consider the unique character of frugal innovations. For example, frugal water treatment systems possess ambiguous regulatory classifications—being too sophisticated for consumer product classifications but too primitive for industrial classification—leading to the slowness in their approval processes (Bergek & Norrman, 2008).

Protection of intellectual property (IP) is the second institutional barrier. Most grassroots innovators are ignorant of the patenting procedure or cannot finance legal hearings. This exposes them to exploitation and makes them incapable of benefiting from the economic gains of their innovations (Bhaduri & Kumar, 2011a, 2011b).

Low institutional trust also hinders the uptake of new technologies. Both consumers and stakeholders will tend to question innovations from the low-cost or informal industries, linking lower prices to lower quality (Boonstra & Bennebroek Gravenhorst, 1998). Such a perception disconnects, along with high standards and certification processes, bars frugal innovations from entering mainstream markets.

9.1 Case Examples

The Jaipur Foot experience demonstrates how structural and financial constraints can delay scale. Even while developing one of the world's cheapest prosthetic limbs, the organization was plagued by bureaucratic delays in funding and logistical issues in exporting the limbs to rural and foreign recipients (Gupta, 2013).

SELCO India, a solar energy firm, was also confronted with initial institutional hurdles as banks showed reluctance to invest in off-grid solar schemes. By innovating not just in terms of the product but also in the delivery mechanism—via collaboration with microfinance institutions—SELCO progressively overcame these impediments.

10 Entrepreneurial Ecosystem Pillars and Their Components

The World Economic Forum identifies eight pillars of entrepreneurial ecosystems, as real contrasts in the business system can exist from one region to another. Examine these pillars and their importance and validity for entrepreneurs in a WEF report (Table 1).

These building blocks mark a dramatic departure from traditional economic models centered on firms and markets, shifting instead toward an architecture based on individuals, their networks, and formal and informal institutions. In this view, value creation is people-led and governed by multiple governance mechanisms, which are all operating in particular institutional environments.

This entrepreneurial ecosystem perspective has proven to be especially valuable in shaping public policy since it sheds light on the government's central function alongside that of private sector enablers and support services. Cultural change, access to talent, and access to financial capital are also repeatedly highlighted as being central.

Even with these contributions, the models tend to be limited in describing the underlying causes of entrepreneurial ecosystems or providing specific recommendations for selective public intervention. The World Economic Forum (2013), for example, lists market access, labor skills, and access to finance as key drivers for the growth and success of entrepreneurial firms, but it fails to explore how these drivers can be built systematically and affected through policy measures. These are likely to be proximate causes rather than root causes of ecosystem success (e.g., human capital and funding are likely to depend on core institutions in terms of education

Table 1 Key pillars and components of an entrepreneurial ecosystem

Pillar	Components
Accessible markets	Domestic market: Large/medium/small companies as customers and governments as customer Foreign market: Large/medium/small Companies as customers and governments as customer
Human capital/workforce	Management talent, technical talent, entrepreneurial company experience, outsourcing availability and access to immigrant workforce
Funding and finance	Friends and family, Angel investors, private equity, venture capital, and access to debt
Support system / mentors	Mentors/advisers, professional services, incubators or accelerators, and a network of entrepreneurial peers
Government and regulatory framework	Ease of starting business, tax incentives business business-friendly legislation or policies, Access to base infrastructure, Access to Telecommunication or broadband, and access to transport
Education and training	Available workforce with pre university education, Available workshop workforce with university education, and those with Entrepreneurship Specific training
Major universities as catalysts	Promoting a culture of respect for entrepreneurship, playing a key role in idea formation for new companies, and playing a role in providing graduates to new companies
Cultural support	Tolerance for risk and failure, preference for self-employment, Success stories, role models, research culture, Positive image of entrepreneurship, and celebration of innovation

Source World Economic Forum (2013, p. 67)

and financial markets), and it is far from clear what the necessary and contingent conditions are for successful ecosystems and what is the role of the government and other public organizations), especially in the more unclear arrangements of the public and private sectors.

11 Barriers to Scaling Up of Frugal Innovations

Entrepreneurship is critical to economic growth, innovation, and job creation globally. Entrepreneurship is difficult to start, but scaling is usually even more challenging. Scaling a business implies expanding operations, expanding into new markets, growing profits, and having a broader impact. Nonetheless, numerous entrepreneurs, particularly from developing nations, such as India and other emerging nations, are confronted with chronic hurdles that hinder the transition. Two of the greatest challenges are particularly important: gaining access to and collaborating with partners in the formal market, and entrepreneurial skills and attitude issues.

Barriers Concerning Approaching and Working with Partners in the Formal Market: Collaborating with existing market players, such as companies, supply chains, banks, and corporate buyers, is crucial for entrepreneurs who desire to expand. This is a very challenging process.

One of the large issues for entrepreneurs, particularly in India and other emerging economies, is that they are not viewed as reliable by formal market participants. Most small and informal entrepreneurs lack formal documents, credit histories, or quality certifications. This creates suspicion by potential partners, who prefer to work with known businesses and known suppliers (OECD, 2005, 2010).

Joining the formal market typically involves complying with complex regulations, such as GST registration, MSME certification, complying with environmental regulations, and complying with labor regulations. This can be notoriously difficult for entrepreneurs who lack law knowledge or have no accounting expertise (Patton, 2002). In India, the stringent regulations can discourage many entrepreneurs from even attempting to formalize their partnerships.

Business owners, particularly in rural or developing regions, lack access to information about markets, lists of potential partners, or business connection sites (Banerjee & Duflo, 2011). In India, government portals such as Udyam Registration and Startup India exist, but they are not utilized to a large extent since people are unaware of them or lack computer skills.

Even if there are partnerships, there are typically uneven levels of power, especially when there are buyer–supplier relations. Large companies can impose strict terms of payment or insist on sole dealings, which can limit the degree of growth of small businesses. In India, small and medium-sized enterprises (SMEs) often experience delayed payment by large customers, which affects their cash flow (Rogers, 2003).

Globally, cultural and linguistic variations also constrain effective partnership formation. Native English-speaking entrepreneurs or indigenous people are confronted with further challenges in building rapport with business partners in formal, frequently Western-dominated, business contexts (Dana, 2007). In India, rural entrepreneurs and corporate business groups are confronted with the same challenges of language barriers.

12 Obstacles to Entrepreneurial Competency and Mindset

In addition to external barriers, internal constraints on entrepreneurial potential, mindset, and psychological paradigms tightly limit scaling.

Most start-ups are started off necessity rather than opportunity; they lack a fundamental understanding of money management, market strategy, and operations. For Indian microentrepreneurs, in accordance with one report by the National Skill Development Corporation, a high percentage lacked necessary skills in such fields as scale of operations, market demand knowledge, and money management. The same goes for African and Southeast Asian low-income economies (Prahalad, 2012). Scaling demands strong decisions, investment, and risk-taking. Entrepreneurs, however, particularly those with thin cushions, do not engage in risk-taking since they fear financial collapse, social stigma, or loss of jobs (Hessels et al., 2011). This holds particularly true for Indian women entrepreneurs, who face more social and economic risks.

It is difficult for entrepreneurs to transition from being "doers" to "leaders." As the company expands, it is extremely crucial to delegate, manage teams, and lead. Most entrepreneurs, particularly in family businesses or informal setups, struggle to let go of control or hire competent workers (Gupta & Mirchandani, 2018). Carol Dweck's "growth mindset" is that trusting that you can learn and get better is critical to success (Prabhu, 2017; Raj, 2020). Fixed-mindset entrepreneurs may shun innovation, shun criticism, or refuse to adapt during adversity, which makes it more difficult to develop their businesses. This psychological barrier is found around the globe but is particularly prevalent in societies that place high social hierarchies, such as in areas of India, where entrepreneurship is not always valued (Sarasvathy, 2001; Ries, 2011).

Role models, peer networks, and mentors can make an entrepreneur more self-assured and confident to expand their business. Incubators and accelerators in defined structures are available in developed nations (Zeschky et al., 2011, 2014). In India, however, these facilities are not readily available except in major cities. According to a worldwide survey by the Global Entrepreneurship Monitor (GEM, 2022), even in developing nations, entrepreneurs have very little access to mentoring facilities in comparison to developed nations.

13 India and World Policy Actions and Recommendations for Innovators

To counter these challenges, governments and private sectors across the globe have undertaken various responses: In India, Startup India offers mentorship, funding, and ease of regulatory compliance, although access is distributed unevenly by geography. Around the globe, initiatives such as UNCTAD's Empretec assist individuals from developing nations in acquiring business skills. The Women Entrepreneurs Finance Initiative (We-Fi) of the World Bank finances women entrepreneurs by providing them with training and market access. Encouraging ecosystem-led development through hubs, cluster programs, and innovation zones has the potential to fill partnership and skills gaps. But scaling takes more than policy. Mindset shift initiatives, education reform, and behavior shift initiatives—like entrepreneurial leadership instruction, simulation-based instruction, and resilience coaching—have to be brought into the entrepreneurship development strategy.

Building successful entrepreneurial businesses is a multifaceted problem influenced by external and internal factors. Failure to properly interact with conventional market players and the absence of entrepreneurial ability and mindsets are among the greatest challenges, particularly in the developing world of India. They are strongly entrenched in enduring cultural and structural contexts. They require more than policy reform; they also involve continuous investment in education, mentoring networks, and cooperation as a community. Equipping entrepreneurs with the capability, mindset, and networks necessary to thrive in formal markets is key to sustainable and inclusive economic growth.

Frugal innovation has been an acknowledged development model in the Global South, particularly in India. Such governmental initiatives as the National Innovation Foundation (NIF), Startup India, and Atal Innovation Mission (AIM) focus on mainstreaming bottom-up innovators by offering mentoring, funding, and scaling assistance. Global entities such as the UNDP and OECD have grown to acknowledge frugal innovators as central in attaining development goals in impoverished environments (Bergek & Norrman, 2008).

Across the globe, efforts of mobilization related to impact investing, circular economy, and inclusive design all respond to the ideals of frugality. Some African and Latin American countries also promote bottom-up innovation support systems, for instance, Kenya's iHub or Brazil's social entrepreneurship initiatives.

Frugal innovators need to be brought to the center stage of development, not as fringe characters but as protagonists of transformation, as central architects of change. Their entrepreneurial attitude, characterized by resilience, empathy, and improvisation, allows them to develop scalable and sustainable solutions. In addition to their innovations, they drive mindset shifts that shift the way societies view innovation, success, and consumption. Policymakers, schools, and funding institutions need to actively include these innovators in mainstream innovation systems and use their influence to create a more sustainable and inclusive world (Bell et al., 2018).

Frugal innovators are not just innovative problem solvers but formidable drivers of inclusive, sustainable, and systemic change. At the nexus of adversity and creativity, they possess a unique entrepreneurial spirit, characterized by resilience, resourcefulness, empathy, and acute sensitivity to local conditions. Their behavioral competencies, which flourish under constraints, allow them to create meaningful innovations with few resources, creating useful, low-cost, and contextually relevant solutions to immediate problems.

Most importantly, frugal innovators shape the way innovation is thought of and done. They challenge traditional top-down, capital-driven models of innovation and cultivate a bottom-up culture of empowerment in which excluded voices are able to make a meaningful contribution to economic and technological advancement. In so doing, they disrupt held assumptions about who is capable of innovation and what constitutes valuable innovation (Zeschky et al., 2011, 2014). Their success stories tend to reframe aspirations within excluded communities, creating a ripple effect that changes attitudes toward entrepreneurship, sustainability, and consumption.

Both in the Indian and international contexts, frugal innovators are being increasingly seen as having the potential to make a significant contribution to the Sustainable Development Goals (SDGs), especially in areas like clean energy, healthcare, education, and sustainable consumption. Government policy, innovation centers, and academic institutions thus need to collaborate and build enabling ecosystems that nurture and scale such grassroots innovations.

With the world looking for inclusive recovery and resilient development models in the wake of climate change, inequality, and post-pandemic crises, putting frugal innovators at the center of change is not an afterthought—it is a strategic necessity. Their approach and behavior not only provide near-term solutions but also drive a deeper cultural transformation toward sustainable living, collaborative problem-solving, and socially responsible innovation. Embracing and amplifying their role will be crucial in building societies that are not just technologically advanced but also equitable, empathetic, and ecologically conscious.

14 Frugal Entrepreneurship: Achieving Sustainable Impact and SDG Synergies Through Enablers and Challenges

Sustainable development, which refers to the fulfillment of present needs without sacrificing the capability of future generations to fulfill theirs, is a growing international issue. The United Nations' 2030 Agenda identifies 17 Sustainable Development Goals (SDGs) that seek to address pressing global issues like poverty, inequality, climate change, and environmental degradation. Attaining these goals, particularly in low- and middle-income nations, necessitates approaches that are inclusive, cost-effective, and resource-frugal. Under such circumstances, frugal innovation, as well as grassroots and social entrepreneurship, is seen to contribute significantly to providing sustainable and impactful change. This part reviews sustainable impact based on the context of the UN SDGs and discusses how synchronizing frugal innovation and entrepreneurship with the SDGs can further sustainable development.

Sustainable impact is the long-term beneficial effects that are consistent with environmental conservation, economic development, and social justice. The SDGs offer a measuring stick for such impact, from poverty eradication (SDG 1), health and education improvement (SDG 3 and 4), access to clean energy (SDG 7), to sustainable consumption (SDG 12) and climate action (SDG 13).

To give an example, Goal 1 (No Poverty) and Goal 8 (Decent Work and Economic Growth) are directly influenced by entrepreneurship-driven job creation, particularly where the focus is on vulnerable groups. Goal 9 (Industry, Innovation, and Infrastructure) is closely associated with the creation of sustainable technologies and solutions with scalability. In the Indian context, innovations such as SELCO's solar solutions for rural household's support Goal 7 (Affordable and Clean Energy) while enabling local entrepreneurs (Bergek & Norrman, 2008).

But in isolation, it is not possible to achieve these goals. True change happens when there is goal synergy, driven by entrepreneurial and innovative strategies. For instance, clean energy (SDG 7) enhances health (SDG 3) by lowering indoor air pollution and improves education (SDG 4) by enabling children to learn after sunset.

Entrepreneurship is the key to scaling thrifty concepts into solutions. Entrepreneurs are change agents who recognize social, environmental, and economic gaps and bridge them using market-based approaches. Social entrepreneurship, in turn, integrates business objectives with social missions, and its efforts contribute directly to the SDGs.

For example, India's Araku Coffee Project unites sustainable farming (SDG 15), economic empowerment of tribal farmers (SDG 8 and 1), and access to global markets. Likewise, Africa's M-KOPA Solar offers pay-as-you-go solar power to off-grid homes, generating employment (SDG 8), renewable energy (SDG 7), and rising living standards (SDG 3).

The synergy between SDGs is realized when entrepreneurs specifically design solutions for multiple goals. A creative entrepreneur developing sustainable sanitary pads in rural India is not only solving women's health (SDG 3), but also education and menstrual hygiene awareness (SDG 4), gender equality (SDG 5), and sustainable production (SDG 12).

Where frugal innovation and entrepreneurship intersect, a strong synergy emerges for driving multiple SDGs simultaneously. These synergies express themselves in the following ways:

Resource Efficiency and Cost Savings (SDG 12, 9, 1): Frugal innovations achieve optimal utilization of resources and avoid waste. They enable necessary services at affordable costs for low-income groups, and as a direct consequence, reduce poverty and enhance access to technology and infrastructure.

Inclusive Growth and Gender Empowerment (SDG 5, 8, 10): Entrepreneurial businesses catering to women and marginalized groups foster inclusivity. Enterprises such as Lijjat Papad and SEWA in India empower women economically, hence attaining SDGs on gender and work (Adams & Neil Adger, 2013).

Solutions for a Local Planet (SDG 11, 13, 3): Most of the sustainable development issues are local in scope. Local, context-specific frugal innovations—from frugal fuel-efficient stoves to affordable diagnostics—solutions to global challenges such as pollution, global warming, and disease avoidance (Sharma & Salvato, 2011).

Resilience and Adaptability (SDG 13, 9, 3): Entrepreneurs tend to respond quickly during crises. During the COVID-19 pandemic, entrepreneurs from around the world came up with low-cost ventilators, PPE, and sanitization products. Their prompt response builds community resilience and supported health and innovation-related SDGs.

Despite its promise, this synergy is challenged. Numerous frugal innovators find it challenging to scale as they have limited access to funding. Impact investing and SDG-conformant funding remain in their infancy in developing economies (WEF, 2020). Regulatory constraints frequently hold back experimentation, especially in areas such as health and energy. Most grassroots innovations are unable to access markets because they lack supply chain infrastructure or brands. To address these, multi-stakeholder alliances—governments, NGOs, universities, and private investors—need to be developed. In India, Atal Innovation Mission (AIM) and Startup India are portals that seek to institutionalize innovation toward lasting impact (Sharma & Iyer, 2012).

Fostering sustainable development requires a shift from single-focused development to holistically integrated, impact-based innovations. Frugal innovation and entrepreneurship offer a strategic route to achieving the UN SDGs, especially when linked to achieve synergistic impacts across multiple goals. By fostering locally led, affordable, and inclusive innovations, societies can progress toward sustainability without straining resources. Governments and ecosystem actors need to drive this change by removing system barriers and incentivizing innovation for SDG priority goals. As the world approaches the 2030 timeline, unleashing the potential of frugal, entrepreneurial strategies is not only an opportunity but a responsibility (Sharma & Salvato, 2011).

In a more resource-scarce and inequality-prone world, frugal innovators are rising as catalysts of change (Singh et al., 2008). Their capacity to come up with cost-efficient, scalable, and sustainable solutions, despite austere constraints in many cases, is the key differentiator that makes them exemplary drivers of inclusive development and social change. These innovators do not just produce products or services; they represent a different entrepreneurial spirit and behavioral capability that impacts collective societal thought. As countries move toward the Sustainable Development Goals (SDGs), it is important to realize the position of frugal innovators as change-makers and influencers of mindset, especially in the Global South, where affordability and optimization of resources are foremost imperatives (Stake, 1995).

15 Entrepreneurial Mindset and Behavioral Capabilities Among Frugal Innovators

The entrepreneurial attitude is shaped by opportunity perception, resilience, creativity, and a bias for action in the face of uncertainty (Alam, 2006). For frugal innovators, such qualities are boosted by limitations such as restricted access to capital, formal education, infrastructure, and regulatory assistance. Their innovation processes are mostly iterative, bottom-up, and rooted in local knowledge (Tracey & Stott, 2017; UNCTAD, 2010).

Frugal innovators exhibit three essential behavioral competencies that place them in the category of entrepreneurial achievement and social significance:

Resource Recombination and Constraint-Driven Ingenuity: Frugal innovators illustrate the philosophy of "jugaad" (an Indian colloquialism for innovative fix or solution), applying constrained resources in non-traditional ways to address basic needs. This action is not only responsive but also opportunity-driven and strategic

(Radjou et al., 2012). As an example, Indian innovator Mansukhbhai Prajapati came up with the Mitticool clay refrigerator—a green, electricity-free method for rural food preservation.

16 Pro-Social Values Guiding Frugal Innovation

In contrast to most traditional entrepreneurs, motivated only by profitability, frugal innovators tend to serve unserved or underserved markets. Frugal innovations tend to aim at social challenges like access to clean water, low-cost healthcare, education, or clean energy—hence balancing economic sustainability with social good (Bound & Thornton, 2012). This two-track orientation serves to imbue a wider sense of mission and accountability.

Frugal innovators are rooted in the society that they serve, so the process of learning is ongoing and extremely adaptive. Flexibility in behavior, receptiveness to criticism, and agile prototyping are visible among grassroots innovators documented by the Honey Bee Network in India (Gupta, 2013). These characteristics not only improve product applicability but also user engagement and scalability.

In addition to developing useful solutions, frugal innovators initiate societal mindset changes—reshaping what innovation is, who innovates, and what value is (Teece, 2010). They disrupt conventional paradigms of high-tech, high-cost innovation and emphasize that significant progress may come from the periphery. Cost-conscious innovators unsettle conventional stories of innovation that feature R&D laboratories, prestigious education, and venture capital. Rather, they make knowledge derived from spontaneous environments, local communities, and common problem-solving environments legitimate (Adams & Neil Adger, 2013). Democratization of innovation creates inclusivity and promotes local involvement in development discourse.

By their innovations, frugal innovators foster a transition from conspicuous to minimalist and sustainable consumption. For example, the extensive adoption of solar lanterns by firms such as d.light in Africa and South Asia not only substitutes kerosene lamps but also creates an affinity for clean energy. In this way, frugal innovations can trigger behavior changes in favor of SDG 12 (Responsible Consumption and Production).

When frugal innovators come from informal economies or rural regions, their success stories become motivational blueprints for others in the same situation. They shape entrepreneurial attitudes toward entrepreneurship as a feasible career and way of life, particularly among youth and women. This can be seen in projects such as SELCO India, which has trained solar entrepreneurs in rural Karnataka, producing ripple effects in mindset transformation and aspiration creation (Alam, 2006).

Frugal innovators tend to recover control over technology and economic discourses. Their innovations focus on self-sufficiency and localized knowledge, subverting top-down models of development. Through this, they reorient societal cultures from dependency to empowerment, especially in postcolonial and backward regions (Bell et al., 2018).

17 Strategic Insights and Future Pathways for Frugal Innovations

Shattering frugal innovation constraints calls for systemic reforms across various fronts. In terms of structure, governments and private sector actors need to invest in peri-urban and rural transport, digital connectivity, innovation clusters, and infrastructure (Bell et al., 2018).

There is a requirement for public–private partnership capital that is specifically designed to fund frugal innovations, including patient capital, low-interest loans, and milestone-based financial models (Bhatti & Ventresca, 2013). Governments can also offer tax benefits to venture capitalists and philanthropic investors who invest in frugal start-ups.

Institutionally, regulatory changes must establish innovation sandboxes to enable low-risk testing of frugal products without the weight of full-scale compliance. Further, government departments can simplify the process of patents and offer legal assistance to frugal innovators. Additionally, raising awareness of consumers and establishing certification programs specifically for low-cost products can increase legitimacy and trust (Abor & Quartey, 2010).

Frugal innovation is not just a cost-effective option—it is the prerequisite for sustainable, inclusive development. But the potential of such innovations is still out of reach for the masses because of interrelated structural, financial, and institutional constraints. Policymakers, financial institutions, research institutions, and industry must collectively break these system bottlenecks. This is when frugal innovations will shift from niche pilots to universal solutions.

The entrepreneurial ecosystem is not yet in possession of a definition to which everyone agrees. However, there has been an increasing effort from scholars to conceptualize it, with definitions commonly being adjusted to suit the particular research purpose. Shared by the majority of its interpretations is the focus on local environments and complex, interdependent relations between actors in the business world that contribute to entrepreneurial performance. They include economic agents, their roles, and the external conditions influencing enterprise activity and innovation in a given area.

The idea itself is intriguing in that it brings entrepreneurial practices together with systems of beliefs that promote economic cooperation. Just as regional clusters can emerge organically (Braunerhjelm & Feldman, 2008), ecosystems tend to be considered developing, adaptive systems that have dynamic feedback loops influencing their continuing development (Isenberg, 2011). In line with ecosystems are made up of a range of different elements, including individuals, practices, and institutions that are not necessarily directly involved with startups. They encompass institutions like universities, large corporations, government ministries, banks, healthcare systems, and capital markets. Of these, entrepreneurial universities tend to be found at the center of building business activity, though some claim their role is overstated (Adams & Neil Adger, 2013).

While they have vital functions, large established organizations are underrepresented in entrepreneurial environment discussions. However, there is substantial evidence that these organizations are likely to create ecosystems by hiring competent staff and creating good environments. In some areas, particularly those with high defense industry concentration, external large organizations play a major role in influencing the local entrepreneurial ecosystem. Such organizations play a significant role in the local business ecosystem of entrepreneurs, although their role is often overlooked in the majority of the entrepreneurial ecosystem literature (Abor & Quartey, 2010).

18 Conclusion

Growing frugal innovation-based ventures provides an excellent route to achieving sustainable development by matching cost-effectiveness with high social and environmental impact. These businesses are designed to maximize value with minimal resources, making them optimal for solving problems in low-income, resource-constrained markets. Frugal innovation-based ventures are also unique in that they offer low-tech, low-cost, simple, and practical solutions that can enkindle real change at the community level, while promoting inclusive and sustainable development in responsible ways. To successfully scale from a local solution to more impactful scale-up models, frugal innovation-based ventures need a productive ecosystem. Together with access to capital funds, mentor networks, policy incentives, and stronger market linkages, a much more supportive ecosystem can allow ventures to scale to new markets. Cooperating across government, corporate, and social networks can only expand the market as well as align interests with the Sustainable Development Goals (SDGs). With a focus on fundamental principles of adaptability, social relevance, and sustainability, frugal innovation-based ventures should be able to scale their business without losing sight of their ultimate aim of delivering products that are affordable and accessible. When frugal innovation-based ventures are successful, they will create jobs, lessen our environmental impacts, and lead all participants on their journeys toward equitable development opportunities. Therefore, scaling frugal innovation-based ventures is not only a compelling entrepreneurial opportunity but also the first step toward an inclusive, resilient, and sustainable future.

References

Banerjee, A. V., & Duflo, E. (2011). Poor economics: A radical rethinking of the way to fight global poverty. *Population and Development Review, 37*(4), 796–797. https://doi.org/10.1111/j.1728-4457.2011.00462.x

Abor, J., & Quartey, P. (2010). Issues in SME development in Ghana and South Africa. *International Research Journal of Finance and Economics, 39*(6), 215–228.

Adams, H., & Neil Adger, W. (2013). The contribution of ecosystem services to place utility as a determinant of migration decision-making. *Environmental Research Letters, 8*(1), Article 015006. https://doi.org/10.1088/1748-9326/8/1/015006

Ahuja, S., & Chan, Y. E. (2016). Digital innovation: A frugal ecosystem perspective.

Alam, I. (2006). Removing the fuzziness from the fuzzy front-end of service innovations through customer interactions. *Industrial Marketing Management, 35*(4), 468–480.

Albert, M. (2019). Sustainable frugal innovation—The connection between frugal innovation and sustainability. *Journal of Cleaner Production,* 117747.

Basu, R., Banerjee, P., & Sweeny, E. (2013). Frugal innovation: Core competencies to address global sustainability. *Journal of Management for Global Sustainability, 1*(2), 63–82.

Bell, E., Bryman, A., & Harley, B. (2018). *Business research methods.* Oxford University Press.

Bergek, A., & Norrman, C. (2008). Incubator best practice: A framework. *Technovation, 28*(1–2), 20–28.

Bhaduri, S., & Kumar, H. (2011a). Extrinsic and intrinsic motivations to innovate: Tracing the motivation of 'grassroot' innovators in India. *Mind & Society, 10*(1), 27–45.

Bhaduri, S., & Kumar, H. (2011b). Frugal innovation for sustainable development: How grassroots innovations are addressing unmet social needs. *Technology in Society, 33*(1–2), 50–61. https://doi.org/10.1016/j.techsoc.2011.03.003

Bhatti, Y. A. (2012). What is frugal? What is innovation? Towards a theory of frugal innovation. *SSRN Electronic Journal.* https://doi.org/10.2139/ssrn.2005910

Bhatti, Y. A., & Ventresca, M. (2013). How can 'frugal innovation' be conceptualized? *Oxford Development Studies, 41*(1), 87–104.

Bhatti, Y., Ramaswami Basu, R., Barron, D., & Ventresca, M. (2018). Towards a theory of frugal innovation. In *Frugal innovation: Models, means, methods* (pp. 101–215). Cambridge University Press.

Boonstra, J., & Bennebroek Gravenhorst, K. M. (1998). Power dynamics and organizational change: A comparison of perspectives. *European Journal of Work and Organizational Psychology, 7*(2), 97–120.

Bound, K., & Thornton, I. (2012). *Our frugal future: Lessons from India's innovation system.* Nesta.

Braunerhjelm, P., & Feldman, M. (2008). Cluster genesis: Technology-based industrial development. *Economic Geography, 84*(2), 245–246. https://doi.org/10.1111/j.1944-8287.2008.tb00409.x

Brem, A., & Ivens, B. (2013). Do frugal and reverse innovation foster sustainability? Introduction of a conceptual framework. *Journal of Technology Management for Growing Economies, 4*(2), 31–50.

Brem, A., & Wolfram, P. (2014). Research and development from the bottom up—Introduction of terminologies for new product development in emerging markets. *Journal of Innovation and Entrepreneurship, 3*(1), 9.

Brown, R., Mawson, S., Rowe, A., & Mason, C. (2018). Working the crowd: Improvisational entrepreneurship and equity crowdfunding in nascent entrepreneurial ventures. *International Small Business Journal, 36*(2), 169–193. https://doi.org/10.1177/0266242617729743

Brussel, M., Zuidgeest, M., Pfeffer, K., & van Maarseveen, M. (2019). Access or accessibility? A critique of the urban transport SDG indicator. *ISPRS International Journal of Geo-Information, 8*(2), 67.

Bushe, B. (2019). The causes and impact of business failure among small to micro, and medium enterprises in South Africa. *Africa's Public Service Delivery and Performance Review, 7*(1), 1–26.

Carlsson, B., Jacobsson, S., Holmén, M., & Rickne, A. (2002). Innovation systems: Analytical and methodological issues. *Research Policy, 31*(2), 233–245. https://doi.org/10.1016/s0048-7333(01)00138-x

Cohen, D., & Crabtree, B. (2006). *Qualitative research guidelines project.*

Cullen, B., Tucker, J., Snyder, K., Lema, Z., & Duncan, A. (2014). An analysis of power dynamics within innovation platforms for natural resource management. *Innovation and Development, 4*(2), 259–275.

Cunha, M. P., Rego, A., Oliveira, P., Rosado, P., & Habib, N. (2014). Product innovation in resource-poor environments: Three research streams. *Journal of Product Innovation Management, 31*(2), 202–210.

Dana, L. P. (2007). Promoting SMEs in Africa: Some insights from an experiment in Ghana and Togo. *Journal of African Business, 8*(2), 151–174. https://doi.org/10.1300/j156v08n02_09

George, G., McGahan, A. M., & Prabhu, J. (2012). Innovation for inclusive growth: Towards a theoretical framework and a research agenda. *Journal of Management Studies, 49*(4), 661–683.

Gupta, A. K. (2013). *Grassroots innovation: Minds on the margin are not marginal minds.* Penguin UK.

Gupta, A. K. (2016). Linking frugal innovation and grassroots entrepreneurship: Exploring overlooked connections. *Oxford Development Studies, 44*(1), 68–83.

Gupta, N., & Mirchandani, A. (2018). Investigating entrepreneurial success factors of women-owned SMEs in the UAE. *Management Decision, 56*(1), 219–232. https://doi.org/10.1108/md-04-2017-0411

Harvard Business Review. (2002). The competitive advantage of corporate philanthropy. *Harvard Business Review, 80*(12), 56–68.

Hartley, J. (2004). Case study research. In *Essential guide to qualitative methods in organizational research* (Vol. 1, pp. 323–333).

Heeks, R. (2012). IT innovation for the bottom of the pyramid. *Communications of the ACM, 55*(12), 24–27.

Hervani, A. A., Sarkis, J., & Helms, M. M. (2017). Environmental goods valuations for social sustainability: A conceptual framework. *Technological Forecasting and Social Change, 125*, 137–153.

Hessels, J., Grilo, I., Thurik, R., & van der Zwan, P. (2011). Entrepreneurial exit and entrepreneurial engagement. *Journal of Evolutionary Economics, 21*(3), 447–471. https://doi.org/10.1007/s00191-010-0190-4

Hossain, M., Simula, H., & Halme, M. (2016). Can frugal go global? Diffusion patterns of frugal innovations. *Technology in Society, 46*, 132–139.

Indd, A. (n.d.). Report summary for the annual meeting of the new champions 2013. *Weforum.org.* Retrieved May 19, 2025, from https://www3.weforum.org/docs/WEF_EntrepreneurialEcosystems_Report_2013.pdf

Ireland, R. D., & Webb, J. W. (2007). A multi-theoretic perspective on trust and power in strategic supply chains. *Journal of Operations Management, 25*(2), 482–497.

Isenberg, D. (2011). The Entrepreneurship Ecosystem Strategy as a New Paradigm for Economic Policy: Principles for Cultivating Entrepreneurship. *Institute of International and European Affairs.*

Jääskeläinen, R. (2010). Think-aloud protocol. In *Handbook of Translation Studies* (Vol. 1, pp. 371–374).

Johnson, S. (n.d.). DARON ACEMOGLU. *Mit.edu.* Retrieved May 19, 2025, from https://economics.mit.edu/sites/default/files/publications/institutions-as-the-fundamental-cause-of-long-run-.pdf

Josephson, A., & Haeussler, C. (2022). Equity crowdfunding and peer-to-peer lending: Are 'funding platforms' more than matchmakers? *Research Policy, 51*(1), Article 104393. https://doi.org/10.1016/j.respol.2021.104393

Kaplinsky, R., & Morris, M. (2001). *A handbook for value chain research.*

Kobayashi, Y., & Suzuki, K. (2018). Innovation and entrepreneurship in developing countries: A systematic review of the literature. *Asia Pacific Journal of Innovation and Entrepreneurship, 12*(3), 258–276.

Koen, P. A., Ajamian, G. M., Burkart, R. J., Clamen, A., Davidson, J., D'Amore, R., Elkins, C. J., Herald, K., Incorvia, M. J., Johnson, A. F., Karol, R. A., Seibert, R., Slavejkov, A., & Wagner, K. (2001). Providing clarity and a common language to the "fuzzy front end." *Research-Technology Management, 44*(2), 46–55.

Krippendorff, K. (2013). *Content analysis: An introduction to its methodology.* Sage.

Langley, A. (1999). Strategies for theorizing from process data. *Academy of Management Review, 24*(4), 691–710.

Leten, B., Belderbos, R., & Van Looy, B. (2016). Entry and strategy of firms in emerging economies: An analysis of corporate patents. *Global Strategy Journal, 6*(3), 142–160.

London, T., & Hart, S. L. (2004). Reinventing strategies for emerging markets: Beyond the transnational model. *Journal of International Business Studies, 35*(5), 350–370. https://doi.org/10.1057/palgrave.jibs.8400099

Markides, C. (2006). Disruptive innovation: In need of better theory. *Journal of Product Innovation Management, 23*(1), 19–25.

Maxwell, J. A. (2005). *Qualitative research design: An interactive approach* (2nd ed.). Sage.

Meyskens, M., Carsrud, A. L., & Cardozo, R. N. (2010). The role of partnerships on the economic, environmental, and social outcomes of social ventures. *Journal of Business Ethics, 94*(1), 103–121.

Miles, M. B., & Huberman, A. M. (1994). *Qualitative data analysis: An expanded sourcebook* (2nd ed.). Sage.

Mishra, R. K. (2014). Frugal innovation and inclusive development: The case of India. *AI & Society, 29*(4), 365–370. https://doi.org/10.1007/s00146-013-0461-8

Nair, A., & Blomquist, T. (2018). Failure prevention and management in complex projects: Role of project governance and governmentality. *International Journal of Project Management, 36*(2), 295–306.

Nelson, R. R. (1993). *National innovation systems: A comparative analysis.* Oxford University Press.

OECD. (2005). *Oslo Manual: Guidelines for collecting and interpreting innovation data* (3rd ed.).

OECD. (2010). *Measuring innovation: A new perspective.* OECD Publishing. https://doi.org/10.1787/9789264059474-en

Patton, M. Q. (2002). *Qualitative research and evaluation methods* (3rd ed.). Sage.

Prahalad, C. K. (2012). *The fortune at the bottom of the pyramid: Eradicating poverty through profits.* Pearson Education.

Prabhu, J. (2017). Frugal innovation: Doing more with less for more. *Philosophy & Technology, 30*(2), 153–155. https://doi.org/10.1007/s13347-017-0252-9

Radjou, N., Prabhu, J., & Ahuja, S. (2012). *Jugaad innovation: Think frugal, be flexible, generate breakthrough growth.* Jossey-Bass.

Raj, S. K. (2020). Role of start-ups and entrepreneurs in Indian economic growth. *International Journal of Management, 11*(4), 97–106.

Ries, E. (2011). *The lean startup: How today's entrepreneurs use continuous innovation to create radically successful businesses.* Crown Business.

Rogers, E. M. (2003). *Diffusion of innovations* (5th ed.). Free Press.

Sarasvathy, S. D. (2001). Causation and effectuation: Toward a theoretical shift from economic inevitability to entrepreneurial contingency. *Academy of Management Review, 26*(2), 243–263.

Schumpeter, J. A. (1934). *The theory of economic development: An inquiry into profits, capital, credit, interest, and the business cycle.* Harvard University Press.

Sharma, A., & Iyer, G. R. (2012). Resource-constrained product development: Implications for green marketing and green supply chains. *Industrial Marketing Management, 41*(4), 599–608.
Sharma, S., & Salvato, C. (2011). Cross-national organizing of family firms as a response to institutional constraints. *Entrepreneurship Theory and Practice, 35*(3), 555–572.
Singh, R. K., Garg, S. K., & Deshmukh, S. G. (2008). Strategy development by SMEs for competitiveness: A review. *Benchmarking: An International Journal, 15*(5), 525–547.
Stake, R. E. (1995). *The art of case study research.* Sage.
Teece, D. J. (2010). Business models, business strategy, and innovation. *Long Range Planning, 43*(2–3), 172–194. https://doi.org/10.1016/j.lrp.2009.07.003
Tracey, P., & Stott, N. (2017). Social innovation: A window on alternative ways of organizing and innovating. *Innovation, 19*(1), 51–60.
UNCTAD. (2010). *Information Economy Report 2010: ICTs, enterprises and poverty alleviation.* United Nations.
UNDP. (2014). *Empowered lives. Resilient nations: Human development report 2014.* United Nations Development Programme.
Weyrauch, T., & Herstatt, C. (2016). What is frugal innovation? Three defining criteria. *Journal of Frugal Innovation, 2*(1), 1. https://doi.org/10.1186/s40669-016-0005-y
Yin, R. K. (2014). *Case study research: Design and methods* (5th ed.). Sage.
Zeschky, M., Widenmayer, B., & Gassmann, O. (2011). Frugal innovation in emerging markets. *Research-Technology Management, 54*(4), 38–45.
Zeschky, M. B., Winterhalter, S., & Gassmann, O. (2014). From cost to frugality: A cross-sectoral typology of frugal innovations. *R&D Management, 44*(2), 114–146.

Dr. Amrita Baid More is a dynamic educator and academic leader with over 15 years of experience in higher education, curriculum development, and student mentorship. Known for her energetic and learner-centered approach, she has consistently played a pivotal role in shaping holistic, future-ready business professionals. Currently serving at Medicaps University, she leads the Incubation and Innovation Cell and co-convenes the Centre for Case Development, inspiring students to think beyond the classroom and embrace entrepreneurial mindsets.

Her career spans esteemed institutions like IIM Indore and is actively involved in designing value-added courses, strengthening alumni engagement, and enhancing institutional quality standards through her roles on committees such as IQAC and NBA. Dr. More believes in experiential learning and simulation-based education as powerful tools for developing critical thinking and real-world application. Her sessions are often remembered not just for their content, but for the enthusiasm and clarity with which they are delivered.

She has been a mentor to numerous students and budding professionals, helping them unlock their potential in marketing, communication, and business strategy. Her work reflects a deep commitment to academic excellence, professional ethics, and the transformational role of education in individual and societal progress.

Dr. Arpan Shrivastava brings over 15 years of teaching experience in Management and International Business, along with six years of industry exposure, creating a strong link between academic theory and practical application. He holds a Ph.D. in Management and has contributed more than 30 research papers published in journals indexed in ABDC, Scopus, and UGC Care. His work explores themes such as international business strategies, organizational development, and evolving trends in management practices. Combining research, teaching, and mentorship, Dr. Shrivastava continues to engage with the academic community to foster deeper insights into global management dynamics.

Circular Economy in Asia: A Comparative Policy and Startup Review

Jacob Stalk and Won-Yong Oh

Abstract This chapter explores the evolving role of startups in advancing the circular economy (CE) across key Asian countries: South Korea, Japan, China, and India. Against a backdrop of rapid population growth, industrialization, and increasing waste, CE principles—reduce, reuse, and recycle—offer a compelling framework for sustainable development. While governments have begun to implement supportive CE policies, progress remains slow, often hindered by limited commitment and policy inertia. Startups, in contrast, are demonstrating agility and innovation in recycling, re-manufacturing, and sustainable packaging, while navigating diverse regulatory and cultural landscapes. Drawing on case studies, this chapter shows that startups are not only enablers of CE practices but also critical intermediaries between policy and behavior. However, their success depends on a supportive ecosystem, including public awareness, government incentives, and technological infrastructure. The findings underscore that CE adoption in Asia is contingent on collaborative networks—between governments setting strategic direction, startups driving implementation, and citizens participating in circular practices. Ultimately, regional CE progress will require knowledge exchange, coordinated efforts, and scalable solutions rooted in local contexts. This chapter highlights the potential of startups to transform sustainability ambitions into practical and community-centered outcomes.

1 Introduction

The circular economy (CE) offers a strategic alternative to the traditional linear model of "take, make, dispose." By prioritizing the principles of reuse, repair, and recycling, CE aims to minimize waste and reduce environmental burdens (Ellen

J. Stalk · W.-Y. Oh (✉)
Lee Business School, University of Nevada, Las Vegas, NV, USA
e-mail: wonyong.oh@unlv.edu

J. Stalk
e-mail: stalkj1@unlv.nevada.edu

T. Endress and Y. F. Badir (eds.), *Business and Management in Asia: Opportunities and Entrepreneurship*, https://doi.org/10.1007/978-981-95-4909-2_6

MacArthur Foundation, 2013). In Asia, rapid urbanization and growing consumer demand have intensified challenges related to resource depletion and waste management. In response, many Asian governments are formulating national CE frameworks and policy roadmaps (Mohan et al., 2024). Simultaneously, the region's startup ecosystem has emerged as a critical driver of CE innovation, often delivering context-specific and scalable solutions tailored to local environmental and socio-economic conditions (e.g., Schröder et al., 2019).

This chapter explores the CE landscape in four Asian countries—South Korea, Japan, China, and India—selected based on their economic influence in the region, distinct policy approaches to CE, and the presence of notable startup-driven innovations. These countries represent diverse governance models, levels of economic development, and environmental challenges, offering rich ground for comparative analysis. It begins by examining each country's national policy environment, comparing government intentions, strategic priorities, and regulatory mechanisms, including the opportunities and challenges that shape CE implementation. Subsequently, the chapter highlights selected case studies of representative startups that are translating CE principles into tangible societal innovations. By combining policy analysis with entrepreneurial case studies, this chapter seeks to provide a holistic understanding of the evolving CE ecosystem in Asia and offer practical insights for policymakers, scholars, and startup practitioners.

This chapter investigates the evolution of CE development across Asia by examining both *top-down* regulatory frameworks established by governments and *bottom-up* innovations introduced by startups. It aims to illuminate the dynamic interplay between national-level policies and grassroots entrepreneurial initiatives, arguing that this interaction is essential to achieving the systems-level transformation required for a lasting and sustainable CE transition. By exploring these dual dimensions, the chapter identifies the best practices and shared obstacles, offering insights into how collaborative synergies can foster more scalable and context-sensitive innovations across the region. Rather than viewing regulatory and entrepreneurial approaches in isolation, this chapter adopts an integrative perspective that contributes to the academic discourse on CE and provides actionable knowledge for policymakers, researchers, and practitioners seeking meaningful impact in Asia's diverse socio-economic and environmental contexts.

This integrative perspective also aligns with the logic of stakeholder theory (Freeman, 1984), particularly in the context of sustainability, which emphasizes the interconnected roles and responsibilities of diverse actors in creating long-term environmental and social values. This perspective further underscores the role of collaborative networks among key stakeholders—governments setting strategic direction, startups driving implementation, and citizens engaging in circular practices. Such networked coordination is essential for realizing systemic CE transitions that are socially inclusive and contextually grounded.

2 Theoretical Background

2.1 *Foundations: Concept and Principles of the Circular Economy*

The CE represents a new paradigm for how we produce, use, and reuse resources. Traditionally, the linear model has followed a "take, make, dispose" pattern—extracting resources, utilizing them, and discarding the waste. In contrast, CE encourages a fundamental rethinking of how to minimize waste, extend the lifecycle of materials, and reduce environmental impact (Oh et al., 2021). It is grounded in three core principles: first, to prevent waste and pollution; second, to keep products and materials in use for as long as possible; and third, to regenerate natural systems (Ellen MacArthur Foundation, 2013). These principles are especially pertinent in rapidly developing regions such as Asia, where accelerated urbanization and industrial growth have led to intensive resource consumption (Tan et al., 2022).

The CE requires sustained innovation in sustainability to support its implementation and scaling. Such innovations may include emerging technologies (e.g., Lee et al., 2024), such as artificial intelligence and digital platforms, that enable more efficient waste management, recycling tracking, and resource optimization. Notably, many of these innovations originate from startups, which, due to their agility and responsiveness, are often able to deliver environmental solutions more rapidly and flexibly than larger corporations or government entities (Mehrotra & Jaladi, 2022).

The effectiveness of the CE depends on the successful integration of its principles into systems that are responsive to specific regional challenges—particularly in densely populated and resource-constrained areas such as those found across Asia (e.g., Herrador & Van, 2024). While governments and large corporations play a critical role in policy development and the establishment of standards, they are often startups that serve as the initial testing ground for CE innovation. These startups take the lead by engaging local communities in pilot projects, experimenting with new business models, and encouraging behavioral changes that help embed CE principles at the grassroots level (Mehrotra & Jaladi, 2022). Entrepreneurial initiatives, combined with technological advancements (e.g., Lee et al., 2024), are thus instrumental in scaling and amplifying circular activities, ultimately contributing to broader environmental and economic goals across the region.

2.2 *Entrepreneurial Ecosystems Driving Circular Economy in Asia*

Entrepreneurial ecosystems in Asia—comprising startups, investors, educational institutions, and enabling regulatory frameworks—are increasingly fostering opportunities within the CE (Asian Development Bank, 2021). According to the Asian

Development Bank (2021), more such ecosystems are emerging to support startups exploring innovations in areas like recycling, sustainable fashion, and clean energy (e.g., Oh et al., 2021). However, despite growing attention and resources dedicated to CE innovation, academic research tends to concentrate predominantly on government policies and large corporate initiatives, often overlooking the dynamic contributions of startups, which play a critical role in identifying and exploiting market opportunities created by sustainability challenges (Cohen & Winn, 2007).

Startups typically face challenging conditions, operating with limited capital and often navigating regulatory uncertainties, while also needing public trust to thrive. Despite these obstacles, startups possess the unique capability to translate the CE principles into concrete, place-based solutions that address both local and regional challenges (e.g., Herrador & Van, 2024). By focusing on these relatively nascent entrepreneurial ecosystems, this chapter aims to offer fresh insights into how startups contribute to the CE landscape across Asia, demonstrating how their agility, creativity, and resilience can support wider policy and societal shifts toward sustainability.

3 Comparative Policy Landscape for Circular Economy in Asia

Asian countries have developed sector-specific policies to promote the CE. Countries such as Japan, South Korea, China, and India share a common goal—to minimize waste and maximize material reuse through recycling—but they employ different tools shaped by their economic priorities, governance structures, and sociocultural norms. These countries were selected due to their substantial economic size, contrasting policy frameworks, and the presence of active startup ecosystems that offer diverse approaches to CE transition in Asia. This section reviews national-level CE policies in these countries, highlighting their challenges and strengths, key focus areas, and summarizing major policy features.

The degree of policy enforcement and collaboration between government and market actors varies significantly across these countries (e.g., Asian Development Bank, 2021). Some have regulations in place but lack consistent enforcement or a continuous policy framework. Others have made limited or inconsistent efforts to implement legislation, with regulations, terminology, and guidelines for startups often lacking clarity or consistency. These variations reflect the diverse social, cultural, and political contexts shaping CE policy (Mohan et al., 2024), underscoring the importance of understanding how national policies translate into concrete actions. Therefore, this section provides a comparative overview of the policy environments in these four countries, aiming to identify, describe, and characterize their distinct structural features, challenges, barriers, strengths, and opportunities for advancing CE initiatives.

3.1 South Korea: Leveraging Digital Innovation and Policy Synergy for CE Transition

South Korea has actively pursued the CE by embedding it within its broader national sustainability strategies (Herrador et al., 2022). A distinguishing feature of Korea's approach lies in its integration of digital technologies with CE principles. The government has developed smart recycling systems, RFID-enabled waste bins, and digital platforms for waste and pollution tracking, all of which enhance transparency, efficiency, and public participation (Lee & Cha, 2020). These digital tools form part of a wider effort to transition from a linear to a data-driven circular waste management system, demonstrating the potential of technologically advanced governance in CE implementation.

In addition to technological innovation, Korea emphasizes public–private partnerships (PPPs) to accelerate CE uptake. Collaborative projects involving startups, industrial actors, and local governments play a key role in piloting new recycling methods, re-manufacturing systems, and consumer engagement platforms. This cross-sectoral coordination highlights the government's recognition that CE success depends not only on regulation but also on entrepreneurial dynamism and societal engagement. However, despite such advancements, disparities persist in access and participation, particularly in rural areas with limited digital infrastructure or public awareness (e.g., Herrador et al., 2020).

Moreover, while the policy framework appears robust, challenges remain in terms of behavioral change and cultural adaptation. Long-term transformation toward CE requires more than technological deployment—it also necessitates consumer education, economic incentives for sustainable practices, and community-based programs to foster a circular mindset (Herrador et al., 2020; Hiquet et al., 2018). Sustainable entrepreneurship thrives when policy, culture, and market conditions align to support new business models that address environmental market imperfections (e.g., Cohen & Winn, 2007).

South Korea's emphasis on innovation and digitalization offers valuable insights for other nations pursuing CE, especially regarding how smart technologies can complement regulatory frameworks. Korea's experience illustrates the evolving synergy between technology, policy, and society in shaping CE outcomes. While significant progress has been made, the conceptual maturity of advanced CE models—such as product-service systems and circular design thinking—is still developing and offers room for further experimentation and refinement. Overall, South Korea presents a compelling case of how a digitally enabled, policy-coordinated, and innovation-driven CE agenda can serve as a blueprint for nations seeking systemic sustainability transformation (Herrador et al., 2022).

3.2 *Japan: Legal Foundations and Long-Term Vision for a CE*

Japan's CE policy landscape is anchored in long-term strategic planning and robust legal frameworks. A central pillar is the Basic Act on Establishing a Sound Material-Cycle Society, enacted in 2000 (Arai et al., 2024), which provides the legislative backbone for Japan's CE system. This law institutionalizes key principles such as waste reduction, reuse, recycling, and promotes resource efficiency across sectors (Arai et al., 2024). Under this Act, Japan has developed a range of sector-specific regulations, including Extended Producer Responsibility (EPR) policies that compel manufacturers to manage the full life cycle of their products (Hotta & Aoki-Suzuki, 2014). Japan's commitment to CE is reinforced through national programs such as the Zero Emission Plan, which sets measurable goals for waste reduction, resource efficiency, and greenhouse gas mitigation. These initiatives reflect the country's cultural inclination toward long-term societal planning and environmental responsibility (Takahashi, 2018). The combination of legally binding standards and a collectivist ethic has made Japan a global exemplar in implementing CE policy frameworks.

Another hallmark of Japan's approach is its emphasis on multi-level governance and public–private collaboration. Industry associations, local governments, and private firms collaborate on CE initiatives, from advanced recycling technologies to public education campaigns (Aoki-Suzuki et al., 2021). These partnerships foster shared responsibility and innovation, as evidenced in Japan's industrial symbiosis zones and urban resource circulation hubs.

Despite these strengths, Japan faces several limitations. While CE policies are highly structured and technologically advanced, they often remain confined within a growth-oriented economic paradigm. Scholars note that Japan's CE transition has largely emphasized reformist and technocratic measures, rather than addressing deeper social transformations or inclusive stakeholder engagement (Arai et al, 2024). Moreover, challenges persist in balancing top-down regulation with grassroots participation, and in adapting policies to reflect evolving stakeholder needs and technological changes.

To address these gaps, researchers suggest that Japan's CE model must broaden its scope to include social justice, stakeholder inclusivity, and behavioral change strategies (Arai et al, 2024; Colley et al., 2024). As Japanese firms increasingly adopt circular business models—such as leasing, product take-back, and remanufacturing—there is a growing need for complementary policy measures that facilitate social innovation and equitable access to CE benefits.

3.3 China: Centralized Governance and Digital Infrastructure Driving CE Innovation

China has progressively initiated CE regulation through comprehensive frameworks (Feng & Lam, 2021), including the Circular Economy Promotion Law (2009) and the 14th Five-Year Plan (2021–2025). These instruments exemplify China's top-down, infrastructure-heavy, and directive governance model for CE (Geng et al., 2012; Yin, et al., 2019). The Circular Economy Promotion Law aims to enhance resource efficiency, minimize waste, and stimulate green innovation. The 14th Five-Year Plan embeds CE into national development strategies, reflecting a formal commitment to sustainable growth and policy integration. China's CE strategy also pressures businesses to innovate, often through mandates for waste reduction and resource efficiency across sectors, from manufacturing to logistics. The 14th Five-Year Plan marks a pivotal shift from pilot initiatives to systemic CE implementation, introducing performance metrics for resource productivity and pollution reduction. This reflects a broader transition from experimentation to institutionalization, enabling rapid deployment of CE practices under China's centralized governance model (Wang et al., 2022).

A defining feature of China's CE model is the strategic use of technology-based solutions. These include digital reuse platforms, second-hand goods marketplaces, and mobile recycling apps designed to match waste generators with recyclers. Such innovations capitalize on China's vast digital infrastructure and user base to facilitate circular practices and alter consumption behavior (Geng et al., 2012). Moreover, Industry 4.0 technologies—such as digital tracking, automation, and artificial intelligence—are increasingly viewed as critical enablers of CE transitions (de Sousa Jabbour et al., 2018). As such, China's integration of digital technologies with strong government support is expected to significantly accelerate its CE transition by 2030 (Wang et al., 2022).

Despite China's strong top-down push for CE integration (Geng et al., 2012; Yin, et al., 2019), substantial challenges remain. A primary concern is the integration of the informal recycling sector, which continues to play a critical role in waste management, especially in urban peripheries and rural regions. Reconciling formal governance structures with informal economic practices is essential (Chi et al., 2011)—not only for improving overall system efficiency, but also for ensuring that the benefits of CE strategies are equitably distributed, particularly among rural and low-income communities. China's path offers unique insights into the possibilities and limits of centralized, technology-driven approaches. It highlights the necessity of balancing national ambition with practical implementation, stakeholder inclusivity, and systemic coordination. The convergence of top-down policy and bottom-up technological innovation remains central to understanding CE trajectories in China (Geng et al., 2012; Yin, et al., 2019).

3.4 India: Navigating Fragmented Policies and Informal Sector Integration in CE

India currently faces a fragmented policy environment for CE, characterized by regulatory gaps that hinder the scaling of formal recycling systems (e.g., Sengupta et al., 2022). While policies addressing recycling, waste management, and sustainability exist, their patchwork nature results in uneven application across regions and sectors. The absence of cohesive national frameworks with clear standards, defined roles, and incentives limits the growth of formal CE systems (Kala & Bolia, 2024). In particular, the informal sector remains central to India's waste management. Millions of waste pickers and small-scale recyclers collect and process vast amounts of waste, yet their contributions remain largely unrecognized by formal regulatory structures (Kala & Bolia, 2024). Although the Indian government has initiated programs to formalize and support informal workers, enforcement remains inconsistent, and most initiatives have yet to provide legal protections, social benefits, or meaningful participation in policy dialogues. This gap between policy intent and implementation reflects the complexities of India's cultural diversity and rapid development.

Additional challenges include limited resources for CE initiatives, low public awareness about recycling, and competing socio-economic priorities that often favor economic growth over environmental sustainability. While government efforts to promote CE are expanding, translating policies into enforceable actions remains difficult (e.g., Fiksel et al., 2021). Particularly, an inclusive CE strategy must address the diverse realities of poor and working-class communities in both urban and rural India.

To tackle these issues, India has initiated national-level action plans on critical areas like plastics, e-waste, and end-of-life vehicles, representing a strategic move toward a more coordinated and scalable CE framework that fosters innovation and inclusive growth (Kambanou et al., 2025). In this evolving landscape, entrepreneurship and innovation are increasingly recognized as key enablers of India's circular transition. Startups, unbound by legacy systems, hold strong potential to drive circular solutions (Mehrotra & Jaladi, 2022).). Yet, current incubators and support programs often overlook the specific needs of circular business models. As Kambanou et al. (2025) suggests, advancing sustainable entrepreneurship through targeted incubation and policy incentives is essential for embedding circularity within India's broader development trajectory. It is also important to acknowledge that resource constraints—such as limited funding, infrastructure gaps, and fragmented policy support—significantly shape how startups in India design and scale their CE initiatives. These limitations often lead to creative but highly localized solutions that differ from those in resource-rich contexts like Japan or South Korea.

3.5 Bridging Policy and Practice: Lessons from Asia's CE Transitions

Despite sharing the common goal of waste reduction and transition to CE, these Asian countries implement CE strategies that reflect their unique economic priorities, governance structures, technological environment, and sociocultural contexts. The varied approaches—from South Korea's digital innovation and public–private partnerships, Japan's legally grounded long-term planning, China's centralized governance combined with technological infrastructure, to India's ongoing efforts to integrate informal sectors amid fragmented policies—illustrate the complexity of translating policy intent into effective, inclusive action. Closing the gap between policy design and on-the-ground implementation requires not only understanding these diverse national circumstances but also fostering entrepreneurship, innovation, and stakeholder engagement to make CE transitions both scalable and socially equitable across Asia (e.g., Mohan et al., 2024).

4 Innovative Startups Driving Circular Economy Transitions

While national policies outline the broad framework for CE development, local municipalities often rely on startups to implement context-specific solutions addressing unique regional challenges. This section presents comparative case studies of leading startups from major Asian countries at the forefront of CE initiatives. Through an analysis of their innovative business models and practical impacts, we explore how these startups operationalize CE principles within their local contexts.

The case studies highlight the role of startups in driving behavioral change among consumers, improving waste management practices, and influencing supply chain dynamics. These localized innovations not only contribute to regional CE transitions but also inform and reinforce broader national policy agendas.

4.1 SuperBin (South Korea)

SuperBin is a South Korean startup leveraging AI-powered smart recycling bins to promote consumer engagement in recycling through monetary incentives. Its core innovation, the Nephron machine, automatically identifies and sorts recyclable materials such as PET bottles and cans, rewarding users with digital points redeemable for cash or coupons (SuperBin, n.d.). This gamified model enhances public participation in recycling by making it more interactive and rewarding (Kim, 2023). Through partnerships with local governments and corporate sponsors, SuperBin has expanded its network across urban areas in South Korea, demonstrating how user-friendly technologies can operationalize CE principles in practice. The company exemplifies how startups can act as effective intermediaries between national CE policy goals and on-the-ground behavioral change by directly engaging the public with incentives and accessible infrastructure. However, challenges remain in scaling this model nationwide and fostering consistent engagement across different social groups. Continuous innovation, targeted public education, and proactive policy support are required to ensure widespread adoption and long-term sustainability (Kim, 2023).

4.2 JEPLAN (Japan)

JEPLAN is a Japanese startup specializing in chemical recycling technologies that convert used apparel and PET bottles into new raw materials, particularly polyester (JEPLAN Inc., n.d.). Its core technology, branded as BRING™, enables the breakdown and repolymerization of polyester waste, allowing it to be reused in new garments and containers (JEPLAN Inc., 2023). JEPLAN collaborates with large retail and manufacturing corporations such as Kao, MUJI, and Aeon to collect discarded clothing and promote recycling awareness among consumers (JEPLAN Inc., 2024). Through these partnerships, JEPLAN not only expands access to recycling infrastructure but also educates the public on how corporate–startup collaboration can drive sustainability.

Supportive national policies—such as Japan's Circular Economy Vision 2020—have helped to create a regulatory environment conducive to innovation in material recovery and reuse (Ministry of the Environment Japan, 2022). JEPLAN's model highlights how startup-driven technologies can scale with the help of public and private cooperation, contributing meaningfully to Japan's national CE goals.

4.3 Xianyu (China)

Xianyu is a Chinese digital platform operated by Alibaba that facilitates the buying and selling of secondhand goods with the aim of promoting reuse and reducing waste (Sun, 2023). Initially launched as a consumer-to-consumer marketplace, Xianyu has grown significantly, helping to normalize secondhand consumption, particularly among younger consumers (Yao & Miao, 2021). By leveraging China's extensive digital infrastructure, the platform offers convenience and affordability, embedding reuse practices into everyday consumption and promoting a growing culture of CE awareness, especially in urban areas (Sun, 2023).

However, Xianyu's model also illustrates persistent challenges associated with informal and small-scale waste markets. Issues such as product quality assurance, fraud prevention, and the regulation of informal sellers continue to hinder consumer trust and raise questions about the reliability of secondhand markets (Sun, 2023).

Building trust between buyers and sellers is a core challenge for platform-based CE models, and platform governance plays a critical role in enabling sustainable engagement and long-term loyalty. Ultimately, the case of Xianyu highlights how large-scale digital platforms can serve as important enablers of behavioral shifts toward sustainability, but their long-term success depends on a supportive institutional ecosystem that bridges digital innovation, trust-building mechanisms, and inclusive regulation (Sun, 2023; Yao & Miao, 2021).

4.4 Recykal (India)

Recykal is a Hyderabad-based digital marketplace that connects waste generators (e.g., households, corporates), aggregators, informal waste pickers (kabadiwalas), and recyclers across India, facilitating transactions, quality checks, real-time tracking, and transparent pricing for materials such as plastic, paper, metal, and e-waste (Meghani, 2020). It integrates informal workers into the formal circular-economy value chain—"like the Uber for Trash"—increasing their income by up to 20 percent through direct payments and digital banking (Khan, 2020; Meghani, 2020).

According to Forbes India (Meghani, 2020), Recykal's digital tools enable price discovery, traceability, and compliance with regulations like Extended Producer Responsibility (EPR), helping brand partners such as Unilever and Coca-Cola report on ESG metrics and recycling outcomes. Its Circularity Marketplace also allows brands to source verified recycled raw materials (e.g., rPET, paper, and metal) with full quality assurance and third-party audits (Outlook Business, 2023).

However, despite its scalable model, Recykal's long-term success depends on continued regulatory support, improved digital literacy among informal workers, and ongoing public education campaigns to enhance adoption and deepen engagement (Bhadra & Mishra, 2021). Its ability to formalize diverse stakeholders using technology illustrates how startups can accelerate circular practices in contexts with fragmented recycling systems.

5 Discussion

The CE is gaining momentum across Asia, driven by diverse actors including governments, startups, and communities. This chapter explores how different countries are navigating the opportunities and challenges inherent in CE adoption, focusing particularly on the role of startups as catalysts for innovation and systemic change. By examining case studies from South Korea, Japan, China, and India, we identify common trends and unique national approaches that shape the evolving CE landscape in the region, as summarized in Table 1.

Table 1 Cross-country review of policies and startup-driven innovation

Country	CE Approach	Startup	Policy Features
Korea	Tech-driven, PPPs	SuperBin: digital gamified recycling	Smart waste bins, RFID, PPP incentives
Japan	Legal framework	JEPLAN: chemical recycling	Extended Producer Responsibility (EPR) policies, long-term planning
China	Centralized, digital	Xianyu: C2C reuse platform	14th Five-Year Plan, informal challenges
India	Fragmented, informal	Recykal: inclusive marketplace	Inconsistent enforcement, digital gaps

5.1 Cross-National Patterns and Divergences in CE Practices

A cross-national examination of CE initiatives across key Asian countries reveals both shared strategies and significant differences. A prominent commonality is the strategic deployment of technology to tackle waste management challenges aligned with CE principles. For instance, South Korea utilizes smart recycling systems such as SuperBin; Japan advances chemical recycling technologies through companies like JEPLAN; China promotes consumer participation in reuse via digital platforms such as Xianyu; and India leverages waste management apps like Recykal. These technological innovations are not isolated solutions but integrative tools embedding CE practices into daily life (e.g., Lee et al., 2024). Governments increasingly recognize the potential of startups in bridging policy goals and citizen-level engagement to operationalize CE strategies.

However, critical differences stem from structural, regulatory, and socio-economic contexts. Japan's highly regulated environment facilitates institutionalized public–private collaborations that help scale CE initiatives. Conversely, India's fragmented waste ecosystem—dominated by informal actors—poses challenges for startups like Recykal, which must navigate regulatory ambiguities and help define operational norms. While China demonstrates technological sophistication, inconsistent regulatory enforcement presents ongoing implementation challenges.

Despite national variation, several common obstacles persist across the region. Most notably, CE startups' growth and sustainability hinge on governmental support and access to funding. Competition for green finance is intense, and startups frequently confront limited resources and fragmented policy environments. Nevertheless, CE movements in Asia are maturing (Mohan et al., 2024), and where governments actively partner with or endorse startups, the potential exists to build systemic models that are both environmentally sustainable and socially inclusive.

5.2 The Role of Startups as Change Agents

Startups have emerged as pivotal actors in Asia's CE landscape (e.g., Mehrotra & Jaladi, 2022; Schröder et al., 2019). Their contributions extend beyond technological innovation—they translate abstract governmental ambitions into actionable, community-level solutions. For example, South Korea's smart recycling initiatives and India's waste apps illustrate startups' ability to operationalize CE strategies in ways that are contextually relevant and citizen-centric.

These efforts bridge the gap among technology, policy frameworks, and habitual consumer behaviors. Moreover, startups contribute to job creation, community networking, and catalyzing shifts toward sustainable daily practices. Their agility and creativity enable them to pilot new ventures, adapt business models, and apply emerging technologies—advantages often unattainable for larger corporations or government bodies.

Crucially, many startups embed social value into their models by connecting small producers with markets, supporting local livelihoods, and reinvesting in communities. This dual focus on innovation and social impact positions startups as key facilitators of inclusive CE models aligned with national sustainability objectives.

5.3 Ecosystemic Challenges and Policy Implications

Despite their promise, CE startups face significant systemic barriers. They often lack access to sufficient funding, enabling regulatory frameworks, and integration into existing infrastructure. Visibility and public awareness also remain low, constraining startups' capacity to scale up impact.

Countries in the region—such as South Korea, Japan, China, and India—adopt varied strategies to address these challenges. Some emphasize top-down policy alignment and public–private partnerships, while others rely more heavily on informal ecosystems or grassroots entrepreneurial networks. These differences underscore that there is no universal "blueprint" for CE policy. Instead, successful models depend on an ecosystemic approach where governments provide regulatory clarity and investment; startups offer innovation and local adaptability; and citizens engage as empowered participants. The synergies among these actors are critical, requiring ongoing collaboration, dialogue, and mutual learning.

Public–private-innovation (PPI) frameworks are evolving as a critical mechanism for advancing circular-economy strategies. These frameworks go beyond traditional public–private partnerships by explicitly incorporating entrepreneurial and innovation-driven actors—such as startups, social enterprises, and research institutions—into the policy design and implementation process. PPI emphasizes tri-sector collaboration, where governments provide strategic direction and regulation, the private sector delivers operational capacity, and startups contribute agile, technology-driven solutions tailored to local needs.

For example, South Korea's SuperBin initiative demonstrates how national policy support (e.g., smart waste policies) can align with municipal cooperation and startup innovation to create gamified recycling infrastructure. Similarly, Japan's JEPLAN shows how chemical recycling technologies can scale through close cooperation among government agencies, corporations, and innovative ventures. These cases illustrate how contextualized PPI frameworks enable experimentation, mutual learning, and more inclusive CE outcomes. Through such localized and multi-stakeholder coordination, PPI frameworks offer countries the ability to align CE strategies with their unique institutional, cultural, and economic contexts—ultimately contributing to more resilient and transferable circular practices across the region.

5.4 *Current Gaps and Future Directions*

Despite strong national commitments, many Asia–Pacific countries still lack comprehensive CE implementation frameworks, particularly at the execution level. Challenges such as insufficient funding, weak policy enforcement, and limited public awareness persist. These gaps highlight the necessity of sustained cross-sector collaboration, the establishment of robust regulatory and financial instruments, and the empowerment of grassroots entrepreneurship.

Startups, positioned at the nexus of innovation, policy, and community engagement, have a central role in translating policy commitments into scalable, actionable CE systems. Their capacity to pilot solutions tailored to local challenges offers valuable lessons for building sustainable circular transitions. Looking forward, it is essential to explore how CE principles can be extended to emerging and resource-intensive sectors, including construction materials, electronics, and ecological farming—fields where waste and resource management pose critical challenges.

6 Conclusion

This chapter illustrates the growing significance of startups as transformative agents in Asia's CE development. By bridging technology, policy, and community engagement, startups create innovative, context-specific solutions that not only advance sustainability but also foster social inclusion through job creation and local empowerment. However, the scaling and sustainability of these initiatives depend on supportive ecosystems encompassing financial resources, enabling regulations, technological infrastructure, and collaborative networks among governments, businesses, and citizens.

From a stakeholder theory perspective (Freeman, 1984), the success of circular initiatives hinges on the active involvement and alignment of diverse actors—ranging from policymakers and investors to local communities and consumers—each of whom holds a legitimate interest in shaping CE outcomes (e.g., Hiquet et al., 2018).

This highlights the importance of participatory governance and value co-creation in building CE ecosystems that are not only efficient but also socially equitable and responsive to local needs.

The diversity of approaches across countries demonstrates that CE development is a multifaceted process requiring adaptable, locally grounded strategies rather than one-size-fits-all policies. As CE practices continue to evolve, further research should investigate emerging sectors and explore how lessons from Asian startups and government collaborations can inform global efforts toward a just and sustainable circular future. Ultimately, fostering inclusive, resilient, and innovative CE ecosystems—guided by stakeholder engagement—offers a promising pathway for systemic transformation that benefits both people and the planet.

References

Aoki-Suzuki, C., Dente, S. M., Tanaka, D., Kayo, C., Murakami, S., Fujii, C., ... & Hashimoto, S. (2021). Total environmental impacts of Japanese material production. *Journal of Industrial Ecology, 25*(6), 1474–1485.

Arai, R., Calisto Friant, M., & Vermeulen, W. J. (2024). The Japanese circular economy and sound material-cycle society policies: Discourse and policy analysis. *Circular Economy and Sustainability, 4*(1), 619–650.

Asian Development Bank. (2021). Asian development outlook 2021: Financing a green and inclusive recovery. https://www.adb.org/sites/default/files/publication/692111/ado2021-highlights.pdf

Bhadra, U., & Mishra, P. P. (2021). Extended producer responsibility in India: Evidence from Recykal, Hyderabad. *Journal of Urban Management, 10*(4), 430–439.

Chi, X., Streicher-Porte, M., Wang, M. Y., & Reuter, M. A. (2011). Informal electronic waste recycling: A sector review with special focus on China. *Waste Management, 31*(4), 731–742.

Cohen, B., & Winn, M. I. (2007). Market imperfections, opportunity and sustainable entrepreneurship. *Journal of Business Venturing, 22*(1), 29–49.

Colley, K., Hague, A., Chen, J., Lorenzo-Arribas, A., Wooldridge, T., Somervail, P.,... & Craig, T. (2024). Putting people at the centre of the circle: an agenda for behavioural research on the circular economy. *Frontiers in Sustainability, 5*, 1423912.

Lopes de Sousa Jabbour, A. B., Jabbour, C. J. C., Godinho Filho, M., & Roubaud, D. (2018). Industry 4.0 and the circular economy: a proposed research agenda and original roadmap for sustainable operations. *Annals of Operations Research, 270*, 273–286.

Feng, K., & Lam, C. Y. (2021). An overview of circular economy in China: How the current challenges shape the plans for the future. *The Chinese Economy, 54*(5), 355–371.

Fiksel, J., Sanjay, P., & Raman, K. (2021). Steps toward a resilient circular economy in India. *Clean Technologies and Environmental Policy, 23*, 203–218.

Freeman, R. E. (1984). *Strategic management: A stakeholder approach.* Cambridge University Press.

Geng, Y., Fu, J., Sarkis, J., & Xue, B. (2012). Towards a national circular economy indicator system in China: An evaluation and critical analysis. *Journal of Cleaner Production, 23*(1), 216–224.

Herrador, M., & Van, M. L. (2024). Circular economy strategies in the ASEAN region: A comparative study. *Science of the Total Environment, 908*, Article 168280.

Herrador, M., Cho, Y., & Park, P. H. (2020). Latest circular economy policy and direction in the Republic of Korea: Room for enhancements. *Journal of Cleaner Production, 269*, Article 122336.

Herrador, M., De Jong, W., Nasu, K., & Granrath, L. (2022). Circular economy and zero-carbon strategies between Japan and South Korea: A comparative study. *Science of the Total Environment, 820*, Article 153274.
Hiquet, R., Brunneder, J., & Oh, W. Y. (2018). From myopia to boycott: Consumer acceptance of, and resistance to, fast fashion. In *Eco-friendly and fair* (pp. 58–68). Routledge.
Hotta, Y., & Aoki-Suzuki, C. (2014). Waste reduction and recycling initiatives in Japanese cities: Lessons from Yokohama and Kamakura. *Waste Management & Research, 32*(9), 857–866.
JEPLAN Inc. (n.d.). About BRING Technology. Retrieved June 18, 2025, from https://www.jeplan.co.jp/en/
JEPLAN Inc. (2023, May 22). BRING Technology: Chemical recycling of polyester from clothes and PET bottles. https://www.jeplan.co.jp/en/bring
JEPLAN Inc., (2024, May). JEPLAN and Kao Collaborate to Achieve Horizontal Recycling in Cosmetics Bottle Demonstration Project. https://www.jeplan.co.jp/en/2024/05/29/15296/
Kala, K., & Bolia, N. B. (2024). Empowering the informal sector in urban waste management: Towards a comprehensive waste management policy for India. *Environmental Development, 49*, Article 100968.
Kambanou, M. L., Hajoary, P. K., & Lindfors, A. (2025). Supporting start-ups in the circular economy: An analysis of university-led incubators in India. *Journal of Industrial Ecology, 29*(3), 997–1012.
Khan, S. (2020, March 9). Recykal: Making money from India's huge waste problem. The Economic Times.
Kim, E. (2023, April 30). Startup brings AI to waste sorting to promote recycling. The Korea Herald. https://biz.heraldcorp.com/article/3115142
Lee, K., & Cha, J. (2020). Towards improved circular economy and resource security in South Korea. *Sustainability, 13*(1), 17.
Lee, S., Oh, W. Y., & Yi, I. (2024). The Emergence of the Nighttime Artificial Intelligence-Robot-Driven Economy. In Artificial Intelligence for Sustainability: Innovations in Business and Financial Services (pp. 55–79). Cham: Springer Nature Switzerland.
MacArthur, E. (2013). Towards the circular economy, economic and business rationale for an accelerated transition. *Ellen MacArthur Foundation: Cowes, UK, 1.*
Meghani, V. (2020, March 9). Uber for trash: How Recykal is cleaning up the mess. *Forbes India.* https://www.forbesindia.com/article/take-one-big-story-of-the-day/how-recykal-is-cleaning-up-the-mess/70177/1
Mehrotra, S., & Jaladi, S. R. (2022). How start-ups in emerging economies embrace circular business models and contribute towards a circular economy. *Journal of Entrepreneurship in Emerging Economies, 14*(5), 727–753.
Ministry of the Environment Japan. (2022). Circular Economy Vision 2020. Retrieved from https://www.meti.go.jp/shingikai/energy_environment/junkai_keizai/pdf/20200522_03.pdf
Mohan, J., Mohanty, C. R. C., Cross, J. S., & Khajuria, A. (2024). Mapping 3R and circular economy policy implementation in Asia and the Pacific. *Circular Economy and Sustainability, 4*(1), 671–692.
Oh, W. Y., Chang, Y. K., Park, J. H., & Han, S. (2021). Toward a sustainable paradigm: Circular economy solutions in the fashion industry. In *Research handbook of innovation for a circular economy* (pp. 47–58). Edward Elgar Publishing.
Outlook Business. (2023, August 8). *Recykal introduces circularity marketplace.* https://www.outlookbusiness.com/sector/e-commerce/recykal-introduces-circularity-marketplace-news-9059
Schröder, P., Anantharaman, M., Anggraeni, K., & Foxon, T. J. (2019). *The circular economy and the Global South.* Routledge. https://doi.org/10.4324/9780429434006
Sengupta, D., Ilankoon, I. M. S. K., Kang, K. D., & Chong, M. N. (2022). Circular economy and household e-waste management in India: Integration of formal and informal sectors. *Minerals Engineering, 184*, Article 107661.
SuperBin. (n.d.). *Company overview.* Retrieved June 18, 2025, from https://www.superbin.co.kr

Sun, B. (2023). *Reading between the lines of the second-hand e-commerce business in China: A study of consumer behaviour Xianyu second-hand platform* (Dissertation). Singapore Management University. https://ink.library.smu.edu.sg/etd_coll/491

Takahashi, W. (2018). Toward a sound material-cycle society: History of Japanese policy and its interaction with international norms. In *Routledge Handbook of Japanese Foreign Policy* (pp. 119–135). Routledge.

Tan, J., Tan, F. J., & Ramakrishna, S. (2022). Transitioning to a circular economy: A systematic review of its drivers and barriers. *Sustainability, 14*(3), 1757.

Wang, D., Ponce, P., Zhang, Y., Ponce, K., & Tanveer, M. (2022). The future of Industry 4.0 and the circular economy in Chinese supply chain: In the era of post-COVID-19 pandemic. *Operations Management Research, 15*(1–2), 342–356.

Yao, G., & Miao, J. (2021). Service value co-creation in digital platform business: A case of Xianyu idle trading platform. *Sustainability, 13*(20), 11296.

Yin, H., Zhang, X., & Wang, F. (2019). Environmental regulations in China. In *Oxford Research Encyclopedia of Environmental Science.*

Jacob Stalk is currently pursuing an M.B.A. at the University of Nevada, Las Vegas (UNLV) and is a committed community leader. He serves on the board of SHARE Village Las Vegas, formerly known as Veterans Village, where he actively supports initiatives focused on veteran welfare and homelessness. He brings substantial professional experience and demonstrates a strong dedication to advancing social impact initiatives.

Dr. Won-Yong Oh is Lee Professor of Strategy and an associate professor at the Lee Business School, University of Nevada, Las Vegas (UNLV), USA. Previously, he was an associate professor at the Haskayne School of Business, University of Calgary in Canada and a visiting faculty at the Faculty of Management, University of Warsaw in Poland. His research interests include corporate social responsibility, corporate governance, sustainability, and strategic leadership. He has published over 70 peer-reviewed journal articles, book chapters, and case studies, with many of his journal publications appearing in outlets included on the Financial Times Top 50 list. He currently serves as an editor for the *Journal of Business Research* and *Corporate Governance: An International Review*.

Circular Economy Initiatives: Harnessing the Potential of Countries in Asia

Tareq Mahbub

Abstract This book chapter has investigated the circular economy from a number of different perspectives. It first examines the circular economy in terms of its origins and definitions, its benefits in relation to economic, environmental and social dimensions and its relevance to the United Nation's sustainable development goals. After setting the background it delves into the topics of the landscape of circular economy in relation to policies with particular emphasis to the Asia–Pacific region, the role of industry 4.0 technologies in promoting circularity, circular economy applications in industry, implementation challenges, and the types of circular economy performance indicators including progress of circular economy policies across the Asia–Pacific region. Additionally, it has recommended policy implications both for the business and the government for the implementation of circular economy including informing on the next frontier of circular economy development for the Asia–Pacific region.

1 Introduction

1.1 Circular Economy Origins and Definition

The British environmental economists, Pearce and Turner first introduced the concept of circular economy drawing on previous studies of ecological economist Boulding (1966). Boulding coined the term "spaceship earth" as a metaphor for the material constraints human faced on earth. He proposed that the industrial society acts like a "cowboy economy" where a herd can simply be moved to a new posture once the grass is grazed. On the contrary, he proposed that the earth is a "single spaceship" without limited reservoirs of anything, either for extraction or for pollution." He argued that in such a "spaceman economy" where resource and sinks are two sides of the same coin, endless growth is not feasible and materials need to circulate as long as possible within the socioeconomic system (Rizos et al., 2017).

T. Mahbub (✉)
Faculty of Business Department, Sakarya University School of Business, Serdivan, Turkey
e-mail: tareq@sakarya.edu.tr

T. Endress and Y. F. Badir (eds.), *Business and Management in Asia: Opportunities and Entrepreneurship*, https://doi.org/10.1007/978-981-95-4909-2_7

Expounding on Boulding's work, British environmental economists, Pearce and Turner, made the first reference to the circular economy in 1990. They suggested that the earth is a circular system in which the economy and the environment cannot be treated in a linear but a circular relationship and suggested a closed cycle of materials within the economy to achieve a "win–win" situation both in the economy and the environment (Su et al., 2013).

The fundamental principle of circular economy is based on the 3R model: reduce, reuse, and recycle (Gebrardt et al., 2022; Okorie et al., 2018; Prieto-Sandoval et al., 2018). A circular economy aims at keeping materials used as long as possible and minimizing waste by designing products for reuse, repair, and recycling. The development of the circular economy is based on two interconnected ideas, the closed-loop economy and design to re-design thinking. It is suggested that in a well-functioning circular economy, all products are made in a way that items can be repaired or reused or easily recycled at the end of the life cycle, ensuring durability and ease of maintenance. In this way, the circular economy works as a regenerative system with minimal energy losses and carbon footprint, as well as minimalized resource intake and waste. This is achieved by slowing, closing and narrowing material and energy loops (Geissdoerfer et al., 2017). When contrasting with a linear economy in which natural resources are extracted, transformed into consumer products through industrial processes, and subsequently disposed of after they have satisfied the customer's demand, for example, "take-make-consume-dispose," on the contrary circular economy assumes that natural resources are limitless, readily accessible, and inexpensive to dispose of. Therefore, this process renders the concept of "end-of-life" obsolete and consequently materials are in a state of perpetual circulation with closed cycles throughout the production process.

Several definitions have been given regarding the circular economy focused on utilizing waste (outputs) into another system's future resource (input). For examples, Kirchherr et al. (2017) describes the circular economy as a business model which replaces the "end-of-life" concept replacing by reducing, reusing, recycling and recovering materials in production, distribution and consumption processes at the meso (eco-industrial parks) and macro (city, region, nation and beyond) with the aim of sustainable development (i.e., better environmental quality, economic prosperity, social equity) benefitting current and future generations. Rood et al. (2017) defines the circular economy as the optimal use of raw materials and products to preserve natural resources. According to this concept, circular economy gives a "second life" to the resources; thus, causing less damage to the environment and adds value to the economy. The Ellen MacArthur Foundation offers a widely accepted definition of the circular economy which states the circular economy is a system where materials never become waste and nature is regenerated. In a circular economy products and materials are kept in circulation through processes like maintenance, reuse, refurbishment, remanufacture, recycling, and composting. It tackles climate change and other global challenges like biodiversity loss, waste and pollution by decoupling economic activity from the consumption of finite resources.

Among the leading nations to first implement circular economy, China and Japan were among the first nations to implement circular economy. For example, Japan

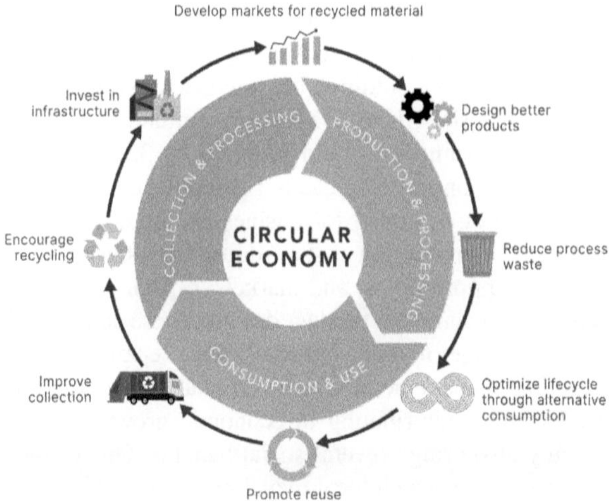

Fig. 1 Circular economy model. *Source* Circular Innovation Council (2025)

put its "Law for the promotion of effective utilization of resources" into force in April 2001 and 2008. China passed a law on closed-loop economy (Geng & Doberstein, 2008; Mathews & Tan, 2011). Following through the European countries have stepped up their efforts to implement circular economy practices. Some EU member states have published policy strategy documents that set out strategies for implementing the circular economy (EU, 2015, 2017; SITRA, 2016).

Figure 1 shows a circular economy model.

1.2 Benefits of Using Circular Economy

The transition to a circular economy offers a multitude of benefits across environmental, economic, and social dimensions. It provides a sustainable alternative, rather than the linear model of the production and management of resources, which has had negative economic, environmental and social consequences; thus, promising a future where economic growth is achieved in harmony with environmental stewardship and social well-being.

One of the most significant benefits of the circular economy is its positive impact on the environment. For example, by adopting the principles of reduce, reuse, and recycle, the amount of waste generated can be drastically reduced. This reduction in waste not only alleviates pressure on landfills and waste management systems but also decreases pollution and greenhouse gas emissions associated with waste disposal. A study conducted by the Ellen MacArthur Foundation and McKinsey Centre for Business Environment (2015) which employed econometric modelling and data gleaned through 150 interviews on three European sectors (i.e., food, mobility, and the built environment) found that the circular economy can decrease greenhouse gas (GHG) emissions up to 48% by 2030 and up to 83% by 2050 (Ellen MacArthur Foundation, 2015; Rizos et al., 2017). Additionally, the study estimated that inter alia in car and construction materials, land use and agricultural water use and fertilizer use, primary-material consumption could decrease by 32% by 2030 and 53% by 2050. Similarly circular economy can lead to substantial cost savings for both businesses and consumers. For example, for businesses, the efficient use of materials and resources can reduce production costs. Additionally, the circular economy can open up new business opportunities, and markets, especially in the fields of recycling, refurbishing, and sustainable product design. These can pave the way for the development of a new range of skills and roles, from repairing and refurbishing to recycling and resource management, which can lead to the creation of a substantial number of jobs; thus, contributing to economic growth and stability. Lastly, the circular economy also brings several social benefits. One of the key aspects is community development for which local recycling and refurbishing initiatives help strengthen community ties and foster a sense of shared responsibility for the environment. These initiatives often involve local businesses and community groups promoting local economic development and social cohesion.

2 Circular Economy and Sustainable Development Goals

The United Nations (UN) SDGs, established in 2015, encompasses a comprehensive set of global objectives aimed at eradicating poverty, safeguarding the planet, and ensuring prosperity for all by 2030. There are 17 SDGs with 169 targets that can be categorized into three broad areas: social, economic, and environmental. The environmental and economic goals (SDGs 7–9 and 11–15 respectively) emphasize affordable and clean energy, decent work and economic growth, industry innovation and infrastructure, sustainable cities, responsible consumption and production, climate action, and the protection of life below water and on land. The social goals (SDGs 1–6, 10, 16) focus on eliminating poverty and hunger, promoting health, and well-being, providing quality education, achieving gender equality, ensuring clear water and sanitation, and reducing inequalities. SDG 17 promotes global partnership to advance all SDGs. Schroeder et al. (2019) suggest that the circular economy contributes directly to achieving several of the SDGs, for example, SDG 6, SDG 7, SDG 8, SDG 12, and SDG 15. The SDGs can be achieved through circular economy activities at various levels: micro (products, companies, consumers), meso eco-industrial parks), and macro (cities, regions, nations, and beyond).

2.1 *The Landscape of Circular Economy Policies in the Asia–Pacific Region*

Circular economy policy development in the Asia–Pacific region started in 1992. These policies could be categorized into seven categories based on each country's level of maturity in developing and implementing policies that promote circularity. These are early-stage policy; in scoping; in development; call to action; roadmap; operational strategy; and actual policy. Figure 1 shows the distribution of circular economy policies in the Asia–Pacific region.

Figure 2 presents the number of circular economy policies in the Asia–Pacific region.

East and North-East Asia has the highest number of policies followed by South-East Asia, the Pacific, South and South-West Asia, and North and Central Asia. In East and North-East Asia–China, Japan, and the Republic of Korea are frontrunners for circular economy policies mostly at the stages of policy implementation and operational strategies. In contrast, policies in Mongolia and Hong Kong are at the "in scoping" and "call to action" stages. The Chinese circular economy promotion laws define circular economy a generic term for the reducing, reusing, and recycling activities conducted in the process of production, circulation, and consumption (CCICED, 2008). On the contrary, other countries such as Europe, Japan, USA, Korea, and Vietnam seem to identify circular economy and its founding principles 3R in more sectoral initiatives majorly related to waste management policies. Likewise, Japan implemented circular economy since 1991 with the law for Effective Utilization of

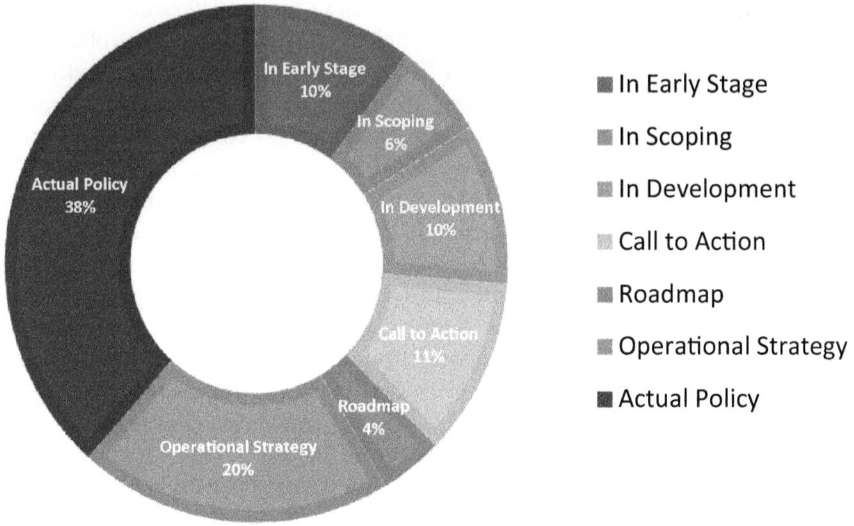

Fig. 2 Illustrates the distribution of circular economy policies in the Asia–Pacific region. *Source* ESCAP (2024)

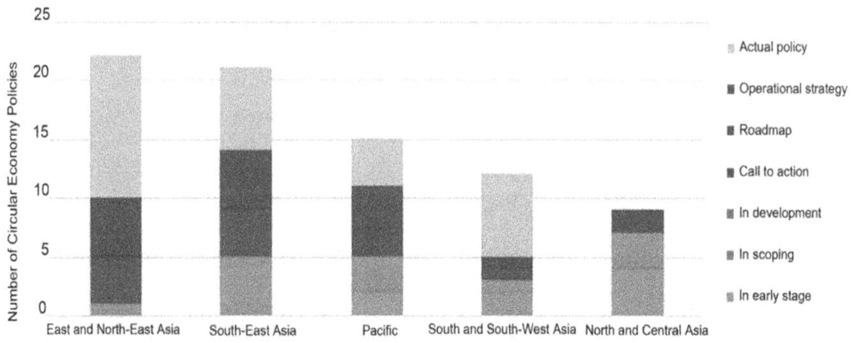

Fig. 3 Presents the number of circular economy policies across regions. *Source* ESCAP (2024)

Recyclables (METI, 2015) and, later on, the Japanese circular economy initiative. In Japan, several policies are in the implementation phase, including the law for the Promotion of Effective Utilization of Resources (2000), the law for the Recycling of Specified Kinds of Home Appliances (2001), and the Basic Act for Establishing a Sound Material-Cycle Society (2000). Additionally, the Ministry of the Environment, the Ministry of Economy, Trade, and Industry, and the Japan Business Federation established the Japan Partnership for Circular Economy to promote circular practices through closed-loop recycling systems for plastic materials and cross-industry collaborations for upcycling waste.

The Republic of Korea has advanced policies focused on resource efficiency and waste reduction, facilitated through a comprehensive Extended Producer Responsibility (EPR) framework that covers electronics, packaging, and hazardous materials. In this vein, China is also at the "policy implementation" stage, with robust EPR system recently reinforced by the 2024 EPR scheme for mobile phones, effective management of e-waste, and promoting the recycling of mobile communication devices. For the case of China, the country seems strongly committed and attracted by circular economy owing to its huge environmental, human health, and social problems in regard to its very rapid and continuous economic development. In China circular economy is promoted as a top-down national political objective and its implementation is structured following a horizontal and a vertical approach, as the Chinese national governmental policy aims to transform not only the industry but also the socioeconomic organization of the society at all levels. At the vertical level, China attempts to shift circular economy from the low level of analysis—micro (i.e., company or single consumer level) to the higher hierarchical levels—meso—(i.e., eco- industrial parks), and macro (i.e., cities, provinces, and regions) while the horizontal dimension relates to a link between "industries, urban infrastructures, cultural environment, and the social consumption system." This is unlike the European Union, Japan, or the USA where circular economy is used as a tool to design bottom up environmental and waste management policies, which are market oriented vis-à-vis China's command and control approach.

Among other countries in East and North-East Asia; Hong Kong, China, is at scoping stage with its "Producer Responsibility Scheme on Plastic Beverage Containers and Beverage Cartons (2021)," while in Mongolia, policies are primarily at the "call to action" and "operational strategy" stages, focusing on resource conservation, waste reduction, and embedding 3R principles (reduce, reuse, recycle) across sectors.

Among North and Central Asian countries, Kazakhstan and Kyrgyzstan are leading the region. For example, Kazakhstan has adopted the "Kazakhstan 2050" strategy which emphasizes sustainable development, energy efficiency, and resource management while Kyrgyzstan has adopted a green economy strategy for 2019–2030 prioritizing energy efficiency, waste management, and the introduction of renewable energy sources.

Among the countries of South and South-West Asia, India is leading the circular economy transition. India has developed a number of steps toward this transition, establishing the Circular Economy Cell in NITI Aayog and implementing sector-specific action plans and policies aimed at promoting resource efficiency and sustainable practices. For example, India's E-Waste Management Rules (2016) mandates businesses to ensure the safe disposal of scrapped electronics items and to recycle a minimum of 30% of the manufactured electronic products. Additionally, to further address e-waste, the EPR e-waste regulations (2022–2023) require businesses involved in the sale, manufacture, purchase, transfer, dismantling, refurbishing, processing, or recycling of e-waste, including its parts and components to comply with the EPR for e-waste management framework. The EPR scheme on Plastic Packaging (2016) strengthens circularity in the use of plastic packaging waste promotes the development of new alternatives to plastics and provides next steps for moving toward sustainable plastic packaging. Furthermore, the Steel Scrap Recycling Policy (2019) attempts to promote circular economy in the steel industry by collecting, dismantling, and processing end-of-life products that are sources of recyclable scraps, thereby promoting resource conservation and energy savings. Similarly, the Battery Waste Management Rules mandate importers take responsibility for the collection, recycling, and refurbishment of waste batteries as well as the use of recovered materials to create new batteries. Finally, the National Circular Economy Framework (2023) has been developed to call for action which emphasizes collaboration, awareness, and targeted actions for a sustainable and prosperous future. Among other countries in South Asia, Bangladesh has implemented the Ship Recycling Act (2008), an industrial circular economy policy that mandates ship cycling only in specific zones and the Zero Waste policy. Turkey has introduced reverse vending machines where citizens can exchange their plastic bottles and cans for public transport credits (KPMG Turkey and France, 2022). Turkey has also implemented the Circular Economy Platform (2018) as an operational strategy, providing companies seeking to accelerate their circular transition with a knowledge hub, an e-commerce platform, measurement tools, training, technical assistance, and consultancy services.

Among the countries in South-East Asia, the only regional policy for circular economy in place is the Regional Policy: Framework for Circular Economy for the

ASEAN Economic Community SEA Circular (2021). Most policies are already in place at the country level while others are operational strategies.

For example, Indonesia's Regulation on Road Map to Waste Reduction by Producers (2019) which requires producers to make a plan and report to reduce packaging and containers (Ministry of Environment and Forestry, 2020); the Extended Producer Responsibility Act (2022); in the Philippines, which is primarily concerned with plastic packaging waste (Keslio, 2024). For example, unlike many EPR systems, the Philippine law includes the recovery of flexible plastic, which are hard to recycle, as it incentivizes people to recover non-recyclable waste. Singapore has implemented the Resource Sustainability Act (2019), which is applying EPR to e-waste, packages, and containers. Vietnam has implemented the Environmental Protection Law, which applies EPR to e-waste, tires, batteries, and vehicles. Furthermore, Thailand has been drafting an EPR scheme primarily targeting at the packaging wastes. Thailand has embraced the circular economy model through the Bio-Circular-Green (BCG) initiative. It is a multifaceted approach that integrates the bioeconomy, circular economy, and green economy to create high-value added products and services that are eco-friendly and resource-efficient. The BCG model in Thailand concentrated on four strategic factors which are agriculture and food, wellness and medicine, energy materials and biochemicals, and tourism and creative economy. A case in point is the Siam Cement Group (SCG), has held the world's number one ranking for a decade in the Dow Jones Sustainability Indices in construction materials and has deployed a wide range of innovations and processes within its workflow for sustainable development (Asian Insiders, 2025).

3 Building a Digital Circular Economy

The concept of a digital circular economy is gaining ground which is in essence combining the traditional principles of the CE with digital technologies such as artificial intelligence (AI), block chain and the internet of things (IoT) to create a more circular industrial system. It is suggested that by integrating these tools, businesses can achieve greater resource efficiency and innovation while also contributing toward a more sustainable economy.

For example, AI as an emergent "Fourth Industrial Revolution" technology, can support and accelerate the pace of innovation to design products, bring together aspects of successful circular economy models, and optimize the infrastructure needed to loop products and materials back into the economy. As the circular economy requires more features to be taken into consideration for the design of products, components, and materials, such as disassembly, upgradability, or recycled content including the wide choice of materials and possibilities of manipulation of structures coupled with 3D printing technology along with other manufacturing technologies; the design options become countless. AI can be helpful to manage this complexity when making decision. Further, a continuous feedback loop in which designers test and refine AI generated design could inform better design outcome in a shorter time span (Sreenivasan & Suresh, 2024). In that vein, to design a new material, scientists need to evaluate large amounts of data about the structures and properties of materials, which AI could analyze quickly to inform new materials. Additionally, by training an algorithm to analyze known chemical data, AI could be potentially be used to predict the toxicity of chemicals or materials where it is not known in a more economic and efficient way. A case in point in this regard is the Accelerated Metallurgy Project run by the European Space Agency in collaboration with a group of leading manufacturers, universities, and designers. In this venture the AI technology was used to produce and test new metal alloys. The outcome was it not only helped develop completely new materials but it happened at a faster rate than ever before. However, one typical concern about AI is that this processing of data often generates an enormous amount of heat (i.e., massive data centers that consume huge amount of energy and water). The Microsoft's AI supercomputer in IOWA, which helped train GPT-4 relies heavily on water cooling, drawing from local rivers to keep servers running at optimal temperatures. In this regard, cooling AI infrastructure is a major environmental concern, as in hot climates these data centers can withdraw millions of gallons per day. To balance this trade-off between the growing demand of AI and also to reduce its environmental footprint, companies like Microsoft, Google and others are investing in renewable energy to adopting alternative cooling technologies. Additionally, some companies are exploring immersion cooling to capture 100% of the heat generated by servers without relying on large amounts of water while others are looking at air-based cooling or even using recycled water, particularly in areas where water is a scarce resource (Langmajer, 2025).

In terms of circularity, blockchain has a wide range of unique uses due to its ease of traceability. In terms of circularity, block chain provides the ability to trace a product from its origin, providing a record of all materials throughout its lifespan so that the rates of reuse, remanufacturing, and recycling can be increased. A case of point is the Suez, a French-based water and waste management company has successfully developed and implemented their own version of block chain centered around the circular economy. Eponymously named "CircularChain," Suez's blockchain helps increase transparency throughout the waste management sector allowing for increased reliability and traceability. Additionally, the European Union is seeking to introduce a "Digital Product Passport" (DPP), which is a digital record that provides comprehensive information about a product and its entire value chain. This includes tracing the origin of the product, materials used, environmental impact, and disposal recommendations. It is a structured digital repository of product-related information including data on traceability, sustainability, and circularity. The passport must be linked to a data carrier with a unique product identifier, physically present on the product, its packaging, or accompanying documentation. For example, in the form of a QR code. The DPP is set for full implementation by 2030. The fashion industry is one of the first industries that has been targeted for a full rollout under this scheme for traceability and transparency (Retraced, 2025; Wan & Jiang, 2025).

For IoT, it is a network in which objects and sensors are interconnected, controlled, monitored, and optimized through wired cables, wireless networks or hybrid systems. This internetworking of physical devices through sensors and electronics can unlock the potential of the circular economy by supporting the monitoring of products and components throughout their lifecycles and facilitating decision-making processes in companies that implement circular economy business models. In this process, it can provide valuable support for business by increasing visibility and control over supply chains and enhancing efficiency and innovation. For example, from a real-world perspective, a manufacturer may seek to incorporate a smart sensor within their equipment, which can alert technicians when a potential issue is detected, allowing for early repair rather than total replacement. When this is paired with cloud computing, huge amounts of data can be stored with relevant ease and shared across long distances in a short period of time. However, despite such advantages, there are several challenges that constrain the widespread adoption of IoT. For example, its implementation is hampered by a lack of structured data, interoperability and technical capabilities (Rejeb et al., 2022). Another consideration is that despite its positive impact on the environment a widespread distribution of the IoT requires a significant increase in electronic devices which may lead to an increase in e-waste. A potential solution to reducing e-waste is to ensure that electronic devices should not have any form of planned obsolescence in their design by providing software updates for older devices and expanding the compatibility of new systems for reducing e-waste (Oraee et al., 2024). Furthermore, when considering disposing old electronics, businesses should partner with certified electronics recyclers who manage unwanted used electronics. Further, they should provide complimentary recycling services for legacy products. A case in point is the Dutch smartphone producer "Fairphone" which addresses the full lifespan of mobile phones which includes use, reuse and safe recycling. Its phones are designed for longevity focusing on durability and containing parts that can be easily replaced by the user if the phone breaks. The company sells spare parts and offers repair tutorials to help make their phones useful for as long as possible including adding dual subscriber identify modules (SIMs) to make them more attractive on the secondhand market. It also works with partners in Ghana to set up projects to improve local waste, collecting efforts and transport discarded phones to Europe for safe recycling. Additionally, Fairphone's Take Back Program ensures that the old mobile phones are reused or properly recycled. It has also partnered with iFixit to create open-source repair guides.

4 Circular Economy Applications in Industries

The circular economy concept has been successfully applied in various industries. For example, in the fashion industry companies like Patagonia and H&M have made significant strides in implementing circular economy practices. Patagonia's Worn Wear Program encourages customers to return used clothing items which are then repaired and resold extending the life cycle of their products. This practice not only reduces waste but also emphasizes the value of durable and repairable clothing (Chamberlin & Boks, 2018). Similarly, the Toronto-based Encircled, one of the few apparel brands in Canada certified for their social and environmental performance.

The company uses eco-friendly fabrics such as "Tencel" and "Modal" which requires less water and energy than traditional cotton products. It also prioritizes ethical manufacturing by producing all garments locally in Canada with a transparent supply chain.

Similarly, circular economy's relevance has been investigated for luxury items. It has been found that there is a link between the basic characteristics of luxury products and the circular economy with respect to high quality and durability that makes these products less disposable. Circular economy also seems to play a key role in the service industry. For example, a number of international hotel chains and resorts have embraced the concept of circular economy with respect to preserving natural resources, mitigating environmental impacts and recycling and water conservation. However, many of these hotels have not made any formal reference to the circular economy in their core business strategies. For example, Marriott International, the Radisson and Best Western hotel groups have emphasized their commitment to recycling but made no formal reference to the circular economy. Counterintuitively, some smaller hotels have employed the circular economy model. For example, Martin's Hotels, the Belgian hotel chain has employed a circular economy model in its purchasing, waste, and renovation projects. In pursuing its purchasing policy, for example, Martin's Hotels gives priority to local, natural, recycled, recyclable, and seasonal products, to minimize the flow of incoming waste and to maximize the recycling of the waste (Peter & Comfort, 2020). Additionally, circular economy has been successfully applied in the building sector, as construction business is one of the sectors that can significantly reduce costs using the circularity practices. In the building sector the practices of remanufacturing and product life-cycle extension are already in use. For example, product life cycle extension in the building sector has been applied to prolong the life of the asset (i.e., designing buildings for a longer lifespan by using durable materials and high construction standards). In this instance, businesses in the construction industry may increase their circularity by paying more attention to the design phase primed for the possibility of reuse and re-purposing parts of the buildings for the future (Rizos et al., 2017). Finally, circular economic practices have been developed in the food sector recently. It is estimated that 40% of food is laid to waste and food waste and food loss span the entire agrifood supply chain with serious environmental, economic, and social implications. To mitigate these effects, platforms such as "Agri Marketplace" a B2B cloud-based digital marketplace that specializes in utilizing e-commerce and food traceability with block chain is facilitating the matching of supply and demand over specific agrifood markets in a bid to make the process of buying and selling agrifood products easier. Similarly, MaGie Creations, a Netherlands-based company upcycles beer grains, which would otherwise be discarded—into fiber and protein-rich-flour.

5 Circular Economy Implementation Challenges

There are a couple of challenges in implementing circular economy in business. For example, it takes significant initial investments in technologies, infrastructure, and training staff to implement circular economy practices. Setting up a recycling facility or redesigning products for reuse or re-cyclability are cost-intensive. In this vein, Indorama Ventures, Thailand's largest private investor in plastics circularity and a leader in PET recycling that allows for the recycling of lower-quality, hard to recycle, post-consumer PET to virgin-grade resin has significantly invested in large-scale recycling facilities which are capital-intensive and takes years to yield financial returns (Indorama Ventures, 2025). It is suggested that such upfront costs create significant barriers to investment for small and medium-sized firms which lack the wherewithal compounded by investors' reluctance to fund circular economy projects due to their perceived risks and longer payback period. Additionally, many businesses that are deeply entrenched in traditional linear models may find it challenging to transition to circular economy practices (Rizos et al., 2021).

Supply chain challenges poses significant barriers to implement circular economy practices. As the circular economy requires businesses to source materials from suppliers adhering to sustainable business practices, it has been found that many of these suppliers use differing environmental and sustainability standards that create challenges for standardization of circular economy practices across companies. This can complicate supply chain management, logistics and transportation, transparency and traceability, and suppliers' capacity. For example, Unilever PLC, sources raw materials from multiple sources such as palm oil from South-East Asia, tea from India and Kenya, and soy from South America. Since each of these suppliers have differing environmental regulations and sustainability standards, it becomes challenging and requires coordination and investment for capacity building of the suppliers.

Another significant challenge in circular economy implementation is the ambiguity and definitions and requirements. For example, one of the challenges facing aluminum industry is the definition of green or low-carbon goods in trade classifications, as different regions and criteria for what constitutes "green and low-carbon aluminum" differs. This lack of standardization can create confusion and difficulty for producers to meet multiple sets of requirements. In this vein, a taxonomy for sustainable activities could be used to address ambiguity in definitions and requirements. This can help in scaling up sustainable investment by creating security for investors, protecting from greenwashing, and helping companies to become more climate friendly. In that instance, several Asia–Pacific region countries have already begun implementing the sustainable taxonomy in global markets which include Singapore, China, Hong Kong, Indonesia, Malaysia, Thailand, the Philippines, and the Republic of Korea.

Similarly, consumer behavior and market demand create challenges for circular economy implementation. Since the circular economy relies on market demand for sustainable products, consumers who are accustomed to linear consumption may resist such changes as circular economy products are perceived to be less convenient or more expensive, as price is prioritized over sustainability. For example, on the supply side the high costs associated with laboratory testing and certification of bioplastic products to meet biodegradability standards are expensive and a major burden to bear for small- and medium-sized companies seeking to compete with conventional plastics. From the Asian perspective for those countries which are rapidly industrializing, the circular economy affords considerable benefits due to their sustainable production, though its implementation is restricted by various barriers. The implementation of circular practices in developing nations exhibits diverse scenarios, geographical location, and the unique circumstances of each country. Though many Asian countries as discussed earlier has shown significant growth in the use of circular economy practices, however, the adoption of circular economy practices in the industrial sector remains in its initial stages in many Asian countries. In that context, Rasheed et al. (2024) investigated the implications of various barriers to circular economy adoption in the Pakistan's industrial sector. Conducing a survey of 310 industrial experts in Pakistan and employing PLS-SEM, the study revealed a number of construct barriers toward CE implementation in Pakistan in the industrial sector and ranked these barriers in the descending manner. These are (i) sociocultural factors and communication barriers; (ii) infrastructure and technological access barriers; (iii) stakeholder perception and resistance barriers; and (iv) economic viability and financial support barriers. The study confirm that barriers related to sociocultural factors and communication barriers and infrastructure and technological access have a positive significant influence on the adoption of CE. Finally, the authors advocate that technological progress could be crucial in facilitating the adoption of CE within industries.

5.1 Circular Economy Performance Indicators

Sustainability and programmatic indicators are necessary for evaluating, monitoring, and improving upon various policies and programs. In this vein, various tools and methodologies have been developed for circular economy adoption. One such indicator is the Material flow accounting or analysis (MFA) used for developing and managing indicators in many developed countries. MFA is a quantitative procedure for determining the flow of materials and energy through the economy on multiple scales, including national, inter-industrial/eco-industrial park, enterprise, and product levels. There are two widely used MFA-derived indicator systems, namely, the European Union (EU) and the Japanese material flow indicator systems. The former was published in "Economy-wide Material Flow Accounts and Derived Indicators—A Methodological guide," prepared by the Statistical Office of the European Commission (EUROSTAT). This system contains three categories—input indicators, consumption indicators, output and balance indicators. The main indicators listed in the input category include (i) direct material input (DMI); (ii) total material input (TMI); (iii) and total material requirement (TMR). In the consumption category, the core indicators are domestic material consumption (DMC) measuring the total amount of material directly used in the economic system and total material consumption (TMC) including the total material requirement of domestic consumption (EUROSTAT, 2001).

Similarly, Japan uses material flow indicators within its various levels. As Japan is largely dependent on imports of raw materials and having limited land space for waste disposal, thus, improving the overall eco-efficiency has been the primary goal of its economic system. Resource productivity (RP), material reuse and recycling rate, and the rate of waste for final disposal are the three core sustainability indicators in the Japanese material flow indicator system.

Here for better clarity, China's CE indicators for both macro and meso level (i.e., industrial park) have been shown with 22 indicators and 12 indicators, respectively. It is to be stated that China is the first country to release nationally focused circular economy indicators and circular economy has been chosen as a national policy for sustainable development. China's national circular economy indicators are based upon the 3R principles (reduction, reuse, and recycle). Different planning and implementation levels of circular economy present some variations in the types of indicators used. Specifically, the published Chinese circular economy evaluation indicator system provides two separate sets of indicators. One set of indicators is uses at macro-level for the general evaluation of the circular economy development for both individual region and national-level analysis. This macro indicator system provides guidance for future CE development planning. The other set of indicators is used for assessing the state of circular economy development at the industrial park (meso) level (Geng et al., 2012). China has enacted national laws and regulations to facilitate the implementation of circular economy principles and national circular economy demonstration projects have been implemented such that national benchmarking activities could be completed. Additionally, quantitative indicators have also been released to help evaluate such projects under circular economy principles.

Table 1 shows the macro circular economy evaluation indicators with 22 indicators categorized into four groups. Here, two indicators are used and listed for resource output, seven are listed for resource consumption, nine are listed for resource integrated utilization, and four are listed for waste disposal and pollutant emission.

Table 2 lists the CE indicators at the industrial park level. At this level, 12 indicators are categorized into four groups. Four indicators are listed for resource output and four are listed for the resource consumption category, two indicators are listed for both resources integrated utilization and two indicators exist for waste disposal and pollutant emission.

Table 1 Circular economy evaluation indicator system (at macro-level)

Group	Indicators
Resource output rate	Output of main mineral resource
	Output of energy
Resource consumption rate	Energy consumption per unit GDP
	Energy consumption per added industrial value
	Energy consumption of per unit product in key industrial sectors
	Water withdrawal per unit of GDP
	Water withdrawal per added industrial value
	Water consumption of per unit product in key industrial sectors
	Coefficient of irrigation water utilization
Integrated resource utilization rate	Recycling rate of industrial solid waste
	Industrial water reuse ratio
	Recycled rate of reclaimed municipal waste water
	Safe treatment rate of domestic solid waste
	Recycling rate of iron scrap
	Recycling rate of non-ferrous metal
	Recycling rate of waste paper
	Recycling rate of plastic
	Recycling rate of rubber
Water disposal and pollutant emissions	Total amount of industrial waste for final disposal
	Total amount of industrial waste water discharge
	Total amount of SO_2 emission
	Total amount of COD discharge

Source Geng et al. (2012)

6 Progress of Policies in Circular Economy Among the Asian Countries

The ensuing discussion will talk about six themes (i.e., infrastructure, regulation, education, finance, innovation and collaboration) that drives the success of circular economy initiatives in Asia. For example, with respect to infrastructure countries like China, Japan, and the Republic of Korea have implemented sustainable infrastructure policies and programs for scaling up circular economy. For example, Shenzhen (China) green building initiative have had a spillover effects in the neighboring cities which also integrates criteria like (energy savings, renewable energy, GHG reductions, waste management, recycled building materials, water conservation, and recycling), Japan's development of the Light-Rail-Transit (LRT) system in

Table 2 Circular economy evaluation indicator system at the industrial park level

Group	Indicators
Resource output rate	Output of main mineral resource
	Output of energy
	Output of land
	Output of water resource
Resource consumption rate	Energy consumption per unit industrial production value
	Water consumption per unit industrial production value
	Energy consumption of per unit key product
	Water consumption of per unit key product
Resource comprehensive utilization rate	Recycling rate of industrial solid waste
Waste disposal and pollutant emission	Industrial water reuse ratio
	Total amount of industrial solid waste for final disposal
	Total amount of industrial wastewater discharge

Source Geng et al. (2012)

Utsunomiya City, and Korea's "Waste Recycling Systems" for the recycling of e-waste for EV batteries and decommissioned solar PV panels which are rapidly rising globally and are technically more complex to recycle vis-à-vis municipal solid waste (UNEP, 2021). However, while making progress, most countries in South and South-East Asia face challenges in implementation of the circular economy due to limited infrastructure. In terms of regulation, China, Japan, the Republic of Korea, Australia, and Vietnam have comprehensive regulations that drive the circular economy practices vis-à-vis countries in South-East Asia are beginning to develop harmonized policies such as the "Framework for Circular Economy in ASEAN Community (2021)"; although its enforcement remains inconsistent and effective implementation is lacking. With respect to educating the general public about the concepts and practices of the circular economy, Japan the Republic of Korea have integrated the circular economy principles in their educational systems promoting sustainability from a young age while India has made specific efforts to introduce circular apparel aspects leading to design and fashion institutes. However, there is a lack of holistic policies in the Asia–Pacific region that address education in promoting circularity. In terms of finance, some countries have implemented taxes on virgin materials offering tax exemptions and providing fiscal incentives for promoting the circular economy. Additionally, there are also green, blue, climate, and sustainability-linked bonds and loans offered by governments and commercial and development banks in several countries in the Asia–Pacific region that support circular economy projects. With respect to innovation, Japan, China, the Republic of Korea, and Singapore are the leaders in driving circular economy innovations. For example, the Suzhou Industrial

Park in China which utilizes industrial symbiosis make companies to collaborate to repurpose each other's by-products and waste materials as inputs for production; thus, achieving significant reductions in waste and emissions while enhancing resource efficiency (UNEP, 2021). Lastly, Japan and Australia are the key players in promoting regional cooperation especially in areas like marine plastic pollution and sustainable resource management.

7 Policy Implications

As discussed in this chapter, the governments of different countries in the Asia–Pacific region have already taken initiatives at the policy level to implement circulate economy practices in their respective countries with different levels of commitment. Likewise, the major businesses in the region have also taken initiative within the control of their supply chains to implement circular activities as relevant to their products and services. However, bold and contextually appropriate actions are still needed to see real impact in the short, medium, and long-term.

The following delineates some specific steps that the government and business can do to promote circular economy practices. For example, there is a need to change the rules of the game and create a playing field to incentivize circular economy practices. The rules of the game should incentivize circular economy practices vis-à-vis linear practices. This will shape the nature and scale of economic activities across countries and industries. Second, Governments can adjust fiscal policies and leverage public budgets and services to create prices that ensure that circular products and services are more valuable and can compete and replace products and services that rely on linear practices. Governments could impose tax that will ensure that prices of goods and services reflect both financial and social and environmental costs. Additionally, incentives for excess material consumption need to be transitioned out. As enforcement of regulations is a challenge in many developing countries, governments need to improve regulations on circular economy practices or other mandatory measure that support circularity (i.e., minimum recycled content, EPR, taxes, and fines). The monitoring and penalties must be strict to ensure compliance. Governments could support circular activities that are higher in the waste hierarchy. For example, recycling and recovery are on the lower end of the waste hierarchy; however, these activities are practiced globally. In this instance, governments could support circular activities that offer higher value for material use and waste prevention such as repairing. These have experienced very low implementation compared to other circular activities.

From the business perspective there is a need to undertake a systematic diagnosis of an organization's value chain in order to understand how to embed a circularity mindset into the organization coupled with finding tangible ways to identify how circularity could address business challenges and add value. This can then be transformed into a strategy that lays out what circular activities should be done; who will lead the implementation of each activity; what resources will be allocated to support, and the value added at the end. Buy-in from top management will ensure that circularity will be an organization-wide priority. Second, companies can establish steering committee forums that comprise key stakeholders to share and learn where they can explore circularity opportunities from alternate design from procurement of sustainable products through operational usage to expanding life expectancy. Lastly, business should learn from the successes of other companies who are leading circularity practices and replicate those successes in their own companies.

8 Summary and Conclusion

This book chapter has evaluated circular economy from a number of different perspectives. First, it has attempted to trace the definition and origin of circular economy including how the circular economy differs from the traditional linear model (take-make-consume-dispose), its benefits related to environmental, economic, and social dimensions and its relation with the SDGs. After setting the background it has attempted to explore the landscape of circular economy policies in the Asia–Pacific region. Additionally, it explores industry 4.0 technologies to bring together successful circular economy models. Further, it explores circular economy applications in industries including some of the leading companies (i.e., Indorama Ventures, MaGie Creations, Agri Marketplace) that are the frontrunners in the circular economy initiative. Finally, it discusses some implementation challenges, progress in policies in the Asia–Pacific region in respect with the six drivers of circular economy (i.e., infrastructure, regulation, education, finance, innovation, and collaboration) and the role of businesses and the governments to implement successful circular economy programs in respect to their needs.

It is assumed that in the next frontier of circular economy, the use of today's linear practices would be a minimum or being used only when all other options are exhausted. As awareness of the circular economy is growing among the general public including the media, government, and private agencies, it becomes a clarion call to have all efforts put together for the implementation of the circular economy tuned to the needs of the Asia–Pacific region. Along this transition there will be certain linear practices that will prevail in the short-term to achieve the long-term gains from the circular economy benefitting the society and the planet. In this vein, resources and willpower need to be drafted from the public and private entities to bring the region into the next frontier of circular economy. The next frontier of the circular economy initiatives will be defined by a level playing field for circular economy products and services primed to be attractive and competitive for the marketplace. In that vein, much of this success will depend on the implementation of the current circular economy initiatives undertaken by the various Asia–Pacific region countries effected through laws, regulations, and supported by economic and fiscal incentives. This will ensure that there will be more policies at the implementation and operational strategy levels and less for "calls to action" or roadmaps in the future.

References

Asian Insiders. (2025). Developing the circular economy in Asia https://asianinsiders.com/2024/02/06/developing-the-circular-economy-in-asia/. Accessed 10 May 2025.

Boulding, K.E. (1966). The economies of the coming spaceship earth. New York, pp. 1–17.

CCICED (2008). Policy recommendations and China's environment and development policies (2007–2008), http://www.cciced.net/ccicedPhoneEN/Events/AGMeeting/2008_3976/meetingplace_3977/201609/t20160922_89704.html

Chamberlin, L., & Boks, C. (2018). Marketing approaches for a circular economy: Using design frameworks to interpret online communications. *Sustainability, 10*(2070), 1–27.

Circular Innovation Council. (2025). Circular economy: Beyond recycling. https://circularinnovation.ca/circular-economy/. Accessed 6 August 2025.

Ellen Macarthur Foundation. (2015). Towards a circular economy: Business rationale for an accelerated transition. https://www.ellenmacarthurfoundation.org/towards-a-circular-economy-business-rationale-for-an-accelerated-transition. Accessed 16 May, 2025.

ESCAP. (2024). Trade, investment and innovation: The secrets to unlocking the next frontier for a circular economy in the Asia-Pacific region. https://sustainability.indoramaventures.com/storage/content/document/environmental/escap-2024.pdf. Accessed 28 May 2025.

EU. (2015). Closing the loop—An EU action plan for the circular economy. Communication from the commission to the European Parliament, the Council, the European Economic and Social committee and the Committee of the regions, European Commission.

European Commission. (2017). On the implementation of the circular economy action plan, 33 final.

EUROSTAT. (2001). Economy-wide material flow account and derived indicators: A methodological guide. Office for official publications of the European communities, Luxembourg.

Gebrardt, M., Spieske, A., & Birkel, H. (2022). The future of the circular economy and its effect on supply chain dependencies: Empirical evidence from Delphi study. *Transportation Research Part E, 157*, Article 102570.

Geissdoerfer, M., Savaget, P., Bocken, N., & Hultink, E. J. (2017). The circular economy—A new sustainability paradigm? *Journal of Cleaner Production, 143*(6), 757–768.

Geng, Y. & Doberstein, B. (2008). Developing the circular economy in China: Challenges and opportunities for achieving 'leapfrog development.' *International Journal of Sustainable Development & World Ecology*, 15(3):231–239, https://doi.org/10.3843/SusDev.15.3:6

Geng, Y., Fu, J., Sarkis, J., & Xue, B. (2012). Towards a national circular economy indicator system in China: An evaluation and critical analysis. *Journal of Cleaner Production, 23*(1), 216–224. https://doi.org/10.1016/j.jclepro.2011.07.005

Indorama Ventures. (2025). Recycling. https://sustainability.indoramaventures.com/en/environmental/recycling/at-a-glance. Accessed 12 May 2025.

Keslio, (2024). A Guide to the Extended Producer Responsibility (EPR) Law in the Philippines. https://www.keslio.com/kesliox/a-guide-to-the-extended-producer-responsibility-epr-lawin-the-philippines

Kirchherr, J., Reike, D., & Hekkert, M. (2017). Conceptualizing the circular economy: An analysis of 114 definitions Resources. *Conservation and Recycling, 127*, 221–232.

Langmajer, M. (2025). ChatGpt is thirsty: How much water does Al really use. https://felloai.com/2025/02/the-real-environmental-impact-of-ai-how-much-water-does-chatgpt-use/. Accessed 11 May 2025.

Mathews, J. A. & Tan, H. (2011). Progress toward a circular economy in China: the drivers (and inhibitors) of eco industrial initiative. *Journal of Industrial Ecology, 15, 435–457, 15*(3). https://doi.org/10.1111/j.1530-9290.2011.00332.x

McDonough, W. Cradle to cradle: Remaking the way we make things. https://mcdonough.com/writings/cradle-cradle-remaking-way-make-things/. Accessed 5 April 2025.

METI (2015). Law for the promotion of effective utilization of resources, https://www.env.go.jp/content/900451446.pdf

Ministry of Environment and Forestry (2020). MOEF Regulation P.75/2019, https://ccet.jp/sites/default/files/2020 10/Indonesia_plastics_web_200626.pdf

Okorie, O., Salonitis, K., Charnley, F., Morenco, M., Turner, C., & Tiwari. A. (2018). Digitisation and the circular economy: A review of current research and future trends. *Energies, 11*, 3009.

Oraee, A., Pohl, L., Geurts, D., & Reichel, M. (2024). Overcoming premature smartphone obsolescence amongst young adults. *Cleaner and Responsible Consumption, 12*, Article 100174.

Peter, J., & Comfort, D. (2020). A circular case: The circular economy and the service industry. *International Journal of Management Cases, 22*(3), 13–123.

Prieto-Sandoval, V., Jaca, C., & Ormazabal, M. (2018). Towards a consensus on the circular economy. *Journal of Cleaner Production, 179*, 605–615.

Rasheed K., Saad S., Zaland, A., Khan, M.W., Ali, Z., Haris, M., Ahammad, S., & Sadiq, T. (2024). Circular economy and critical barriers: Mapping the pathways and success metrics for sustainable circular success in industrialised South Asian developing nations. *Results in Engineering, 24*, 102995.

Rejeb, A., Suhaiza, Z., Rajeeb, K., Seuring, S., & Treiblmaier, H. (2022). The internet of things and the circular economy: A systematic literature review and research agenda. *Journal of Cleaner Production, 350*, Article 131439.

Retraced. (2025). How can you prepare for fashion brand for the digital product passport (DPP)? https://www.retraced.com/blogs/knowledge-hub/digital-product-passport. Accessed 11 May 2025.

Rizos, E., Fujiwara, N., & Stroica, C. (2021). Barriers and enablers for implementing circular economy business models: Evaluation from the electrical and electronic equipment and agri-food value chains. https://cdn.ceps.eu/wp-content/uploads/2021/10/RR2021-01_Barriers-and-enablers-for-implementing-circular-economy-business-models.pdf. Accessed 5 May 2025.

Rizos, V., Tuokko, K., & Behrens, A. (2017). The circular economy: A review of definitions, processes and impacts. https://cdn.ceps.eu/wp-content/uploads/2017/04/RR2017-08_CircularEconomy_0.pdf. Accessed 20 April 2025.

Rood, T., Muilwijk, H., & Westhoek, H. (2017). *Food for the circular economy*. PBL Netherlands Environmental Assessment Agency: Hague, The Netherlands. https://www.pbl.nl/sites/default/files/downloads/PBL-2017-Food-for-the-circular-economy-2878.pdf. Accessed 20 April 2025.

Schroeder, P., Anggraeni, K., & Weber, U. (2019). The relevance of circular economy practices to the sustainable development goals. *Journal of Industrial Ecology, 23*, 77–95.

SITRA. (2016). Finnish roadmap to a circular economy 2016–2025. https://www.sitra.fi/en/projects/leading-the-cycle-finnish-road-map-to-a-circular-economy-2016-2025/. Accessed 5 August 2025.

Sreenivasan, A., & Suresh, M. (2024). Design thinking and artificial intelligence: A systematic literature review exploring synergies. *International Journal of Innovation Studies, 8*, 297–312.

Su, B., Heshmati, Y., Geng, Y., & Yu, X. (2013). A review of the circular economy in China: Moving from rhetoric to implementation. *Journal of Cleaner Production, 42*, 215–227.

UNEP. (2021). Scaling up circular economy through sustainable infrastructure: Case studies from China, Japan and Korea. https://www.greenpolicyplatform.org/sites/default/files/downloads/best-practices/Scaling%20up%20Circular%20Economy%20Through%20Sustainable%20Infrastructure-20220505.pdf. Accessed 12 May 2025.

Wan, P. K. F., & Jiang, S. (2025). Enabling a dynamic information flow in digital product passports during product use phase: A literature review and proposed framework. *Sustainable Production and Consumption, 54*, 362–374.

Tareq Mahbub is an Associate Professor at the Business Department at Sakarya University, Serdivan, Turkey. He completed his Ph.D. in management from the Asian Institute of Technology (AIT), Bangkok, and M.B.A. in International Business from Carleton University, Ottawa. His areas of interest are foreign direct investment (FDI), FDI and intellectual property rights, international market entry modes, and FDI and renewable energy. He has over 10-years of experience in the pharmaceutical sector working as Business Development Manager for a top-notch US FDA and UK MHRA certified international pharmaceutical company in the areas of new market development, contract manufacturing, under-licensing and strategic alliances both in the regulated and moderately regulated markets.

Foodmandu: From Clicks to Cuisine in Nepal's Food Industry

Jashim Uddin Ahmed, Anisur R. Faroque, Samsul Islam, and Shashi Shekhar Acharya

Abstract Foodmandu is Nepal's first food delivery service platform, aimed at addressing the time constraints and logistical challenges faced by busy professionals and individuals. With an intuitive digital interface for ordering from a wide range of restaurants in the Kathmandu Valley, Foodmandu has steadily expanded its network. The company's innovative business model combines both "business-to-consumer" (B2C) and "business-to-business" (B2B) strategies, integrating restaurant partnerships, logistics, and delivery operations. Beyond providing convenience, the company has contributed to Nepal's digital transformation, local employment generation, and the evolution of the e-commerce ecosystem. This case study traces Foodmandu's growth trajectory from its inception to becoming a market leader, examining its strategic innovations, operational challenges, and future prospects. Emphasis is placed on the importance of technological adaptation, customer-centric service design, and resilience in navigating market volatility. As Foodmandu expands into new verticals such as grocery delivery, its story offers critical insights into the dynamics of digital entrepreneurship in emerging markets.

J. U. Ahmed (✉)
Department of Management, School of Business and Economics, North South University, Dhaka, Bangladesh
e-mail: jashim.ahmed@northsouth.edu

A. R. Faroque
School of Marketing and Communication, University of Vaasa, Vaasa, Finland
e-mail: anisur.faroque@uwasa.fi

S. Islam
JR Shaw School of Business, Northern Alberta Institute of Technology (NAIT), Edmonton, AB, Canada
e-mail: mislam@nait.ca

S. S. Acharya
Nepal Administrative Staff College, Jawalakhel, Lalitpur, Nepal
e-mail: shashi.acharya@nasc.org.np

T. Endress and Y. F. Badir (eds.), *Business and Management in Asia: Opportunities and Entrepreneurship*, https://doi.org/10.1007/978-981-95-4909-2_8

1 Introduction

The government's adoption of mainframe computers in the 1950s for census data collection marked the beginning of Nepal's information and communication technology (ICT) journey. With the establishment of the Ministry of Science and Technology in 1996, the country's science and technology budget saw a significant increase. The policy, prepared by the Royal Nepal Academy of Science and Technology (RONAST), was formally endorsed by the Government of Nepal in 1989 through the Nepal Gazette for implementation. After the economic liberalization in the 1990s, computers became essential for education, business, and progress. The Internet was first introduced into Nepal in 1993 in a venture of the RONAST and a private company, Mercantile Office Systems (MOS) (Karki, 2019). From the 1950s to the mid-1990s, most graduates and high-level manpower were trained and educated in various countries, including communist as well as capitalist blocs of the world, under scholarship schemes. This diverse international exposure enriched Nepal with technological insights from multiple systems and ideologies (Singh & Bhuju, 2001). In 2019, Nepal's Ministry of Communication and Information Technology introduced a "Digital Framework" comprising 80 digital initiatives aimed at achieving digital-driven social and economic prosperity. The framework highlighted the potential of the e-commerce sector to act as a catalyst for the growth of small and medium-sized enterprises and the creation of greater employment opportunities.

Despite the presence of approximately 500 startup companies, the framework acknowledged that Nepal was still lagging behind due to challenges related to financing, a limited customer base, and the overall tech readiness of consumers. Startups play a crucial role in generating tech-based job opportunities, which in turn supports the growth of Nepal's broader technology sector. However, low levels of digital literacy, concerns about data security, and an underdeveloped ICT infrastructure remain significant barriers to realizing the vision of a digital Nepal (Ministry of Communication and Information Technology, 2019).

As of 2025, the number of fiber broadband internet users in Nepal has surpassed 3.05 million. Similarly, fixed wired broadband connections now cover 45.74% of the population (Nepal Telecommunications Authority, 2025). The mobile revolution of 2000s ushered in affordable internet and mobile banking, further accelerating digital transformation. Thamel.com (www.thamel.com) became Nepal's first e-commerce company. Between 2000 and 2010, the country witnessed significant growth with the establishment of several key companies that helped shape the digital marketplace. Popular startups from that era included NepBay.com-later rebranded as Thulo Market in 2007. In 2009, eSewa was established as one of the pioneering online payment platforms, which changed the shape of digital payment in Nepal. In the same period, companies like Sastodeal, founded in 2011, emerged alongside other e-commerce platforms. The advent of new technology has made it easier for people to order food online through various platforms and apps (Ahmed et al., 2021). This timeframe marked a critical shift in the country's digital landscape, with internet penetration growing from 0.2% to 7.9% over the decade, setting the stage for the rapid expansion of e-commerce and online services in Nepal.

2 Online Food Delivery Market Overview and Growth

The online food delivery industry in Nepal has witnessed substantial growth in recent years, catalyzed by increasing internet accessibility, the proliferation of smartphones, and the evolving lifestyle of urban consumers who increasingly seek convenience in their daily routines. In 2025, the sector is projected to generate approximately USD 343.2 million in revenue, with a compound annual growth rate (CAGR) of around 14.7% expected through 2030. By then, the market is forecasted to nearly double, reaching an estimated USD 682 million (Research and Markets, 2023; Statista, 2025).

The Kathmandu Valley—including Kathmandu, Lalitpur, and Bhaktapur—remains the epicenter of this transformation. Over 120,000 online food delivery orders are processed monthly in this region alone, with Foodmandu, the market leader, handling more than 100,000 orders per month. This represents a 35% year-on-year growth in order volume (Tamang, 2024). Other key players, including Bhojdeals, Bhokmandu, and Foodmario, are also rapidly scaling operations to meet growing demand (Bhattarai & Paudel, 2024). Increased app-based service adoption and digital payment usage have further streamlined the customer experience, reinforcing a shift toward tech-enabled food services. This expansion is strongly aligned with consumer behavior trends, which are influenced by ease of use, time savings, and growing trust in digital platforms. Studies have shown that perceived usefulness, app reliability, and promotional offers are significant factors affecting consumer intentions and actual usage behavior in Nepal (Cuong, 2024). Furthermore, service quality-including timely delivery, food packaging, and customer support has a direct and positive impact on customer satisfaction, which in-turn fosters loyalty and repeat use (Karki, 2023).

While the current market is largely urban-centric, particularly concentrated in Kathmandu Valley, there is strong potential for growth in tier two cities[1] such as Pokhara, Biratnagar, and Bharatpur. As logistical infrastructure improves and awareness of online platforms increases, these regions are expected to contribute more significantly to the national food delivery landscape (Sharma & Adhikari, 2024).

[1] In Nepal, "Tier two cities" is not an official term but is commonly used in urban planning, real estate, and socio-economic contexts to describe sub-metropolitan cities—regional hubs with growing populations, infrastructure, and economic activity that rank just below the major metropolitan cities.

3 Case: Foodmandu

3.1 Background

Manohar Adhikari (hereafter Adhikari), who was working as a software developer in Kathmandu, faced frequent time constraints during his lunch break. In 2010, there were only a limited number of restaurants offering quality food, and due to insufficient time to dine out, Adhikari often had to settle for a few nearby eateries—and sometimes, he had to go without lunch altogether. This personal frustration made him realize that many other professionals in urban areas were facing similar issues. This shared experience sparked the idea of creating a food delivery service tailored for busy people like him.

3.2 Inception

In 2010, after extensive market research Adhikari founded Foodmandu with the sole purpose of creating a platform that would allow customers to easily order food from their favorite restaurants while staying at home within the Kathmandu Valley. Foodmandu provides a larger choice of restaurants to its customer base. The early days were challenging, as Adhikari had to contend with skepticism from restaurant owners and slow partnership development. His perseverance and ability to build relationships with restaurant owners carried him through. Adhikari also invested significant time in understanding customer behavior, which proved essential in navigating the difficulties of the startup phase. His focus on patience, strategic planning, and market insight laid the groundwork for Foodmandu's growth and success. The creation of Foodmandu demonstrates how personal frustration, combined with determination and a deep understanding of market needs, can drive innovation. Adhikari's experience highlights the role of personal insight in launching a business that addresses widespread challenges and improves daily life.

4 Feeding Nepal's Urban Appetite

Foodmandu is the first company in Nepal to offer a multi-restaurant food ordering and delivery service. The updated distribution of Foodmandu's registered restaurant partners across various districts in Nepal is as follows: as of the latest count, a total of 2,295 restaurants are affiliated with the platform. The majority are located in Kathmandu (1,458), followed by Lalitpur (462), Pokhara (153), Bhaktapur (92), Chitwan (70), and Butwal (60). This regional categorization reflects the platform's strong presence in key urban centers throughout the country.

Foodmandu was established with the goal of becoming Nepal's leading food delivery service by offering high-quality meals at affordable prices, providing a wide selection of restaurants, creating employment opportunities for self-employed individuals, and ensuring fast and reliable delivery to customers. Customers can conveniently place orders through its website, mobile app, or, in the early days, via phone calls. The platform provides a user-friendly interface for browsing restaurants, viewing menus, and placing orders.

Foodmandu has created value by delivering a wide variety of meals efficiently within the Kathmandu Valley and expanding its services to other areas such as Bhaktapur, Lalitpur, and surrounding regions, ensuring convenience and choice for its customers (Sharesansar, 2024). It has become a go-to platform for those seeking quality meals at home or at work, especially during busy schedules, without the need to dine out. As one of Nepal's pioneering online food delivery services, Foodmandu has adapted to the competitive market by offering value-added services such as seasonal promotions and a diverse array of restaurant options that cater to various tastes and dietary needs. While its loyalty program is yet to be launched, it is scheduled to start around April/May 2026. In addition to its expansive network of partner restaurants, Foodmandu collaborates with local food vendors and small businesses, thereby supporting the local economy.

To enhance customer experience, Foodmandu has integrated features such as a rating and review system, allowing users to share feedback on their dining and delivery experiences. The company has continuously upgraded its technology infrastructure to ensure seamless service, including real-time delivery tracking, secure payment options, and responsive customer support. Foodmandu has cultivated a loyal customer base, including busy professionals, event organizers, families, and others who value timely access to quality meals. Most recently, the company has expanded its market reach to include restaurant partners from Pokhara, Bharatpur, and Butwal, further strengthening its national presence and service coverage.

5 Target Market

Identifying and effectively reaching the right target market is crucial to the success of any business organization (Ahmed, 2017). Foodmandu targets all kinds of customer segments, primarily focusing on individuals and groups who face time constraints, such as busy professionals, families, and those who cannot cook or visit restaurants due to their hectic schedules. It also targets those individuals who crave food from high-end restaurants yet cannot dine out. This shows that Foodmandu tries to address the distinct needs of a diverse group of customers. It also provides services to big groups, parties, seminars, meetings or even office lunches, which shows the flexibility of the company and its ability to respond to different demands. Foodmandu also delivers convenience along with tasty food, saving customers' time that would otherwise be spent on meal preparation or traveling to a restaurant. Foodmandu frees the schedule for busy people because they neither need to prepare meals nor go out for dinner. Saving time has become one of the most important values in contemporary consumer behavior—something Foodmandu effectively addresses.

Foodmandu also shows its flexibility by serving both individual meal orders and larger group events. This flexibility expands the company's scope, from meeting the needs of an individual seeking a quick meal to those of organizations requiring catering services. It is positioned as a service that addresses time scarcity, reliably and efficiently helping customers manage their daily dining needs without compromising on quality. Addressing the need for convenience, time-saving, and flexibility, Foodmandu solves many problems for its target audience and puts forward a relevant solution in today's scenario.

6 Business Model of Foodmandu

Foodmandu operates on a hybrid business model that integrates both restaurant-to-consumer and platform-to-consumer delivery systems, thereby offering a comprehensive and efficient service experience to its users. These models are commonly seen in the online food delivery ecosystem, where digital platforms act as intermediaries between customers and foodservice providers (Research & Markets, 2023).

6.1 Platform-to-Consumer Model (Aggregator Model)

At the core of Foodmandu's operations lies the platform-to-consumer model, in which Foodmandu serves as an intermediary between customers and a wide variety of restaurants. Customers place their orders through the Foodmandu mobile app or website, which acts as a centralized digital platform showcasing numerous restaurants, cuisines, and menu options. Foodmandu manages the entire delivery logistics—receiving the orders, confirming the details, selecting delivery personnel, and ensuring the food reaches the customers in a timely manner. This model benefits customers through ease of use, variety, and convenience, while restaurants gain access to a larger customer base without having to invest in their own delivery infrastructure.

6.2 Business-to-Customer (B2C) Operations

Foodmandu's B2C component enables customers to browse restaurant listings, customize orders, and make payments digitally. The workflow begins when a customer places an order via the app or website. The platform's system automatically processes the order, verifies details, and assigns a delivery personnel through an algorithm. Restaurants receive the order details, prepare the food, and coordinate with delivery staff for pickup. Real-time updates and order tracking enhance customer experience. If payment is not made online, the delivery personnel may handle cash transactions upon delivery. This digital-to-physical interface represents a seamless journey from digital order to doorstep delivery.

6.3 Business-to-Business (B2B) Restaurant Onboarding

On the supply side, Foodmandu follows a B2B approach (as shown in Fig. 1) to collaborate with restaurants. Interested foodservice providers can apply for registration through the platform by submitting key business details. Foodmandu's internal evaluation team reviews each application, considering the quality of food, type of cuisine, and ability to fulfill orders reliably. Only those restaurants meeting the company's standards are listed on the platform. This careful curation ensures high-quality service for customers and strengthens the brand's reputation.

Foodmandu has not formally identified or promoted a dedicated restaurant-to-consumer delivery model. However, some restaurants and cloud kitchens on the platform operate their own delivery services alongside using Foodmandu, offering them greater operational flexibility while still benefiting from the platform's reach and technological support.

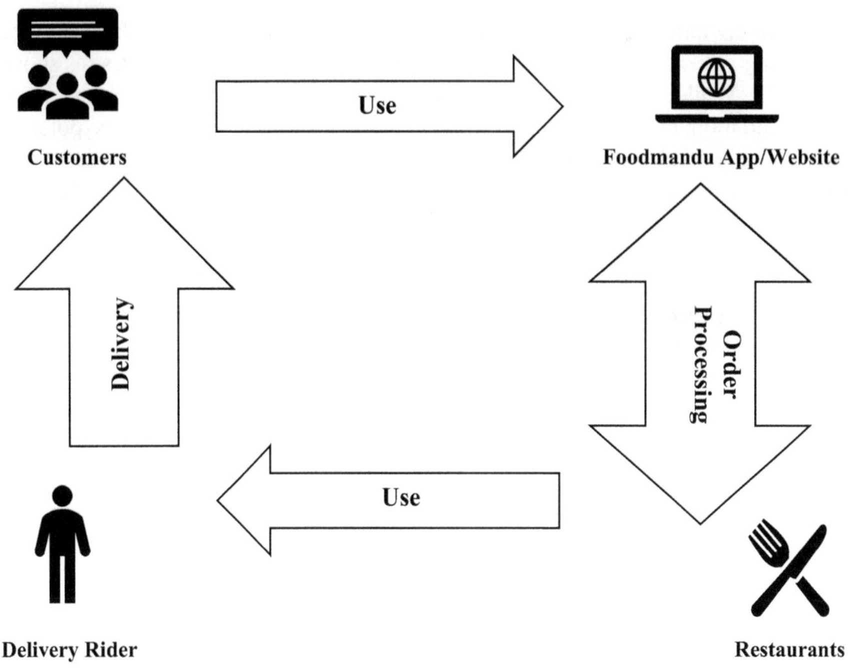

Fig. 1 Workflow of ordering food through the Foodmandu app/website

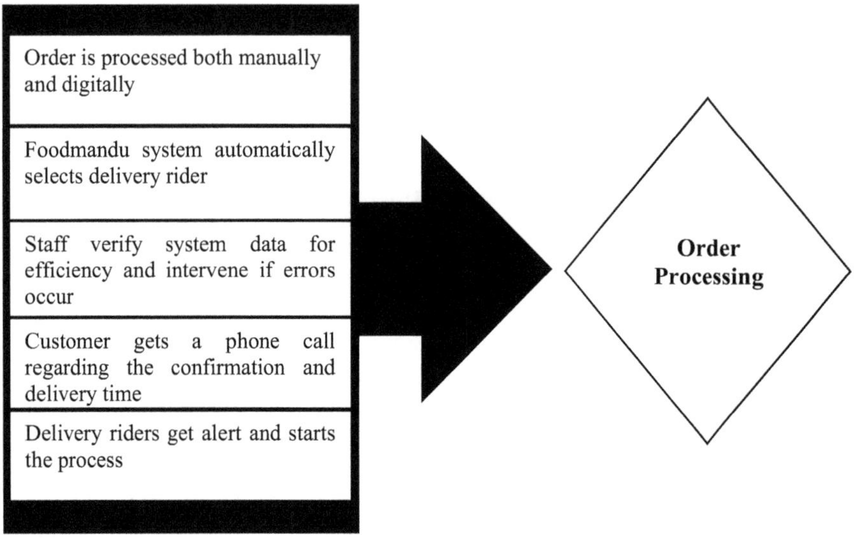

Fig. 2 Illustrations by the authors', 2025

6.4 Hybrid Order Processing System

To ensure operational efficiency and accuracy, Foodmandu employs a hybrid order-processing system that integrates both automated and manual procedures (as shown in Fig. 2). While the platform automates delivery personnel selection[2] and initial order validation, human staff oversee the system data to detect and resolve potential errors. The team also makes confirmation calls to customers regarding order details and delivery timeframes. This hybrid system combines the efficiency of technology with the personalized assurance of human oversight, resulting in enhanced customer satisfaction and trust.

By adopting a multi-faceted emerging business model (Bhul, 2025), Foodmandu strategically positions itself as both a service facilitator and a market connector. The combination of platform-to-consumer and restaurant-to-consumer frameworks—enhanced by hybrid processing, a robust B2C interface, and B2B partnerships with vetted restaurants—enables Foodmandu to deliver a scalable, customer-centric, and operationally efficient food delivery experience in Nepal's rapidly evolving digital marketplace.

[2] All of Foodmandu's delivery riders are employed under an official employment contract. This approach provides stable employment along with the associated benefits of being a contracted employee.

7 Revenue Generation

Foodmandu operates a multi-dimensional revenue generation model, similar to other e-commerce platforms, with various income streams that contribute to covering operational costs and driving profitability. One of the primary sources of revenue is the listing fee charged to restaurants for inclusion on the Foodmandu platform. This approach not only offers customers a broad selection of dining options but also enables restaurants to increase their visibility and attract more orders. This mutually beneficial arrangement ties the success of Foodmandu and its partner restaurants closely together. Additionally, Foodmandu earns revenue through a platform service fee on orders placed through the platform. Partner restaurants are charged a percentage of each transaction, which supports financial sustainability for both parties while incentivizing high-quality service and customer satisfaction to encourage repeat business. Another significant revenue stream comes from advertising. Restaurants can pay to display ads on the Foodmandu app and website, boosting their visibility while providing an additional income source for Foodmandu—mirroring common practices among major e-commerce platforms.

Foodmandu also charges a delivery fee, calculated based on the total value of the order and the road distance between the restaurant and the delivery address. This transparent pricing model helps cover delivery-related expenses, including rider salaries, and promotes operational efficiency. It also encourages restaurants to consider delivery feasibility based on location.

8 Modes of Service and Delivery

Foodmandu charges a Rs. 100 fee per order for fresh orders. Delivery charges for restaurants and stores are determined based on the total bill amount and the approximate road distance between the selected restaurant and the delivery location. For deliveries within 1 km, the charge is Rs. 20. For distances exceeding 1 km, there is an additional charge of Rs. 20 per km (Foodmandu, 2020a, 2020b). Customers can pay using various digital payment methods or in cash to the delivery agent upon food delivery to their location. Once the food is ordered using the system, customers cannot directly pick up food from the restaurant, as this service has been disabled. Allowing customers to personally pick up their orders, rather than utilizing the delivery service, could result in a loss of revenue from delivery charges, negatively impact customer satisfaction due to reduced convenience, disrupt operational efficiency in terms of logistics and order processing, and potentially harm the company's brand image by diminishing its identity as a delivery-focused service.

The delivery of an order generally takes between 45 min and 1 h, with the time frame influenced by various factors, including the distance between the customer's location and the restaurant, prevailing traffic conditions, the availability of delivery rider, the restaurant's order volume at the time, as well as the type and size of the order. While every effort is made to ensure timely delivery, to mitigate any potential delays, it is advisable for customers to place their orders in advance, even several hours ahead of the intended delivery time. This approach can help ensure the food arrives within the desired time frame.

9 Foodmandu's Strategic Rollout of OneMart

A strategic rollout is a carefully planned and phased implementation of a service or initiative, designed to maximize impact, ensure efficiency, and facilitate smooth adoption. The aim is to achieve effectiveness while minimizing disruption for all stakeholders. Recently, Foodmandu's expansion of its grocery delivery service, OneMart, into Kathmandu and Lalitpur exemplifies this approach—demonstrating a calculated effort to scale rapid delivery solutions while addressing the everyday challenges faced by urban consumers (Foodmandu, n.d.). OneMart offers the delivery of essential groceries, snacks, beverages, and household supplies within 20 to 30 min, providing a convenient alternative to traditional in-store shopping. By eliminating the need to visit physical stores, the service reduces consumer exposure to crowded streets, long queues, and parking issues. Initially launched within a 3-km radius of Foodmandu's Gairidhara hub, the service has now extended its reach to key locations in Lalitpur, such as Jawalakhel, Lagankhel, Sadobato, Imadol, Sanepa, Dhobighat, Bhaisepati, Nakkhu, and Balkumari. Plans are underway to further expand coverage throughout the Kathmandu Valley (Business360, 2025).

Foodmandu leverages its operational experience to enhance urban lifestyles by promoting speed, convenience, and reliability in daily shopping practices. Customers can access the service through the Foodmandu mobile application by selecting the OneMart feature, which enables them to purchase a wide range of items, including fresh produce and cleaning products, from the comfort of their homes (Foodmandu, n.d.).

10 Foodmandu's Multifaceted Impact

Foodmandu has created many positive impacts beyond just food delivery service provisions. Since its inception, it has paved the way for the emergence of various other platforms, including online payment services such as Khalti, iPay, and Esewa; on-demand delivery service Aayoexpress; laundry service Chamkilo; and ride-sharing platforms Tootle and Pathao (Hamal & Huijsmans, 2022). Besides promoting local enterprise, Foodmandu has played a vital role in the growth of e-commerce in Nepal by breaking barriers for traditionally small markets. By providing a convenient online platform, Foodmandu has opened new doors for restaurants and consumers to engage with different varieties of food.

Foodmandu has launched its midnight food delivery service, extending ordering hours until midnight to meet the growing demand of its customers. Initially, the service is available within Kathmandu's ring road area, with plans to expand to other locations in the near future (Sharesansar, 2025). With its growth, the company has created many jobs by hiring delivery personnel and providing work opportunities that help decrease unemployment in the community. This also relates to the company's ability to lower food costs because the e-commerce model of dining makes eating more affordable, especially for those who might find dining out too expensive. Improvement in customer experience has a significant bearing on the current growth; easy online ordering boosts loyalty to the company and enhances its brand. The affordability and improved accessibility of Foodmandu have played a key role in its expansion throughout the valley and into several major towns in Nepal. This growth not only boosts the company's profitability but also supports broader economic development through higher demand and consumption. The efficiency in the cost model allows a cut in costs related to the operations of food delivery, thereby streamlining and facilitating the use of the service to more and more people. People either stay in their homes or at workplaces for lunch instead of hitting the road for restaurants; this reduces congestion and pollution, making the environment more sustainable. The reduced traffic congestion means fewer vehicles on the roads, which overall helps reduce the carbon footprint. It innovatively models better convenience for customers, contributes to economic growth and job creation, ensures environmental sustainability, and increases access to more affordable food, making Foodmandu a game-changing company in the food delivery industry in Nepal.

11 The 4C Strategic Framework for Tech Startups in Asia

The 4C Strategic Matrix—Customer centricity, Collaboration, Convenience, and Continuity—offers a comprehensive approach for tech startups to thrive in dynamic markets.

Foodmandu's journey can be synthesized into a practical "4C Strategic matrix" (as shown in Table 1) applicable across Asia's developing economies. The first "C," Customer centricity, refers to Foodmandu's personalized services such as loyalty programs and real-time tracking, which built trust and engagement (Ahmed et al., 2021). The second, Collaboration, emphasizes partnerships with local vendors and restaurants to expand service reach and community impact. The third "C," Convenience, underscores the firm's digital interface, app features, and instant delivery model that cater to the fast-paced lifestyle of urban consumers. Lastly, Continuity captures Foodmandu's crisis resilience—from surviving cyberattacks and natural disasters to scaling new verticals during competitive pressure (Foodmandu, 2020a, 2020b; MyRepublica, 2020). This 4C Strategic matrix can serve as an adaptable tool for managers seeking to balance growth with operational challenges in similar settings. Together, these four pillars create a solid foundation for sustainable growth and lasting customer loyalty.

Table 1 4C Customer-centric Strategic Matrix

Customer centricity	Collaboration
• Loyalty initiatives • Real-time order tracking • Personalized experience • Trust and reliability	• Partnership with restaurants • Community engagement • Ecosystem partnerships • Shared value creation
Convenience	Continuity
• Fast-delivery network • Intuitive mobile app • User-friendly app/interface • Tailored to urban pace	• Cybersecurity resilience • Disaster recovery plans • Scalable business model • Strategic flexibility

Source Illustrations by the authors, 2025

12 Setbacks and Challenges

Foodmandu, Nepal's pioneering online food delivery platform, encountered several challenges throughout its journey toward becoming a market leader. As an early entrant in a nascent digital ecosystem, the company faced resistance from both customers and partner restaurants unfamiliar with the concept of online food delivery. Educating stakeholders and gaining trust in a market that lacked prior exposure to e-commerce became one of the initial and most critical hurdles (Foodmandu, 2020a, 2020b).

In its formative years, Foodmandu struggled with limited financial and human resources. Small teams, constrained capital, and a lack of robust infrastructure made it difficult to manage logistics efficiently. The challenge of coordinating delivery riders and ensuring timely order fulfillment was particularly acute in the early stages, resulting in operational inefficiencies. The dependency on restaurant partnerships further exposed the platform to disruptions in the supply chain, which often affected food variety and order reliability.

Moreover, the company had to weather multiple external shocks that significantly affected its operations and reputation. The 2015 earthquake disrupted Kathmandu's business ecosystem, and later, the COVID-19 pandemic forced rapid operational adaptations. A significant cybersecurity breach on March 7, 2020, further tested Foodmandu's resilience. Hackers claimed to have compromised personal data of approximately 50,000 customers, including names, contact details, and location coordinates. The company promptly acknowledged the incident and confirmed the resolution of the security loophole the following day (MyRepublica, 2020). Although the breach temporarily damaged public confidence, Foodmandu's transparent communication and rapid response helped mitigate long-term reputational harm.

Since the onset of COVID-19 in Nepal, the food delivery industry has experienced rapid growth. Numerous emerging food delivery companies have entered the market, partnering with a wide range of restaurants to expand their delivery services. As a result, Foodmandu now faces significantly more competition than in the past. However, with the gradual return to normalcy, consumer preferences are shifting—many people are increasingly inclined to dine out and enjoy the ambience of nearby restaurants rather than ordering food online (Neupane, 2020). Additionally, operational challenges during peak demand periods revealed further vulnerabilities. For instance, during festive seasons such as Dashain and Tihar, managing restaurant closures and inventory updates became highly complex. According to Neupane (2020), tasks such as contacting restaurant partners, updating system dashboards, and ensuring accurate menu and delivery time information required exceptional coordination between sales, data, and marketing departments.

Despite these obstacles, Foodmandu's founder, Manohar Adhikari, remained steadfast in his commitment to the venture. Initially managing the platform alongside his software company, he made a pivotal decision in 2015 to devote himself fully to Foodmandu. This strategic shift enabled a focused effort on scaling the platform, enhancing service quality, and reinforcing customer trust. Notably, in its early phase, the company benefitted from limited direct competition, which allowed for continuous experimentation and innovation.

Over the years, Foodmandu has evolved by emphasizing customer service, strategic partnerships, and internal capacity building. Its response to crises—ranging from natural disasters to global pandemics—demonstrates the company's adaptability. The implementation of safety protocols, training of staff, and technological enhancements have further strengthened its position in Nepal's increasingly competitive food delivery landscape.

13 Managerial Implications and Strategic Takeaways

The case of Foodmandu offers several valuable insights for business professionals operating in emerging Asian markets. One major lesson is the importance of personal experience in identifying market gaps. Adhikari's struggle to find quality food during working hours helped him recognize a larger unmet need among Kathmandu's urban population. This reinforces the idea that entrepreneurial ideas often stem from personal inconvenience, a concept echoed in entrepreneurial literature on opportunity recognition (Shane & Venkataraman, 2000). Furthermore, Foodmandu's hybrid order-processing system—balancing automation with manual oversight—serves as a blueprint for ensuring operational efficiency without compromising service quality (Ahmed et al., 2021). This hybrid approach helped mitigate issues like delivery inaccuracies and system glitches, offering a practical model for similar logistics-dependent startups in resource-constrained settings.

Foodmandu's experience also highlights the need for flexible and inclusive customer targeting strategies. By serving both individuals and organizations—from busy professionals to corporate clients—Foodmandu demonstrated that e-commerce platforms can scale by catering to diverse consumer profiles (Ahmed, 2017). The company also embraced real-time customer feedback mechanisms and loyalty programs to deepen engagement. These tactics are increasingly recognized as essential in enhancing customer retention and building brand equity in digital marketplaces (Kumar & Reinartz, 2016; Sheth & Uslay, 2022). Importantly, Foodmandu's ability to turn adversity into innovation, such as expanding into grocery delivery through OneMart after market saturation in food delivery, reflects an agile approach to business model evolution that is vital for startups in dynamic markets (Blank, 2020).

14 Regional Relevance: Lessons for Asia's E-Commerce Landscape

Nepal's online food delivery industry is rapidly evolving, supported by favorable demographic shifts, digital transformation, and changing consumer expectations. While still modest by global standards, the sector's robust growth trajectory and alignment with broader trends in South Asia underscore its strategic importance within Nepal's emerging digital economy.

Foodmandu's trajectory mirrors the growth patterns of similar e-commerce firms in the region. Its evolution resembles the rise of HungryNaki in Bangladesh and Zomato in India, both of which leveraged digital innovation to meet urban consumers' changing food habits (Ahmed, 2017; Ahmed et al., 2021). Like its counterparts, Foodmandu had to educate a low-digital-literacy customer base, establish logistics in cities with infrastructure deficits, and build payment trust through cash-on-delivery and mobile wallets. These shared experiences affirm that digital startups in Asia must prioritize user trust, scalable operations, and local customization to thrive in rapidly urbanizing economies (Kshetri, 2010). Foodmandu's use of app-based services, flexible pricing, and expansion beyond food delivery offers a valuable blueprint for tech-driven service innovation across developing Asia.

15 Way Forward

Foodmandu's growth into Butwal and the introduction of its grocery delivery service, Foodmandu OneMart, reduce dependence on the competitive food delivery market and open new customer segments. This aligns with shifting customer choices for comfort and integrated services inside a single platform. Strong partnerships with local restaurants provide Foodmandu a competitive edge, presenting a diverse food variety. Its involvement in high-profile events, like the Kathmandu Music Festival, boosts visibility, brand loyalty, and market presence. The "Fantastic 14 Sales" campaigns have fueled both customer acquisition and retention, contributing to 40% year-on-year growth and reinforcing Foodmandu's market position. Moving forward, Foodmandu needs to focus on technological innovation, customer satisfaction, and operational efficiency. The company should invest in scalable technologies for logistics, data management, and consumer experience to keep up with its geographical growth and diversification of offerings. It will also need to operate effectively so that the quality and level of service to customers is not compromised. With increased competition, Foodmandu will have to be agile and responsive to ongoing changes in the marketplace. In fact, continuous innovation and meeting the needs of dynamic customers will be vital for their leadership in the meal delivery market of Nepal. Embracing innovation, knowing customer preference, and ensuring operational excellence, Foodmandu has been in a good position to continue growth and explore new markets. In the future, Foodmandu needs to balance the challenges of expansion with its core mission: effectively delivering food. With further strategic diversification, technological advancement, and customer-centricity, Foodmandu is poised to lead the food delivery business in Nepal and create a sound foundation for sustained growth.

References

Ahmed, J. (2017). HungryNaki: Challenges of an emerging online food delivery service in Bangladesh. *Sage Business Cases*. https://doi.org/10.4135/9781526409997

Ahmed, J. U., Faroque, A. R., Jannat, U. M. U., Anika, F. H., & Majid, M. A. (2021). Khan's kitchen: Feeding the city dwellers. *Sage Business Cases*. https://doi.org/10.4135/9781529763300

Bhattarai, R., & Paudel, K. (2024). Online food delivery services in Nepal: An emerging urban culture. *Journal of Business and Knowledge Culture, 4*(1), 42–53.

Bhul, B. (2025). The Gig Economy Revolution in Nepal: Analyzing Challenges and Opportunities for Digital Governance. *Prashasan: The Nepalese Journal of Public Administration, 57*(1), 137–157.

Blank, S. (2020). *The four steps to the epiphany: Successful strategies for products that win*. Wiley.

Business360. (2025). Foodmandu OneMart brings instant grocery delivery to busy residents of city. https://www.b360nepal.com/detail/24832

Cuong, D. T. (2024). Factors affecting consumer intentions and actual behavior: A case of food delivery applications. *Innovative Marketing, 20*(2), 29–39.

Foodmandu. (2020, November 11). *A message from the founder*. https://blog.foodmandu.com/a-message-from-the-founder/

Foodmandu. (2020, November 11). FoodMandu. https://blog.foodmandu.com/a-message-from-the-founder/

Foodmandu. (n.d.). OneMart: Instant grocery delivery service. https://www.foodmandu.com/

Hamal, P., & Huijsmans, R. (2022). Making markets gendered: Kathmandu's ride-sharing platforms through a gender lens. *Gender, Place & Culture, 29*(5), 670–692.

Karki, H. (2019). A brief history of public education, information & communication technology (ICT) and ICT in public education in Nepal. *Deerwalk Journal of Computer Science and Information Technology*, 78–103.

Karki, N. (2023). Effect of service quality on customer satisfaction: A study on food delivery apps in Kathmandu. *Valley State College Journal, 2*(1), 15–25.

Kshetri, N. (2010). *The global cybercrime industry: Economic, institutional and strategic perspectives*. Springer.

Kumar, V., & Reinartz, W. (2016). Creating enduring customer value. *Journal of Marketing, 80*(6), 36–68.

Ministry of Communication and Information Technology. (2019). Digital Nepal Framework. https://mocit.gov.np/application/resources/admin/uploads/source/EConsultation/ENpercent20Digitalpercent20Nepalpercent20Frameworkpercent20V8.4percent2015percent20Julypercent20percent202019.pdf

MyRepublica. (2020, March 9). *Cyberattack exposes personal details of thousands of Foodmandu users*. https://myrepublica.nagariknetwork.com/index.php/news/cyberattack-exposes-personal-details-of-thousands-of-foodmandu-users

Nepal Telecommunications Authority (2025). Nepal Telecommunications Authority Telecommunication Indicators Falgun, 2081. https://nta.gov.np/uploads/contents/MIS%20_Falgun%20%E0%A5%A8%E0%A5%A6%E0%A5%AE%E0%A5%A7.pdf

Neupane, N. (2020). Analysis of Food Delivery during COVID-19 Pandemic at Foodmandu. *Cooperative Education Report*. Faculty of Business Administration, Siam University, Thailand.

Research and Markets (2023). Online Food Delivery Market Report and Forecast 2023–2028. https://www.researchandmarkets.com/reports/5775104/online-food-delivery-market-report-forecast

Shane, S., & Venkataraman, S. (2000). The promise of entrepreneurship as a field of research. *Academy of Management Review, 25*(1), 217–226.

Sharesansar (2025, May 5). Foodmandu launches midnight food delivery service in Kathmandu. https://www.sharesansar.com/newsdetail/foodmandu-ylaunches-midnight-food-delivery-service-in-kathmandu-2025-05-05

Sharesansar. (2024, November 12). Foodmandu celebrates 14 years of service with new grocery delivery service and exciting anniversary campaign. https://www.sharesansar.com/newsdetail/foodmandu-celebrates-14-years-of-service-with-new-grocery-delivery-service-and-exciting-anniversary-campaign-2024-11-12

Sharma, S., & Adhikari, T. (2024). Regional expansion of digital platforms in Nepal. *Digital Development Journal, 1*(2), 10–18.

Sheth, J. N., & Uslay, C. (2022). Creating enduring customer value. *Journal of Creating Value, 8*(2), 241–252.

Singh, R. M., & Bhuju, D. R. (2001). Development of science and technology in Nepal. *Science, Technology and Society, 6*(1), 159–178.

Statista. (2025). *Online food delivery—Nepal: Market revenue forecast (2025–2030)*. https://www.statista.com/outlook/emo/online-food-delivery/nepal

Tamang, A. (2024). *Top 10 fastest growing businesses in Nepal*. ArunTamang.com.np. https://aruntamang.com.np/fastest-growing-business-in-nepal

Thamel.com. (2024). thamel.com—About us. https://www.thamel.com

Jashim Uddin Ahmed , Ph.D., is a Professor of Strategy in the Department of Management, School of Business and Economics, North South University, Bangladesh. He is the founder of InterResearch, a leading research organization in Bangladesh. He has been awarded his Ph.D. in Management Sciences from the University of Manchester Institute of Science and Technology (UMIST, currently known as The University of Manchester), UK. He has achieved Master degrees in both Marketing and Management from the University of Northumbria, UK. He also studied in the University of Reading and the University of Lincolnshire and Humberside, UK. His research interests include social innovation, higher education, strategic management, and contemporary issues in marketing and management. He has published over 250 research articles and business cases in reputable journals.

Anisur R. Faroque , D.Sc. (International Business), Ph.D. (International Business & Entrepreneurship), is an Associate Professor (tenure track) in the School of Marketing and Communication at the University of Vaasa, Finland. Having teaching and research experience in four different countries in Europe, Asia, and Oceania endows him with cross-cultural literacy and the understanding of the unique needs of diverse students. His research interests are in the marketing, international business and entrepreneurship domains, and include research topics such as opportunity recognition, strategic orientations, and entrepreneurial decision making.

Samsul Islam Ph.D., is an academic and researcher at the Northern Alberta Institute of Technology (NAIT), JR Shaw School of Business, in Canada. He has an extensive academic background in both the theoretical and applied areas of Operations Management, Transportation, and Supply Chain Management. He studied at the University of Gothenburg, Sweden, and the University of Auckland, New Zealand. He has published research on truck-sharing constraints, transportation modeling, and other topics in peer-reviewed journals and conference papers.

Shashi Shekhar Acharya is a Training and Research officer at Nepal Administrative Staff College (a national level autonomous institution). He has completed his Masters of Computer Science and Information Technology (MSc CSIT) from Tribhuvan University. He is also engaged as a part-time lecturer on different constituent campuses of Tribhuvan University. He has also served as an IT consultant in different government offices in Nepal. He also has the experience of working for international and national IT companies as a developer. His research interests include information technology, artificial intelligence, machine learning, and public service innovation and procurement.

Invisible Enterprises: The Unrecognized Contribution of Home-Based Women Entrepreneurs in Nepal

Shradha Adhikari and Krishna Khanal

Abstract This chapter explores the largely unrecognized yet vital role of home-based women entrepreneurs in Nepal's informal economy. Across kitchens, courtyards, and increasingly digital platforms, millions of Nepali women operate micro-enterprises that sustain household livelihoods, preserve traditional skills, and strengthen community resilience. Yet, these "invisible enterprises" are often absent from official statistics and excluded from financial systems and policy agendas due to intersecting structural, cultural, and institutional barriers. In response, the chapter introduces a context-sensitive empowerment framework, known as the "SEE" model—Support (financial and regulatory inclusion), Equip (skills and technology access), and Elevate (market linkages and public visibility). This model is anchored in local practice and scalable through multi-stakeholder engagement involving banks, NGOs, retailers, and government agencies. Ultimately, recognizing and investing in these invisible enterprises is not only a matter of gender equity. It is a strategic lever for inclusive and sustainable economic transformation in Nepal and South Asia.

1 Introduction: The Hidden Engine of Asia's Emerging Economies

Entrepreneurship refers to the process of identifying opportunities, taking calculated risks, organizing resources, and creating something of economic value (Khanal & Prajapati, 2023; Ratten, 2023). The word "entrepreneur" comes from the French term "entreprendre," meaning "to undertake." This is a definition that captures the spirit of those who lead ventures into the unknown. Joseph Schumpeter (1934), a pioneer in economic thought, has defined entrepreneurs as innovators who disrupt the status quo

S. Adhikari
Kathmandu University School of Management, Lalitpur, Nepal
e-mail: 25902_shradha@kusom.edu.np

K. Khanal (✉)
King's College, Kathmandu, Nepal
e-mail: Krishna@kingscollege.edu.np

T. Endress and Y. F. Badir (eds.), *Business and Management in Asia: Opportunities and Entrepreneurship*, https://doi.org/10.1007/978-981-95-4909-2_9

and drive economic progress through "creative destruction." Over time, scholars have highlighted various traits that define entrepreneurship: innovation, proactiveness, resilience, and the ability to navigate uncertainty. (Hisrich & Peters, 2017; Neupane et al., 2025). In modern economics, entrepreneurship is celebrated not only as a path to personal success but also as a national development strategy (Prajapati & Khanal, 2023; Wiklund et al., 2019). It generates employment, encourages innovation, fosters local industries, and expands markets (Rashid et al., 2025).

This is true both in developed economies and in low and middle-income countries where small-scale, informal, and micro-entrepreneurship drives a large portion of local economic activity. According to the Asian Development Bank (ADB, 2024), in South Asia, the informal economy accounts for over 60% of total employment, with micro-entrepreneurship being a major contributor to livelihoods, particularly for women. Yet, mainstream definitions of entrepreneurship have often overlooked the quiet but powerful forms of enterprise that happen in homes and alleyways, particularly led by women. Across Asia, particularly in countries like Nepal, Bangladesh, and India, economic value is not just created in factories and offices. It is crafted in living rooms, kitchens, and courtyards (Ojediran & Anderson, 2020).

In a society structure where patriarchal norms, limited job opportunities, and socioeconomic contractions shape women's daily lives, entrepreneurship often takes unconventional forms (Cinar, 2019; Xheneti et al., 2018). It is not about venture capital or high-growth startups. Instead, it is about turning a courtyard into a tailoring center, a kitchen into a food business, or a Facebook page into an online thrift shop. The invisible enterprises run by home-based women entrepreneurs in Nepal. These women do not always consider themselves "entrepreneurs," nor are they typically included in national surveys or business statistics. Yet, they contribute to household incomes, support children's education, revive traditional skills, and sustain local markets. Their enterprises are often small, informal, and home-bound, but their impact is large, compounding, and long-lasting (Muhammad et al., 2021a, 2021b).

According to the International Labour Organization (ILO, 2022), home-based work constitutes a substantial portion of informal employment in Nepal, particularly for women, who are often excluded from public-facing work. UN Women (2023) further notes that "home-based income is the economic lifeline for women with restricted mobility." These findings align with everyday observations in Nepali towns and villages: from women selling sel roti at bus stops, to elderly grandmothers running vegetable shops, to young girls reselling clothes online by marketing them as sustainable to pay for college. These are not just survival strategies; they are entrepreneurial adaptations to environments with limited opportunities (Sah, 2020). In urban areas like Kathmandu and Pokhara, the gig economy and digital platforms have added new layers to this ecosystem.

As Xheneti and Madden (2024) argue, women's entrepreneurship in such settings is deeply "socio-spatial," meaning that their work emerges from, and is shaped by, the space of home, community dynamics, and cultural expectations. The relevance of this topic is further underscored by the COVID-19 pandemic, which accelerated both the need for income diversification and the expansion of digital micro-enterprises. Evidence from Nepal shows that women's informal businesses served as economic lifelines during the crisis, particularly as male out-migration and job loss increased household vulnerabilities. (ADB, 2024; World Bank, 2021) Digital platforms like Instagram, Facebook Marketplace, and mobile wallets have emerged as alternative economic spaces, albeit with uneven access due to digital literacy and affordability issues. This chapter covers these overlooked and undervalued enterprises in greater detail. It highlights why recognizing and supporting home-based women entrepreneurs is essential for inclusive economic development, gender equity, and local sustainability. It begins by defining the practical context of home-based women entrepreneurship in Nepal, then maps their economic, social, and cultural contributions. It also outlines the core challenges they face, such as limited access to finance, digital illiteracy, and legal invisibility, and ends with a proposed framework for empowering them in more systematic, scalable ways. Nepal's economic future cannot rely solely on large-scale industrialization or foreign direct investment. It must also invest in the grassroots systems that already exist in kitchens, courtyards, and community networks and that continue to power livelihoods for millions. It is an economic necessity to highlight them.

2 Practical Context: Defining Home-Based Women Entrepreneurship in Nepal

When we talk about home-based women entrepreneurs in Nepal, we are talking about women who run small businesses from available resources, generally their own homes. They are often one-woman setups, sometimes with the help of family, by using whatever spaces and resources they already have. In many cases, their businesses may range from food preparation to textile production and social media-based reselling, yet they are largely unregistered and excluded from formal economic data (Anwar & Daniel, 2016).

Recent studies highlight how these entrepreneurs operate within overlapping systems like the informal economy, the gig economy, and microenterprise sectors (Chen, 2016; Gómez et al., 2020; Khan et al., 2024). For instance, handmade textile producers in Bhaktapur keep the traditional crafts and culture associated with them alive while earning an income, home-based food sellers in Pokhara meet neighborhood demand for ready-to-eat snacks, and over time, online thrift sellers in Kathmandu creatively use Instagram to reach young urban buyers.

According to the International Labour Organization (2022), more than 80% of female employment in Nepal remains informal, and a significant portion of that is home-based. These women are not formally recognized as workers or business owners in any official records, yet they contribute directly to household income, neighborhood economies, and the preservation of traditional crafts and foodways, The World Bank (2021) also points out that women in South Asia, including Nepal, often participate in economic life through what are termed "invisible enterprises"-small, home-managed activities that respond to local demand but exist entirely outside tax and regulatory frameworks.

Nepal has seen stories like this unfold across generations. One such example is who began her clothing business 50 years ago with just NRS 18. Over time, she has trained more than 5000 people in sewing and weaving. Right now, in her eighth decade of human life, she is continuing to sew with her own hands. She says, "As long as your hands and feet work, you should never stop working hard." Let's take this as a spirit of women entrepreneurship, as this mirrors the spirit of countless other women quietly powering the economy from home. At the same time, entrepreneurship is also a path taken out of necessity.

In the commercialized capital of Nepal, the city of temples, you can observe teenage girls running a tea stall in the temples or places with people before heading to school. These cases often go unnoticed by the media. The money she earns helps her to cover school fees and supplies. Isn't the girl demonstrating early what it means to identify the market need and meet it? Clearly, yes, although informal setup and minimal resources, but just like any other entrepreneur. A recent IFC case study (2024) highlights how women like Bismriti Paudel in Kathmandu left formal banking jobs to run home-based caregiving enterprises due to the lack of institutional child care. Her venture, "Homecare Nepal," now provides domestic health workers to over 100 clients, while employing more than a dozen women informally trained on the job. This kind of enterprise, born out of unmet need and resourcefulness, represents a shift in how entrepreneurship can emerge from social responsibilities (IFC, 2024). Similarly, in Rukum, groups like the Ratamata Women Farmers Cooperative have pooled seed grants to launch goat farming operations and revive food security in post-earthquake settings without ever entering formal registries or trade groups (Kathmandu Post, 2024).

Phillips once said, "Entrepreneurship is not just about creating something new, it's about responding to unmet needs with creative and practical solutions." That's exactly what happened in Kathmandu around 2017, when a Tibetan dish known as Laughing exploded in popularity thanks to the social media boom. People couldn't get enough of it. As simple as the dish may sound, it wasn't easy to prepare for a beginner. However, that didn't stop local panipuri stall owners, especially women, from rising to meet the demands. These were mostly small-scale vendors near schools and colleges, where street food is a post-class favorite activity. They learned quickly, adapted their recipes, and scaled up. What started as a food trend became a livelihood. These vendors, often operating from temporary setups, exemplify how informal entrepreneurs respond swiftly to market shifts.

Analyzing street food vendors in Kathmandu's New Bus Park and Ratna Park areas found that the street food trade is a growing sector, providing low-cost food to urban populations and serving as a significant income source for many urban poor, including women. The research highlighted that street food vending is predominantly a self- and family-based activity led by women, offering employment opportunities in the informal sector. Moreover, the informal nature of street vending in Kathmandu allows for flexibility and adaptability, enabling vendors to meet the specific demands of their communities. The World Bank (2021) further shows that during the COVID-19 pandemic, many women in Nepal started small food delivery and clothing reselling ventures on Facebook and Instagram. For many, these ventures were not only temporary coping strategies. They evolved into sustainable income streams even after the lockdowns ended.

One such woman, interviewed anonymously in this study, explained how a single Instagram story could generate dozens of orders overnight—"without a shop, without a signboard." This trend is particularly significant in urban areas where space is expensive and mobility is limited. As the notes state, "home-based work is an economic lifeline for women with restricted mobility," and enables them to participate in markets without leaving their domestic spheres.

Despite their contributions, these enterprises often go unrecognized due to a lack of formal registration and limited access to markets, credit, and training (Sharma & Paudel, 2025). Meanwhile, the rise of Nepal's gig economy has opened new channels of economic activity. According to the Asian Productivity Organization (2024), this economy is "empowering women to engage in productive labor while accommodating domestic responsibilities," particularly through flexible, tech-enabled platforms. Digital tools such as mobile wallets, WhatsApp, and Facebook are reshaping how women run their businesses informally yet efficiently. As we argue, women's entrepreneurship in informal settings must be understood not just economically but socio-spatially as a response to the constraints and possibilities within their homes and communities (Henderson & Ross, 2025). These enterprises thrive because women adapt, innovate, and organize their labor around the household. This is not just survivalist entrepreneurship but also strategic.

3 Contribution to Economic and Social Development

Home-based women entrepreneurs, though often "invisible" in official records, make substantial economic, social, and cultural contributions in Nepal. Collectively, these micro-enterprises increase household incomes and help lift families out of poverty. Women's home-based businesses create employment not only for the proprietors themselves but sometimes for neighbors and family, spurring local commerce and reducing job scarcity in the community (Muhammad et al., 2021a, 2021b). The additional income generated improves living standards by enabling better access to education and healthcare for family members. In this way, women's entrepreneurship at the household level fosters a positive cycle of reinvestment in communities, contributing to poverty reduction and local economic growth. Moreover, as these businesses expand the range of goods and services in the village markets from handcrafted textiles to homemade food products, they add diversity to local commerce and supply chains.

This economic diversification makes local economies more resilient to shocks, an outcome that benefits all market actors in those areas. Equally important are the social gains. Home-based enterprises advance women's agency and empowerment within traditionally patriarchal communities (Al-Dajani & Marlow, 2010). Earning an income gives women greater say in household financial decisions and boosts their confidence and status in society.

Many women entrepreneurs report enhanced decision-making roles at home and in the community, as their business challenges gradually change traditional gender norms. For instance, studies in Pokhara find that women-led enterprises empower women by elevating their role from passive homemakers to active contributors to the family's economy. These entrepreneurs also tend to form informal support networks, where, through local cooperatives, self-help groups, or microfinance circles, they reinforce social bonds and trust. Nepal's thriving microfinance sector, entrepreneurs, providing community-based finance and peer networking. Such networks allow women to exchange business knowledge, pool savings, and collectively address common challenges, thereby building social capital at the grassroots (Bhandar, 2021). The rise of women's business associations and cooperatives further extends these informal networks into more organized platforms that can interface with banks and markets. In short, home-based businesses not only economically empower women but also strengthen community cohesion and inclusion, as women connect with the support of one another's ventures. Culturally, home-based women entrepreneurs play a pivotal role in preserving Nepal's rich heritage of crafts and culinary skills.

Many of these businesses are built on inherited skills passed down through generations (Pokhrel, 2025). For example, women in rural areas engage in traditional handloom weaving, knitting, pottery, and embroidery, producing artisanal goods that reflect Nepal's cultural identity. By commercializing these crafts from their homes, they ensure that ancient techniques and designs continue to be practiced and valued in modern markets. This has broader economic significance: by producing cultural handicraft products that are often sold domestically and even exported, women artisans contribute to the preservation of cultural heritage while directly adding to Nepal's GDP.

A similar pattern appears in the culinary realm. Home-based food businesses- such as making pickles (achar), spices, dried foods, or traditional snacks- allow women to monetize their family recipes and kitchen skills. These ventures keep age-old culinary traditions alive. For instance, a recent skills program in western Nepal trained women to make a dozen varieties of local pickles (from timur pepper to akbare chili) with proper preservation and packaging techniques. The training not only enhanced the quality of marketability of these traditional products but also empowered participants to earn additional income from a culturally rooted craft. This illustrates how home-based female entrepreneurs act as custodians of cultural knowledge, turning heritage crafts, and cuisine into viable products.

For business leaders in sectors like tourism, retail, and handicrafts, these women offer an opportunity to source unique, authentic Nepali products from handwoven textiles to homemade gourmet pickles—that can enrich companies' product lines while supporting cultural preservation.

4 Why Business Leaders Should Care?

Given these multifaceted contributions, why should Nepal's business leaders (companies, banks, and development organizations) care about home-based women entrepreneurs? The answer lies in the mutual benefits of engagement. First, these women-led enterprises represent an untapped supply chain opportunity. Progressive companies can practice inclusive sourcing by integrating women's micro-enterprises into their procurement networks (Dhaubhadel & Modi, 2022). For example, handicraft exporters or boutique retailers could partner with women's cooperatives to source hand-loomed fabrics, incense, knitted goods, and other local products. Such partnerships not only diversify a company's supply chain but also enhance its resilience and community relationships.

There is evidence that when home-based producers are given market access and support, their income rises significantly (Aku et al., 2018; Ma et al., 2024). Organizations like SABAH Nepal (a women-focused cooperative) have shown that linking rural women artisans allows goods to reach both local and foreign markets. Companies that engage with these networks can benefit from a stable source of distinctive products and a positive brand reputation for supporting women's livelihoods. Second, engaging women entrepreneurs opens up new customer segments and markets. As women's enterprises grow, they elevate household purchasing power and create new demand in local economies, for everything from farming supplies to telecommunications.

Banks and microfinance institutions, in particular, stand to gain by tailoring financial services to women entrepreneurs. Currently, there are 5.99 million members in a total of 77 microfinance companies in Nepal, and of those, 96 percent are women who provide small loans without collateral, enabling women to engage in small-scale businesses like farming, handicrafts, and retail (Acharya, 2020). This hints at a vast client base for formal financial institutions that can offer SME loans, insurance, and digital banking suited to these entrepreneurs' needs.

Some government and banking initiatives have begun tapping this market (for instance, concessional loan schemes have mobilized financing for tens of thousands of women-owned businesses), but much more can be done to bring "invisible" enterprises into the formal financial fold. Similarly, technology firms and telecom providers have a stake: if women entrepreneurs are capable of utilizing smartphones and internet connectivity for business, they become active users of digital services. This creates an opportunity for tech companies to expand into rural markets with mobile banking, e-commerce platforms, and training apps designed for semi-literate users.

Finally, partnering with home-based women entrepreneurs aligns with broader corporate social responsibility (CSR) and sustainability goals. Supporting these businesses can help companies meet gender inclusion targets and demonstrate a commitment to community development. It can also foster goodwill and brand loyalty among Nepal's growing female consumer base. Development agencies and NGOs, on the other hand, can amplify their impact by involving the private sector-for example, by facilitating corporate mentorship programs, market linkages, or "inclusive business" models that invest in women-led value chains. The bottom line is that the economic and social contributions of Nepal's home-based women entrepreneurs translate into tangible business advantages for those who choose to collaborate with them. By recognizing these "invisible" enterprises as vital partners in development, business leaders can not only do good but also do well, leveraging a powerful engine of growth that has long been operating behind closed doors (Gustavsson, 2021).

5 Key Challenges: Where Intervention Is Needed

A significant barrier for women entrepreneurs in Nepal is the limited access to formal financial services (Agrawal et al., 2023). With only 27% of women having access compared to 35% of men, the disparity is evident. The lack of property ownership among women-nearly 80% do not own fixed assets, further hampers their ability to secure loans, as collateral is often required. Consequently, many women rely on personal savings or informal lenders, which can be unsustainable and limit business growth (Sharma & Paudel, 2025). Moreover, over half of women-owned small businesses report challenges in accessing finance, highlighting the need for more inclusive financial policies and products.

Digital literacy remains a critical challenge. Only 28% of rural women own smartphones, and less than 10% utilize them for business purposes. This digital divide restricts women's ability to market their products online, access digital financial services, and participate in e-commerce platforms. Additionally, women constitute only 43.6% of Nepal's social media users, indicating underrepresentation in digital spaces that are increasingly vital for business visibility and networking.

The majority of home-based women entrepreneurs operate informally, with less than 7% of such businesses being formally registered. This legal invisibility excludes them from government support programs, formal financial systems, and legal protections. Furthermore, only 13% of SMEs are fully or partially owned by women, reflecting systematic barriers to formal business ownership and growth (UN Women, 2023). Formal registration can provide access to a wider range of resources, but the process must be made more accessible and supportive for women entrepreneurs.

Cultural and societal norms in Nepal often dictate women's roles, limiting their mobility and time available for entrepreneurial activities. Women are frequently expected to prioritize household responsibilities, which restricts their ability to attend training, network, or manage business operations effectively (Khanal & Prajapati, 2023). These norms not only limit women's participation in entrepreneurship but also affect their confidence and societal support, making it challenging to sustain and grow their businesses.

6 Actionable Framework for Empowering Home-Based Women Entrepreneurs: The "SEE" Model

Despite their critical role in local economies, most home-based women entrepreneurs in Nepal remain outside the radar of formal markets and development interventions. To bridge their gap, the "SEE" model—Support, Equip, Elevate—offers a practical, scalable framework that recognizes the lived realities of these women and proposes interventions grounded in policy, technology, and community-based ecosystems. Each step is designed not only to address systemic constraints but also to create synergies among government, private sector, and civil society actors. This framework is not theoretical; it draws from real, field-tested practices across Nepal and suggests scalable adaptations that public, private, and nonprofit stakeholders can implement.

Support: At the heart of women's economic empowerment lies the capacity to access credit and formal identity as entrepreneurs. In Nepal, the finance gap remains one of the most persistent barriers. As of 2022, less than 19% of women in Nepal legally own land or property- a key prerequisite for accessing collateral-based loans through traditional banks (World Bank, 2021) The rigidity of these systems excludes most home-based women entrepreneur, who often have no business registration, no formal bookkeeping and no access to financial history records, many reply on informal lenders charging interest rates exceeding 26% annually, creating debt cycles rather than business growth. To counter this, decentralized, mobile-enabled financial services are gaining traction. Esewa, Nepal's leading digital wallet, has partnered with microfinance institutions to enable mobile-based microloans for rural women entrepreneurs. In early 2023, Prabhu Bank and Sajilo Finance jointly piloted a program in Surkhet and Kaplivastu districts, offering credit as low as NPR 10,000 (approx. USD 75) with flexible repayment schedules linked to harvest and festival season.

Equally crucial is access to a legal identity as a business. As of 2023, fewer than 7% of home-based businesses in Nepal were formally registered. Recognizing this gap, Lalitpur Metropolitan City launched mobile "Enterprise Registration Camps" in five wards between June and September 2023, enabling 178 women-led businesses to obtain official registration with support for filling digital forms, acquiring PAN Numbers, and accessing concessional loan schemes. These Camps offer templates for provincial replication. Banks and fintech firms have the opportunity to develop dedicated "micro-home business accounts" with simplified Know Your Customer (KYC) norms. These could bundle mobile banking, credit scoring via transaction data, and savings incentives into a single low-barrier product for women micro-entrepreneurs. With over 4 million Nepali women enrolled in cooperatives and savings groups, the financial sector stands to benefit enormously from this under-leveraged demographic.

Equip: If support mechanisms provide a foundation, capacity-building equips women to operate and expand their businesses confidently. Yet, a significant digital divide persists, particularly among rural women. According to UN Women (2023), only 20% of rural Nepali women entrepreneurs own smartphones, and fewer than

10% use digital tools for business (UN Women Nepal, 2023). Low digital literacy-compounded by gendered access norms-prevents women from utilizing social media, digital wallets, or e-commerce platforms that could significantly improve reach and efficiency. Innovative, localized training programs are starting to change that. In Chitwan, the NGO Code for Nepal (2023) conducted WhatsApp Business literacy circles in 2022, teaching 150 women how to send product images, conduct pricing discussions, and manage inventory using simple apps like Google Keep and voice notes. Participants reported an average 25% increase in weekly orders after the training, particularly for food and clothing products sold via Facebook Marketplace and Viber groups. Meanwhile, Room to Read and ChangeFusion Nepal have co-developed a voice-navigated bookkeeping app called SmartBanjiya, tailored for semi-literate women traders. This app allows for icon-based inventory recording, expense calculation, and verbal summaries of cash flow. A 2023 pilot in Bardibas revealed that women using the app were 3× more likely to separate business and household income, improving financial planning and reinvestment capacity.

Equipping women also requires layering business training onto digital literacy. Organizations like SABAH. Nepal have successfully run modular courses combining food safety, packaging, pricing strategy, and negotiation skills. Their women's cooperatives now produce export-quality crafts and species, supported by buyer standards manuals and collective bargaining with retailers. Private-sector actors-particularly mobile operators and tech firms-can play a transformative role by bundling business tools with mobile access: offering SIM + smartphone packages bundled with business training modules, or call-center support in regional languages. These are not charity efforts- they expand customer base while advancing equity.

Elevate: Even with support and skills, home-based entrepreneurs struggle to access wider markets-especially women who lack mobility, networks, or formal business profiles (Thapa Karki et al., 2021). They often remain locked into hyperlocal sales, earning marginal profits. Without visibility, women's products, it handmade candles, fermented pickles, or woolen hats, are underpriced and underappreciated.

Several promising initiatives have started to bridge this last mile. The "Miteri Bazar" initiative in Biratnagar, supported by the Biratnagar Municipal Office and Women for Human Rights, hosts bi-monthly pop-up markets specifically for home-based women entrepreneurs. Participants receive free stalls, digital marketing support, and payment facilitation via eSewa or Khalti. According to the 2023 monitoring report, vendors at Miteri Bazar recorded average earnings of NPR 8000–12,000 per event, with 60% of attendees being first-time sellers.

A transformative next step would be the development of an "e-Haat Bazar," a nationwide, multilingual digital platform exclusively for verified women-led micro businesses. Backed by the government or donors, and linked with post offices and rural collection centers, this system could ensure delivery, payment, and customer feedback loops. Such a platform would give informal women entrepreneurs the kind of exposure usually reserved for urban brands. Corporate and retain actors can strengthen this elevation by integrating inclusive sourcing policies pledging that 5 to 10% of procurement will come from home-based, women-led suppliers. Donors can co-fund mentorship pipelines, where mid-sized women entrepreneurs coach home-based producers in brand building, pricing, and export readiness. The SEE Framework- Support, Equip, Elevate- presents a sequential, integrative approach to unlocking the power of home-based women entrepreneurs.

These women are not "hidden" by choice but by systems that were never built with them in mind. From mobile-based credit and doorstep business registration to WhatsApp marketing and an inclusive e-commerce platform, the pathways to empowerment already exist—they just need to be scaled, sustained, and supported across sectors. For governments, this means decentralizing economic services and embedding gender-responsive budgeting. For financial institutions, it offers a growing, loyal, and under-tapped customer base. For NGOs and CSR programs, it outlines replicable blueprints for women-led transformation.

7 Conclusions

Home-based women entrepreneurs in Nepal are not new to entrepreneurship; what's new is the growing recognition of their economic, cultural, and social impact. Yet, this recognition must go beyond words and lead to action. These women often operate in the informal economy out of necessity, not preference, excluded from systems that require collateral, legal documents, and digital literacy. What they need is not charity, but fair access to tools, training, and markets. Their enterprises are often rooted in tradition but can evolve into growth engines if supported properly. A holistic policy approach must begin with finance. As of 2022, only 19% of Nepali women own land (World Bank, 2021), making conventional loans inaccessible. Mobile-based microfinance, like that supported by UNCDF and Sparrow Pay, has begun bridging the gap, offering doorstep credit tailored to informal women entrepreneurs (UNCDF, 2023). Financial tools must be paired with digital inclusion. UN Women Nepal (2023) reports that fewer than one-third of rural women own smartphones. Initiatives like SABAH Nepal's mobile training centers and Code for Nepal's WhatsApp business modules are helping women engage with technology on their terms.

Legal visibility also matters. Many women-led enterprises remain unregistered, leaving them out of grants, protections, and government support. Programs like Biratnagar's "business registration camps" are a low-cost way to bring formalization to their doorsteps. Social norms, the invisible thread through all of this, need to evolve, too. Showcasing success stories, engaging families, and building community-based cooperatives, as seen in SEWA India and BRAC Bangladesh, are proven methods for long-term change (BRAC, 2023). These entrepreneurs have shown resilience, innovation, and impact. Now it's time for policymakers, businesses, and civil society to match that energy. Supporting home-based women entrepreneurs is not just inclusion-it's nation-building.

References

Acharya, G. (2020). Impact of micro-finance on income change of women in Chandragiri municipality. *Tribhuvan University Journal, 35*(1), 181–192.

Agrawal, R., Bakhshi, P., Chandani, A., Birau, R., & Mendon, S. (2023). Challenges faced by women entrepreneurs in South Asian countries using interpretive structural modeling. *Cogent Business & Management, 10*(2).

Aku, A., Mshenga, P., Afari-Sefa, V., & Ochieng, J. (2018). Effect of market access provided by farmer organizations on smallholder vegetable farmers' income in Tanzania. *Cogent Food & Agriculture, 4*(1).

Al-Dajani, H., & Marlow, S. (2010). Impact of women's home-based enterprise on family dynamics: Evidence from Jordan. *International Small Business Journal, 28*(5), 470–486. https://doi.org/10.1177/0266242610370392

Anwar, M. N., & Daniel, E. (2016). The role of entrepreneur-venture fit in online home-based entrepreneurship: A systematic literature review. *Journal of Enterprising Culture, 24*(4), 419–451. https://doi.org/10.1142/S0218495816500151

Asian Development Bank. (2024). *Social protection for the informal economy in South Asia.* Asia Pathways / ADB Institute Blog. Available at: https://www.asiapathways-adbi.org/2024/08/social-protection-for-the-informal-economy-in-south-asia/

Asian Productivity Organization. (2024). *Digital transformation in Asian economies: Enhancing productivity, socioeconomic impacts, and policy insights.* Asian Productivity Organization. https://www.apo-tokyo.org/wpcontent/uploads/2024/07/Digital-Transformation-in-Asian-Economies_PUB.pdf

Bhandar, M. (2021). Women and business networking: A social capital view. In W. Leal Filho, A. M. Azul, L. Brandli, A. L. Salvia, & T. Wall (Eds.), *Gender equality* (Encyclopedia of the UN Sustainable Development Goals). Springer.

BRAC. (2023). *Annual report: Empowering women through enterprise development.* BRAC. https://www.brac.net/wp-content/uploads/2023/12/BRAC-Annual-Report-2023.pdf

Chen, M. A. (2016). The informal economy: Recent trends, future directions. *New Solutions: A Journal of Environmental and Occupational Health Policy, 26*(2), 155–172. https://doi.org/10.1177/1048291116652613

Cinar, K. (2019). Women's entrepreneurship in patriarchal societies: The case of women's cooperatives in Turkey. In F. Tomos, N. Kumar, N. Clifton, & D. Hyams-Ssekasi (Eds.), *Women entrepreneurs and strategic decision making in the global economy* (pp. 79–98). IGI Global Scientific Publishing. https://doi.org/10.4018/978-1-5225-7479-8.ch005

Code for Nepal. (2023). *Digital inclusion for women entrepreneurs: WhatsApp business training report.* Code for Nepal.

Dhaubhadel, S., & Modi, D. K. (2022). Management practice of women in entrepreneurship activities of micro enterprise running in Parbat District, Nepal. *Nepal Journal of Multidisciplinary Research, 5*(2), 20–31.

Gómez, G. M., Chawla, S., & Fransen, J. (2020). Exploring the entrepreneurial ecosystem within the informal economy with a multifactor framework. In M. Iftikhar, J. Justice, & D. Audretsch (Eds.), *Urban studies and entrepreneurship* (pp. 185–204). Springer. https://doi.org/10.1007/978-3-030-15164-5_10

Gustavsson, M. (2021). The invisible (woman) entrepreneur? Shifting the discourse from fisheries diversification to entrepreneurship. *Sociologia Ruralis, 61*(4), 787–805. https://doi.org/10.1111/soru.12343

Henderson, S., & Ross, E. (2025). Informal entrepreneurship and women's empowerment: An asset-based perspective on the lived experiences of Swati women. *Development Southern Africa, 42*(3), 423–441. https://doi.org/10.1080/0376835X.2025.2474240

Hisrich, R. D., & Peters, M. P. (2017). *Entrepreneurship* (10th ed.). McGraw-Hill Education.

International Finance Corporation. (2024). Empowering women SMEs and promoting financial inclusion. https://www.ifc.org/en/stories/2024/empowering-women-entrepreneurs-himalayas

International Labour Organization & Government of Nepal, Ministry of Labour, Employment and Social Security. (2022). *Diagnostic report on the extent, circumstances, causes, factors, and nature of informality in Nepal.* ILO. https://www.ilo.org/sites/default/files/wcmsp5/groups/public/%40asia/%40ro-bangkok/%40ilokathmandu/documents/publication/wcms_884823.pdf

Kathmandu Post. (2024). *Women's cooperatives revive goat farming to rebuild livelihoods in Rukum.* Kathmandu Post.

Khan, M. H., Williams, J., Williams, P., & Mayes, R. (2024). Caring in the gig economy: A relational perspective of decent work. *Work, Employment and Society, 38*(4), 1107–1127. https://doi.org/10.1177/09500170231173586

Khanal, K., & Prajapati, B. (2023). Influence of demographic factors on the entrepreneurial intentions of business students in Nepal. *Journal of Economic Sciences, 2*(1), 1–12. https://doi.org/10.55603/jes.v2i1.a1

Ma, W., Rahut, D. B., Sonobe, T., & Gong, B. (2024). Linking farmers to markets: Barriers, solutions, and policy options. *Economic Analysis and Policy, 82*, 1102–1112. https://doi.org/10.1016/j.eap.2024.05.005

Muhammad, S., Ximei, K., Saqib, S. E., & Beutell, N. J. (2021a). Women's home-based entrepreneurship and family financial position in Pakistan. *Sustainability, 13*(22), 12542. https://doi.org/10.3390/su132212542

Muhammad, S., Kong, X., Saqib, S. E., & Beutell, N. J. (2021b). Entrepreneurial income and wellbeing: Women's informal entrepreneurship in a developing context. *Sustainability, 13*(18), 10262. https://doi.org/10.3390/su131810262

Neupane, S. M., Bhattarai, P. C., & Lowery, C. L. (2025). Personality traits in describing entrepreneurial intentions: A sequential mixed methods study. *Journal of Innovation and Entrepreneurship, 14*, 50. https://doi.org/10.1186/s13731-024-00459-4

Ojediran, F., & Anderson, A. (2020). Women's entrepreneurship in the Global South: Empowering and emancipating? *Administrative Sciences, 10*(4), 87. https://doi.org/10.3390/admsci10040087

Pokhrel, R. K. (2025). Prosperity through tradition: Traditional skills and level of income generation in Nepal. *Teacher Half-Yearly Journal, 17*(1), 191–201.

Prajapati, B., & Khanal, K. (2023). Perception of entrepreneurial ecosystem factors: Comparison among students and entrepreneurs. *Asian Journal of Management Studies, 3*(1), 79–102. https://doi.org/10.4038/ajms.v3i1.61

Rashid, M., Anser, M., Shah, S., & others. (2025). Fostering entrepreneurship: Analyzing the influence of access to finance, innovation investment, educational attainment, infrastructure development, and regulatory environment. *Future Business Journal, 11*, Article 140. https://doi.org/10.1186/s43093-025-00557-z

Ratten, V. (2023). Entrepreneurship: Definitions, opportunities, challenges, and future directions. *Global Business and Organizational Excellence, 42*(5), 79–90. https://doi.org/10.1002/joe.22217

SABAH Nepal. (2023). *Annual report: Home-based work and market access.* SABAH Nepal.

Sah, B. N. (2020). Home-based workers and their ownership in Nepal. *Patan Pragya, 7*(1), 255–267. https://doi.org/10.3126/pragya.v7i1.35250

Schumpeter, J. A. (1934). *The theory of economic development: An inquiry into profits, capital, credit, interest, and the business cycle.* Harvard University Press. (Original work published in 1911)

Sharma, L. K., & Paudel, V. (2025). The role of SMEs in enhancing women's employment opportunities in Nepal: A data-driven perspective. *Cognition: Journal of Psychology and Education, 7*(1). https://doi.org/10.3126/cognition.v7i1.74727

Thapa Karki, S., Xheneti, M., & Madden, A. (2021). To formalize or not to formalize: Women entrepreneurs' sensemaking of business registration in the context of Nepal. *Journal of Business Ethics, 173*(4), 687–708. https://doi.org/10.1007/s10551-020-04541-1

UNCDF. (2023). *Empowering women-led small businesses in Nepal to go digital.* United Nations Capital Development Fund. https://www.uncdf.org/article/7828/empowering-women-led-small-businesses-in-nepal-to-go-digital

UN Women. (2023). *Towards inclusive MSME sector growth in Nepal.* United Nations Entity for Gender Equality and the Empowerment of Women. https://asiapacific.unwomen.org/sites/default/files/2023-07/np-towards-inclusive-msme-sector-growth-in-nepal-s.pdf

Wiklund, J., Nikolaev, B., Shir, N., Foo, M.-D., & Bradley, S. (2019). Entrepreneurship and well-being: Past, present, and future. *Journal of Business Venturing, 34*(4), 579–588. https://doi.org/10.1016/j.jbusvent.2019.01.002

World Bank. (2021). *Women's non-farm employment in Nepal: A landscape review of organizations and interventions.* World Bank. https://documents1.worldbank.org/curated/en/880741611555598446/pdf/Women-s-Non-Farm-Employment-in-Nepal-A-Landscape-Review-of-Organizations-and-Interventions.pdf

Xheneti, M., Karki, S. T., & Madden, A. (2018). Negotiating business and family demands within a patriarchal society—The case of women entrepreneurs in the Nepalese context. *Entrepreneurship & Regional Development, 31*(3–4), 259–278.

Xheneti, M., & Madden, A. (2024). Women's entrepreneurship in the informal economy: A socio-spatial perspective. *Human Relations.*

Shradha Adhikari is a graduate student of Business and Economics at Kathmandu University School of Management. She has worked with AIESEC in Nepal for four years and currently contributes as a freelancer across areas of business development and research projects. She aspires to become an economist focused on research and policy that uplifts communities in Nepal and the Global South. She is committed to learning, contributing meaningfully through research, and building a career rooted in service, equity, and impact.

Krishna Khanal is an Assistant Professor of Marketing and ethics at King's college. He was previously working as a Research analyst at Nanyang Technological University, Singapore. He has also worked for various multinationals like BOSCH GmbH and AXA in various managerial roles. His teaching philosophy is focused on provoking the students to question the basic narratives of business models in society.

Catalyzing Asian Women's Entrepreneurship in the E-Commerce Ecosystem: A Case Report and Policy Analysis of Cambodia

Rongtitya Rith and Riccardo Spinelli

Abstract Advancements in information and communication technology (ICT) provide tremendous potential for micro, small, and medium-sized enterprises (MSMEs) to utilize e-commerce and enhance their digital business practices. In Southeast Asia, the regional digital economy has witnessed a surging increase in electronic businesses (e-businesses) on both social media and e-commerce platforms. Since the emergence of COVID-19, female entrepreneurs increasingly utilize and optimize social media and e-commerce platforms to sustain and innovate their business-to-business (B2B) and business-to-consumer (B2C) activities. This study aims to provide a case report and policy analysis of Cambodia concerning its entrepreneurial landscape for women conducting e-businesses. The key findings provide a narrative analysis of the salient features and characteristics of the e-commerce environment of Cambodia, as well as the existing opportunities, challenges, and initiatives for women-led MSMEs. The commentary discussion highlights certain policy recommendations surrounding the issues of data collection and research efforts, business registration and formalization, access to digital training, access to finance, incentivization and support, and digital infrastructure.

1 Introduction: Research Background and Context

In Southeast Asia (SEA), recent technological advancements and adoptions of information and communication technologies (ICTs) have tremendous potential in reinforcing and empowering entrepreneurial intentions and participations among women. Specifically, social media (e.g., Facebook, Instagram, Telegram, TikTok, etc.) and e-commerce platforms (e.g., AliExpress, Taobao, Temu, Shein, Lazada, Shopee, etc.) have emerged and expanded rapidly in SEA both during and after the COVID-19

R. Rith (✉) · R. Spinelli
Department of Economics, University of Genoa, Genoa, GE, Italy
e-mail: rongtitya.rith@edu.unige.it

R. Spinelli
e-mail: riccardo.spinelli@unige.it

T. Endress and Y. F. Badir (eds.), *Business and Management in Asia: Opportunities and Entrepreneurship*, https://doi.org/10.1007/978-981-95-4909-2_10

pandemic, bringing both disruptive and positive changes to how women-led businesses are conducted (Braun et al., 2023; Chikh-Amnache & Mekhzoumi, 2024; Guelich & Xavier, 2017; Roscoe & Ntim, 2022). Consequently, female entrepreneurs increasingly utilize and optimize those social media and e-commerce platforms to sustain and innovate their business-to-business (B2B) and business-to-consumer (B2C) activities (Braun et al., 2023; Chikh-Amnache & Mekhzoumi, 2024).

During the rampant COVID-19 pandemic and subsequent lockdowns on socio-economic activities, e-commerce emerged as a lifeline for businesses of all sizes, including micro, small, and medium-sized enterprises (MSMEs), to prevail and redefine their purposes and values (Chan, 2022). The COVID-19 pandemic has highlighted the essence of e-commerce as a mechanism for sustaining and innovating businesses (UNCTAD, 2020). Consequently, it becomes even more imperative and urgent for women-led businesses, particularly the micro and small ones, to optimize e-commerce to accommodate their needs and those of the business markets. This perspective is crucial in practice to align with the objectives, set forth by UNESCAP[1] (2017) in the "Regional Roadmap for Implementing the 2030 Agenda for Sustainable Development Goals (SDGs) in Asia and the Pacific", which have emphasized gender equality and women empowerment as key issues in the policy agenda. Despite the optimistic outlook, women's entrepreneurship has not reached its pinnacle in the increasingly complex and competitive e-commerce environment in SEA (Braun et al., 2023; Chikh-Amnache & Mekhzoumi, 2024; Guelich & Xavier, 2017). It is also noteworthy that there is limited research that specifically addresses women's entrepreneurial capabilities and successes in the broader e-commerce ecosystem, particularly in developing Asian countries (Braun et al., 2023; Chikh-Amnache & Mekhzoumi, 2024; Sörensson & Ghannad, 2024).

In SEA, women's entrepreneurship, despite some successes, remains an underutilized catalyst for social and economic progress. Various recent studies and research reports have largely indicated that female entrepreneurs in less developed countries in SEA and the Pacific face barriers and challenges in accessing financial capital and ICTs needed to grow and innovate their businesses (e.g., Braun et al., 2023; Chikh-Amnache & Mekhzoumi, 2024; Guelich & Xavier, 2017; Roscoe & Ntim, 2022; UNESCAP, 2018, 2019, 2022, 2023). While the socio-economic landscape of SEA has become more inclusive for female entrepreneurs in recent years (UNDP,[2] 2020; UNESCAP, 2022, 2023; UN Women,[3] 2018), this study proposes that it is timely and imperative to determine the status quo concerning the existing opportunities, challenges, and characteristics of the broad e-commerce ecosystem in SEA. In the case of Cambodia, roughly 60% of businesses are run by women, among which, 26% of businesses classified as small or medium in size, while 62% of them are micro-sized and women-led (UNESCAP, 2023). The e-commerce market capitalization has been estimated to surpass $1 billion in 2024 and keep growing exponentially at a compound annual growth rate (CAGR) of almost 10% from 2024 to 2029 to reach almost $2

[1] UNESCAP—United Nations Economic and Social Commission for Asia and the Pacific.

[2] UNDP—United Nations Development Programme.

[3] UN Women—United Nations Entity for Gender Equality and the Empowerment of Women.

billion (ADB,[4] 2024; Profitence, 2025). Although women-led businesses represent a considerable segment of the country's e-commerce market, the influential role of women's entrepreneurship remains as an under-utilized catalyst for the long-term economic growth and development of the country.

Considering the afore-mentioned perspectives, the framing of this study is also characterized by the theoretical underpinnings of the digital divide perspective. In the contexts of women's digital entrepreneurship and ICT utilization, the extant research has yielded inconclusive results on a global scale (Hilbert, 2011). While some scholars claim that women are rather more technophobic than men in certain developing countries in the Global South, others assert that women also embrace ICTs more in the Global North (e.g., Ahmed, 2024; Al Jamil & Ahmed Ismail, 2024; Al-Omoush et al., 2023; Brahem & Boussema, 2023; Chatterjee et al., 2020; Gupta & Butt, 2024; Liao et al., 2021; Salmizi & Abd Aziz, 2023; Yu & Cui, 2019). Hilbert (2011) stated that the digital divide against women is tied to their unfavorable conditions with respect to employment, education, and income. On a positive note, some scholars (e.g., Hilbert, 2011; Van Deursen, 2017; Van Dijk, 2017) also presented the alleged digital divide as an opportunity to further cultivate women's affinity for and access to ICTs and consequently tackle persistent gender inequality issues in developing countries. This perspective is central to this study and worth elucidating amid the continuous growth of digital entrepreneurship. In terms of accessibility, the digital divide has provided insights into the determinants and consequences of access to ICTs (Van Dijk, 2017). Simultaneously, the growth of ICTs also demands digital and media literacy to enable individuals to participate more effectively in the wider society (Van Deursen, 2017). In this study, the digital divide notion is contextualized in the women's entrepreneurship field. This implies that if female entrepreneurs perceive social media and e-commerce platforms as accessible, usable, and beneficial for their businesses, they are more likely to leverage the digital tools to advance their business operations. In fact, certain studies have shown that positive attitudes toward digital entrepreneurship significantly influence female entrepreneurs' decisions to engage with the platforms (e.g., Ahmed, 2024; Al Jamil & Ahmed Ismail, 2024; Al-Omoush et al., 2023; Brahem & Boussema, 2023; Chatterjee et al., 2020; Gupta & Butt, 2024; Liao et al., 2021; Salmizi & Abd Aziz, 2023; Yu & Cui, 2019).

2 Research Aim and Objectives

The aim of this study is to conduct a case study report and policy analysis of a specific country context (i.e., Cambodia) concerning its entrepreneurial landscape for women conducting businesses on social media and e-commerce platforms. Specifically, the principal research purpose is to enhance the knowledge and capacity of female entrepreneurs in their application and utilization of social media and e-commerce

[4] ADB—Asian Development Bank.

platforms to facilitate their businesses and participate in the local, regional, or even international global supply chain networks.

This qualitative case report contributes to the nascent field of Asian women's entrepreneurship research and responds to the appeals from Ahi et al. (2023), Samy et al. (2023), and Sörensson and Ghannad (2024) whose empirical works advocate for a closer examination of existing opportunities and challenges catalyzed through women's entrepreneurial participation in the digital economy. Thus, the following research objectives are outlined. First, this chapter aims to characterize Cambodia's entrepreneurial landscape to inform about the know-how of female entrepreneurs conducting businesses on social media and e-commerce platforms. Second, this study intends to explicate their perceived importance of a digitally enhanced business model with a proper consideration of the existing opportunities and challenges. The third and final objective is to inform about the relevant policies and initiatives that are currently reinforcing and fostering women's entrepreneurial participation at a country-level analysis.

The remainder of this study is organized as follows. The next section outlines the qualitative case report methodology. The key findings concerning Cambodia's digital economy and e-commerce landscape for women, as well as the prevalent opportunities and challenges are presented in the following section. Then the next following section discusses the policy implications and existing government initiatives. Finally, the last section concludes by reiterating the key findings and highlighting the implications of the study.

3 Methodology

This study utilizes a qualitative case report method. In essence, *a case report* provides a detailed and insightful examination of a specific situation by drawing connections to relevant knowledge and potentially offering solutions or recommendations (Rashid et al., 2019). While *case study* research is more systematic as a stringent methodological framework for developing an in-depth understanding of one or more case(s) that represent(s) bounded systems (Yin, 2018), Marin-Garcia et al. (2022) denote that a case report, as an alternative strategy, is useful for presenting a story in a narrative manner to include concerns, conditions, interventions, and outcomes of a phenomenon or context, and "the narrative should include a discussion of the rationale for any conclusions and lessons learned" (p. 108). In this regard, this study is structured in the said format of a case report with an aim to synthesize important insights and implications in existing studies, project reports, organizational or institutional documents, and policy documents, focusing on entrepreneurial capacity building for women-led e-businesses in Cambodia. Those organizational or institutional documents may come from a variety of sources, including but not limited to, the *Asian Development Bank (ADB)*, *Cambodia Development Resource Institute (CDRI)*,

Cambodia Investment Review (CIR), Open Development Cambodia (ODC), Organisation for Economic Co-operation and Development (OECD), United Nations Development Programme (UNDP), United Nations Economic and Social Commission for Asia and the Pacific (UNESCAP), World Trade Organization (WTO), etc.

In total, 33 documents have been specifically analyzed (see Appendix 1). The documents are beneficial for providing up-to-date empirical evidence in various forms of institutional reports, longitudinal studies, policy documents and briefs, project outcomes, etc. Analyzing such documents in case report research typically involves a systematic approach to extract meaningful insights (Ibarra et al., 2023). Through an inductive content analysis technique, important implications in those documents were collected and recorded in a research note. As the dataset comprises a large corpus of textual data, the open coding process was intended to specifically characterize Cambodia's e-commerce ecosystem in the context of women's entrepreneurship, along with the existing opportunities, challenges, and relevant policies and initiatives in the country's digital economy. This implies a thorough examination of the country case itself, while also synthesizing other relevant implications in the existing literature, as well as those embedded in other similar country settings (Houghton et al., 2017). This perspective is in line with that of Yin (1994, p. 151) who has noted that such a case report "must be composed in an engaging manner" with sufficient evidence to support its findings. This approach to gathering insights, as well as any empirically driven data embedded within the documents, is essential for ensuring the study's rigor and quality.

4 Findings

In this section, the key findings are presented in the three following sub-sections to elucidate on: "Cambodia's Digital Economy and E-Commerce Landscape for Women", "Opportunities and Initiatives", and "Challenges."

4.1 Cambodia's Digital Economy and E-Commerce Landscape for Women

According to the Economic Census of Cambodia's Ministry of Planning (2022), the country has had over 750,000 business establishments, with women owning over 69% of them. Majority of those businesses are micro, small, and medium-sized enterprises (MSMEs) with a low record of employees. According to Chhorn (2025), a recent survey conducted by Cambodia Development Research Institute (CDRI), in partnership with the Asian Development Bank (ADB), using primary data from 414 MSMEs and 32 key informant interviews, highlighted that businesses in Cambodia are mostly small and informal. Almost 50% of the businesses are individual-run, and many lack formal registration, a persistent barrier that keeps limiting their access to finance, business networks, and other resources. This informality specifically affects women-led businesses, holding back their ability to scale, innovate, and adopt digital tools and practices.

The Asian Development Bank (ADB, 2024) has projected that the Cambodian e-commerce market value in 2024 has reached approximately $1.12 billion. In the near future, the market is anticipated to grow at a compound annual growth rate (CAGR) of 9.98% from 2024 to 2029, potentially reaching a volume of $1.81 billion by 2029 (Profitence, 2025). Nevertheless, Cambodian MSMEs remain uncompetitive due to limited organizational capacity, insufficient productivity, and a lack of access to information (ADB, 2024). The whole e-commerce ecosystem remains sub-par in online presence despite a huge and young consumer market with increasing access to the Internet and mobile phone services (Datareportal, 2024). As a result, access to finance remains a challenge for most MSMEs. Promoting the internationalization of MSMEs by strengthening their participation in global value chains is one way to unlock productivity and inclusive growth (Ahi et al., 2023). However, very few Cambodian MSMEs trade internationally or are integrated into the regional value chains of SEA.

Notably, several large-scale nation-wide projects, conducted by ADB (2024), IFC[5] (2019), UNESCAP (2019), etc., have emphasized the potential of digitalization as a force that equips enterprises, particularly the micro and small ones, with opportunities to grow, innovate, access new markets, and compete by improving access to information. Digital technology, as a linking element, also plays an important role in fostering regional commerce and trade. However, Cambodian MSMEs have yet to fully embrace digitalization. In 2021, Cambodia ranked 92nd out of 146 countries on the Cisco Digital Readiness Index (ADB, 2024). Many Cambodian entrepreneurs lack awareness of the benefits of digitalization, perceiving it as complex and costly, with little practical relevance to their businesses. On another note, MSMEs also lack awareness of the initiatives, solutions, and policy guidance provided by the public (i.e., government) and private (i.e., business) sectors, as well as other national or international institutions that provide financial assistance, skill building, capacity building, etc. This persistent issue poses a knowledge gap between all the entities involved in contributing and operating in the whole digital economy.

Considering these dynamics, significant transformations in the digital economy and workforce are necessary. In this regard, the shift toward digital business practices is crucial for a sustainable growth, particularly within women-owned MSMEs, which represent a prolific segment and a cornerstone of the country's economy. Female entrepreneurs, particularly in micro and small enterprises, represent considerable yet under-utilized potential within this sector. Although Cambodia boasts a higher incidence of female entrepreneurs compared to men, women-owned businesses tend to be smaller, have lower average sales, and have fewer employees (IFC, 2019; UNESCAP, 2018, 2019, 2022, 2023). Advances in disruptive technologies do not

[5] IFC—International Finance Corporation.

always translate into advances in gender equality, and to date, there is limited research that has addressed women's entrepreneurial participation in e-commerce.

4.2 Opportunities and Initiatives

In recent years, Cambodia's digital economy has been undergoing a profound transformation, driven by rapid technological advancements, increasing consumer access to social media platforms, and concerted efforts to strengthen the regulatory and institutional landscape (ADB, 2024). At the core of this transformation is e-commerce, which has emerged as a key enabler of economic growth, business competitiveness, market access, and opportunities for MSMEs. The expansion of the Cambodian e-commerce sector reflects the government's stronger commitment toward digital transformation, as outlined in the Pentagonal Strategy Phase I and the Digital Economy and Society Policy Framework 2021–2035 (Profitence, 2025). It becomes more apparent that significant progress has been made in recent years, with noticeable improvements in digital payment systems, logistics, and consumer trust mechanisms.

As Cambodia continues to deepen its digital integration, the evolution from e-commerce to a broader digital trade ecosystem will be instrumental in ensuring long-term economic resilience and global competitiveness, particularly within SEA. The Ministry of Commerce is also taking decisive steps to become more fit-for-purpose in supporting Cambodia's e-commerce and digital trade ambitions since 2021 (Profitence, 2025). By strengthening its institutional capacity, the ministry aims to provide more dedicated support to industries, ensuring that both businesses and consumers can fully leverage arising opportunities presented by digital transformation (Profitence, 2025). The Cambodia Digital Trade Policy, which was still being formulated in 2024, will further enhance e-commerce in the nation's digital economy, providing a clear strategic direction to foster innovation, improve digital readiness, and create a more dynamic and prolific environment for MSMEs (Profitence, 2025).

Overall, opportunities to remain resilient for enterprises depend on the economic and social environment in which female entrepreneurs operate, as well as the government policies and programs that enable inclusive development (Kuckerz & Brändle, 2021). In this regard, the support system for women's entrepreneurship in Cambodia can be theorized as an entrepreneurial ecosystem that may create a favorable environment for inclusive growth. Thus, a conducive culture is needed for a more accessible and inclusive entrepreneurial ecosystem for Cambodian female entrepreneurs which may include availability of appropriate finance for entrepreneurial start-ups, quality human capital, market access, and a range of institutional and policy supports. Considering these notions, policy advancements have been more apparent in recent years to foster the digital economy of Cambodia. Table 1 outlines the key initiatives on e-commerce and digital trade put forward and implemented by the Cambodia's government within the last three years (2022–2024).

Another noteworthy point is the Cambodian women's labor force participation rate (80% in 2019), which is one of the highest rates in the world, and women own 65%

Table 1 Cambodia's e-commerce policy advancements

2022	2023	2024
- MoC has signed an MOU with Swiss contact to initiate a project entitled "SeT4SME" - Draft: Personal Data Protection Law - Cambodia goes digital: CamDX - Draft Cyber-Security Law - CamDigiKey: Easy yet secure - Mobile Authentication Service - CamDL elevates Cambodia's fintech sector - Government has started to implement e-commerce VAT - Cambodia Digital Government Policy 2022–2035 - Cambodiatrade.com to promote e-commerce and prepare to export to foreign markets	- Digital Technology Strategic Plan 2023–2027 - ASEAN launches negotiations of the world's first regional Digital Economy Framework Agreement (DEFA) - FinTech Development Policy (2023–2028) - Government Pentagonal Strategy Phase I (2023–2028)	- Cambodia launches the national single window for trade facilitation - Draft: Cambodia Digital Trade Policy - Draft: Cambodia E-commerce Trustmark Scheme - Establishment of Trade Policy Advisory Board (TPAB) - Cambodia Trade Policy Framework Toward 2030 (CTPF) - EU-German Gate (2024–2028) - Cambodia launches Tourist App with KHQR Payments - New government e-invoicing system boosts the digital economy - Bakong expands to more Asian countries - Cambodia introduces a digital platform for informal business registration - Cambodia launches first Digital, Media, and Information Literacy Framework - Cambodia Digital Skill Development Roadmap (2024–2035) - Draft: Code of conduct for intermediaries and e-commerce service providers

Source Profitence (2025)

of the country's MSMEs, a rate unparalleled in other Southeast Asian economies (Profitence, 2025). Demographically, Cambodia is home to the second youngest population in SEA with a median age of 26 (Profitence, 2025). This demographic feature offers a prolific ecosystem for online businesses catered to consumers who are younger, tech-savvy, and in favor of online retailing and shopping. In fact, micro-sized enterprises typically use smart phones and basic digital tools for sales and marketing but lack the necessary infrastructure for broader digitalization. In contrast, small and medium-sized enterprises (SMEs) tend to adopt a wider range of digital tools, and interestingly, the adoption of digital practices does not show significant gender differences when comparing businesses of similar sizes.

On a similar note, as it is relatively convenient and cost-effective enough to utilize the internet to conduct business, even micro and small firms can participate in e-commerce (OECD, 2019a, 2019b). With user-friendly platforms, those smaller firms can set up operations without the full range of traditional in-house resources such as extensive and sophisticated ICT equipment, a marketing and sales department, and the expertise to establish and maintain a website presence (UNCTAD, 2015). E-commerce also helps MSMEs by removing the traditional geographic distance barriers and dramatically lowering information acquisition costs.

Regardless of ownership, MSMEs adopt similar levels of digital technologies. Notably, Facebook and TikTok have reshaped Cambodia's sales and advertising landscape, empowering women-led businesses and stimulating the e-commerce market for both MSMEs and big corporations. According to Datareportal (2024), Facebook remains as Cambodia's leading social networking platform, with almost 12 million users, reaching 70% of the population in 2024. Facebook has been serving as a primary channel for online purchases, driven by live sales and small business pages. Likewise, TikTok has reached 9.96 million users (90% of Cambodian adults). According to the most recent study on Cambodia's e-commerce landscape by Profitence (2025), Facebook is the most used social media site for online purchases, followed by TikTok, Telegram, and Instagram, etc. Notably, fashion and apparel, beauty and cosmetics, and food are the most dominant product categories in online purchases, followed by electronics, healthcare, transportation, etc. (Profitence, 2025). The study also reveals that promotions and convenience drive purchases, while quality, authenticity, fraud, and payment security remain as key concerns in purchasing online.

On a separate note, there are two noteworthy initiatives that focus on empowering women's participation in e-commerce, namely Accelerate and SHE Investments. The "Accelerate Women's Entrepreneurship and Access to Capital" initiative or *Accelerate* is a project funded by the VISA Foundation and implemented by The Asia Foundation (2023). The initiative aims to provide training of digital skills to women-led micro and small businesses in Cambodia and the Philippines. The training courses include financial literacy training, business skills and financial planning, and the use of e-commerce and social media platforms. The project also aims to link women entrepreneurs with financial institutions and services. Likewise, *SHE Investments*, is the first gender-focused, culturally tailored incubator for women-owned micro and small business entities in Cambodia. Launched in 2015, the social enterprise offers a range of business incubators, accelerators, and investment-readiness programs designed specifically for women micro-entrepreneurs. The initiative has also introduced innovative digital tools to help women improve their financial management. SHE Investments is one of 15 innovative fintech start-ups supported by the Catalyzing Women's Entrepreneurship project of UNESCAP (2022).

4.3 Challenges

Notwithstanding the progress, it is equally important to note the existing challenges manifesting within the contemporary landscape of MSMEs in Cambodia. Despite the importance of this sector, micro and small businesses face a variety of growth challenges, including access to finance, market access, low productivity, and a need for more qualified and skilled labor. These issues also disproportionately affect women-led enterprises. Access to capital is one of the most significant barriers for Cambodian MSMEs, and the issue can limit their growth, success, and competitiveness in local and international markets.

In the context of e-commerce, a persistent challenge many Cambodian women-led businesses face is understanding and accessing finance. While women make up the ownership majority of MSMEs, they face systematic challenges including informal business registration, restricted access to information, limited opportunities for skills training and capacity-building programs, financial constraints, and barriers to business aspirations and networking (IFC, 2019, 2023). Additional challenges may include insufficient infrastructure, cyber-security concerns, and limited regulatory frameworks to support the adoption of digital tools. Smaller firms, which are dominated by female ownership, tend to rely more on manual processes and use fewer digital tools in their business operations (OECD, 2021). Although those entrepreneurs have adequate access to e-payment systems to operate their e-businesses, the sophistication and development of e-payment systems are still lacking and not widely accessible to some women-led businesses. Thus, this study is supportive of and in line with the notion of ICT readiness to incorporate the influence of technological complexities on small businesses (Dyerson et al., 2016).

Another issue primarily concerns the fact that Cambodia's MSMEs also have limited market access. Some MSMEs, including those owned by women, operate in remote and rural areas (Profitence, 2025). This is compounded by weak logistics infrastructure, making transporting goods to market complex and costly. Most MSMEs also lack international quality standards to compete in foreign markets. Furthermore, MSMEs in Cambodia may face regulatory and compliance challenges due to a growing yet complex regulatory environment that can be difficult to navigate.

In addition, today's digital business climate requires digital literacy comprising meta competencies ranging from digital know-how, to understanding business models, negotiation and communication skills (Braun, 2010). E-commerce carries a higher risk of dropping out for many Asian women, who tend to possess lower digital skills and have less time to engage in online activities due to disproportionate household responsibilities (OECD, 2021). Especially for women-led MSMEs and informal enterprises in developing countries, pivoting to an e-commerce model can be challenging due to the lack of ICT literacy, stable internet access, e-business skills, and e-payment capabilities.

5 Discussion

In addition to providing an in-depth analysis of the current e-commerce landscape of Cambodia, along with its salient characteristics, opportunities, and challenges, this study also intends to characterize Cambodia's e-commerce public policy, highlight its digital divide, and provide policy recommendations.

5.1 Government Policy for Fostering Entrepreneurial Ecosystems

Government policy is seen as an important pillar to build a strong entrepreneurial ecosystem for women. Ecosystem policy is always contextual and thus embedded in the social, cultural, and political institutions of its environment (Yousafzai et al., 2015). There is a well-established body of literature on how well entrepreneurial ecosystem policies support women-led MSMEs (e.g., Braun, 2018; Brush et al., 2019; Foss et al., 2019; Orser et al., 2019). In Cambodia, the institutional environment influences entrepreneurial activities and business trajectories. This regard, Cambodian women's participation in the digital economy is predicated on this approach.

While in theory, entrepreneurs are assumed to benefit equally from resources within their respective ecosystem, this is not often the case (Brush et al., 2019). Indeed, research has shown that entrepreneurial ecosystems do not support female entrepreneurs to the extent that they do with male entrepreneurs (Brush et al., 2019). While women-led MSMEs in Cambodia are not intrinsically less productive, an inherent gender bias obstructs female entrepreneurs from equal access to ecosystem resources such as finance and markets. Gender and international trade research domains similarly point toward the role of government and weak collaborations within ecosystems in deterring female entrepreneurs from equal access to ecosystem pillars (Braun, 2018; Orser et al., 2019). Thus, it is timely and imperative to reiterate the importance of effective e-commerce policymaking that specifically cultivates and sustains entrepreneurial ecosystems.

This study also re-affirms that there is still little empirical evidence indicating that contemporary policies in Cambodia address gender inequalities to increase women's participation in the digital economy. Nor do calls for inclusive economic development appear to be heeded to achieve the sustainable development agenda. At present, women's entrepreneurship policies in Cambodia are not sufficiently underpinned by knowledge and a framework that engage and support women within their business ecosystems, making the extant policies remain unresponsive.

5.2 The Importance of E-Commerce Public Policy

Public policies are actions that governments undertake to set goals and utilize means or tools to achieve such goals (Howlett & Cashore, 2020). Public policymaking is a dynamic process that is usually the result of a set of inter-related decisions that cumulatively contribute to an outcome (Howlett & Cashore, 2014). In the context of e-commerce, governments can allocate resources to the development and growth of ICT infrastructure and provide access to reliable and affordable ICT services (UNCTAD, 2019). This is important as ICT is a key building block of the digital economy which facilitates and drives e-commerce for Cambodia (OECD, 2017). Through public policy, the Cambodian government can also design, implement, and communicate up-to-date legal and regulatory frameworks that provide a supportive and inclusive business environment for e-commerce. Such frameworks may include laws and regulations for electronic documents and e-signature, electronic payments, customer protection measures such as the right of withdrawal (procedures for returning products), and privacy and data protection regulations, including safeguards for the use of personal information (OECD, 2017). These policies can provide an adequate legal and regulatory framework that mitigates transaction risks and provides transparency within e-commerce (OECD, 2017, 2019a, 2019b).

In the e-commerce context, there remains a large variation in e-commerce and digital trade policies across countries. At the same time, there is a paucity of academic research on public policy related to e-commerce, with majority of existing studies adopting a firm-level perspective (Braun et al., 2023). However, digital transformation is not driven only by private decision-making; this study proposes that the role of government policy plays a pivotal role in the process, particularly in the context of women-led e-businesses. In this regard, many governments, including that of Cambodia, have recognized the importance of policy frameworks as a driver of e-commerce participation, and that e-commerce has since become a top priority for policymakers at national, regional, and global levels since the mid-1990s (OECD, 2019a, 2019b).

The availability and quality of ICT infrastructure, as well as the necessary capabilities with respect to the deployment of new technologies, play an important role in the e-commerce diffusion within a country (Shih et al., 2005). The extent to which these factors are available is arguably the main driver of the e-commerce adoption gap between developed and developing countries (Ahi et al., 2023). Concerning the e-commerce setting of Cambodia, it appears that the digital divide as noted by Norris (2001) persists today. Although there has been promising progress in women's entrepreneurial intention and participation during the last several years in Cambodia, it is imperative that this study also reiterates certain challenges that persist in today's digital economy. As noted in various research reports and extant studies, although ICT infrastructure and digital literacy are important factors in the growth of the e-commerce sector, they need to be complemented by high-quality public policies

(Okoli et al., 2010; Oxley & Yeung, 2001; Shih et al., 2005). However, governments in developing and least developed countries tend to require help from international bodies with the development of such policies. This is applicable to the case of Cambodia as well, and to promote e-commerce and its inclusion of women-led MSMEs, certain initiatives have been launched over the past several years as illustrated above. On a global scale, there has been multi-stakeholder initiatives that aim to help developing countries participate more efficiently in e-commerce, including the "eTrade for All" initiative launched in 2016 during a UNCTAD (2016) conference.

5.3 *The Digital Divide Perspective*

In the digital divide perspective, when applied to women's digital entrepreneurship in Cambodia, the notion highlights the gap in access to and usage of digital technologies that hinders women's business growth and economic empowerment. This divide, in line with the perspective of Hilbert (2011), is not solely about access to technology, but also encompasses issues like affordability, digital literacy, and socio-cultural norms that can limit Cambodian women's ability to fully leverage digital tools for their ventures. The so-called digital divide was simply about the uneven distribution of access to the Internet, manifesting in exclusion and inequality due to socio-economic and cultural norms that persist in Cambodia's wider society at large. While technological inventions were believed to be beyond women's capabilities in the past (Eastin et al., 2015), this kind of digital divide is now referred to as a first-level digital divide (Scheerder et al., 2017). With the arrival of high-speed broadband Internet and telephone connectivity in Cambodia, the focus of the digital divide discourse emphasizes a second-level digital divide which includes a wider array of digital skills. In the Fourth Industrial Revolution (4IR) driven by groundbreaking technologies such as Artificial Intelligence (AI), Internet of Things (IoT), Blockchain and Virtual Reality (VR), Cambodia can reap the greatest benefits by reinforcing female entrepreneurs to adapt to the digital environment and acquire the digital literacy skills to navigate the e-business environment.

A decade ago, the role of ICT in the digital economy, not only in terms of optimized production processes, but also in terms of information and knowledge management, product consumption, distribution and trade, appeared to provide significant economic opportunities for women entrepreneurs (Braun, 2010). However, when it came to using digital technologies, there proved to be a glaring digital divide for women-led enterprises in terms of equal access to the internet and digital e-commerce platforms. In line with the perspective of Braun (2010) and Van Deursen et al. (2016), disadvantages experienced by women entrepreneurs in Cambodia were attributable not only to a lack of local or regional access to technology and infrastructure, but also to a lack of comprehensive digital and strategic skills to conduct e-businesses. This created a clear gendered order in technology, whereby women became frequently positioned as end users and men as primary innovators and designers. It also created a wide-spread perception that women were under-represented in the technology sector which, in turn, triggered a range of government initiative to attract, promote, and retain women to study and pursue careers in ICTs (Bernhardt et al., 2018).

5.4 Policy Recommendations: The Case of Cambodia

To align with Cambodia's long-term development goals, the growth of MSMEs must embrace digital transformation. In the context of women's entrepreneurship in the e-commerce sphere, gender inclusivity is essential for unlocking the full potential of the workforce, fostering innovation, sustainability, and economic resilience (Chhorn, 2025). Considering the afore-mentioned implications associated with the essence of e-commerce policy and the alleged digital divide perspective, the Cambodian digital entrepreneurial landscape possesses distinctive features that comprise both strengths vis-à-vis opportunities and weaknesses vis-à-vis threats that shape and influence its own institutional policy. Notably, underdeveloped logistics, outdated payment systems, digital illiteracy, etc. remain persistent to hinder growth. While Cambodia is dominated by a younger demographic who are more tech-savvy to ICTs, supportive policies are growing accordingly in the last several years to foster both domestic and international e-commerce and foreign investment. Table 2 illustrates an analysis of the strengths, weaknesses, opportunities, and threats (SWOT) of the Cambodia's e-commerce ecosystem.

In this study, the following policy recommendations are proposed with an aim to support the digital transition of MSMEs with a proper consideration of women's entrepreneurial participation in the digital economy.

More Data Collection and Research Effort: Formalization may be a significant challenge, given that the majority of MSMEs in Cambodia operate informally and lack registration. However, the immediate priority should be on strengthening data collection efforts to better understand the landscape. Conducting regular surveys with both formal and informal MSME owners, particularly the female ones, will provide valuable insights into the challenges they face and their reluctance to register. Additionally, establishing dedicated research bodies or entities to analyze MSME trends, inform policy decisions, and track progress on formalization efforts will be crucial in designing effective strategies for sustainable growth and integration into the formal economy.

Encouraging Registration and Promoting Formalization: Promoting stronger links between economic development and MSMEs in Cambodia begins with a well-defined strategy for MSMEs formalization. Formalization serves as the foundation for effective economic governance, enabling the government to collect essential data on SMEs challenges, opportunities, and needs. This, in turn, informs evidence-based policymaking and facilitates targeted investments in infrastructure and human capital, benefiting businesses of all sizes, not just large enterprises. To encourage MSMEs to register, administrative burdens should be reduced, and tax benefits or financial incentives should be introduced. Strengthening linkages between MSMEs and foreign investment will allow formalized businesses to integrate into supply

Table 2 SWOT analysis of Cambodia's e-commerce ecosystem

Strengths	**Opportunities**
- *Rapid Digital Penetration*: A growing number of Cambodians have access to smart phones and the internet, driving online consumer engagement - *Young, Tech-Savvy Population*: The predominantly young demographic is quick to utilize digital platforms for online shopping - *Supportive Government Policies*: Recent initiatives and strategies (e.g., the E-Commerce Strategy 2023–2030) are fostering growth - *Rising Social Media Usage*: High levels of social media engagement facilitate e-businesses	- *Untapped Market Potential*: With a rising middle class and an increasing disposable income, there is room for market expansion - *Cross-Border E-Commerce*: Regional trade agreements and a growing integration in Southeast Asia open opportunities for cross-border business activities - *Foreign Investment and Innovation*: Enhanced digital infrastructure and supportive policy frameworks attract both local and international investors - *Expanding Digital Ecosystem*: Continued improvements in digital payment systems and growing tech solutions can further boost consumer confidence
Weaknesses	**Threats**
- *Underdeveloped Logistics*: Distribution and delivery networks, particularly in rural areas, remain insufficient for fast and reliable service - *Payment Trust Issues*: Many consumers still prefer cash-on-delivery over digital payments due to low trust in online transaction systems - *Regulatory and Infrastructure Gaps*: While policies are emerging, inconsistent enforcement and infrastructural limitations pose challenges - *Digital Literacy Variances*: Despite having a high overall internet penetration, disparities in digital skills can hinder e-commerce adoption among certain segments	- *Intense Regional Competition*: Established e-commerce platforms from neighboring countries may intensify competition - *Cyber-Security Risks*: Increased online transactions raise concerns over data breaches and fraud - *Economic and Regulatory Uncertainty*: Volatile economic conditions and potential shifts in regulatory frameworks can affect growth - *Poor Infrastructure*: Continued gaps in logistics and rural connectivity may pose a challenge

Source Profitence (2025)

chains and access larger markets. While this perspective implies a long-term ambition, it is crucial for the concerned policy to ensure inclusivity for enterprises operating on smaller scales in remote areas as they face significant barriers concerning market access, financial capital, and digital infrastructure.

Enhancing Access to Digital Training and Capacity Building: Expanding digital training and capacity-building initiatives is essential for promoting the growth of MSMEs, particularly among female entrepreneurs. Gender-responsive training programs on digital tools, financial management, and economic benefits of technological adoption should be developed in collaboration with educational institutions and non-governmental organizations (NGOs) to ensure inclusivity. Additionally, networking and mentorship programs can play a crucial role in supporting women entrepreneurs as they adopt digital solutions, providing them with guidance, peer support, and business development opportunities.

Expanding Access to Finance: Expanding access to finance is essential for supporting MSMEs, particularly those led by women, and ensuring that business owners can use loans effectively for productive purposes. To facilitate this, targeted loan programs with affordable rates and flexible terms should be developed, particularly for women-led MSMEs. In addition, financial literacy training should be promoted alongside streamlined access to credit, ensuring that business owners can make informed borrowing decisions with minimal risks.

Accelerating Digital Transformation in MSMEs: To accelerate the digital transformation of MSMEs, targeted support should be provided for micro and small-sized enterprises to transition from manual processes to digital administration. This includes implementing digital solutions for record-keeping, e-payments, online marketing, and business functions such as planning, sales, and supply chain management. For medium-sized enterprises, it is important to promote the adoption of a diverse range of the latest digital tools, such as smart phones, tablets, laptops, security cameras, and cloud-based management software, as well as AI-driven analytics to enhance operational efficiency. While this suggestion is widely endorsed, it is equally crucial for the concerned policymaking and regulation to consider any arising ethical concerns and privacy and data protection issues that come along with the so-called digital transformation.

Establishing a Digital Roadmap for Women-led MSMEs: To drive digital transformation in women-led MSMEs in Cambodia, the roadmap should focus on improving digital infrastructure, offering gender-responsive digital literacy programs, and streamlining the formalization process with incentives like tax benefits. Targeted financial support, such as low-interest loans, should be provided for digital tool adoption. This approach will foster the growth and competitiveness of women-led MSMEs.

Considering the above-mentioned perspectives, female entrepreneurs in Cambodia continue to lag in their abilities, skills, and confidence levels to access, use, and afford digital tools. The so-called digital divide, affecting women of all ages in Cambodia and across international boundaries, has certain underlying causes. Those causes may include affordability of access to digital technologies, limited digital literacy, and safety concerns due to inherent biases and social norms. These causes are often inter-related. Women continue to face cultural barriers and stereotypes, reinforcing existing digital divide gaps and limiting women's engagement in e-commerce (OECD, 2019a, 2019b). When transforming entrepreneurial ecosystems and creating gender-responsive policies, it is essential to think beyond access to ICTs and technical skills. While the latter two are immensely important and vastly unequal in both developed and developing countries, technology is not an isolated artifact but rather an enabler within an entrepreneurial ecosystem that should be both innovative and responsive (Braun, 2018).

6 Conclusion

This study provides a case study report of Cambodia's e-commerce within the context of women-led businesses, along with a descriptive analysis of the current e-commerce public policy that may benefit and inform the digital economy of Cambodia as a whole. This study has highlighted that the e-commerce landscape of Cambodia has both potential opportunities and challenges, especially for women-led micro and small businesses, and that the continuing growth of them should be complemented by effective e-commerce policymaking. The importance of empowering female entrepreneurs and minimizing the digital divide phenomenon in developing countries is relevant for future research endeavors to take note of existing opportunities and challenges across different entrepreneurial ecosystems. This perspective appeals for more substantial empirical data to advance the status quo of women in e-commerce. Future studies may take into consideration a wide array of underlying socio-cultural factors that not only limit women's entrepreneurial opportunities, but also hinder the associated policy. In addition to the growing proliferation of firm-level studies, this study also advocates for more longitudinal and cross-country studies, as well as those involving inter-organizational actors between different types of enterprises and institutional actors and entities. In line with previous research, this study contributes to the limited literature strand on women's entrepreneurship and e-commerce capacity building in emerging economies (e.g., Braun et al., 2023; Chikh-Amnache & Mekhzoumi, 2024; Guelich & Xavier, 2017; Roscoe & Ntim, 2022; Samy et al., 2023; Sörensson & Ghannad, 2024). Furthermore, this study provides key learning perspectives to both current and prospective female entrepreneurs to be proactive toward current opportunities and challenges in the contemporary e-commerce ecosystem of not only Cambodia, but also those of other similar Asian country contexts. On another note, this study provides policy implications by advocating the business of case of women empowerment and shedding light on the existing and relevant policies that support women in enhancing their business aptitude and capabilities in a more digitally enhanced business landscape. This study also advances the closely intertwined concepts of e-commerce and women empowerment, while reiterating the need for a more inclusive entrepreneurial ecosystem.

Appendix 1: Institutional Sources and Documents

1. ADB. (2024). Kingdom of Cambodia: Supporting the adoption of digital technologies and fostering innovation in micro, small, and medium-sized enterprises. Asian Development Bank (ADB). https://www.adb.org/sites/default/files/project-documents/55255/55255-004-tar-en.pdf#:~:text=Cambodian%20businesses%20are%20insufficiently%20digitalized.%20Digitalization%20can,operational%20costs%2C%20increasing%20productivity%2C%20and%20improving%20qua

2. B2B Cambodia. (2024). Boosting women entrepreneurs to drive Cambodia's economic growth. B2B Cambodia. https://b2b-cambodia.com/articles/boosting-women-entrepreneurs-to-drive-cambodias-economic-growth-amcham/?fbclid=IwY2xjawEgCkpleHRuA2FlbQIxMAABHa49rr9y5p90GMOsyR2F7_Hh41-A8JmpEg-Lu5LfwHm8UVQ8h0-rcIc6yA_aem_G3DXgc_zt11OwhYYEJ8dQ
3. GIZ. (2021). Online training on e-commerce and business promotion for women entrepreneurs in Cambodia. Deutsche Gesellschaft für Internationale Zusammenarbeit (GIZ). https://connecting-asia.org/activities/online-training-e-commerce-and-business-promotion-to-women-entrepreneurs-in-cambodia/
4. iBAN. (2022). Cambodia Women Entrepreneurs Association: Supporting women-led inclusive businesses in Cambodia. InclusiveBusiness.net (iBAN). https://www.inclusivebusiness.net/clued-in/19/article/5487
5. IFC. (2019). Exploring the opportunities for women-owned SMEs in Cambodia. International Finance Corporation (IFC). https://documents1.worldbank.org/curated/en/654951573044863479/pdf/Exploring-the-Opportunities-for-Women-owned-SMEs-in-Cambodia.pdf
6. IFC. (2023). Revolutionizing e-commerce: How Evermos is creating entrepreneurship opportunities and expanding market access through social commerce. International Finance Corporation (IFC). https://openknowledge.worldbank.org/handle/10986/40731
7. Mekong Institute (2023). Market access through e-commerce promotion for women-led SMEs. Mekong Institute. https://mekonginstitute.org/wp-content/uploads/2023/04/Women-Led_SMEs_06Oct_Project_Brochure.pdf
8. Ministry of Planning, Cambodia (2022). Economic census of Cambodia 2022: National report on consensus results. National Institute of Statistics, Ministry of Planning, Cambodia. https://www.nis.gov.kh/nis/EC2022/National%20Report%20on%20Final%20Census%20Results%20Economic%20Census%20of%20Cambodia%202022.pdf
9. Narayan, S. (2022). "Cambodia's e-commerce market is crucial"- Cambodian Women Entrepreneurs Association (CWEA). The Better Cambodia. https://thebettercambodia.com/cambodias-e-commerce-market-is-crucial-cambodian-women-entrepreneurs-association-cwea/
10. OECD. (2017). Aid for trade at a glance 2017: Promoting trade, inclusiveness and connectivity for sustainable development. Organisation for Economic Co-operation and Development (OECD). https://doi.org/https://doi.org/10.1787/aid_glance-2017-en
11. OECD. (2019a, 2019b). Unpacking e-commerce: Business models, trends and policies. Organisation for Economic Co-operation and Development (OECD). https://doi.org/https://doi.org/10.1787/23561431-en
12. OECD. (2021). The digital transformation of SMEs. In OECD Studies on SMEs and Entrepreneurship. Organisation for Economic Co-operation and Development (OECD). https://doi.org/https://doi.org/10.1787/bdb9256a-en

13. Phurik-Callebaut, R. (2021). Women entrepreneurs in Cambodia: Study on support programs for innovation and startup. Deutsche Gesellschaft für Internationale Zusammenarbeit (GIZ). https://www.khmersme.gov.kh/wp-content/uploads/2022/05/WOMEN-ENTREPRENEURS-IN-CAMBODIA-STUDY-ON-SUPPORT-PROGRAMS-FOR-INNOVATION-AND-STARTUP.pdf
14. Profitence. (2025). E-commerce in Cambodia 2024. A comprehensive overview on the e-commerce landscape in Cambodia: Addressing challenges, initiatives and opportunities. Profitence. https://data.opendevelopmentcambodia.net/en/dataset/5f990019-a98f-4730-864e-c79b08c4a537/resource/7afad0c3-a117-44bc-8cfd-abcb8bdc0f78/download/e-commerce_in_cambodia_2024.pdf
15. SheTrades (2024). Cambodia outlines steps to advance gender in trade policy. ITC SheTrades. https://www.shetrades.com/story/cambodia-outlines-steps-to-advance-gender-in-trade-policy/
16. SheTrades (2024). SheTrades outlook 2024. ITC SheTrades. https://outlook.shetrades.com/admin/upload/publications/documents/STO%20Policy%20Brief%20Cambodia_Digital_English%20(4).pdf
17. SPF. (2024). Women entrepreneurs' challenge: Solving social issues through entrepreneurship, Vol. 4 – E-commerce business opportunities in Cambodia. Sasakawa Peace Foundation (SPF). https://www.spf.org/en/gender/women_entrepreneurs/20240411.html
18. The Asia Foundation (2023). Accelerate women's entrepreneurship and access to capital in Cambodia: Lessons and recommendations. The Asia Foundation. https://asiafoundation.org/wp-content/uploads/2024/08/Accelerate-Womens-Entrepreneurship-and-Access-to-Capital-in-Cambodia.pdf
19. UN Women. (2018). UN Women annual report 2018–2019. United Nations Entity for Gender Equality and the Empowerment of Women (UN Women). https://www.unwomen.org/sites/default/files/Annual%20Report/Attachments/Sections/Library/2019/UN-Women-annual-report-2018-2019-en.pdf
20. UN Women. (2022). Building gender-transformative innovation ecosystems supporting women's entrepreneurship. United Nations Entity for Gender Equality and the Empowerment of Women (UN Women). https://www.unwomen.org/sites/default/files/2022-12/EP.4_Patrice%20Braun.pdf
21. UNCTAD. (2015). Information economy report: Unlocking the potential of e-commerce for developing countries. United Nations Conference on Trade and Development (UNCTAD). https://unctad.org/system/files/official-document/ier2015_en.pdf
22. UNCTAD. (2016). e-Trade for All: A new multi-stakeholder initiative to boost global gains from e-trade. United Nations Conference on Trade and Development (UNCTAD). https://unctad.org/system/files/official-document/dtlstictmisc2016d6_en.pdf
23. UNCTAD. (2017). Cambodia rapid eTrade readiness assessment. United Nations Conference on Trade and Development (UNCTAD). https://unctad.org/system/files/official-document/dtlstict2017d2_en.pdf

24. UNCTAD. (2019). Rapid e-trade readiness assessments of least developed countries: Policy impact and way forward. United Nations Conference on Trade and Development (UNCTAD). https://unctad.org/system/files/official-document/dtlstict2019d7_en.pdf
25. UNCTAD. (2020). Covid-19 and e-commerce: Impact on businesses and policy responses. United Nations Conference on Trade and Development (UNCTAD). https://unctad.org/system/files/official-document/dtlstict2020d12_en.pdf
26. UNCTAD. (2023). E-commerce from a gender and development perspective. United Nations Conference on Trade and Development (UNCTAD). https://unctad.org/system/files/official-document/ditc2023d1_en.pdf
27. UNDP. (2020). E-commerce strategy: Cambodia. United Nations Development Programme (UNDP). https://www.undp.org/cambodia/publications/e-commerce-strategy
28. UNESCAP. (2017). Regional road map for implementing the 2030 agenda for SDGs. United Nations Economic and Social Commission for Asia and the Pacific (UNESCAP). https://www.unescap.org/sites/default/files/publications/SDGs-Regional-Roadmap.pdf
29. UNESCAP. (2018). Fostering women's entrepreneurship in ASEAN. United Nations Economic and Social Commission for Asia and the Pacific (UNESCAP). https://www.unescap.org/sites/default/files/publications/SSD-Gender-FWE-report_0.pdf
30. UNESCAP. (2019). Selected issues in cross-border e-commerce development in Asia and the Pacific. United Nations Economic and Social Commission for Asia and the Pacific (UNESCAP). https://repository.unescap.org/server/api/core/bitstreams/60532c50-f7fb-4795-9c11-c4d34a47bffb/content
31. UNESCAP. (2022). Catalyzing women's entrepreneurship: Creating a gender responsive entrepreneurial ecosystem. Cambodia: Policy initiatives. United Nations Economic and Social Commission for Asia and the Pacific (UNESCAP). https://www.unescap.org/sites/default/d8files/2022-02/CambodiaPolicyIniativesJan2022.pdf
32. UNESCAP. (2023). A woman entrepreneur's journey to financial inclusion and agribusiness success in rural Cambodia. United Nations Economic and Social Commission for Asia and the Pacific (UNESCAP). https://www.unescap.org/story/woman-entrepreneurs-journey-financial-inclusion-and-agribusiness-success-rural-cambodia
33. UNESCAP. (2023). Cambodian social enterprise tackles challenges faced by women-owned micro and small enterprises. United Nations Economic and Social Commission for Asia and the Pacific (UNESCAP). https://www.unescap.org/story/cambodian-social-enterprise-tackles-challenges-faced-women-owned-micro-and-small-enterprises

References

ADB. (2024). *Kingdom of Cambodia: Supporting the adoption of digital technologies and fostering innovation in micro, small, and medium-sized enterprises.* Asian Development Bank (ADB). https://www.adb.org/sites/default/files/project-documents/55255/55255-004-tar-en.pdf#:~:text=Cambodian%20businesses%20are%20insufficiently%20digitalized.%20Digitalization%20can,operational%20costs%2C%20increasing%20productivity%2C%20and%20improving%20qua.

Ahi, A. A., Sinkovics, N., & Sinkovics, R. R. (2023). E-commerce policy and the global economy: A path to more inclusive development? *Management International Review, 63*(1), 27–56. https://doi.org/10.1007/s11575-022-00490-1

Ahmed, A. (2024). Empowering women entrepreneurs: The role of social media in enhancing financial and professional achievement. *Commerce Research Review, 1*(2), 58–67. https://doi.org/10.21844/crr.v1i02.1113

Al Jamil, A. A., & Ahmed Ismail, A. (2024). The use of 'ecommerce' and 'social commerce in emerging markets': Omani female millennials' experiences. *Information Development, 40*(3), 461–477. https://doi.org/10.1177/02666669221145411

Al-Omoush, K.S., Yaseen, S., Al-Qirem, R., AL-Khatib, A.W. (2023). Women empowerment in the age of social commerce: An empirical study. In S. G. Yaseen (Ed.),*Cutting-edge business technologies in the big data era. Studies in big data.* Springer. https://doi.org/10.1007/978-3-031-42463-2_13

Bernhardt, S., Braun, P., & Thomason, J. (2018). *Gender inequality and the potential for change in technology fields.* IGI Global.

Brahem, M., & Boussema, S. (2023). Social media entrepreneurship as an opportunity for women: The case of Facebook-commerce. *The International Journal of Entrepreneurship and Innovation, 24*(3), 191–201. https://doi.org/10.1177/14657503211066010

Braun, P. (2010). A skilling framework for women entrepreneurs in the knowledge economy. In C. Henry & S. Marlow (Eds.),*Innovating women: Contributions to technological advancement. Contemporary issues in entrepreneurship research* (pp. 35–53). Emerald.

Braun, P. (2018). Developing gender-responsive trade ecosystems in the Asia-Pacific. In S. Yousafzai, A. Lindgreen, S. Saeed, & C. Henry (Eds.), *Contextual embeddedness of women's entrepreneurship: Going beyond a gender neutral approach* (pp. 91–105). Taylor & Francis.

Braun, P., Birdthistle, N., & Flynn, A. (2023). Beyond COVID-19: Women entrepreneurs and e-commerce policy in the Asia-Pacific. In C. Henry, S. Coleman, & K. Lewis (Eds.),*Women's entrepreneurship policy* (pp. 192–213). Edward Elgar. https://doi.org/10.4337/9781800374652.00016

Brush, C., Edelman, L., Manolova, T., & Welter, F. (2019). A gendered look at entrepreneurship ecosystems. *Small Business Economics, 53*, 393–408. https://doi.org/10.1007/s11187-018-9992-9

Chan, R. (2022). An analysis of Cambodia's e-commerce and way forward. *Journal of Management, Economics, and Industrial Organization, 6*(3), 88–100. https://doi.org/10.31039/jomeino.2022.6.3.6

Chatterjee, S., Gupta, S. D., & Upadhyay, P. (2020). Technology adoption and entrepreneurial orientation for rural women: Evidence from India. *Technological Forecasting and Social Change, 160*, Article 120236. https://doi.org/10.1016/j.techfore.2020.120236

Chhorn, D. (2025, February 28). *Driving Cambodia's long-term vision through women-led and digital MSME development.* Cambodia Development Resource Institute. https://coc2025.cdri.org.kh/blogs/driving-cambodias-long-term-vision-through-women-led-and-digital-msme-development

Chikh-Amnache, S., & Mekhzoumi, L. (2024). The influence of socioeconomic factors on female entrepreneurship in Southeast Asian countries. *Journal of Entrepreneurship in Emerging Economies, 16*(1), 33–70. https://doi.org/10.1108/JEEE-12-2022-0371

Datareportal. (2024). *Digital 2024: Cambodia.* Datareportal. https://datareportal.com/reports/digital-2024-cambodia

Dyerson, R., Spinelli, R., & Harindranath, G. (2016). Revisiting IT readiness: An approach for small firms. *Industrial Management & Data Systems, 116*(3), 546–563. https://doi.org/10.1108/IMDS-05-2015-0204

Eastin, M. S., Cicchirillo, V., & Mabry, A. (2015). Extending the digital divide conversation: Examining the knowledge gap through media expectancies. *Journal of Broadcasting and Electronic Media, 59*(3), 416–437. https://doi.org/10.1007/s11187-018-9992-9

Foss, L., Henry, C., Ahl, H., & Mikalsen, G. (2019). Women's entrepreneurship policy research: A 30-year review of the evidence'. *Small Business Economics, 53*(1), 1–21. https://doi.org/10.1007/s11187-018-9993-8

Guelich, U., & Xavier, S. R. (2017). Women's entrepreneurship within the ASEAN Economic Community: Challenges and opportunities. In T. S. Manolova, C. G. Brush, L. F. Edelman, A. Robb, & F. Welter (Eds.),*Entrepreneurial ecosystems and growth of women's entrepreneurship: A comparative analysis* (pp. 15–43). Edward Elgar. https://doi.org/10.4337/9781785364624.00007

Gupta, A., & Butt, A. A. (2024). Investigating women entrepreneurs: Navigation of online marketplaces and e-commerce platforms. *Journal of East-West Thought, 14*(3), 154–163. https://jetjournal.us/index.php/journals/article/view/43

Hilbert, M. (2011). Digital gender divide or technologically empowered women in developing countries? A typical case of lies, damned lies, and statistics. *Women's Studies International Forum, 34*(6), 479–489. https://doi.org/10.1016/j.wsif.2011.07.001

Houghton, C., Casey, D., & Smyth, S. (2017). Selection, collection and analysis as sources of evidence in case study research. *Nurse Researcher, 24*(4), 36–41. https://doi.org/10.7748/nr.2017.e1482

Howlett, M., & Cashore, B. (2020). Public policy: Definitions and approaches. In G. Capano & M. Howlett (Eds.),*A modern guide to public policy* (pp. 10–21). Springer. https://doi.org/10.4337/9781789904987.00007

Howlett, M., Cashore, B. (2014). Conceptualizing public policy. In I. Engeli & C. R. Allison (Eds.), *Comparative policy studies. Research methods series* (pp. 17–33). Palgrave Macmillan. https://doi.org/10.1057/9781137314154_2

Ibarra, E. A. D., Pinzón, J. A. A., & Medina, Y. F. (2023). Methodology: How to develop a case report or case series report. *Revista Colombiana De Reumatología, 30*(2), 129–136. https://doi.org/10.1016/j.rcreu.2021.05.022

IFC. (2019). *Exploring the opportunities for women-owned SMEs in Cambodia.* International Finance Corporation (IFC). https://documents1.worldbank.org/curated/en/654951573044863479/pdf/Exploring-the-Opportunities-for-Women-owned-SMEs-in-Cambodia.pdf

IFC. (2023). *Revolutionizing e-commerce: How Evermos is creating entrepreneurship opportunities and expanding market access through social commerce.* International Finance Corporation (IFC). https://openknowledge.worldbank.org/handle/10986/40731

Kuckerz, A., & Brändle, L. (2021). Creative reconstruction: A structured literature review of the early empirical research on the COVID-19 crisis and entrepreneurship. *Management Review Quarterly, 72*, 281–307. https://doi.org/10.1007/s11301-021-00221-0

Liao, S. H., Widowati, R., & Hsieh, Y. C. (2021). Investigating online social media users' behaviors for social commerce recommendations. *Technology in Society, 66*, Article 101655. https://doi.org/10.1016/j.techsoc.2021.101655

Marin-Garcia, J. A., Garcia-Sabater, J. P., & Maheut, J. (2022). Case report papers guidelines: Recommendations for the reporting of case studies or action research in business management. *WPOM—Working Papers on Operations Management, 13*(2), 108–137. https://doi.org/10.4995/wpom.16244

Ministry of Planning, Cambodia (2022). *Economic census of Cambodia 2022: National report on consensus results*. National Institute of Statistics, Ministry of Planning, Cambodia. https://www.nis.gov.kh/nis/EC2022/National%20Report%20on%20Final%20Census%20Results%20Economic%20Census%20of%20Cambodia%202022.pdf

Norris, P. (2001). *Digital divide: Civic engagement, information poverty, and the internet worldwide*. Cambridge University Press. https://doi.org/10.1017/CBO9781139164887

OECD. (2017). *Aid for trade at a glance 2017: Promoting trade, inclusiveness and connectivity for sustainable development*. Organisation for Economic Co-operation and Development (OECD). https://doi.org/10.1787/aid_glance-2017-en

OECD. (2019a). *The role of education and skills in bridging the digital gender divide. Evidence from APEC economies*. Organisation for Economic Co-operation and Development (OECD). https://www.oecd.org/sti/education-and-skillsin-bridging-the-digital-gender-divide-evidence-from-apec.pdf

OECD. (2019b). *Unpacking e-commerce: Business models, trends and policies*. Organisation for Economic Co-operation and Development (OECD). https://doi.org/10.1787/23561431-en

OECD. (2021). *The digital transformation of SMEs*. OECD Studies on SMEs and Entrepreneurship. Organisation for Economic Co-operation and Development (OECD). https://doi.org/10.1787/bdb9256a-en.

Okoli, C., Mbarika, V. W. A., & McCoy, S. (2010). The effects of infrastructure and policy on e-business in Latin America and Sub-Saharan Africa. *European Journal of Information Systems, 19*(1), 5–20. https://doi.org/10.1057/ejis.2009.48

Orser, B., Riding, A., & Li, Y. (2019). Technology adoption and gender-inclusive entrepreneurship education and training. *International Journal of Gender and Entrepreneurship, 11*(3), 273–298. https://doi.org/10.1108/IJGE-02-2019-0026

Oxley, E. J., & Yeung, B. (2001). E-commerce readiness: Institutional environment and international competitiveness. *Journal of International Business Studies, 32*(4), 705–723. https://doi.org/10.1057/palgrave.jibs.8490991

Profitence. (2025). *E-commerce in Cambodia 2024. A comprehensive overview on the e-commerce landscape in Cambodia: Addressing challenges, initiatives and opportunities*. Profitence. https://data.opendevelopmentcambodia.net/en/dataset/5f990019-a98f-4730-864e-c79b08c4a537/resource/7afad0c3-a117-44bc-8cfd-abcb8bdc0f78/download/e-commerce_in_cambodia_2024.pdf

Rashid, Y., Rashid, A., Warraich, M. A., Sabir, S. S., & Waseem, A. (2019). Case study method: A step-by-step guide for business researchers. *International Journal of Qualitative Methods, 18*. https://doi.org/10.1177/1609406919862424

Roscoe, A., & Ntim, C. B. (2022). *Women and e-commerce in Southeast Asia: Executive summary*. World Bank Group. http://documents.worldbank.org/curated/en/099909308052234068

Salmizi, A. N., & Abd Aziz, N. N. (2023). Exploratory factor analysis of technology-organization-environment and e-commerce adoption among urban women entrepreneurs. *Journal of Academic Research in Business & Social Sciences, 13*(3), 661–671. https://doi.org/10.6007/IJARBSS/v13-i3/16462

Samy, Y., Adedeji, A., Iraoya, A., Dutta, M. K., Fakmawii, J. L., & Hao, W. (2023). Trade and women's economic empowerment: Qualitative analysis of SMEs from Cambodia and Vietnam. In *Trade and Women's Economic Empowerment* (pp. 59–103). Palgrave Macmillan. https://doi.org/10.1007/978-3-031-39039-5_3

Scheerder, A., Van Deursen, A., & Van Dijk, J. (2017). Determinants of internet skills, uses and outcomes. A systematic review of the second- and third-level digital divide. *Telematics and Informatics, 34*(8), 1607–1624. https://doi.org/10.1016/j.tele.2017.07.007

Shih, C.-F., Dedrick, J., & Kraemer, K. L. (2005). Rule of law and the international diffusion of e-commerce. *Communications of the ACM, 48*(11), 57–62. https://doi.org/10.1145/1096000.1096005

Sörensson, A., & Ghannad, N. (2024). Entrepreneurial opportunities and difficulties under COVID-19 for women entrepreneurs in Asia and Europe. *Journal of Entrepreneurship in Emerging Economies, 16*(1), 119–133. https://doi.org/10.1108/JEEE-02-2023-0052

The Asia Foundation. (2023). *Accelerate women's entrepreneurship and access to capital in Cambodia: Lessons and recommendations.* The Asia Foundation. https://asiafoundation.org/wp-content/uploads/2024/08/Accelerate-Womens-Entrepreneurship-and-Access-to-Capital-in-Cambodia.pdf

UN Women. (2018). *UN Women annual report 2018–2019.* United Nations Entity for Gender Equality and the Empowerment of Women (UN Women). https://www.unwomen.org/sites/default/files/Annual%20Report/Attachments/Sections/Library/2019/UN-Women-annual-report-2018-2019-en.pdf

UNCTAD. (2015). *Information economy report: Unlocking the potential of e-commerce for developing countries.* United Nations Conference on Trade and Development (UNCTAD). https://unctad.org/system/files/official-document/ier2015_en.pdf

UNCTAD. (2016). *e-Trade for All: A new multi-stakeholder initiative to boost global gains from e-trade.* United Nations Conference on Trade and Development (UNCTAD). https://unctad.org/system/files/official-document/dtlstictmisc2016d6_en.pdf

UNCTAD. (2019). *Rapid e-trade readiness assessments of least developed countries: Policy impact and way forward.* United Nations Conference on Trade and Development (UNCTAD). https://unctad.org/system/files/official-document/dtlstict2019d7_en.pdf

UNCTAD. (2020). *Covid-19 and e-commerce: Impact on businesses and policy responses.* United Nations Conference on Trade and Development (UNCTAD). https://unctad.org/system/files/official-document/dtlstict2020d12_en.pdf

UNDP. (2020). *E-commerce strategy: Cambodia.* United Nations Development Programme (UNDP). https://www.undp.org/cambodia/publications/e-commerce-strategy

UNESCAP. (2017). *Regional road map for implementing the 2030 agenda for SDGs.* United Nations Economic and Social Commission for Asia and the Pacific (UNESCAP). https://www.unescap.org/sites/default/files/publications/SDGs-Regional-Roadmap.pdf

UNESCAP. (2018). Fostering women's entrepreneurship in ASEAN. United Nations Economic and Social Commission for Asia and the Pacific (UNESCAP). https://www.unescap.org/sites/default/files/publications/SSD-Gender-FWE-report_0.pdf

UNESCAP. (2019). Selected issues in cross-border e-commerce development in Asia and the Pacific. United Nations Economic and Social Commission for Asia and the Pacific (UNESCAP). https://repository.unescap.org/server/api/core/bitstreams/60532c50-f7fb-4795-9c11-c4d34a47bffb/content

UNESCAP. (2022). *Catalyzing women's entrepreneurship: Creating a gender responsive entrepreneurial ecosystem. Cambodia: Policy initiatives.* United Nations Economic and Social Commission for Asia and the Pacific (UNESCAP). https://www.unescap.org/sites/default/d8files/2022-02/CambodiaPolicyIniativesJan2022.pdf

UNESCAP. (2023). *Cambodian social enterprise tackles challenges faced by women owned micro and small enterprises.* United Nations Economic and Social Commission for Asia and the Pacific (UNESCAP). https://www.unescap.org/story/cambodian-social-enterprise-tackles-challenges-faced-women-owned-micro-and-small-enterprises

Van Deursen, A. J. (2017). Digital divide: Impact of media literacy. *The International Encyclopedia of Media Effects,* 1–8. https://doi.org/10.1002/9781118783764.wbieme0044

Van Deursen, A., Helsper, E., & Eynon, R. (2016). Development and validation of the Internet Skills Scale (ISS). *Information Communication Society, 19*(6), 804–823. https://doi.org/10.1080/1369118X.2015.1078834

Van Dijk, J. A. G. M. (2017). Digital divide: Impact of access. *The International Encyclopedia of Media Effects, 1,* 1–11. https://doi.org/10.1002/9781118783764.wbieme0043

Yin, R. K. (1994). Discovering the future of the case study. Method in evaluation research. *Evaluation Practice, 15,* 283–290. https://doi.org/10.1016/0886-1633(94)90023-X

Yin, R. K. (2018). *Case study research and applications: Design and methods* (6th Eds.). Sage.

Yousafzai, S., Saeed, S., & Muffatto, M. (2015). Institutional theory and contextual embeddedness of women's entrepreneurial leadership: Evidence from 92 countries. *Journal of Small Business Management, 53*(3), 587–604. https://doi.org/10.1111/jsbm.12179

Yu, H., & Cui, L. (2019). China's e-commerce: Empowering rural women? *The China Quarterly, 238*, 418–437. https://doi.org/10.1017/S0305741018001819

Rongtitya Rith , Ph.D., is a post-doctoral research fellow at the Department of Economics, University of Genoa (Italy). He holds a Master's Degree in Accounting, Finance, and Regulation from Glasgow Caledonian University (UK), and a PhD degree in Security, Risk, and Vulnerability (Curriculum: Management and Security) from the University of Genoa. His primary fields of research encompass the topics of corporate social responsibility (CSR), business ethics, sustainability strategies, and strategic communication. Formerly, he was a visiting researcher at Temple University (US) School of Sport, Tourism, and Hospitality Management, conducting research on legitimacy management strategies and CSR practices within professional football clubs. His current research works primarily focus on CSR and sustainability strategies in both professional and non-profit sport organizations.

Riccardo Spinelli , Ph.D., is an associate professor of management at the Department of Economics, University of Genoa (Italy). He holds a Master's Degree in Economics and Commerce and a Ph.D. degree in Economics and Management from the same university. He also serves as a board member of the Ph.D. Security, Risk, and Vulnerability program. He also serves as the head of the BA program in Tourism Sciences: Business, Culture, and Territory. His teaching expertise and research interests include tourism management and marketing, nautical tourism, sustainable tourism, corporate social responsibility (CSR), international strategies and marketing, and the application of information technology (IT) in small and medium enterprises (SMEs).

From Istanbul to Singapore: Insider's Headquarters Relocation and Strategic Positioning in Asia's Tech Ecosystem

Deniz Tunçalp

Abstract This study examines the strategic relocation of Insider headquarters, a Turkish-born marketing technology unicorn, from Istanbul to Singapore, providing a longitudinal perspective on cross-border scaling from an emerging-market context. Drawing on an embedded single-case study design, the research integrates primary interviews with secondary archival data to trace Insider's trajectory from its 2012 founding to its post-relocation global expansion. The findings show how relocating to a global innovation hub can simultaneously address institutional constraints in the home ecosystem and unlock access to advanced resources, high-value networks, and symbolic legitimacy in global markets. It pursued a distinct scaling pathway, where it retained core technical and operational functions in its origin country while embedding executive and strategic functions in an advanced financial and entrepreneurial ecosystem. This configuration extends existing theories of internationalization and scaling by highlighting how emerging-market ventures leverage geographic repositioning not as a terminal stage of global expansion, but as a dynamic strategy that reshapes governance, market access, and entrepreneurial identity. The study offers theoretical insights into the interplay between institutional ecosystems, strategic geography, and digital entrepreneurship. It provides practical guidance for policymakers and entrepreneurs managing the challenges of global scaling from relatively resource-constrained environments.

1 Introduction

Founded in Istanbul in 2012, Insider has become a leading player in the global marketing technology (MarTech) sector, providing AI-driven solutions for customer engagement, personalization, and cross-channel marketing optimization. By 2022, the company had reached unicorn status with a valuation exceeding $1 billion, a milestone that placed it among Türkiye's most prominent technology ventures (Insider, 2022) and highlighted the potential for startups from emerging markets to succeed in

D. Tunçalp (✉)
Department of Management Engineering, Istanbul Technical University, Istanbul, Türkiye
e-mail: tuncalp@itu.edu.tr

T. Endress and Y. F. Badir (eds.), *Business and Management in Asia: Opportunities and Entrepreneurship*, https://doi.org/10.1007/978-981-95-4909-2_11

innovation-intensive industries. Its trajectory offers an analytically valuable example of how a firm originating in a relatively resource-constrained ecosystem can achieve sustained international growth despite the structural and institutional limitations typically faced by enterprises from emerging markets (Khanna & Palepu, 2010; Li & Zahra, 2012).

Insider's path is distinctive for the way it addressed typical ecosystem-level constraints, including limited late-stage funding, regulatory uncertainty, and the saturation of the domestic market, through a strategic relocation of its global headquarters (HQ) to Singapore. This move, supported by substantial international financing rounds, including a $121 million Series D in 2022, a $105 million convertible note in 2023, and a Series E investment from General Atlantic in 2024 (Insider, 2022, 2024; Tatler Asia, 2022), was not merely a geographic shift. It reflected a deliberate reconfiguration of the company's operational base, investor networks, and market positioning. By situating its HQ in Singapore, Insider gained proximity to institutional capital, regional enterprise clients, and high-growth markets in Southeast Asia and beyond. Today, the company has 28 offices across six continents, employing 1100+ people.

This chapter uses Insider's HQ relocation as a case study to explore cross-border scaling, defined here as the process by which high-growth ventures from emerging markets establish or shift strategic functions across national boundaries to overcome contextual limitations, access global resources, and reposition themselves competitively in international markets (Cavusgil & Knight, 2015; Luo & Tung, 2007).

Two research questions guided the analysis:

1. Why did Insider relocate its HQ to Singapore?
2. How does this relocation illuminate broader patterns of cross-border scaling and digital entrepreneurship among emerging-market startups?

Addressing these questions contributes to scholarship on emerging-market scaling pathways (Ramamurti, 2012; Zahra et al., 2000) by illustrating how strategic and economic geography, institutional ecosystems, and digital entrepreneurship intersect to shape global expansion strategies (Autio et al., 2014; Mudambi, 2008; Nambisan, 2017), engaging with the literature on internationalization from emerging markets (Luo & Tung, 2007; Matthews, 2006).

2 Theoretical Framing

Scaling for globally oriented startups is no longer a linear extension of operations from a domestic base; instead, it increasingly involves strategic relocation from an emerging to an advanced entrepreneurial ecosystem to overcome systemic constraints. Startups from emerging economies often encounter insufficient capital markets, regulatory volatility, and limited global recognition, which make domestic scaling problematic for sustained growth, calling for early internationalization of new ventures (Autio et al., 2000; Oviatt & McDougall, 2005; Zahra et al., 2000).

In Türkiye, for example, gaps in later-stage financing, fragmented support infrastructures, and macroeconomic volatility create an environment in which high-potential ventures often need to internationalize early to secure growth capital and maintain a competitive position (Lavine, 2023). In this context, strategic relocation becomes a deliberate mechanism. These transitions enable ventures from institutionally constrained environments to reposition themselves in global innovation hubs, acquiring advanced resources, networks, and symbolic legitimacy (Saxenian, 2006). Such relocations serve not only as operational adjustments but also as symbolic interventions in entrepreneurial identity work, enabling startups to construct and project credible organizational narratives that resonate with the evaluative schemas of key audiences, including investors, partners, and clients (Wry et al., 2011).

2.1 Institutional Logics and Scaling Constraints in Emerging Markets

Institutional logics shape how entrepreneurs interpret opportunities and mobilize resources (Thornton et al., 2012). In emerging markets, gaps in market-supporting structures, such as reliable capital provision, enforceable contracts, and professional intermediaries (institutional voids) often constrain these logics (Khanna & Palepu, 1997). Turkish startups operate within a logic that values rapid early growth and cost efficiency. However, the ecosystem lacks the entrepreneurial capital to sustain the scaling of startups beyond the Series B stage. Türkiye's persistent late-stage venture capital gap and macroeconomic challenges such as currency volatility and high inflation reflect this issue (World Bank, 2020).

In contrast, Singapore operates under a logic of institutional maturity, where state-supported innovation policies, transparent regulation, and global financial integration create favorable conditions for startup growth (Asian Development Bank, 2023). The city-state ranks among the top jurisdictions in the *Doing Business Index* for ease of starting a business, protecting minority investors, and legally enforcing contracts (World Bank, 2020). These conditions make it a natural pull destination for emerging-market startups seeking to transition into global markets.

2.2 Entrepreneurial Ecosystems in Asia: Emerging vs. Advanced

Entrepreneurial ecosystems are dynamic configurations of finance, talent, knowledge, and regulation that collectively influence the scaling of ventures (Spigel & Harrison, 2018; Stam, 2015). Across Asia, ecosystems differ markedly in their ability to support high-growth entrepreneurship, creating divergent opportunity structures for scaling ventures.

Türkiye's entrepreneurial ecosystem offers strong technical talent and cost advantages. However, inconsistent regulatory enforcement, fragmented accelerator networks, and an underdeveloped growth-stage funding market hinder its potential. According to the Global Startup Ecosystem Report 2025, Istanbul ranks third among Emerging Startup Ecosystems globally and ninth among European cities, marking a rapid ascent driven by a 423% surge in funding activity from 2023 to 2024, a 142% increase in total VC funding from \$2.6 billion to \$6.3 billion, and significant gains in performance, market reach, and exit activity (Startup Genome, 2025). In contrast, Singapore sits among the world's leading startup ecosystems, ranked within the global top 10, anchored by deep venture capital pools, robust global connectivity, and institutional programs designed to attract tech startups, including initiatives like the Startup SG platform and strong IP protection frameworks that support world-class innovation (Startup Genome, 2025).

2.3 Strategic Legitimation, Digital Identity, and Scaling Logic

HQ relocation is both a resource acquisition strategy and a strategic legitimation process. Legitimacy must be actively constructed in line with the expectations of powerful external audiences (Suchman, 1995). For startups from emerging economies, geographic repositioning is often a central part of their growth strategy. Relocating to a globally recognized innovation hub not only signals alignment with international governance standards and advanced technological capabilities but also serves as a deliberate act of cultural entrepreneurship, enabling ventures to craft and project narratives that conform to the legitimacy criteria of global markets and influential stakeholders (Wry et al., 2011).

3 Methodology

This study employs a qualitative, longitudinal, single-case design (Yin, 2018) to examine the strategic and organizational implications of the Insider's relocation from Istanbul to Singapore. The longitudinal orientation is central to the research design because the relocation decision was not an isolated event but rather the culmination of more than a decade of organizational evolution. By tracing developments from the company's founding in 2012 to its Series E funding in 2024, the study captures the dynamic interplay between institutional constraints, access to funding, and entrepreneurial identity work across multiple strategic inflection points.

Choosing Insider as a theoretical and revelatory case is deliberate. The company stands out as one of the first Turkish startups to secure late-stage investment from globally recognized venture capital firms such as Sequoia Capital India, Riverwood Capital, and General Atlantic, and to relocate its HQ to Singapore as part of a deliberate cross-border scaling strategy. The company's trajectory, encompassing early bootstrapping, multiple funding rounds, two acquisitions, and a carefully staged entry into Southeast Asia and other global markets, provides a rich empirical setting for investigating how an emerging-market technology venture leverages strategic geography for scaling.

3.1 Data Collection

Data for the study were assembled from a triangulated combination of primary interviews, archival sources, and investor and ecosystem databases, allowing for a comprehensive and cross-validated account of Insider's scaling journey. The study generated primary data through semi-structured interviews conducted between January and June 2025 with eight current and former employees of Insider, including executives, product managers, and regional leads, four venture capital professionals with direct or indirect involvement in the company's funding rounds, and four startup ecosystem observers, including journalists, analysts, and accelerator managers. These conversations provided insight into the firm's decision-making, investor engagement, and organizational restructuring before and after the relocation to Singapore.

The study draws on archival materials from publicly available and reputable news sources, as well as industry blogs, press releases, and official corporate statements spanning the period from 2012 to 2024, to provide contemporaneous accounts of product launches, funding announcements, acquisitions, and strategic partnerships. To supplement and validate the primary and archival material, the study also incorporated data from investor and startup ecosystem databases, including Startups.Watch, Crunchbase, and PitchBook. This data allowed for precise reconstruction of the company's funding and acquisition history, including key events such as the $8 million Series B led by Sequoia Capital India in March 2018, the $32 million Series C in July 2020 backed by Wamda Capital, Riverwood Capital, and Sequoia Capital India, and the $121 million Series D in February 2022 that elevated Insider to unicorn status with a valuation of $1.22 billion. Subsequent developments included a $105 million convertible note in May 2023 involving the Qatar Investment Authority and Esas Private Equity, and the Series E funding in November 2024 led by General Atlantic, accompanied by a secondary transaction in which early investors such as 212 Fund I, Galata Business Angels, and e2vc Fund I exited. Acquisition data were also integrated, including the 2018 purchase of InfiniteSoft and the January 2023 acquisition of MindBehind. The use of multiple data sources reduced the risk of retrospective bias. It ensured that the study could corroborate informant accounts with independent evidence.

3.2 Timeline Construction

The study developed an event timeline to organize Insider's trajectory from its founding in 2012 to the Series E round in 2024. This reconstruction enabled the identification of how earlier strategic choices influenced later developments.

The first phase, spanning from 2012 to 2017, was characterized by product development in Istanbul, early customer acquisition, and seed-to-Series A growth, all within the constraints of the Turkish market. The second phase, from 2018 to 2020, marked the beginning of international funding and early market entry, including the Series B and C rounds, as well as the acquisition of InfiniteSoft, which facilitated expansion into the MENA region and pilot markets in the Asia–Pacific. The third phase, spanning 2021 to 2024, was defined by global scaling and HQ relocation, culminating in unicorn status following the Series D in 2022, the acquisition of MindBehind in 2023, the strategic move of HQ to Singapore, expansion into Southeast Asian and Indian enterprise markets, and the Series E investment in 2024.

3.3 Analytical Strategy

The analysis unfolded in three iterative stages. First, the study used the chronological reconstruction to map the company's growth trajectory, highlighting the interdependence of funding events, acquisitions, market entries, and strategic relocations. Second, the study applied thematic coding to interview transcripts and secondary materials. This combined inductive coding, which allowed new patterns to emerge from the data, with abductive coding, which aligned emergent themes with relevant theoretical frameworks from institutional theory, cross-border scaling, and strategic entrepreneurship (Timmermans & Tavory, 2012). Key analytical themes included ecosystem repositioning, strategic legitimation, investor proximity, and shifts in organizational identity. Third, pattern matching and explanation building were employed to interpret the findings through institutional logics (Thornton et al., 2012) and the institutional voids (Khanna & Palepu, 1997, 2010), as well as the literature on scaling in emerging markets, which highlights how ventures respond resource constraints, institutional gaps, and legitimacy deficits in their growth trajectories (Ahlstrom & Bruton, 2006, 2010; Bruton et al., 2008). Particular attention was paid to the role of institutional maturity, defined as the extent to which an entrepreneurial ecosystem offers stable regulatory frameworks, deep capital markets, and global connectivity, in shaping strategic relocation decisions in advanced entrepreneurial ecosystems (Spigel, 2017; Stam, 2015).

By integrating longitudinal depth, multi-source triangulation, and theoretically informed interpretation, this methodological design enables a longitudinal understanding of how Insider reconfigured governance, talent distribution, and brand positioning to transform from a nationally embedded Turkish SaaS startup into a globally recognized MarTech platform.

4 Results

This section presents the empirical findings of the study, tracing Insider's trajectory from its inception in Istanbul to its post-relocation operations in Singapore. The analysis is structured chronologically to reflect the firm's evolution across distinct strategic phases, while also highlighting thematic patterns that emerged from the data. These patterns relate to the interaction between entrepreneurial decision-making and the institutional contexts in which the company operated. The section begins with the company's founding and early expansion within Türkiye's relatively resource-constrained but technically skilled ecosystem, then examines the relocation decision and the challenges encountered in transitioning to a new institutional environment. The section concludes by exploring how Insider has positioned itself within Asia's broader technology and innovation networks, offering insights into the firm's adaptation strategies and the strategic benefits derived from its geographic repositioning.

4.1 Insider's Origins and Pre-relocation Growth

Insider was founded in 2012 in Istanbul by Hande Çilingir and a team of entrepreneurs to transform customer engagement through technology. The founders leveraged Türkiye's deep and relatively affordable engineering talent pool for product development. Istanbul's urban economy and growing tech ecosystem provided fertile conditions for finding early product–market fit. From inception, the founders embraced a "zero optionality" mindset, framing international scaling as a non-negotiable requirement for survival (Tatler Asia, 2022).

The company's first offering was a web-based engagement and on-site optimization platform. Over time, this evolved into an AI-powered growth management suite capable of predictive marketing, hyper-personalized customer journeys, and real-time segmentation across multiple channels. By 2018, Insider's ability to integrate personalization with omnichannel orchestration positioned it to compete with global MarTech providers (TechCrunch, 2018). Early enterprise clients in Europe and the MENA region validated the scalability of its product and demonstrated potential beyond the domestic market.

However, limitations in Türkiye's entrepreneurial ecosystem began to surface as Insider sought later-stage funding. The scarcity of growth-stage venture capital led the company to raise $11 million in Series B funding in 2018 from Sequoia Capital India, marking a globally prestigious investor backing a Turkish MarTech startup (Insider, 2018; Ünsal, 2018). This investment underscored the importance of global capital access for sustaining high-growth trajectories. From 2019 onward, Asia's mobile-first environment began shaping Insider's product strategy. In the developing Asia Pacific region, there is a notable expansion of 5th generation mobile Internet (5G) coverage, alongside significant mobile internet penetration (GSMA, 2025). To meet the needs of these markets, Insider prioritized mobile SDK development, push notification functionality, and in-app personalization tailored to mobile-native consumers. These capabilities accelerated traction in Asia–Pacific and later influenced Western market offerings. Insider also pursued strategic acquisitions to broaden its product suite. In 2018, the acquisition of InfiniteSoft strengthened enterprise software capabilities. In 2023, the acquisition of conversational commerce startup MindBehind expanded AI-powered customer service functions (Insider, 2023). These moves supported a diversified value proposition for global enterprise clients.

Between 2021 and 2024, Insider's funding trajectory reflected its growing global momentum. In 2022, the company raised $121 million in a Series D led by Qatar Investment Authority, Sequoia Capital, and Riverwood Capital, achieving unicorn status with a valuation exceeding $1 billion (Insider, 2022). In 2024, Insider secured a Series E investment from General Atlantic to accelerate expansion in the United States, reinforce its operations in the Asia–Pacific region, and invest in generative AI and cross-channel automation (Insider, 2024).

4.2 Singapore as a Strategic Pivot

Insider's relocation of its global HQ from Istanbul to Singapore was driven by the interplay of domestic ecosystem constraints and the growth potential in Southeast Asia and the broader Asia–Pacific region. While Türkiye offered technical talent and cost advantages, it also posed challenges such as regulatory uncertainty, macroeconomic volatility, and a limited pool of late-stage venture capital (World Bank, 2020). In contrast, Singapore provided a stable regulatory framework, predictable governance, and strategic positioning as a regional business hub.

The move placed Insider in a time zone that enabled real-time collaboration with Asia–Pacific clients while maintaining partial overlap with European operations. Singapore's status as a hub for multinational corporations in sectors such as retail, aviation, and finance has created opportunities for enterprise clients and partnerships. This geographic repositioning also enhanced Insider's credibility with global investors, aligning with major funding milestones, including the 2022 Series D and 2024 Series E rounds (Insider, 2024).

Following relocation, the Singapore base enabled a more agile organizational model. Customer-facing roles and business development functions were increasingly decentralized, with local teams established in different countries across the region. Meanwhile, Istanbul continued to serve as the R&D hub, leveraging cost-effective and high-quality engineering resources. This dual-anchored model allowed Insider to combine centralized product excellence with localized market responsiveness.

The HQ shift also enabled access to leadership talent experienced in scaling SaaS products across culturally diverse and institutionally complex markets. In parallel, acquisitions like MindBehind deepened Insider's integration into clients' digital ecosystems by adding conversational AI and customer service automation capabilities.

By 2024, Insider had evolved from a regional innovator into a global MarTech platform with a governance, talent, and market structure optimized for cross-border scaling. The relocation to Singapore stands as a strategic inflection point that not only opened new market opportunities but also reshaped organizational strategy, investor relationships, and product development priorities.

4.3 *Strategic and Organizational Implications*

Relocating the HQ to Singapore placed senior decision-makers in closer proximity to strategic markets, investors, and high-value clients, enabling rapid alignment between product strategy and market feedback. This co-location enhanced Insider's ability to respond to market changes in real-time and to secure enterprise contracts in competitive bidding environments.

The shift also institutionalized a hybrid operational model. Istanbul's engineering base continued to serve as the primary center for product development, benefiting from Türkiye's relatively competitive labor costs and technical expertise. Meanwhile, regional teams in Asia–Pacific handled client relations, business development, and localized marketing. This structure struck a balance between global brand consistency and market-specific adaptability, supporting Insider's expansion in the region.

In governance terms, the move improved investor relations. Being headquartered in Singapore provided institutional credibility and reassured investors about regulatory stability and operational predictability, factors that were especially important for late-stage funding rounds. Furthermore, positioning the HQ in a hub with advanced mobile commerce adoption, like Singapore, reinforced Insider's mobile-first innovation trajectory, ensuring its product remained competitive across multiple global regions.

The organizational learning from this timeline highlights how emerging-market SaaS firms can leverage ecosystem repositioning as a strategic tool to integrate talent advantages, investor access, and market proximity into a coherent global scaling model (see Table 1).

4.4 *Insider's Strategic Positioning in Asia's Tech Ecosystem*

Insider's relocation to Singapore positioned the company at the heart of Asia's rapidly expanding technology landscape, enabling it to integrate into a multi-layered ecosystem of investors, corporate partners, and innovation networks. Asia–Pacific, particularly Southeast Asia, has emerged as one of the most dynamic regions for digital commerce and mobile-first innovation.

A defining feature of Insider's positioning has been its deliberate integration into the region's platform economy. Technology and solution partnerships with regional leaders enabled the company to embed its personalization and AI-driven customer

Table 1 Timeline of Insider's key milestones (2012–2024)

Year	Milestone	Key event/development	Strategic significance
2012	Founding	Insider was founded in Istanbul by Hande Çilingir and the cofounders' team	Established roots in Türkiye's tech ecosystem; leveraged local engineering talent
2013	Seed	Raised $200,000 from Galata Business Angels, Fırat İşbecer	First investment received from outside cofounders
2013	Seed	Raised $685,000 from Hasan Aslanoba	The post-money valuation reached $6,850,000
2013–2014	Product Launch	Released initial web-based customer engagement and on-site optimization tools	Established MVP and secured early enterprise clients in Türkiye
2015	Geographic Expansion	First international offices in the MENA region	Tested product-market fit outside Türkiye
2016	Funding (Series A)	Raised $2,200,000 from 212 (Fund I), Wamda Capital, Öncü, Erinç Özada, Melih Ödemiş	The post-money valuation reached $12,200,000
2016	Product Pivot	Introduced AI-driven personalization and predictive marketing features	Strengthened competitive positioning against global MarTech platforms
2017	Bridge	Raised $200,000 from 500 Global, e2vc (Fund I)	Post-money valuation reached $12,410,000
2017	Funding (Series A)	Raised $2,050,000 from Wamda Capital, 212 (Fund I), Öncü, Melih Ödemiş, Erinç Özada	The post-money valuation reached $22,050,000 before the HQ moved to Singapore
2017	Partnership	Secured enterprise clients in Europe	Validated cross-border scalability in regulated markets
2018	Funding (Series B)	Raised $8 million led by Sequoia Capital India; acquisition of InfiniteSoft	First significant global VC investment in a Turkish MarTech startup after HQ move to Singapore; expanded technical capabilities
2019	Geographic Expansion	Opened offices in Singapore, London, and Tokyo	Began embedding in advanced and diverse digital ecosystems

(continued)

Table 1 (continued)

Year	Milestone	Key event/development	Strategic significance
2020	Funding (Series C)	Raised $32 million from Riverwood Capital, Sequoia India, and others	Accelerated global hiring and market expansion
2020	Product Enhancement	Rolled out advanced mobile SDKs and in-app personalization tools	Positioned as a mobile-first solution provider, especially for the Asia–Pacific markets
2021	Funding (Series D)	Raised $121 million from Riverwood Capital, Sequoia India, and others	Accelerated global hiring and market expansion
2021	Unicorn Status	Achieved $1B+ valuation after Series D	Increased global investor visibility; strengthened employer brand
2023	Convertible Note	Raised $105 million from Qatar Investment Authority, Esas Private Equity, and others	Accelerated global hiring and market expansion
2023	Acquisition	Acquired MindBehind (conversational commerce platform)	Expanded into conversational AI and messaging commerce
2024	Funding (Series E)	Raised $500 million led by General Atlantic; expansion into India and ANZ	Cemented position as Asia-Pacific MarTech leader; scaled enterprise partnerships

engagement tools directly into dominant consumer touchpoints. This ecosystem integration created network effects that accelerated market penetration.

In parallel, Insider leveraged Singapore's central location to orchestrate a *hub-and-spoke* operational model across the Asia–Pacific region. Country offices in Bangkok, Ho Chi Minh City, Jakarta, Kuala Lumpur, Manila, Seoul, Sydney, Taipei, and Tokyo were supported by centralized leadership in Singapore and core R&D capabilities in Istanbul. This configuration enabled the simultaneous localization of market strategies and the maintenance of a unified, globally competitive product architecture. By doing so, Insider could address the heterogeneous needs of Asia's diverse economies while sustaining the product innovation cadence expected in these markets.

The company's ability to adapt its value proposition to Asia's institutional and cultural diversity has been critical to sustaining growth. In mature markets such as Japan and Australia, Insider emphasized enterprise-grade integration and compliance. In contrast, in fast-growing emerging markets like Vietnam and the Philippines, it prioritized rapid deployment, mobile-first features, and performance-driven ROI metrics. This duality has not only broadened Insider's client base. However, it has also positioned itself as a reference case for how emerging-market firms can embed themselves in, and help shape, one of the world's most competitive technology ecosystems.

5 Discussion: Implications for Entrepreneurship in Asia

5.1 Key Lessons for Digital Entrepreneurs Scaling from Emerging Markets

Insider's relocation to Singapore illustrates a path-dependent yet strategic response to the structural and institutional limitations of its home ecosystem. Originating from Türkiye's entrepreneurial landscape, the firm encountered familiar scaling obstacles for emerging-market ventures: scarcity of late-stage capital, regulatory uncertainty, and constraints on global brand legitimacy. Relocation was not a reactive escape but a deliberate strategic move to embed the company in a regional hub that could amplify its growth trajectory.

From a capital access perspective, the firm's financing pathway shows the importance of staged, diversified fundraising. In 2023, Insider utilized a convertible note to bridge the gap between growth phases, minimizing dilution while sustaining expansion momentum. In 2024, the Series E round, led by General Atlantic with participation from existing investors, solidified its valuation above $1.2 billion, reaffirming market confidence in its global scaling capabilities. These moves demonstrate that internationalization can unlock not only geographic proximity to markets but also sustained access to high-quality capital sources otherwise unavailable in the home country.

Equally important, the case highlights that geography is a strategic lever only when paired with leadership vision. Insider's founders articulated a global orientation from the outset, aligning their narrative and operations to the expectations of globally active VCs such as Sequoia Capital India. This alignment facilitated trust, ensured that capital came with market access and mentorship, and accelerated Insider's integration into Asia–Pacific's enterprise networks.

The firm's journey highlights that relocation does not necessitate abandoning the domestic base. By retaining its engineering hub in Istanbul, Insider benefited from cost-effective technical talent and cultural cohesion while leveraging Singapore's market credibility. This hybrid scaling model provides a replicable template for founders seeking to strike a balance between global reach and local strengths. Table 2 summarizes key lessons from Insider's cross-border scaling journey.

Table 2 Key lessons from Insider's cross-border scaling journey

Lesson	Practical insight
1. Treat location as a growth lever, not an afterthought	Relocating strategic functions to a global hub such as Singapore should be part of a planned scaling roadmap, with explicit objectives for market access, credibility, and capital raising
2. Pair relocation with narrative transformation	Reframe the venture's identity to align with the expectations of global investors and enterprise clients by adjusting the headquarters designation, branding language, and affiliations with high-trust local networks
3. Use hybrid scaling to retain home advantages	Maintain core technical or operational functions in the home country to leverage cost advantages, talent familiarity, and ecosystem ties while situating leadership and investor relations in a global hub
4. Structure funding strategically for continuity	Bridge growth phases with instruments such as convertible notes to preserve momentum and founder control, paving the way for later large equity rounds
5. Leverage success for ecosystem spillover	Use high-profile global investment wins to shift perceptions of the home ecosystem, attract follow-on capital for other ventures, and strengthen the local entrepreneurial brand

5.2 *How Regional Hubs Like Singapore Shape Entrepreneurial Narratives*

Regional hubs, such as Singapore, operate as both operational grounds and legitimacy engines. They provide infrastructure, regulatory predictability, and deep investor pools, but equally important, they enable narrative transformation. For startups emerging from ecosystems burdened by perceived instability or limited global brand visibility, relocating can reframe their identity in ways that influence investor perception, customer trust, and partnership opportunities.

For Insider, positioning itself as a Singapore-headquartered MarTech company allowed it to shift the discourse from "a promising Turkish startup" to "a global SaaS platform embedded in Asia's innovation capital." Concrete practices reinforced this: adjusting corporate messaging, listing Singapore as the headquarters in investor communications, and emphasizing enterprise readiness in marketing materials. These symbolic acts were not superficial; they actively reshaped how global stakeholders assessed the company's risk profile and growth potential. This narrative reframing was particularly valuable for winning large Asia–Pacific enterprise clients, such as Singapore Airlines, where institutional credibility often plays a decisive role in procurement decisions. In turn, the enhanced client roster further reinforced investor interest, creating a self-reinforcing cycle of legitimacy and growth.

5.3 Recommendations for Founders, Investors, and Policy Actors

For founders, three practical recommendations emerge. First, treat location strategy as a deliberate dimension of scaling, not a byproduct of market entry. Relocating HQ functions to a hub like Singapore should be accompanied by explicit signaling to global investors, emphasizing governance maturity, readiness for enterprise markets, and a roadmap for regional expansion. Second, utilize hybrid models that separate strategic and operational functions. Insider's retention of Istanbul-based engineering teams, combined with leadership embedded in Singapore, maximized both cost efficiency and credibility. Third, structure funding with strategic continuity in mind, bridging mechanisms like convertible notes can sustain momentum between major equity rounds while preserving founder control.

For investors, relocation decisions can serve as important signals of a venture's adaptability, ambition, and governance capability. Investors evaluating emerging-market startups should assess whether founders have matched location changes with operational readiness, capital strategy, and market timing. Insider's Series E round, preceded by years of strategic market embedding, demonstrates how relocation, when timed well, can translate into outsized returns.

For policymakers, Insider's trajectory points to two critical imperatives. First, strengthen domestic late-stage capital markets to reduce the need for outbound HQ relocation. Second, invest in international branding and investor outreach to reduce the credibility gap that drives firms to seek external legitimacy. Even so, one should not underestimate the ecosystem spillover from successful hybrid ventures. Following Insider's success, global investors such as General Atlantic, Sequoia Capital India, and Riverwood Capital have shown increased interest in Türkiye-based ventures. The 2024 secondary acquisition of 212's Insider shares by General Atlantic sent a strong signal of long-term investor confidence in the Turkish pipeline, encouraging follow-on investments into other local startups backed by 212, Esas Ventures, and Endeavor.

In short, Insider's journey demonstrates that hybrid scaling, which involves anchoring core technical talent domestically while situating strategic functions in global hubs, can yield firm-level growth and ecosystem-level credibility gains. For stakeholders across the entrepreneurial landscape, recognizing location decisions as fundamental to competitiveness is essential. Where others see a venture that belongs to them, it can be as decisive as what it builds.

6 Conclusion

Insider's relocation from Istanbul to Singapore illustrates how emerging-market startups can use *ecosystem relocation* and *strategic geography* as deliberate levers to overcome institutional constraints and accelerate global scaling. Rather than treating geography as a passive condition, the firm reconfigured it as a resource, embedding itself in a high-trust, innovation-oriented hub while retaining its engineering base in Türkiye. This hybrid scaling model allowed Insider to combine the operational efficiency of its home base with the institutional legitimacy, investor access, and client proximity of Singapore's entrepreneurial ecosystem.

The case demonstrates that such relocation strategies are not merely logistical moves but also symbolic acts of *narrative reconfiguration*. By repositioning itself within an advanced market ecosystem, Insider was able to signal governance maturity, global ambition, and reduced investment risk to venture capitalists, exemplified by its securing of capital from globally prominent investors such as Sequoia Capital India and General Atlantic. This reframing of identity, supported by branding choices, network affiliations, and market-facing communications, enabled the firm to transcend the liability of origin often faced by startups from emerging markets.

From a theoretical perspective, the study contributes to the understanding of *strategic geography* in entrepreneurial scaling by highlighting three interconnected dynamics. First, *ecosystem relocation* can restructure a venture's institutional environment, providing access to late-stage capital, enterprise clients, and global recognition. Second, *hybrid scaling models*, splitting operational and strategic functions across geographies, offer a sustainable path for emerging-market ventures to remain anchored in their home ecosystems while integrating into global markets. Third, *symbolic repositioning* plays a crucial role in reinforcing operational gains, as relocation becomes both a practical and a performative tool for scaling. These findings also underscore the *ecosystem spillover* effects that high-profile relocations can generate, such as shifting investor perceptions and encouraging follow-on funding for other domestic startups.

For practitioners, several actionable lessons emerge. Founders in emerging markets should treat geography as an integral component of their growth strategy, utilizing relocation or multi-location models to leverage the strengths of both their home and host ecosystems. Signaling readiness to global venture capitalists, through governance practices, strategic ecosystem choice, and alignment with international norms, can enhance access to capital and partnerships. Investors evaluating startups from volatile or resource-constrained contexts should pay close attention to how entrepreneurs use geography to mitigate risk and build credibility. Policymakers, meanwhile, must recognize that retaining scaling-stage startups requires not only fostering early-stage innovation but also addressing capital gaps, building brand infrastructure, and ensuring macroeconomic stability to reduce the pressure to relocate strategic functions abroad.

Insider's trajectory reinforces that geography is not destiny. However, startups can actively manage it as a strategic asset to unlock growth, legitimacy, and global integration. By coupling operational competence in its home base with the institutional advantages of a global hub, the firm created a durable competitive position while contributing positively to the reputation and connectivity of its domestic entrepreneurial ecosystem. This dual anchoring, home and hub, offers a model for other emerging-market startups seeking to reconcile local roots with global ambitions. Future research should investigate the long-term organizational, governance, and identity dynamics of such hybrid scaling strategies, including how firms manage tensions between their home and host ecosystems, as well as how ecosystem spillovers evolve across sectors and regions.

References

Ahlstrom, D., & Bruton, G. D. (2006). Venture capital in emerging economies: Networks and institutional change. *Entrepreneurship Theory and Practice, 30*(2), 299–320. https://doi.org/10.1111/j.1540-6520.2006.00122.x

Ahlstrom, D., & Bruton, G. D. (2010). Rapid institutional shifts and the co-evolution of entrepreneurial firms in transition economies. *Entrepreneurship Theory and Practice, 34*(3), 531–554. https://doi.org/10.1111/j.1540-6520.2010.00373.x

Asian Development Bank. (2023). *Why Singapore's ecosystem for technology startups is among the best*. Development Asia. https://development.asia/insight/why-singapores-ecosystem-technology-startups-among-best

Autio, E., Kenney, M., Mustar, P., Siegel, D., & Wright, M. (2014). Entrepreneurial innovation: The importance of context. *Research Policy, 43*(7), 1097–1108. https://doi.org/10.1016/j.respol.2014.01.015

Autio, E., Sapienza, H. J., & Almeida, J. G. (2000). Effects of age at entry, knowledge intensity, and imitability on international growth. *Academy of Management Journal, 43*(5), 909–924. https://doi.org/10.5465/1556419

Bruton, G. D., Ahlstrom, D., & Obloj, K. (2008). Entrepreneurship in emerging economies: Where are we today and where should the research go in the future. *Entrepreneurship Theory and Practice, 32*(1), 1–14. https://doi.org/10.1111/j.1540-6520.2007.00213.x

Cavusgil, S. T., & Knight, G. (2015). The born global firm: An entrepreneurial and capabilities perspective on early and rapid internationalization. *Journal of International Business Studies, 46*(1), 3–16. https://doi.org/10.1057/jibs.2014.62

GSMA. (2025). *The Mobile Economy Asia Pacific 2024*. GSMA Intelligence. https://www.gsma.com/solutions-and-impact/connectivity-for-good/mobile-economy/asiapacific/

Insider. (2018). Sequoia India leads US$11M Series B in Insider, a growth management platform for marketers. *Insider Newsroom*. https://useinsider.com/news/singapore-marketing-startup-insider-secures-us11m-sequoia/

Insider. (2022, March 7). Trusted by 1/3 of the Fortune Global 500, unlocks unicorn status and announces $121M Series D with a $1.22B valuation. https://useinsider.com/news/insider-unlocks-unicorn-status-and-announces-121m-series-d/

Insider. (2023). Insider acquires mindbehind signaling a new era in end-to-end conversational commerce & messaging. https://useinsider.com/news/insider-acquires-mindbehind/

Insider. (2024, November 1). Insider announces $500M Series E led by General Atlantic to accelerate AI investments, fuel U.S. expansion, and continue to scale global operations. https://useinsider.com/news/insider-announces-500m-series-e-led-by-general-atlantic/

Khanna, T., & Palepu, K. (1997). Why focused strategies may be wrong for emerging markets. *Harvard Business Review, 75*(4), 41–51.

Khanna, T., & Palepu, K. (2010). *Winning in emerging markets: A road map for strategy and execution*. Harvard Business School Publishing.

Lavine, R. (2023). *Turkey: Can CVC remove the funding roadblocks for startups*? Global Venturing. https://globalventuring.com/corporate/asia/turkey-startup-ecosystem-funding/

Li, Y., & Zahra, S. A. (2012). Formal institutions, culture, and venture capital activity: A cross-country analysis. *Journal of Business Venturing, 27*(1), 95–111. https://doi.org/10.1016/j.jbusvent.2010.06.003

Luo, Y., & Tung, R. L. (2007). International expansion of emerging market enterprises: A springboard perspective. *Journal of International Business Studies, 38*(4), 481–498. https://doi.org/10.1057/palgrave.jibs.8400275

Matthews, J. A. (2006). Dragon multinationals: New players in 21st-century globalization. *Asia Pacific Journal of Management, 23*(1), 5–27. https://doi.org/10.1007/s10490-006-6113-0

Mudambi, R. (2008). Location, control and innovation in knowledge-intensive industries. *Journal of Economic Geography, 8*(5), 699–725. https://doi.org/10.1093/jeg/lbn024

Nambisan, S. (2017). Digital entrepreneurship: Toward a digital technology perspective of entrepreneurship. *Entrepreneurship Theory and Practice, 41*(6), 1029–1055. https://doi.org/10.1111/etap.12254

Oviatt, B. M., & McDougall, P. P. (2005). Toward a theory of international new ventures. *Journal of International Business Studies, 36*(1), 29–41. https://doi.org/10.1057/palgrave.jibs.8400128

Ramamurti, R. (2012). What is really different about emerging market multinationals? *Global Strategy Journal, 2*(1), 41–47. https://doi.org/10.1002/gsj.1025

Saxenian, A. (2006). *The new Argonauts: Regional advantage in a global economy.* Harvard University Press.

Spigel, B. (2017). The relational organization of entrepreneurial ecosystems. *Entrepreneurship Theory and Practice, 41*(1), 49–72. https://doi.org/10.1111/etap.12167

Spigel, B., & Harrison, R. (2018). Toward a process theory of entrepreneurial ecosystems. *Strategic Entrepreneurship Journal, 12*(1), 151–168. https://doi.org/10.1002/sej.1268

Stam, E. (2015). Entrepreneurial ecosystems and regional policy: A sympathetic critique. *European Planning Studies, 23*(9), 1759–1769. https://doi.org/10.1080/09654313.2015.1061484

Startup Genome. (2025). *The Global Startup Ecosystem Report 2025.* https://startupgenome.com/report/gser2025/introduction

Suchman, M. C. (1995). Managing legitimacy: Strategic and institutional approaches. *Academy of Management Review, 20*(3), 571–610. https://doi.org/10.5465/amr.1995.9508080331

Tatler Asia. (2022). *"There's Zero Optionality": Insider's Hande Çilingir on Building a Billion-Dollar Company.* https://www.tatlerasia.com/gen-t/leadership/theres-zero-optionality-and-that-gives-us-unbeatable-focus-insiders-hande-%C3%A7ilingir-on-building-a-bil

TechCrunch. (2018). *Insider raises $11M to help internet marketers do better internet marketing.* https://techcrunch.com/2018/04/02/insider-raises-11m/

Thornton, P. H., Ocasio, W., & Lounsbury, M. (2012). *The institutional logics perspective: A new approach to culture, structure, and process.* Oxford University Press.

Timmermans, S., & Tavory, I. (2012). Theory construction in qualitative research: From grounded theory to abductive analysis. *Sociological Theory, 30*(3), 167–186. https://doi.org/10.1177/0735275112457914

Ünsal, S. (2018). *Şubat ayinda 7 girişim 7.1 milyon dolar yatirim aldi (Seven startups received $7.1 million in investment in February).* https://www.milliyet.com.tr/yazarlar/serkan-unsal/subat-ayinda-7-girisim-7-1-milyon-dolar-yatirim-aldi-2619590

World Bank. (2020). *Doing business 2020: Comparing business regulation in 190 economies.* Washington, D.C.: World Bank Group. https://openknowledge.worldbank.org/bitstream/handle/10986/32436/9781464814402.pdf

Wry, T., Lounsbury, M., & Glynn, M. A. (2011). Legitimating nascent collective identities: Coordinating cultural entrepreneurship. *Organization Science, 22*(2), 449–463. https://doi.org/10.1287/orsc.1100.0613

Yin, R. K. (2018). *Case study research and applications: Design and methods.*

Zahra, S. A., Ireland, R. D., & Hitt, M. A. (2000). International expansion by new venture firms: International diversity, mode of market entry, technological learning, and performance. *Academy of Management Journal, 43*(5), 925–950. https://doi.org/10.5465/1556420

Deniz Tunçalp is Professor of Management at Istanbul Technical University, specializing in entrepreneurship, digital transformation, and innovation in emerging markets. His research focuses on startup ecosystems, technology management, and the interplay between institutional environments and entrepreneurial growth strategies. He has published in leading international journals, including the *Journal of Business Ethics*, *Organizational Research Methods*, and the *Journal of Family Business Management*. He is also Senior Associate Editor at *Management Decision*. In addition to his academic work, Tunçalp has held leadership roles in technology transfer and R&D commercialization, notably as the CEO of *ITU ARI Teknokent*, and as the founding General Manager of both 1773 ITU Technopark and the *1773 ITU Technology Transfer Office*. He has also consistently ranked among the most impactful people in the Turkish entrepreneurship ecosystem and actively mentors technology startups.

Benchmarking Supply Chain Performance for Entrepreneurial Growth: Financial Insights from Key Industries in India

Ananya Hadadi Raghavendra

Abstract In today's hyper-competitive and digitally evolving landscape, supply chain performance is no longer a backend operational concern but a strategic differentiator—particularly in Asia's dynamic entrepreneurial markets. This chapter presents a benchmarking framework tailored for Indian enterprises, emphasizing how operational efficiency rooted in financial data can drive sustainable growth, innovation, and entrepreneurial scalability. Focusing on five vital industries—Automotive, Electronics, Healthcare, Pharmaceutical, and Food & Beverage—this study analyzes 10 leading firms from each sector (totaling 50 companies) over a 10-year period, offering a longitudinal perspective rarely captured in Asian entrepreneurship research. By introducing three original supply chain indicators—Total Length of Chain (aggregate inventory days), Supply Chain Inefficiency Ratio (cost-to-sales), and Supply Chain Working Capital Productivity (sales-to-capital efficiency)—the study benchmarks firm performance and captures strategic shifts across two key sub-periods. The findings reveal significant inter- and intra-industry variations in supply chain efficiency, highlighting top performers such as Hyundai, BEL, Manipal Hospitals, Sun Pharma, and ITC. These companies exemplify how data-driven operational strategies can enhance market competitiveness, resource utilization, and entrepreneurial agility. Aligned with the book's mission to uncover new entrepreneurial opportunities in Asia, this chapter showcases how financial statement-driven benchmarking can empower startups, SMEs, and large firms alike to identify inefficiencies, adopt best practices, and strengthen resilience. The study contributes to both academic discourse and managerial practice by offering actionable insights and advocating for greater transparency, strategic benchmarking, and digital adaptation within Asia's evolving entrepreneurial ecosystems.

A. H. Raghavendra (✉)
Great Lakes Institute of Management, Chennai, India
e-mail: ananya.hr20ph@iimranchi.ac.in

T. Endress and Y. F. Badir (eds.), *Business and Management in Asia: Opportunities and Entrepreneurship*, https://doi.org/10.1007/978-981-95-4909-2_12

1 Introduction

As Asia emerges as a dynamic hub of entrepreneurial growth, the efficiency and adaptability of supply chains have become vital levers for competitive advantage and innovation. In the context of Asia's vibrant entrepreneurial resurgence, especially within India's fast-evolving industrial landscape, supply chain efficiency has become a decisive factor for entrepreneurial success. Today's ventures operate not only under heightened global competition but also amid digital disruptions that require agile and data-driven decision-making. In this context, operational excellence is critical for survival. It is measured through supply chain robustness and serves as a key growth enabler.

In today's competitive environment, effective supply chain management (SCM) is crucial for organizational success. SCM encompasses a broad range of activities—from sourcing raw materials and production to distribution and delivery—that collectively determine a firm's ability to meet customer demand efficiently. Companies are increasingly challenged by cost pressures, global competition, and complex, multi-tier supply networks. Monitoring and improving supply chain performance has thus become unavoidable for firms seeking to maintain healthy profit margins. Prior research has identified numerous factors influencing successful SCM implementation, including customer expectations, globalization, information technology, and e-business adoption. In particular, benchmarking has emerged as a widely used tool to assess and enhance supply chain performance by comparing key performance metrics against peers or industry leaders (Raghavendra et al., 2024). According to global management surveys, over 70% of companies utilize benchmarking as a management tool, reflecting its ubiquity in practice (Rigby, 2001). Benchmarking is explicitly encouraged in quality frameworks such as the Malcolm Baldrige National Quality Award, underscoring its significance across diverse sectors (Wong & Wong, 2008). However, despite its widespread use, there remains a notable lack of comprehensive theory and frameworks to guide benchmarking, particularly in the context of supply chain management. This gap makes it challenging for organizations to systematically identify and implement best practices in their supply chains.

Benchmarking in supply chain management involves comparing performance metrics—often derived from financial and operational data—against those of competitors or industry standards. Financial statements, in particular, provide valuable insights into supply chain performance by quantifying elements such as cost of goods sold, inventory levels, and working capital. Managers worldwide have leveraged financial metrics as a proxy to benchmark supply chain efficiency and effectiveness. For example, cost-of-sales figures and inventory turnover ratios can indicate how well a firm manages its procurement and inventory processes, while metrics like order fulfillment rates and on-time delivery (when available) reflect customer service performance. By benchmarking these metrics, companies can pinpoint areas where they outperform competitors or, conversely, lag behind. Such comparative analysis enables organizations to learn from the successes of others and drives continuous improvement. Indeed, studies have shown that firms adopting rigorous benchmarking practices often achieve superior operational and financial outcomes. Classic cases include Xerox in the 1980s, which famously used benchmarking to overhaul its supply chain and regain market share from Japanese competitors. Subsequent benchmarking studies have reaffirmed that organizations employing best-in-class supply chain practices tend to realize higher efficiency and profitability. Stewart's (1995) early benchmarking study, for instance, revealed key drivers of supply chain excellence such as leadership commitment and technology adoption, while more recent works continue to link effective SCM to improved business performance.

Despite the evident benefits, supply chain benchmarking is underutilized in certain contexts. In reviewing the literature, it is apparent that few studies have systematically benchmarked supply chain performance of Indian companies using published financial data. Much of the extant research has focused on developed economies or specific sectors, leaving a gap in understanding how Indian industries compare in supply chain efficiency. Moreover, prior studies often examine a narrow timeframe or a limited set of metrics. There is a need for longitudinal analysis to capture performance trends over time. The *research gaps* identified include: (1) a lack of studies analyzing multi-year supply chain performance of a broad cross-section of Indian companies—many benchmarking studies in supply chain have been conducted in other countries but not comprehensively in India; (2) limited exploration of sustainability and long-term trends in supply chain efficiency, as companies often prioritize short-term profitability over sustainable practices; and (3) the novelty of comparing direct competitors on supply chain performance using common financial metrics. Addressing these gaps is important for both academia and industry. Companies operating in India's dynamic market can benefit from understanding how their supply chain performance stacks up against peers, while researchers can gain insights into the applicability of financial metric-based benchmarking in emerging economies.

Accordingly, this study aims to benchmark the supply chain performance of key industries in India using published financial statements, thereby extending the knowledge frontier on supply chain benchmarking in an Indian context. We focus on five critical sectors of the Indian economy: Automotive, Electronics, Healthcare, Pharmaceutical, and Food & Beverage. These industries have been chosen due to their significant contribution to India's GDP and their diverse supply chain structures (ranging from heavy manufacturing to fast-moving consumer goods). By analyzing multiple industries, the study provides a comparative perspective that can highlight sector-specific strengths and weaknesses in supply chain management. The research is structured around a core hypothesis: firms that excel in supply-chain-related financial metrics (such as efficient inventory management and low supply chain costs) tend to achieve superior profitability. This hypothesis aligns with the proposition that a well-managed supply chain reduces costs and improves service, which should translate into better financial results. While a formal statistical test of this hypothesis is beyond the scope of the current benchmarking analysis, it provides a conceptual foundation—motivating the expectation that companies with high supply chain efficiency will, on average, perform better financially (through higher profit margins or ROI) than their less efficient counterparts.

The objectives of this study are fourfold: (1) to develop a framework for using financial statement data to benchmark supply chain performance across industries; (2) to apply this framework to measure and compare the supply chain performance of ten prominent companies in each of five industries over a 10-year period; (3) to identify best-in-class companies in each industry and distill the best practices or strategic decisions that contribute to their superior performance; and (4) to provide recommendations for how companies (especially those lagging behind) can improve their supply chain performance based on the insights gained. In pursuing these objectives, the study constructs and utilizes composite metrics that capture different dimensions of supply chain performance from financial data (inventory levels, cost efficiency, and working capital utilization).

The significance of this study lies in its practical and academic contributions. For practitioners, it offers a ready methodology to benchmark their firm's supply chain using publicly available data, which can be a cost-effective alternative to internal operational audits. By highlighting specific areas (e.g., inventory days, cost ratios) where a company deviates from industry benchmarks, the findings enable managers to formulate targeted improvement strategies. The approach demonstrates that financial statements can be leveraged beyond traditional financial analysis, serving as a window into operational efficiency and effectiveness. Firms can evaluate where they are performing better or worse than competitors and learn from peers' successes to adopt new practices. In an era where data-driven decision-making is paramount, such benchmarking provides an evidence-based foundation for supply chain enhancements. For academia, this study fills a gap by focusing on Indian industries, thereby adding to the global benchmarking literature a perspective from an emerging market. It also tests the applicability of supply chain performance measures (originally developed in other contexts) within the Indian business environment, contributing to the generalizability of those measures.

This study highlights that financial-statement-based benchmarking offers entrepreneurs a practical, low-cost method to assess and enhance supply chain efficiency—crucial for scaling businesses in competitive Asian markets. By identifying sector-specific best practices and top-performing firms, the framework provides actionable insights that support data-driven decision-making and operational excellence in emerging economies like India. For students, scholars, and practitioners interested in Asian entrepreneurship, this article provides empirical grounding for how financial insights can drive operational strategy. For policymakers and ecosystem enablers, it highlights the importance of encouraging transparent reporting and supply chain benchmarking as part of national innovation strategies. Ultimately, the study repositions supply chain performance not as a back-end function, but as a cornerstone of sustainable, scalable, and inclusive entrepreneurship in Asia. Figure 1 presents the conceptual framework of this study, outlining the step-by-step flow from industry selection through metric computation, benchmarking, and cross-industry comparison to the development of actionable insights. This framework ensures a structured approach that aligns with both academic rigor and practical relevance for business professionals.

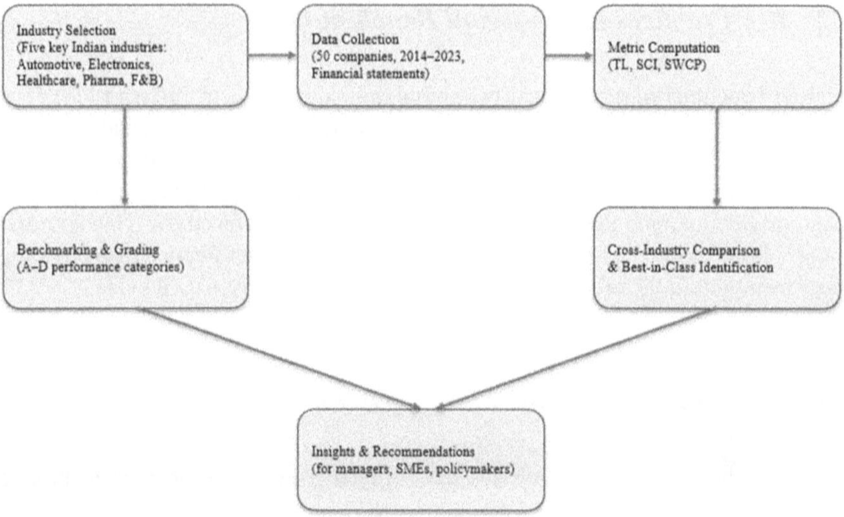

Fig. 1 Conceptual framework of the study

2 Literature Review

Benchmarking in supply chain management has attracted extensive scholarly attention, with researchers exploring diverse performance measures, frameworks, and evolving contexts. The literature broadly underscores benchmarking as a dynamic tool to enhance supply chain performance, identify best practices, incorporate sustainability, and adapt to emerging challenges.

2.1 Enhancing Supply Chain Performance

Benchmarking plays a pivotal role in driving supply chain improvements. Gilmour (1998) emphasized that benchmarking facilitates the identification of inefficiencies and fosters continuous improvement through a performance feedback loop. Wong and Wong (2008) underscored the necessity of choosing appropriate metrics and maintaining adaptable benchmarking systems that evolve with market and technological shifts. Simatupang and Sridharan (2004) empirically linked supply chain collaboration—via shared information and synchronized decision-making—to superior performance. These works collectively argue that benchmarking is not a one-off assessment but an ongoing strategic activity necessary for supply chain excellence.

2.2 Key Practices and Internal Benchmarking

Internal benchmarking is critical for optimizing supply chains. Stewart (1995), in a foundational study, identified leadership, technological integration, and customer-centricity as hallmarks of high-performing supply chains. Shah and Singh (2001) developed an internal benchmarking framework, promoting alignment of procurement, production, and distribution with broader business objectives. This approach enables firms to uncover internal bottlenecks, stressing that effective benchmarking starts from within the organization before external comparisons are made.

2.3 Evolving Metrics and Value Creation

The focus of benchmarking metrics has evolved from cost-efficiency to broader indicators. Gopal and Thakkar (2012) observed a shift from traditional cost/output metrics to those emphasizing responsiveness, flexibility, and customer satisfaction. Brandenburg and Seuring (2011) further connected superior supply chain performance with increased firm valuation, linking operational excellence to shareholder value. In the Indian context, Patel and Patel (2018) benchmarked tire manufacturers, demonstrating how industry-specific characteristics can inform customized benchmarking. Piotrowicz et al. (2011) synthesized various measurement frameworks, reinforcing that benchmarking strategies must reflect the complexity of modern supply chains.

2.4 Sustainability and Green Supply Chain Benchmarking

Incorporating sustainability into benchmarking has become a key theme. Hervani et al. (2005) proposed integrating environmental performance metrics (e.g., waste reduction, carbon footprint) into benchmarking systems. Yakovleva et al. (2012) applied this to the food industry, showing how sustainability benchmarking improves both ecological and operational efficiency. Bichou (2006) proposed supplementing traditional port benchmarks with supply-chain-based and environmental metrics to capture sustainability more holistically. Hines (1998), though not directly focused on sustainability, highlighted global variations by comparing Toyota's supply chains in Japan and the UK, establishing international best practice benchmarks. Colicchia et al. (2011) added that sustainability metrics should be sector-specific, as environmental priorities differ across industries.

2.5 Environmental Metrics and Collaboration

Shaw et al. (2010) developed environmental benchmarking metrics such as carbon footprint per delivery unit, enabling performance comparison on green parameters. Andersen et al. (1999) used benchmarking to identify replicable best practices via inter-organizational learning. Fawcett et al. (2009) emphasized information-sharing as a critical enabler of superior performance, suggesting benchmarking should evaluate relational as well as operational dimensions. These studies collectively argue that benchmarking should also assess collaborative processes and not just outcomes.

2.6 Diverse Applications of Benchmarking

Benchmarking is applicable across diverse supply chain contexts. Acquaye et al. (2014) benchmarked carbon emissions, advocating eco-efficiency as a competitive differentiator. Lewis and Naim (1995) benchmarked post-sales service supply chains, linking improved aftermarket performance to customer satisfaction. Gonzalez et al. (2008) applied benchmarking to design supply chain curricula using Quality Function Deployment (QFD). Sutton (2004) compared Chinese and Indian auto-component supply chains, highlighting competitive gaps and areas for mutual learning. Rizet et al. (2012) benchmarked carbon and energy efficiency across supply chains, showing challenges in data standardization. Kumar et al. (2015) used an Analytical Hierarchy Process (AHP) to benchmark technology transfer barriers, showing how benchmarking supports strategic decision-making in supply chains.

2.7 Resilience, Risk Mitigation, and Performance Measurement

Recent literature has broadened benchmarking to include resilience and risk management. Kaviani et al. (2020) benchmarked supply chain resilience in the automotive sector by analyzing vulnerability and recovery metrics. Tarei et al. (2020) assessed the effectiveness of various risk mitigation strategies like safety stock and supplier diversification. Mor et al. (2018) applied Interpretive Structural Modeling (ISM) to benchmark interdependencies among dairy supply chain KPIs. Manning et al. (2008) benchmarked the poultry supply chain, emphasizing cold chain logistics. Keebler and Plank (2009) stressed logistics metrics (e.g., delivery times, fill rates) as central to effective supply chain benchmarking.

2.8 Agility, Sustainability, and Global Contexts

Feizabadi et al. (2019) highlighted the "Triple-A" framework—agility, adaptability, and alignment—as essential benchmarking themes. Faisal (2009) benchmarked risk response strategies, and Brockhaus et al. (2016) integrated system dynamics modeling for sustainable product benchmarking. Tseng et al. (2014) introduced eco-efficiency under uncertainty, while Uluskan and Godfrey (2018) benchmarked supply chain structures in Haiti vs. China, revealing the importance of localization in benchmarking. Mangla et al. (2018) employed fuzzy Failure Mode and Effects Analysis (FMEA) to benchmark green supply chain risks in India.

2.9 Emerging Trends and Innovations

New data sources and technologies are shaping benchmarking practices. Gao et al. (2021) extracted benchmarking data from corporate websites to evaluate green practices. Hossain and Thakur (2021) benchmarked Industry 4.0 technology readiness in Indian hospital supply chains using fuzzy-AHP-DEMATEL methods, highlighting digital transformation as a benchmarkable domain. Tuominen et al. (2009) benchmarked food supply chains between Russia and Finland, noting infrastructure's role. Banomyong and Supatn (2011) developed benchmarking tools for Thai SMEs, showing that smaller firms need tailored, accessible benchmarking frameworks. Singh et al. (2006) surveyed benchmarking maturity in Indian firms, revealing inconsistent adoption. Lapide (2000) questioned metric relevance and urged firms to align benchmarking with strategic goals.

Recent research underscores the role of digital transformation in enabling resilient, high-performing supply chains. For instance, Ivanov (2023) introduces an *Intelligent Digital Twin (iDT)* framework that supports stress-testing, disruption prediction, and proactive resilience building. Additionally, Zhao (2023) empirically maps the influence of supply chain digitalization through absorptive, response, and recovery capabilities, linking it to enhanced performance. On the strategic front, Ocicka et al. (2022) highlight the significance of organizational ambidexterity—balancing exploitation and exploration—for achieving resilience during and after the COVID-19 crisis. Finally, Zamani et al. (2022), in their systematic review, demonstrate how AI and big data analytics collectively support supply chain resilience across multiple phases.

3 Methodology

This study employs a quantitative benchmarking approach to evaluate supply chain performance across five key Indian industries—Automotive, Electronics, Healthcare, Pharmaceutical, and Food & Beverage. These sectors were selected for their economic significance and availability of consistent financial data. From each industry, ten major companies were chosen based on market prominence and data availability, yielding a total sample of 50 firms. Financial data were primarily sourced from the Capitaline database, with cross-verification from company annual reports, Screener, and CMIE to ensure accuracy and completeness. All data were reported in Indian Rupees and reflect consolidated figures to capture full supply chain operations.

The analysis spans a ten-year period (2014–2023), divided into two equal sub-periods: Period 1 (2014–2018) and Period 2 (2019–2023). For each firm, financial data were averaged over each five-year span to smoothen year-on-year volatility and provide a representative view of performance. This temporal division also enables benchmarking a firm's progress over time, while accounting for major disruptions such as the COVID-19 pandemic during 2020–2021.

Three key performance indicators (KPIs) were derived from financial statements to measure supply chain efficiency:

Total Length of Chain (TL): Represents inventory holding time across the supply chain, calculated as the sum of days of inventory for raw materials, WIP, and finished goods. Lower TL implies faster inventory turnover and operational efficiency.

Supply Chain Inefficiency Ratio (SCI): Measures the proportion of net sales consumed by supply chain costs (distribution costs and inventory carrying costs). Lower SCI indicates better cost efficiency in supply chain operations.

Supply Chain Working Capital Productivity (SWCP): Evaluates how effectively supply chain working capital (inventory + receivables − payables) is converted into revenue. Higher SWCP signifies greater financial efficiency.

All metrics were computed for both periods for all 50 companies, producing 300 data points. Plausibility checks were performed to identify outliers or extreme values—such as notably negative SWCP ratios—resulting from high payables. These anomalies were flagged for qualitative discussion but retained in the quantitative analysis.

Performance grading was conducted within each industry using a four-level system (A to D). Companies showing consistent improvements or top-tier metrics were graded "A," while those with declining or below-average performance were graded "D." This relative classification highlights leaders and laggards within each industry (see Table 2).

Additionally, cross-industry comparisons were made using average metrics across all 10 companies in each sector. This allowed identification of industry-level strengths and weaknesses, as well as top performers across all industries in individual metrics—offering insights into potential best practices (e.g., JIT systems or central warehousing).

While grounded in quantitative analysis, qualitative factors—such as sector-specific regulations or strategic decisions like inventory buffering—were considered during interpretation. This ensures that benchmarking results are both analytically robust and contextually meaningful.

By integrating consistent data sources, clearly defined metrics, and a structured grading system, this methodology provides a reliable and actionable framework for evaluating supply chain performance across diverse industries in India.

Table 1 presents the formulas for these variables and a brief description for clarity. All financial inputs for these formulas were obtained from the data sources mentioned, and calculated for each company and period.

Table 1 Benchmarking formulas for key supply chain performance metrics

Metric (abbreviation)	Formula	Description (financial elements)
Total Length of Chain (TL)	DRM = (RM × 365)/CRMDWIP = (SFG × 365)/CPDFG = (FG × 365)/CSTL = DRM + DWIP + DFG	*Inventory days at various stages:* DRM = Days of Raw Material Inventory (RM = raw material inventory; CRM = annual cost of raw materials consumed); DWIP = Days of Work-in-Process (SFG = semi-finished goods inventory; CP = cost of production); DFG = Days of Finished Goods (FG = finished goods inventory; CS = cost of sales). TL is the sum of these, representing total inventory holding time in the supply chain
Supply Chain Inefficiency Ratio (SCI)	SCC = DC + (INV × ICC)SCI = SCC/NS	*Supply chain cost relative to sales:* SCC = Supply Chain Cost (DC = distribution cost; INV = total inventory; ICC = inventory carrying cost rate, estimated if not directly given); NS = Net Sales. SCI is the fraction of sales lost to internal supply chain costs (warehousing, distribution, inventory financing). Lower SCI indicates better cost efficiency in the supply chain
Supply Chain Working Capital Productivity (SWCP)	SWC = INV + AR − APSWCP = NS/SWC	*Revenue per unit of working capital in supply chain:* SWC = Supply Chain Working Capital (INV = inventories; AR = accounts receivable; AP = accounts payable). NS = Net Sales. SWCP reflects how effectively a company's supply chain working capital is turned into revenue. Higher SWCP is better; a very high or undefined SWCP can result if AP significantly exceeds INV + AR (indicating the supply chain is largely vendor-financed)

Table 2 Grading criteria for company performance within each industry

Grade	Performance Description
A	Best-performing company (benchmark leader) in the industry—showed significant improvements or top performance across all metrics
B	Better-than-average performance—company improved or performed well on most metrics, though not at the absolute top on all
C	Average or mixed performance—some metrics may have improved while others stagnated or declined; overall performance is moderate
D	Declining or poor performance—company underperformed relative to peers, with declines in most metrics over time

Table 2 summarizes the general meaning of each grade. This grading approach is similar to peer grouping in benchmarking—it provides a quick way to identify leaders and laggards in each cohort.

After grading within industries, we also conducted a **cross-industry comparison**. Here, we aggregated performance by industry (using mean or median of the companies' metrics) to see how the five industries compare to one another on average. This revealed, for example, which industry tends to maintain the shortest supply chain cycle times, or which has the lowest cost inefficiency on average. Additionally, we identified the *best-performing company in each metric across all industries*. These "global" benchmarks show if any company significantly outperforms not just its industry peers but also all other firms in the sample on a given metric. The best-in-metric findings are used to discuss best practices. For instance, if one company has an exceptionally low TL or SCI, its strategies (such as just-in-time adoption, central distribution model, etc.) are inferred and discussed as potential best practices that other firms might emulate.

It is important to note that while the analysis is heavily quantitative, the interpretation of results considers qualitative factors that might explain the numbers. Industry-specific dynamics (like regulatory environment for pharmaceuticals, or demand volatility in electronics) and company-specific strategies (like a company deliberately holding high inventory as a strategic buffer) are taken into account when discussing findings. The grading and benchmarking outcomes are thus contextualized with these insights to ensure that conclusions and recommendations are meaningful and actionable.

By following this methodology, we maintain consistency with benchmarking principles—using reliable data, standardized metrics, and clear comparison criteria—thereby ensuring that the results provide a fair and insightful evaluation of supply chain performance across the selected Indian industries. The next section presents the results of this benchmarking study, detailing the performance of each industry and highlighting key observations from the data.

4 Results

This benchmarking analysis provides insights into supply chain performance across five key Indian industries, based on three financial metrics: Total Length of Chain (TL), Supply Chain Inefficiency Ratio (SCI), and Supply Chain Working Capital Productivity (SWCP). The findings reveal performance patterns, link metric improvements to potential financial benefits, and suggest best practices for companies aiming to enhance supply chain efficiency.

4.1 Interpreting Performance Patterns

Performance varied across industries and companies, with Healthcare and Automotive showing the most improvement. In healthcare, firms like Manipal Hospitals and HealthCare Global (HCG) significantly reduced TL and SCI while boosting SWCP, indicating efficient inventory and cost management. This supports existing literature emphasizing that the healthcare sector has moved toward professionalized supply chain management to reduce treatment costs. For example, systems like hospital inventory automation and centralized procurement are likely drivers.

In the automotive sector, firms like Hyundai and Maruti Suzuki leveraged lean practices and Just-In-Time (JIT) systems, a methodology that minimizes inventory holding by aligning production schedules with demand, thereby reducing inventory days and improving working capital productivity. Hyundai, in particular, made dramatic improvements across all metrics. This aligns with findings from Stewart (1995) and Lee (2004) that link disciplined operational processes and agility to supply chain excellence.

Electronics presented a mixed picture. Bharat Electronics Ltd. (BEL) made strong gains, whereas firms like Micromax and Voltas experienced major setbacks, including surging inventory and declining efficiency. This divergence underscores the volatility and complexity of electronics supply chains, which face rapid product cycles and demand uncertainty. Firms like Micromax likely struggled to adjust inventory levels quickly, pointing to the importance of agility in fast-changing sectors.

Across sectors, the trade-off between inventory reduction and service levels became apparent. While many firms aggressively cut TL to reduce costs, some strategically increased inventory to support market expansion or product diversification. Parle Agro's doubling of TL, accompanied by improved SWCP, is one such example—suggesting inventory growth can be beneficial if it supports proportional sales growth. In contrast, Britannia increased TL without matching efficiency gains, leading to weaker performance.

These findings resonate with Fisher's (1997) distinction between functional products (where lean supply chains work best) and innovative products (where buffer stock may be necessary). For instance, FMCG firms like HUL and Nestlé kept relatively stable inventories, while firms with more variable demand, like Glenmark (pharma) or Parle (F&B), experienced fluctuations.

4.2 Linking Supply Chain and Financial Performance

A core hypothesis of the study was that better supply chain metrics correlate with better financial performance. While profitability was not measured directly, inferred links are evident. Companies with high SCI, such as Micromax or Fortis, likely face margin pressures, while firms like Manipal, Hyundai, and Sun Pharma—who drastically improved SCI and SWCP—likely enjoy better profitability and cash flow.

Grade A performers consistently showed stronger financial health in recent years. Conversely, many Grade D companies (e.g., Lupin, Biocon) have faced challenges, suggesting that supply chain inefficiency contributes to financial strain. This is consistent with prior research (e.g., Brandenburg & Seuring, 2011) linking supply chain performance to firm value. However, some exceptions exist: Coca-Cola India, for example, maintained financial stability despite supply chain inefficiencies, likely due to strong brand power and market position. This indicates that supply chain metrics are strong contributors—but not sole determinants—of financial performance.

4.3 Best Practices from Top Performers

Successful companies in the study exhibited common best practices:

Inventory Optimization: Firms like Hyundai, Manipal, and BEL drastically reduced TL, likely through production planning improvements, lean inventory systems, and vendor collaboration. This supports the view that aggressive inventory control, when balanced with service needs, boosts efficiency.

Cost Management: SCI improvements in firms such as HUL and Sun Pharma suggest effective control of logistics and warehousing costs. These firms may use centralized distribution systems and real-time tracking to reduce overhead.

Working Capital Efficiency: Significant gains in SWCP among top performers (e.g., Dr. Reddy's, Manipal) imply tighter receivables management and better credit terms with suppliers—key financial supply chain strategies. These firms may have used techniques like dynamic discounting, consignment stock, or supply chain finance.

Technology Adoption: Many of the best-performing firms likely leveraged Enterprise Resource Planning (ERP) systems, demand forecasting tools, or inventory optimization software. Healthcare firms like HCG and Artemis, for example, may have adopted hospital inventory systems that link consumption with automated reordering.

Supply Chain Integration: Collaboration across the supply chain was also a key differentiator. BEL and Sun Pharma possibly benefitted from closer supplier coordination and centralized procurement strategies, reducing redundancy and delays.

Figure 2 visually summarizes the best practices identified from Grade A companies across industries. These practices—ranging from inventory optimization and cost management to advanced technology adoption and supply chain integration—highlight the operational strategies that underpin superior supply chain performance. The mind map format allows readers to quickly capture the interrelated nature of these practices.

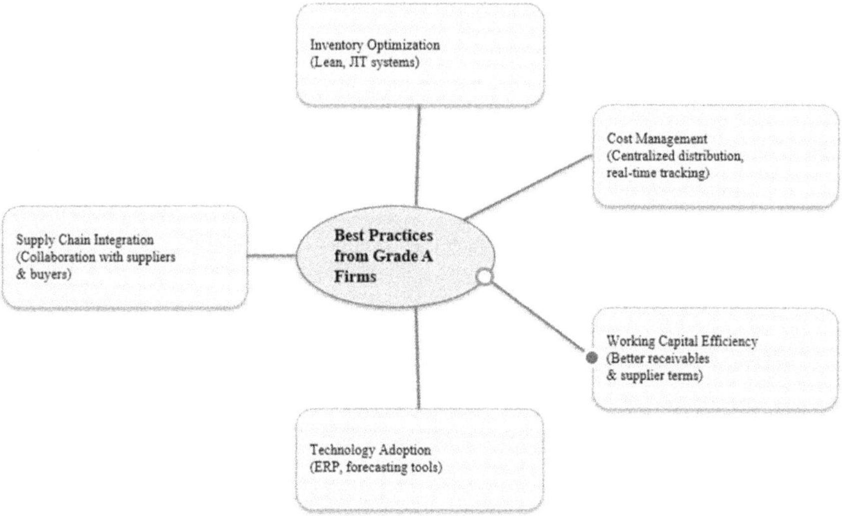

Fig. 2 Best Practices from Grade A companies

4.4 Recommendations for Laggards

Firms with lower performance can draw lessons from their industry leaders. For instance:

- Toyota Kirloskar could benchmark Hyundai's lean practices.
- Micromax may need agile supply chain systems and better demand forecasting to avoid excess inventory.
- Fortis Healthcare should explore centralized procurement models used by Manipal.
- Biocon and Lupin may benefit from optimizing their production planning and renegotiating supplier terms to reduce TL and SCI.

In the FMCG space, Dabur might reduce its TL by streamlining its multi-tier distribution network—possibly adopting a direct-to-retail replenishment model like HUL. In general, lagging firms should create internal benchmarking teams and actively study best-in-class peers using these standardized metrics.

5 Conclusion

The benchmarking results highlight that supply chain performance, when measured using well-defined financial indicators, can offer a strategic edge. Companies that systematically reduced inventory, controlled costs, and managed capital efficiently consistently outperformed peers. The top performers demonstrated that both operational discipline and financial prudence are essential for long-term success. These findings reaffirm the relevance of benchmarking in supply chain management and its strategic value across industries.

6 Implications

In today's hyper-competitive and digitally evolving landscape, supply chain performance is no longer a backend operational concern but a strategic differentiator—particularly in Asia's dynamic entrepreneurial markets. This chapter presents a benchmarking framework tailored for Indian enterprises, emphasizing how operational efficiency rooted in financial data can drive sustainable growth, innovation, and entrepreneurial scalability. Focusing on five vital industries—Automotive, Electronics, Healthcare, Pharmaceutical, and Food & Beverage—this study analyzes 10 leading firms from each sector (totaling 50 companies) over a 10-year period (2014–2023), offering a longitudinal perspective rarely captured in Asian entrepreneurship research.

Beyond firm-level outcomes, the proposed benchmarking framework has wider societal and policy implications. For policymakers, institutionalizing such benchmarking practices can improve national supply chain resilience, enhance competitiveness, and support industrial growth strategies aligned with Sustainable Development Goals (SDGs). Industry associations can leverage aggregated benchmarking results to set sectoral performance benchmarks and disseminate best practices across members. For the academic community, the framework opens avenues for cross-country comparative studies, longitudinal impact assessments, and integration with emerging paradigms such as AI-enabled supply chain optimization. These multi-level implications ensure that the research findings contribute not only to immediate business improvement but also to the broader agenda of economic resilience and sustainability.

By introducing three original supply chain indicators—Total Length of Chain (aggregate inventory days), Supply Chain Inefficiency Ratio (cost-to-sales), and Supply Chain Working Capital Productivity (sales-to-capital efficiency)—the study benchmarks firm performance and captures strategic shifts across two key sub-periods. The findings reveal significant inter- and intra-industry variations in supply chain efficiency, highlighting top performers such as Hyundai, BEL, Manipal Hospitals, Sun Pharma, and ITC. These companies exemplify how data-driven operational strategies can enhance market competitiveness, resource utilization, and entrepreneurial agility.

7 Practical Contributions

The study contributes to both academic discourse and managerial practice by offering actionable insights and advocating for greater transparency, strategic benchmarking, and digital adaptation within Asia's evolving entrepreneurial ecosystems. These findings urge policymakers and industry leaders to institutionalize benchmarking frameworks within national innovation strategies, while encouraging entrepreneurs to view supply chain analytics not merely as an operational tool but as a critical enabler of scalable, sustainable business models in a rapidly digitizing economy.

From a managerial standpoint, the framework allows firms to move beyond intuition-driven decision-making and adopt a data-centric approach to supply chain optimization. Identifying inefficiencies in inventory, cost structures, and working capital allows organizations to reconfigure operations. This improves cash flow, reduces waste, and enhances customer responsiveness—critical elements for entrepreneurial success.

For emerging startups and SMEs, the insights provide a practical roadmap for achieving operational excellence even with limited resources. Understanding how industry leaders leverage financial data for supply chain performance enables smaller firms to adopt leaner, more adaptive models that mitigate risk and enhance growth potential.

Academically, the study lays the groundwork for future research in performance benchmarking by offering a replicable model applicable across different geographies and sectors. It opens new avenues to explore the relationship between supply chain agility and innovation outcomes, especially in resource-constrained environments typical of many Asian economies.

Finally, in an era where ESG compliance and responsible capitalism are gaining prominence, the emphasis on financial efficiency as a measure of sustainable supply chain performance encourages businesses to align profitability with accountability—turning supply chains into levers of both economic and ethical value creation.

Aligned with the book's mission to uncover new entrepreneurial opportunities in Asia, this chapter showcases how financial-statement-driven benchmarking can empower startups, SMEs, and large firms alike to identify inefficiencies, adopt best practices, and strengthen resilience. The study contributes to both academic discourse and managerial practice by offering actionable insights and advocating for greater transparency, strategic benchmarking, and digital adaptation within Asia's evolving entrepreneurial ecosystems.

References

Acquaye, A., Genovese, A., Barrett, J., & Lenny Koh, S. C. (2014). Benchmarking carbon emissions performance in supply chains. *Supply Chain Management: An International Journal, 19*(3), 306–321.

Andersen, B., Fagerhaug, T., Randmæl, S., Schuldmaier, J., & Prenninger, J. (1999). Benchmarking supply chain management: Finding best practices. *Journal of Business & Industrial Marketing, 14*(5/6), 378–389.

Banomyong, R., & Supatn, N. (2011). Developing a supply chain performance tool for SMEs in Thailand. *Supply Chain Management: An International Journal, 16*(1), 20–31.

Bichou, K. (2006). Review of port performance approaches and a supply chain framework to port performance benchmarking. *Research in Transportation Economics, 17*, 567–598.

Brandenburg, M., & Seuring, S. (2011). Impacts of supply chain management on company value: Benchmarking companies from the fast moving consumer goods industry. *Logistics Research, 3*, 233–248.

Brockhaus, S., Fawcett, S., Kersten, W., & Knemeyer, M. (2016). A framework for benchmarking product sustainability efforts: Using systems dynamics to achieve supply chain alignment. *Benchmarking: An International Journal, 23*(1), 127–164.

Colicchia, C., Melacini, M., & Perotti, S. (2011). Benchmarking supply chain sustainability: Insights from a field study. *Benchmarking: An International Journal, 18*(5), 705–732.

Faisal, M. N. (2009). Benchmarking supply chains on risk dimensions. *International Journal of Services and Operations Management, 5*(3), 402–427.

Fawcett, S. E., Wallin, C., Allred, C., & Magnan, G. (2009). Supply chain information-sharing: Benchmarking a proven path. *Benchmarking: An International Journal, 16*(2), 222–246.

Feizabadi, J., Maloni, M., & Gligor, D. (2019). Benchmarking the triple-A supply chain: Orchestrating agility, adaptability, and alignment. *Benchmarking: An International Journal, 26*(1), 271–295.

Fisher, M. L. (1997). What is the right supply chain for your product? *Harvard Business Review, 75*, 105–117.

Gao, S., Qiao, R., Lim, M. K., Li, C., Qu, Y., & Xia, L. (2021). Integrating corporate website information into qualitative assessment for benchmarking green supply chain management practices for the chemical industry. *Journal of Cleaner Production, 311*, Article 127590.

Gilmour, P. (1998). Benchmarking supply chain operations. *Benchmarking for Quality Management & Technology, 5*(4), 283–290.

Gonzalez, M. E., Quesada, G., Gourdin, K., & Hartley, M. (2008). Designing a supply chain management academic curriculum using QFD and benchmarking. *Quality Assurance in Education, 16*(1), 36–60.

Gopal, P. R. C., & Thakkar, J. (2012). A review on supply chain performance measures and metrics: 2000–2011. *International Journal of Productivity and Performance Management, 61*(5), 518–547.

Hervani, A. A., Helms, M. M., & Sarkis, J. (2005). Performance measurement for green supply chain management. *Benchmarking: An International Journal, 12*(4), 330–353.

Hines, P. (1998). Benchmarking Toyota's supply chain: Japan vs UK. *Long Range Planning, 31*(6), 911–918.

Hossain, M. K., & Thakur, V. (2021). Benchmarking health-care supply chain by implementing Industry 4.0: A fuzzy-AHP-DEMATEL approach. *Benchmarking: An International Journal, 28*(2), 556–581.

Ivanov, D. (2023). Intelligent digital twin (iDT) for supply chain stress-testing, resilience, and viability. *International Journal of Production Economics, 263*, Article 108938. https://doi.org/10.1016/j.ijpe.2023.108938

Kaviani, M. A., Tavana, M., Kowsari, F., & Rezapour, R. (2020). Supply chain resilience: A benchmarking model for vulnerability and capability assessment in the automotive industry. *Benchmarking: An International Journal, 27*(6), 1929–1949.

Keebler, J. S., & Plank, R. E. (2009). Logistics performance measurement in the supply chain: A benchmark. *Benchmarking: An International Journal, 16*(6), 785–798.

Kumar, S., Luthra, S., & Haleem, A. (2015). Benchmarking supply chains by analyzing technology transfer critical barriers using AHP approach. *Benchmarking: An International Journal, 22*(4), 538–558.

Lapide, L. (2000). What about measuring supply chain performance. *Achieving Supply Chain Excellence through Technology, 2*(2), 287–297.

Lee, H. L. (2004). The triple-A supply chain. *Harvard Business Review, 82*(10), 102–113.

Lewis, J. C., & Naim, M. M. (1995). Benchmarking of aftermarket supply chains. *Production Planning & Control, 6*(3), 258–269.

Mangla, S. K., Luthra, S., & Jakhar, S. (2018). Benchmarking the risk assessment in green supply chain using fuzzy approach to FMEA: Insights from an Indian case study. *Benchmarking: An International Journal, 25*(8), 2660–2687.

Manning, L., Baines, R., & Chadd, S. (2008). Benchmarking the poultry meat supply chain. *Benchmarking: An International Journal, 15*(2), 148–165.

Mor, R. S., Bhardwaj, A., & Singh, S. (2018). Benchmarking the interactions among performance indicators in dairy supply chain: An ISM approach. *Benchmarking: An International Journal, 25*(9), 3858–3881.

Ocicka, B., Mierzejewska, W., & Brzeziński, J. (2022). Creating supply chain resilience during and post-COVID-19 outbreak: The organizational ambidexterity perspective. *Logistics, 6*(4), 74. https://doi.org/10.3390/logistics6040074

Patel, H. J., & Patel, K. J. (2018). Measuring supply chain performance of tyre manufacturers in India: An empirical investigation. *International Journal of Supply Chain and Inventory Management, 3*(1), 1–17.

Peng Wong, W., & Yew Wong, K. (2008). A review on benchmarking of supply chain performance measures. *Benchmarking: An International Journal, 15*(1), 25–51.

Piotrowicz, W., Cuthbertson, R., & Islei, G. (2011). *Performance measurement and benchmarking in the supply chain: literature review* (Working Paper). University of Oxford, UK.

Raghavendra, A. H., Bala, P. K., & Mukherjee, A. (2024) Strategic Insights for Improved Performance: Leveraging Data in CEO CSR Communications. *California Management Review.*

Rigby, D. (2001). Management tools and techniques: A survey. *California Management Review, 43*(2), 139–160.

Rizet, C., Browne, M., Cornelis, E., & Leonardi, J. (2012). Assessing carbon footprint and energy efficiency in competing supply chains: Review—Case studies and benchmarking. *Transportation Research Part d: Transport and Environment, 17*(4), 293–300.

Shah, J., & Singh, N. (2001). Benchmarking internal supply chain performance: Development of a framework. *Journal of Supply Chain Management, 37*(4), 37–47.

Shaw, S., Grant, D. B., & Mangan, J. (2010). Developing environmental supply chain performance measures. *Benchmarking: An International Journal, 17*(3), 320–339.

Simatupang, T. M., & Sridharan, R. (2004). Benchmarking supply chain collaboration: an empirical study. *Benchmarking: An International Journal, 11*(5), 484–503.

Singh, A., Narain, R., & Yadav, R. C. (2006). Benchmarking and performance measurement of supply chain management practices: A survey of Indian organisations. *International Journal of Services and Operations Management, 2*(4), 313–334.

Stewart, G. (1995). Supply chain performance benchmarking study reveals keys to supply-chain excellence. *Logistics Information Management, 8*(2), 38–44.

Sutton, J. (2004). *The auto-component supply chain in China and India: A benchmarking study* (Economics Discussion Paper). London School of Economics.

Tarei, P. K., Thakkar, J. J., & Nag, B. (2020). Benchmarking the relationship between supply chain risk mitigation strategies and practices: An integrated approach. *Benchmarking: An International Journal, 27*(5), 1683–1715.

Tseng, M. L., Tan, K. H., Lim, M., Lin, R. J., & Geng, Y. (2014). Benchmarking eco-efficiency in green supply chain practices in uncertainty. *Production Planning & Control, 25*(13–14), 1079–1090.

Tuominen, T., Kitaygorodskaya, N., & Helo, P. (2009). Benchmarking Russian and Finnish food industry supply chains. *Benchmarking: An International Journal, 16*(3), 415–431.

Uluskan, M., & Godfrey, A. B. (2018). Business environment-supply chain framework and benchmarking supply chain structures: Haiti versus China. *Benchmarking: An International Journal, 25*(8), 3021–3044.

Yakovleva, N., Sarkis, J., & Sloan, T. (2012). Sustainable benchmarking of supply chains: The case of the food industry. *International Journal of Production Research, 50*(5), 1297–1317.

Zamani, E. D., Smyth, C., Gupta, S., & Dennehy, D. (2022). *Artificial intelligence and big data analytics for supply chain resilience: A systematic literature review*. Advance online publication. https://doi.org/10.1007/s10479-022-04983-y

Zhao, N. (2023). Impact of supply chain digitalization on supply chain resilience and performance. *Sustainability, 15*(3), 2305. https://doi.org/10.3390/su15032305

Ananya Hadadi Raghavendra is an assistant professor in Information Systems and Business Analytics at the Great Lakes Institute of Management Chennai, India. She has completed her PhD in Information Systems and Business Analytics from the Indian Institute of Management Ranchi. She has worked in Infosys Limited, India as a Software Engineer before joining the doctoral program. Her research interests include text analytics, natural language processing, and data mining. She has presented her research work in multiple reputed national and international management conferences including India, Indonesia, the USA, and Australia.

Agritech Ventures in India: Impact of Entrepreneurial Ecosystem on Smart Digital Solutions

Sujana Adapa and Subba Reddy Yarram

Abstract This book chapter sets out to explore the smart innovations that proliferated within the context of India by effective integration of technology to offer digital solutions in the domain of agriculture. More specifically, the chapter provides background information on the context, the agriculture sector, relevance of various stakeholders, emergence of an entrepreneurial ecosystem and the growth of agritech firms in the country. In doing so, 100 agritech firms were selected based on the inclusion criteria, and secondary data analysis was progressed using qualitative content analysis. Results obtained highlighted various opportunities and challenges linked to the growth of agritech firms, which prioritised the development of smart innovative solutions in India. Opportunities identified were linked to the main themes of sophistication, sustainability, sourcing and scalability, and challenges were linked to the thematic categories of funding, integration, replication and hesitancy. The chapter also outlines important implications for practice and policy improvement.

1 Introduction

India presents a unique case and is predominantly identified as an agrarian society. Over the past few years, Indian government has focused upon prolific dissemination of the public campaigns titled 'Digital India', 'Make in India' and 'Startup India'. As a result, startup ideas, growth of new ventures and entrepreneurial mindset are on the rise. Furthermore, interest in entrepreneurial education, training and support heightened. Many stakeholders are also diverting their attention to the integration of sustainable measures in their startups and new ventures. Indian government offers support for incubators (support the establishment of new ventures) and accelerators (connect startups with key networks to accelerate business development), which help new

S. Adapa (✉) · S. R. Yarram
University of New England, Armidale, NSW, Australia
e-mail: sadapa2@une.edu.au

S. R. Yarram
e-mail: syarram@une.edu.au

T. Endress and Y. F. Badir (eds.), *Business and Management in Asia: Opportunities and Entrepreneurship*, https://doi.org/10.1007/978-981-95-4909-2_13

ventures with an overarching motive of the attainment of sustainable development goals (SDGs) by 2030 (Chillakuri et al., 2020).

In India, as an agrarian economy, 54.6% of the total workforce is dependent on agriculture. The agriculture sector contributes to 16.5% of the country's gross domestic product (GDP). Agriculture sector showcased a growth rate of 4.9% over the past 5 years (Suresh et al., 2024). The total value of agricultural production in India is estimated at USD 435.9 billion. The relative importance attributed to technology and technological innovations, garnered significant attention since 2010. One example is the exponential increase in the use of smartphones by individuals in India irrespective of their educational and occupational backgrounds. Since the COVID-19 pandemic, the apprehensions around the adoption of technologies have minimised. As a result, conversations around digital inclusion and fintech started to gain momentum (Kaue et al., 2024). Technology integration and links to precision farming at a global scale are valued at USD 6.96 billion, and available information indicates an expansion rate of 12.8% by 2030 (Balkrishna et al., 2023).

It is at this juncture of sector domination and technological advancements, the entrepreneurial ecosystem started to strengthen in India (Adapa & Yarram, 2023). The focus of entrepreneurial ecosystem is to nurture new ventures and contribute to the country's economic growth (Acs et al., 2018). The entrepreneurial environment is growing in India, and the entrepreneurial ecosystem in the country is ranked as the third largest in the world (World Economic Forum, 2014). Despite the dominance of agriculture, rapid adoption of technological advancements and thriving entrepreneurial ecosystem, farming communities face many internal and external challenges (Xie et al., 2021). Therefore, the critical importance of offering innovative and affordable solutions to solve farmers' problems has been at the forefront of the government and non-government organisations. Ecosystem to support agritech ventures or firms took the prominence in the recent 2023 Union Budget and Economic Survey. Agritech firms contribute to 46.76% of the total startups in India with the key priorities of transformational practices, increased productivity and enhanced profitability (Paranjpe, 2023).

The section below presents the most important theoretical underpinnings of the study followed by the method employed to select the sample of agritech firms. Then the content analysis and the thematic analysis progressed identifies the opportunities and challenges experienced by the agritech firms in the Indian context. Each of the macro theme identified under opportunities and challenges also is linked to micro thematic categories of relevance. Finally, conclusion section outlines certain recommendations alongside limitations and avenues for further research.

2 Theoretical Underpinnings

Innovation is linked to technology advancements, and diffusion of innovations is critical for the uptake and use of innovations by the end users. Start-up agritech firms focus on the integration of technological innovations with the purpose of offering solutions to the farming community. These innovations can be linked to product, service, market, process and/or logistics. Established agritech firms focus on continued innovations with minor or major incremental changes embedded to solve the problem at hand in a different way. Agricultural technology innovations as a key focus of agritech firms proliferated over the past decade. It is not only important for the agritech firms to innovate, but from the firms' point of view, the diffusion of innovations to end users, ultimately leading to the adoption and use of technological advancements in a meaningful way, is crucial.

Diffusion of innovations model prioritises the type of innovation, the communication of the innovation, time it takes for the innovation to be adopted and the critical mass by whom the innovation is adopted (Rogers, 2003). Factors that influence the adoption and use depend upon relative advantage, compatibility, complexity, trialability and observability, which will provide assurance to the users that the innovation is above and beyond the existing alternatives, aligns with their values, easy to use, allows for active experimentation and benefits of the innovation are visible to others (Rogers, 2003). Furthermore, based on the willingness to adopt innovations, adopter categories include innovators (first to adopt), early adopters (adopt early and influence others), early majority (adopt before the average person), late majority (adopt after the majority) and laggards (last to adopt). Firms need to ensure that the technological innovations resulting in product, service, process, market and/or logistics improvement must adhere to the diffusion of innovations theoretical considerations for effective deployment of the innovations.

From the user perspective, the theoretical underpinnings of the technology acceptance model (TAM) are relevant in understanding users' acceptance and adoption of new technologies. TAM model relies on two beliefs, such as the perceived usefulness and perceived ease of use of the technological innovation under considerations and the benefits pertaining to performance, efficiency and effort (Davis, 1989). The beliefs will then lead to users' intentional behaviour and then to the actual use of technological innovations. Several modifications and extensions of TAM exist leading to TAM 2 (extended TAM model) (Venkatesh & Davis, 2000), TAM3 (addition of social and cognitive factors) and the Unified Theories of Acceptance and Use of Technology (UTAUT) to understand the deeper effects of other moderating factors (Venkatesh & Bala, 2008; Venkatesh et al., 2003). UTAUT model was later extended to UTAUT2 by adding hedonic motivation, price quality and habit to enhance the explanatory power (Venkatesh et al., 2012). Versions of TAM were used by scholars to understand the adoption and use of digital tools in various domains with wider applications (Deng & Yu, 2023; Luo et al., 2021; Wang et al., 2022). Agritech firms link the diffusion of innovations to users' acceptance and use of digital applications.

Extant literature elicits the relevance of entrepreneurial opportunities in the uptake of innovations, and the work carried by Shane (2003) is regarded as invaluable. The general theory of entrepreneurship bridges the gap between theory and application (Casson, 2005). Shane (2003) explains the individual-opportunity nexus and links to growth sectors, nature of innovation, individual personality factors and risk assessment which will lead to business setup and outcomes (Huang et al., 2023). It is envisaged that opportunities arise due to technology, external environment and demographical shifts (Ohlert et al., 2025). Better information available to the individual leads to opportunities through life experiences, social networks and better search processes. And, individuals with better cognitive abilities, high intelligence and absorptive capacities tend to use the information available to them in a logical manner resulting in job creation and business outcomes (Schlichte & Junge, 2024). Resource acquisition and the inspections of psychological factors intersecting individual's personality characteristics are integral to critically understand the uptake of innovations.

3 Method and Sample Selection

A sample of 100 agritech firms was identified based on the criteria: (1) integration of technology to improve efficiencies in the agriculture-related outcomes; (2) the agritech firm must be in India; and (3) the agritech firms were established in the last ten years. Following a qualitative approach, a website analysis of the publicly available information was conducted to understand the agritech firms' profiles, product and/or service offerings, website features and user interactions. Content analysis was the starting point to identify patterns, meanings and themes (Bengtsson, 2016). Furthermore, text, sentences, images, audio and video content were also reviewed systematically and then, supplementary analysis was carried out to identify themes of macro and micro relevance (Berg, 2001). The categorisation of themes of importance allowed for the identification of major opportunities presented to agritech firms and significant challenges faced by the agritech firms. The agritech firms increased in absolute numbers in the Indian context. However, at a global level, the number of agritech firms and the nature and type of products and/or services provided by agritech firms when mapped to meeting the requirements of the farming communities, the agritech firms falls into infancy category.

4 Opportunities

The opportunities that agritech firms pursued in the Indian context, leading to their success, are identified to be centred around four macro thematic categories of relevance such as sophistication, sustainability, sourcing and scalability. The following discussion unpacks each of the macro theme and associated micro themes of importance.

4.1 Sophistication

Almost half of the agritech firms identified as part of this study use sophisticated technology to improve the system's efficiencies, reach to the market and/or productivity or yield (Pham & Stack, 2018). By sophistication, authors mean that the agritech firms use data-enabled solutions, integration of advanced technological options like Artificial Intelligence (AI), Internet of Things (IoT) and blockchain methodologies to find solutions for the identified problems. For example, Aarav Unmanned Systems uses drone technology for inspection, surveying and mapping functionalities to promote precision agriculture. Similarly, AgriCXLab uses machine learning to assess the product quality. The other half of the agritech firms use simple technology to offer solutions to pressing issues by bringing together different stakeholders, building relationships and creating long-lasting relationships to solve problems at hand. For example, SfarmsIndia from Hyderabad uses an online portal effectively to connect buyers and sellers and eliminates middlemen. The online portal offers services that allow for the listing of agricultural land for lease or sale, and the process is managed through digital contracts. Whether the agritech firms use sophisticated or simple technologies to offer creative solutions, utmost care is taken to keep the communication clear, simple and concise so that the stakeholders are fully aware of the benefits. The process to realise benefits and solve problems is also explained to the users in simple steps. The efficiency gains in monetary and non-monetary terms are further explained with clarity to the users.

4.2 Sustainability

Sustainability is prioritised by many agritech firms in India. Wicked problems such as climate change, loss of biodiversity and urban expansion created enormous pressure in tackling food security, agricultural production, waste management, and emissions reduction, to name a few. Therefore, focusing on the sustainable production and management of agricultural farmlands is essential. Almost all agritech firms included in this study focused upon sustainable solutions, predictive modelling and informed decision-making (Finger et al., 2019). For example, Farm2Fam offers organic food direct to customers, and the food is produced without the use of pesticides and herbicides. Aibono uses precision farming and farm intelligence to increase the yield and productivity. Agrowave uses sustainable supply chain practices to offer the best price to farmers for their produce. In using sustainable agricultural practices, agritech firms' orientation is to reduce waste production, to increase outputs with minimal inputs and to ensure effective management practices. These agritech companies position farmers at the front and centre and make sure that the management practices are effective, which result in efficiency and monetary gains for the farming community.

4.3 Sourcing

Strategic sourcing is another area of focus for agritech firms for achieving operational efficiencies. Value aspects are embedded throughout the management of supply chain in drawing upon optimal use of available resources and risk mitigation (Birner et al., 2021). Decisions made by agritech firms are of long-term value with attention diverted to creating long-lasting sustained relationships amongst supply chain actors (Lezoche et al., 2020). Adequate mapping to ensure that the supply chain actors meet the needs of the firm is carried out on a continued and frequent basis using various types of evaluation and monitoring techniques. For example, Crofarm agritech firm focuses on optimising supply chain networks and promotes business to business (B2B) and business to customer (B2C) relations through creative partnership arrangements. Similarly, Ergos connects farmers directly to the cold storage owners with focus diverted to achieve post-harvest supply chain efficiencies. Another agritech firm Waycool also connects farmers directly with the cold storage owners to foster enhanced relationships amongst the supply chain actors. Through the implementation of strategic sourcing, agritech firms prioritised direct connections, resource optimisation and effective supply chain management practices.

4.4 Scalability

Agritech in India is a growth area coupled with government's initiatives; the focus is shifting towards increasing the reach. As such agritech firms tend to capture the unique opportunities with attention drawn towards thoughtful expansion. Digital platforms allow for a wider reach beyond increase in firm size thus connecting a wider range of farmers and consumers to value-added services (Agarwal et al., 2022). For example, Ninjakart connects farmers to several businesses and customers, thus providing accessibility to different markets prioritising income generation for farmers and reducing transportation costs. Another agritech firm DeHaat uses backend analytics and offers personalised recommendations to farmers on farming practices and input management. Thus, the strategic scalability approaches allow the agritech firms to market accessibility, wider reach, potential optimisation and personalised approaches. A vast number of agritech firms suffer from premature scaling and lack of profitability, which result in unrealised commercialisation opportunities (Jimenez et al., 2019). Sustainable business models, optimum resource management and collaborative ecosystem development are essential to foster scalable agritech firms.

5 Challenges

The most important challenges that the agritech firms face in the Indian context are identified as the macro thematic categories. Linked to the macro themes are the micro themes of importance outlined below.

5.1 Integration

Technology integration remains a key challenge as smart agricultural practices leading to precision are dependent on software logic, geospatial systems, sensor installation, satellite data, manned/unmanned drones, artificial intelligence (AI), etc. (Beriya, 2020). Most recent integration of AI-enabled drone technology for effective weed management, weather monitoring, disease management, crop growth and irrigation efficiency received greater appreciation (Tzachor, 2021). Available evidence suggests that the uptake and use of such advanced technologies is more visible with the young farming cohort in comparison to the mature farming cohort, citing reasons such as self-efficacy and proficiency in smart technology (Balkrishna et al., 2023). Agritech companies offer specialised service offerings to tackle a specific farm problem, which creates adequate uncertainties for farmers to handle other identified farm-related problems on their own or look for solutions elsewhere. Therefore, effective integration of different smart technologies must be taken into consideration by the agritech firms with an aim to offer smart integrated farm solution with universal standards directed towards quality and safety aspects (Asfaw et al., 2018). The focus of agritech firms in rendering such types of integrated solutions to farmers will result in effective decision-making, efficiencies in monitoring and traceability concerns.

5.2 Replication

Totally new innovations are less visible in the solutions that agritech firms offer, which lead to the problem of replication. Beyond demographic and geographic concerns flagged in the uptake of smart technologies for obtaining farming efficiencies, available information suggests that a majority of agritech firms offer replicating services rather than distinctive solutions (Waughray & de Cleene, 2019). Such offer of overlapping services by agritech firms causes confusion and apprehension amongst farmers, which impacts their decision-making and limits their adoption and usage of smart technological applications. Many agritech firms also provide fragmented initiatives to farmers with an overpromise of addressing all the problems encountered through the agricultural value chain. However, in real-world practice, such initiatives turn out to be under-delivering thus profoundly impacting farmers' experience with the agritech firms and smart technologies. Over three-quarters of the agritech firms included in the present study focus on services linked to crop advisory, yield management, weather monitoring, buyer-seller networks, soil health, market efficiencies, farm equipment lease and soil health. Some agritech firms prioritised integrated fertiliser management or integrated pesticide management or integrated disease management practices. Very few agritech firms prioritised distinctive offerings such as differentiation between pre-harvest, harvest and post-harvest smart solutions, which are directed towards the attainment of sustainability and precision goals.

5.3 Hesitancy

Data-driven digital agriculture and precision farming prioritised by a majority of agritech firms led to enhanced productivity (Balkrishna et al., 2023). Agritech firms also recorded financial success as the uptake of the services offered by these firms increased year on year in absolute numbers. The uptake of agritech firms service offerings by farmers is attributed to key domains of sustainability, food security, data analytics and precise administration (Chandra & Colis, 2021). Despite of the increase in the uptake of the agritech firms service offerings, digital agriculture and precision farming in India are identified to be at its infancy. Demographic and geographic concerns persist. For example, younger farmers tend to adopt and implement smart technologies relatively quickly and much faster than the older farmers. Similarly, farmers from remote and rural areas tend to adopt and implement smart technologies in farming relatively later than the farmers who hold farming land relatively closer to the metro cities and somewhat mid-sized towns. Many smallholder farmers remain to implement traditional agricultural practices and show hesitancy in the adoption and implementation of smart technologies in agriculture (Trendov et al., 2019). Such hesitancies exhibited by the farmers are attributed to the lack of sufficient knowledge, non-availability of training and lack of accessibility (Braun et al., 2018).

5.4 Funding

Funding support to agritech firms, particularly to start-ups increased over the past few years in the Indian context (Tzachor, 2021). The government directed significant funding towards start-ups with digital solutions to agricultural problems over the past decade. Government schemes, programs and projects suffer from regulation, infrastructure and accessibility related obstacles. Yet, agritech firms experience limited access to capital, attraction of secured investors and commercialisation of digital solutions. Additionally, agritech firms in early stages encounter risks related to minimum viable product and/or service offerings coupled with inadequate market clarity. Funding constraints limit agritech firms in the development of differentiated smart solutions to solve farm problems at hand thus resulting in standardised product and/or service offerings with minimum customisation. Access to finance and awareness to secure finance must be prioritised so that agritech firms focus more on the research and development efforts, scalable approaches and effective navigation of identified funding issues. Therefore, increased and targeted support from the government may help agritech firms to overcome funding constraints. Furthermore, investments from financial institutions and public-private partnerships could be more carefully assessed for the progress of investments in agritech firms.

6 Conclusion

The chapter presents the relative importance of agritech firms within the Indian context and outlines the theoretical underpinnings around smart technology acceptance, adoption and implementation by the end users. Opportunities and challenges faced by agritech firms are identified in addressing the farming problems. The identified opportunities relate to sophistication, sustainability, sourcing and scalability. Agritech firms possess the capacity and capability of using sophisticated technology. However, effective integration and solution focus remain underdone due to standardised product and/or service offerings. Additionally, from the end user perspective, sophisticated technologies suffer active uptake and use, which links to the address of demographic, geographic, behavioural and contextual issues to realise the full potential. The focus of agritech firms on precision and evidence-based solutions allows for long-term sustainable farming practices with co-benefits realised for farmers and agritech firms. Furthermore, agritech firms focus on initiatives result in sourcing efficiencies throughout farming operations, value chains and stakeholder networks. Agritech firms present a significant opportunity around scalability due to rapid growth, optimisation and market efficiencies. Realisation of commercialisation opportunities remains untapped. Government interventions through targeted policies and schemes may potentially close the identified gaps.

The identified challenges include funding, integration, replication and hesitance. Formulation of targeted government policies, financial incentives and stakeholder partnerships may help agritech firms to overcome funding-related constraints. Time, money and efforts by agritech firms directed towards enhancing research and development capabilities to enhance scalability and affordability will address problems around smart technology integration. The progress of gap and overlapping analyses on a continued and frequent basis will potentially allow for addressing the challenges identified around replication and foster innovations. Investment by agritech firms in the development of human capital and capacity building may increase the self-efficacy levels of farmers to overcome problems linked to hesitancy. The study presents certain limitations. The generalisation and transferability of the study findings are context-specific. The study findings are based on secondary information sourced from publicly available information. Future studies need to focus on data gathering through primary data collection methods and the progress of qualitative or quantitative or mixed methodological approaches to validate the findings obtained from this study. Cross-cultural studies of agritech firms might result in interesting findings.

References

Acs, Z. J., Szerb, L., & Lloyd, A. (2018). *The Global Entrepreneurship Index 2018.* The Global Entrepreneurship and Development Institute.

Adapa, S., & Yarram, S. R. (2023). Entrepreneurial ecosystem in India. In S. Adapa, T. McKeown, M. Lazaris, & T. Jurado (Eds.), *Small and medium-sized enterprises, and business uncertainty—Just surviving or thriving?* Palgrave Macmillan.

Agarwal, R., Gupta, H., & Kohli, A. (2022). *What's next for Indian agri-tech? Emerging opportunities and the way forward for India's agricultural technology sector.* FSG Global Report.

Asfaw, D., Black, E., Brown, M., Nicklin, K. J., Out-Larbi, F., Pinnington, E., Challinor, A., Maidment, R., & Quaife, T. (2018). TAMSAT-ALERT v1: A new framework for agricultural decision support. *Geoscientific Model Development, 11*, 2353–2371.

Balkrishna, A., Pathak, R., Kumar, S., Arya, V., & Singh, S. K. (2023). A comprehensive analysis of the advances in Indian digital agricultural architecture. *Smart Agricultural Technology, 5*, Article 100318.

Bengtsson, M. (2016). How to plan and perform a qualitative study using content analysis. *NursingPlus Open, 2*, 8–14.

Berg, B. L. (2001). *Qualitative research methods for the social sciences.* Allyn and Bacon.

Beriya, A. (2020). *Digital agriculture: Challenges and possibilities in India* (ICT India Working Paper # 35).

Birner, R., Daum, T., & Pray, C. (2021). Who drives the digital revolution in agriculture? A review of supply-side trends, players and challenges. *Applied Economic Perspectives and Policy, 43*, 1260–1285.

Braun, A. T., Colangelo, E., & Steckel, T. (2018). Farming in the Era of Industrie 4.0. *Procedia CIRP, 72*, 979–984.

Casson, M. (2005). The individual-opportunity nexus: A review of Scott Shane: A general theory of entrepreneurship. *Small Business Economics, 24*, 423–430.

Chandra, R., & Colis, S. (2021). Digital agriculture for small-scale producers: Challenges and opportunities. *Communications in the ACM*, 64.

Chillakuri, B., Vanka, S., & Mogili, R. (2020). Linking sustainable development to startup ecosystem in India—A conceptual framework. *International Journal of Business and Globalisation, 25*(2), 139–153.

Davis, F. D. (1989). Perceived usefulness, perceived ease of use, and user acceptance of information technology. *MIS Quarterly, 13*(3), 319–340.

Deng, X., & Yu, Z. (2023). An extended hedonic motivation adoption model of TikTok in higher education. *Education and Information Technologies.* Retrieved 8 June 2025 from https://doi.org/10.1007/s10639-023-11749-x

Finger, R., Swinton, S. M., El Benni, N., & Walter, A. (2019). A precision farming at the nexus of agricultural production and the environment. *Annual Review of Resource Economics, 11*, 313–335.

Huang, Y., Li, P., Chen, L., & Wang, J. (2023). Opportunity or necessity entrepreneurship? A study based on the national system of entrepreneurship. *Journal of Innovation & Knowledge, 8*(4), Article 100448.

Jimenez, D., Delerce, S., Dorado, H., Cock, J., Munoz, L. A., Agamez, A., & Jarvis, A. (2019). A scalable scheme to implement data-driven agriculture for small-scale farmers. *Global Food Security, 23*, 256–266.

Kaue, M., Ahmad, W., Hari, K. S., & Kattumuri, R. (2024). FinTech entrepreneurial ecosystem in India: Role of incubators and accelerators. *Global Finance Journal, 60*, Article 100933.

Lezoche. M., Hernandez, J. E., Diaz, M. D. M. E. A., Panetto, H., & Kacprzyk, J. (2020). Agri-food 4.0: A survey of the supply chains and technologies for the future agriculture. *Computers in Industry, 117*, 103187.

Luo, Y. Z., Xiao, Y. M., Ma, Y. Y., & Li, C. (2021). Discussion of students' e-book reading intention with the integration of Theory of Planned Behavior and Technology Acceptance Model. *Frontiers in Psychology, 12*, Article 752188.

Ohlert, S., Laibach, N., Harms, R., & Broring, S. (2025). Opportunities recognition in the tension field of knowledge and learning: The case of converging industries. *Journal of Business Research, 186*, Article 114993.

Paranjpe, S. (2023). *Landscape review: Innovation gaps in India's agritech startup ecosystem.* Centre for Social and Environmental Innovation, Ashoka Trust for Research in Ecology and the Environment.

Pham, X., & Stack, M. (2018). How data analytics is transforming agriculture. *Business Horizons, 61*, 125–133.

Rogers, E. M. (2003). *Diffusion of Innovations* (5th ed.). Free Press.

Schlichte, F., & Junge, S. (2024). The concept of entrepreneurial opportunities: A review and directions for future research. *Management Review Quarterly*. https://doi.org/10.1007/s11301-024-00466-5

Shane, S. (2003). *A general theory of entrepreneurship: The individual-opportunity nexus.* Edward Elgar.

Suresh, D., Choudhury, A., Zhang, Y., Zhao, Z., & Shaw, R. (2024). The role of data-driven agritech startups—The case of India and Japan. *Sustainability, 16*(11), 4504.

Trendov, N. M., Varas, S., & Zeng, M. (2019). *Digital technologies in agriculture and rural areas.* Retrieved 10 June 2025 from www.openknowledge.fao.org

Tzachor, A. (2021). Barriers to AI adoption in Indian agriculture. *International Journal of Innovation in Digital Economy, 12*, 30–44.

Venkatesh, V., & Bala, H. (2008). Technology acceptance model 3 and a research agenda on interventions. *Decision Sciences, 39*(2), 273–315.

Venkatesh, V., & Davis, F. D. (2000). A theoretical extension of the technology acceptance model: Four longitudinal field studies. *Management Science, 46*(2), 186–204.

Venkatesh, V., Morris, M. G., Davis, G. B., & Davis, F. D. (2003). User acceptance of information technology: Toward a unified view. *MIS Quarterly*. Retrieved 5 July 2025 from https://doi.org/10.2307/30036540

Venkatesh, V., Thong, J. Y., & Xu, X. (2012). Consumer acceptance and use of information technology: Extending the unified theory of acceptance and use of technology. *MIS Quarterly, 36*(1), 157–178.

Wang, Y., Yu, L. H., & Yu, Z. G. (2022). An extended CCtalk technology acceptance model in EFL education. *Education and Information Technologies, 27*(5), 6621–6640.

Waughray, D., & de Cleene, S. (2019). *Innovation with a purpose: Improving traceability in food value chains through technology innovations.* World Economic Forum.

World Economic Forum. (2014). *Entrepreneurial ecosystems around the globe and early-stage company growth dynamics.*

Xie, Z., Wang, X., Xie, L., & Duan, K. (2021). Entrepreneurial ecosystem and the quality and quantity of regional entrepreneurship: A configurational approach. *Journal of Business Research, 128*, 499–509.

Dr. Sujana Adapa is a Professor in Management and currently she holds Executive Dean role for the Faculty of Science, Agriculture, Business and Law (SABL) at the University of New England, Australia. She was the Head of UNE Business School for 5 years. She principally taught Marketing units in the UNE Business School. She was a recipient of the Office of Learning and Teaching (now AAUT) Citation for outstanding contributions to student learning (2026); a recipient of the Australian and New Zealand Academy of Management (ANZAM) Educator of the year award (2016); and is also UK Higher Education Academy's (HEA) Senior Fellow. Her research expertise covers both Marketing and Management areas. Her research interests include gender, entrepreneurship, adoption and SMEs. Her research has been published in high-ranked journals, and she has also secured research grants from various internal and external sources. She was one of the Board Directors and was also a treasurer for the Small Enterprise Association of Australia and New Zealand (SEAANZ). She held the Associate Editor role for 2 years for the Small Enterprise Research journal. She is currently serving on the DEI (Diversity, Equity and Inclusion) Division's 5-year leadership team, Academy of Management (AOM).

Dr. Subba Reddy Yarram is an Associate Professor in the UNE Business School at the University of New England, Australia. He teaches Corporate Finance in the UNE Business School. He was a recipient of the Office of Learning and Teaching (now AAUT) Citation for outstanding contributions to student learning (2025). His research interests include gender, entrepreneurship, corporate governance and SMEs. His research has been published in high-ranked academic journals such as the *Journal of Cleaner Production, Personnel Review and Applied Economics*. He has attracted research grants to explore the challenges and opportunities faced by the small and medium-sized businesses in Australia.

Automating Finance: The Role of Robotic Process Automation

Deepika Dhingra and Jaskiran Arora

Abstract In a rapidly digitizing world, Robotic Process Automation (RPA) has emerged as a transformative force, particularly within banking and financial services. This chapter explores how RPA streamlines repetitive processes, reduces operational costs by 30%–70%, and enhances both efficiency and accuracy by minimizing human intervention. Financial institutions increasingly rely on automation for tasks such as loan processing, compliance, fraud detection, and customer data management. By leveraging data from multiple service channels, RPA aids in fraud prevention through automated threat detection, anomaly identification, and real-time monitoring. The chapter also delves into use cases in accounting and finance, showcasing tangible organizational benefits from RPA adoption.

1 Introduction

The financial services market is going through a radical change, accelerated by fast-changing technology and the increasing need to have greater efficiency in operations. The rise of new digital technologies like cloud computing, artificial intelligence (AI), blockchain, and robotic process automation (RPA) has challenged the conventional paradigm and has also opened the market to new paths of innovation and service offering. The most promising among them, RPA, has become the most popular, automating routine, rule-based work fast and accurately, and without the use of manual labor, with a better level of reliability in the process (Accenture, 2022; van der Aalst et al., 2018; Willcocks et al., 2021).

Automation is becoming a regular part of business processes to enable organizations to remain competitive in this environment of changing customer demands, regulatory requirements, and cost-reduction realities. In line with its increased level

D. Dhingra (✉)
School of Management, BML Munjal University, Kapriwas, Haryana, India
e-mail: deepika.dhingra@bmu.edu.in

J. Arora
Education Quality, BML Munjal University, Kapriwas, Haryana, India
e-mail: Jaskiran.arora@bmu.edu.in

T. Endress and Y. F. Badir (eds.), *Business and Management in Asia: Opportunities and Entrepreneurship*, https://doi.org/10.1007/978-981-95-4909-2_14

of prominence as a business strategy of continuous improvement and digitalization, a 2020 report by Deloitte indicated that 53% of global businesses had already implemented their RPA journey and that an additional 19% have plans to implement it within any of the next 2 years (Deloitte, 2020).

RPA illustrates a digital force multiplier in banking and accounting. Financial institutions are engaged in heavy volumes of transactions, compliance, and legacy systems in an environment that is the perfect setup to automate. Some banks and other financial institutions have seen their cost reduction by 30%–70%, and better accuracy and efficiency of offloading repetitive data entry, reconciliation, loan processing, and compliance reporting tasks using software bots, a fraction of the time they used to take in the past (McKinsey & Company, 2021). According to Edlich and Sohoni (2017), organizations can unlock significant productivity gains by integrating end-to-end automation into core business processes.

RPA has become the most widely adopted automation approach in financial services, automating routine, rule-based work quickly and accurately while improving process reliability process (Accenture, 2022; van der Aalst et al., 2018; Willcocks et al., 2021).

What is interesting about RPA is that it permeates beyond operational enhancements. It also enhances compliance and risk reduction because it reduces errors that may occur when attended by human beings, and under constant observation, it is possible to observe the financial operations immediately. In the case of fraud detection, the bots are able, for example, to review data across a variety of sources to spot unusual activity and raise alarms, improving how an institution reacts to threats (Gotthardt et al., 2020). Second, RPA enables the flexibility of keeping pace with fast-evolving financial regulations and security measures and, therefore, is the basis of future-proof finance processes.

This chapter explores the influence of RPA on banking and financial services, focusing on improvements in operational efficiency, risk mitigation, fraud detection, and the emergence of entrepreneurial opportunities. Another issue that it dwells upon is the increasing complementarity between the RPA technologies and the emergence of startup ecosystems, and the parity adjustment that intelligent automation presents to smaller companies. Based on the latest case studies, surveys, and expert opinions, the chapter offers an in-depth perspective of the way RPA is transforming the idea of finance and not just as an automation means but as a strategy-transforming tool.

2 Literature Review

Robotic Process Automation (RPA) has emerged as a significant driver of operational transformation in finance, accounting, and auditing over the past decade. Robotic Process Automation (2018) defines RPA as a configurable software tool that automates rule-based processes across applications. Its adoption has been accelerated by the convergence of cloud computing, artificial intelligence (AI), and advanced data analytics, enabling organizations to automate rule-based, high-volume tasks without major infrastructure overhauls.

Willcocks et al. (2021) identify RPA as a pivotal technology in streamlining repetitive tasks, improving process accuracy, and increasing reliability, especially in highly regulated environments like financial services. Le Clair (2017) emphasizes that enterprises progress through defined stages of RPA maturity, from basic task automation to scaled, intelligent automation.

The literature also reflects the growing integration of RPA with AI to create "intelligent automation" solutions that can learn, adapt, and improve over time (Forrester, 2021; Kumar & Balaramachandran, 2018). While RPA handles structured, rule-based processes, AI augments its capabilities by interpreting unstructured data, identifying patterns, and supporting decision-making in complex scenarios (PwC, 2023). This hybrid approach is increasingly seen as a strategic asset for organizations aiming to remain competitive in rapidly evolving financial markets.

In addition to technological benefits, studies highlight the broader organizational implications of RPA adoption. Lacity and Willcocks (2016) note that automation can shift workforce priorities from transactional tasks to strategic, value-added activities. However, EY (2022) warns that 30–50% of RPA implementations fail due to poor process design, unrealistic expectations, or inadequate governance frameworks. This underscores the importance of change management, cross-functional collaboration, and long-term scalability planning in automation strategies.

3 Research Gaps

Despite extensive discussion of RPA's benefits, current literature reveals several gaps. First, most studies focus on case-specific or sector-specific deployments, with limited cross-industry comparisons in the financial services sector. Second, there is insufficient empirical research on the long-term impacts of RPA on workforce roles, skill requirements, and organizational structures. Third, the integration of RPA with AI is still underexplored from a governance, ethics, and regulatory compliance perspective. This chapter addresses these gaps by providing a holistic analysis of RPA's role in finance—covering operational efficiency, compliance, entrepreneurial opportunities, policy recommendations, and the skills required for sustainable adoption.

4 Understanding RPA in the Financial Sector

What is RPA?

Robotic Process Automation (RPA) refers to the use of software bots that automate structured, rule-based, and repetitive tasks by emulating human interactions with digital systems. These bots can perform tasks such as data extraction, form filling, reconciliation, and reporting across multiple systems without requiring human intervention. Unlike traditional IT automation, RPA is non-invasive and can function across existing IT infrastructure without requiring major modifications (Willcocks et al., 2021).

Core Features

RPA (Robotic Process Automation) offers several core features that enhance business efficiency. It operates on rule-based execution, using predefined logic and business rules to carry out tasks. RPA bots mimic human interactions with graphical user interfaces (GUIs), enabling seamless automation across various systems. With its scalability, RPA can be deployed across departments or functions to optimize operations. Additionally, bots are available 24/7, providing continuous productivity without downtime. Every action performed by RPA is auditable, ensuring compliance and enabling robust monitoring. RPA is particularly valuable in environments where processes are stable, digital, and governed by strict rules, such as in financial workflows. FinTech firms increasingly embed RPA into core operations, treating automation as a foundation for innovation rather than just cost reduction (Dadgar, 2024).

4.1 Types of Bots: Attended vs. Unattended

RPA deployments are generally categorized into attended and unattended automation.

Attended Bots: Work alongside employees and are triggered by specific user actions. They are useful in front-office scenarios such as customer service or advisory functions, where a human-in-the-loop is beneficial (UiPath, 2022).

Unattended Bots: Operate independently without human interaction, typically in back-office processes like report generation, account reconciliation, or transaction processing. These bots run on scheduled intervals or event-based triggers and are central to high-volume operations.

More recently, vendors have introduced hybrid bots, which combine the capabilities of both, offering more flexibility and adaptability (Automation Anywhere, 2023).

Why Finance and Banking Are Ideal for RPA

The finance and banking sectors are exceptionally well-suited to RPA for several reasons:

High Transaction Volume: Finance involves millions of repetitive transactions, such as processing payments, loan applications, and journal entries—perfect candidates for automation (PwC, 2023).

Regulatory Pressure: Financial institutions are heavily regulated and must maintain consistent compliance with standards like KYC, AML, and SOX. RPA improves compliance by providing real-time audit trails and consistent rule-based execution (KPMG, 2022).

Legacy Systems: Banks often operate on outdated systems that are difficult to replace. RPA acts as a bridge, interacting with these systems through the user interface, without requiring replacement or reengineering (Gartner, 2023).
Error Sensitivity: Manual financial operations are highly prone to error, especially in data entry and reconciliation. RPA significantly reduces such risks by eliminating human variability (EY, 2022).
Cost Efficiency and Scalability: According to McKinsey (2023), financial firms that have deployed RPA solutions report process cost reductions of 30–70%, with full ROI often achieved in under 12 months.

4.2 RPA vs Traditional IT Automation

While both Robotic Process Automation (RPA) and traditional IT automation are designed to improve operational efficiency, they differ significantly in terms of implementation, complexity, and adaptability. RPA operates at the user interface level, mimicking human actions such as clicks, data entry, and navigation across systems. This non-invasive approach enables RPA to integrate with existing applications without requiring deep changes to the underlying IT infrastructure. In contrast, traditional IT automation typically involves system-level integration through APIs or direct backend connections, which demands more technical expertise and often results in substantial modifications to enterprise systems. A comparison of both approaches is illustrated in Fig. 1.

RPA solutions can be implemented within weeks, allowing organizations to quickly realize value. Traditional IT automation projects, on the other hand, may take several months to complete due to their complexity and dependencies on IT teams. Flexibility is another area where RPA excels—business users with limited technical backgrounds can configure and manage bots through user-friendly platforms. Traditional automation usually requires highly skilled IT personnel to develop and maintain scripts or workflows, limiting its accessibility across departments.

Moreover, RPA causes minimal disruption to daily operations since it overlays on top of current systems, whereas traditional IT automation often necessitates system downtime or restructuring, which can be costly and risky. The best use cases for RPA are rule-based, repetitive, and transactional tasks such as invoice processing, report generation, and data reconciliation. In contrast, traditional automation is more suitable for complex processes that require deep system integration or involve dynamic logic.

It enables institutions to automate high-volume processes quickly, maintain audit trails, and adapt to changes without overhauling core systems. Traditional IT automation remains vital for broader system integration projects, but its rigidity and longer timeframes can pose challenges in rapidly evolving financial environments (Forrester, 2021).

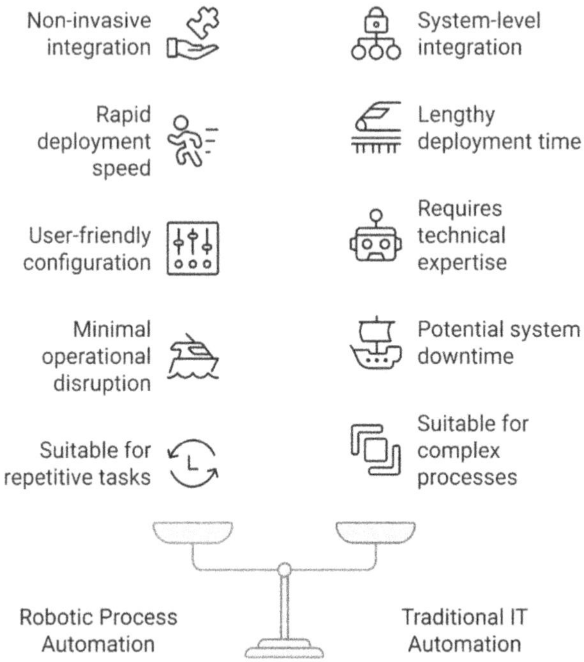

Fig. 1 RPA vs traditional IT automation. *Source* Authors Own creation

5 Use of AI/RPA Technology in Accounting and Auditing

Robotic Process Automation and Artificial Intelligence are two very different but closely-knitted terms that have and will continue to make a big impact on the automation in accounting and auditing practices. Professionals will be required to equip themselves with specialization and the use of technology. The application of RPA in accounting and finance processes is among the most likely ones to be supported or taken over by software robots. The adoption of new technologies such as Robotic Automation and AI will save time and reduce the error ratio and will make the accounting processes easier to automate as they follow prescribed rules and procedures. Generally, revenue is a high-risk zone in auditing activities, and with the automation of tasks where the judgment of an auditor is not required, the audit quality can be improved by reallocation of the auditor's work to analyze the variations generated by the RPA software. The banking sector now has years of data related to customers and employees, thanks to RPA (Kumar & Balaramachandran, 2018). Financial institutions are among the earliest adopters of RPA, applying it in compliance, transaction processing, and auditing contexts (Jacobus & Schneider, 2024).

5.1 RPA Use Cases in Finance and Accounting

Robotic Process Automation (RPA) has been extensively deployed across organizations, particularly in finance and accounting, where structured, rule-based processes dominate. RPA use cases are defined as documented procedures within finance functions that are ripe for automation. These cases simplify the movement of data between systems, reduce manual intervention, and increase accuracy and efficiency, especially in areas like taxation, auditing, and reporting.

Accounting and finance roles are well-suited for automation due to the need for high accuracy, repetitive manual transactions, and data integration across disconnected systems. Key use cases include:

- **Accounts Payable**: Bots transcribe invoice data (e.g., invoice number, date, amount) from PDFs into ERP systems like SAP, reducing cycle time by up to 60%.
- **Controller Function**: Automated validation of current invoices against historical data flags anomalies for human review.
- **Cost Allocation**: Tasks involving data compilation and distribution, which previously required hours using Excel and email, can now be completed in minutes.
- **Financial Close and Reporting**: RPA has achieved an 85% reduction in manual effort by automating spreadsheet integration and regulatory reporting.
- **Accounting Reconciliation**: Bots reconcile entries across platforms like QuickBooks and Excel in a fraction of the time taken manually.

These examples illustrate how RPA transforms finance from a manual, error-prone function into a streamlined, intelligent operation that enhances accuracy and allows professionals to focus on more strategic tasks.

6 Why RPA Is Preferred by the Firms, Especially by the Startups and the Emerging Businesses

6.1 RPA Empowers Startup Growth

Startups increasingly recognize the value of Robotic Process Automation (RPA) as a catalyst for scaling and innovation. By automating repetitive, rule-based tasks, RPA streamlines operations, reduces manual effort, and enhances accuracy—all while lowering costs. This efficiency allows entrepreneurs to focus on customer experience, product development, and strategic decision-making. Importantly, scaling with RPA does not require proportional increases in staff or infrastructure, enabling rapid adaptation to shifting market demands and faster onboarding in compliance-driven environments.

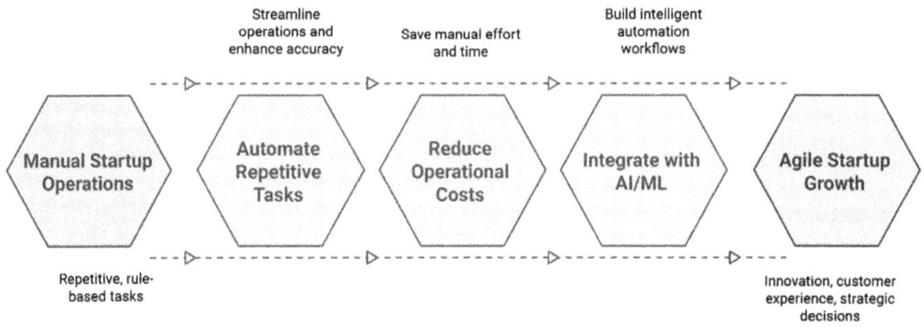

Fig. 2 RPA empowers startup growth. *Source* Authors own Creation

The key drivers of startup scalability through automation are depicted in Fig. 2. Partnerships with RPA solution providers or in-house development can further open doors to new markets, attract investors, and deliver a competitive edge. Many vendors support startups through early access programs, integrations, and innovation credits (UiPath, 2021). Low-code platforms lower the entry barrier, allowing non-technical teams to prototype and deploy bots quickly, fostering experimentation in early-stage environments (Deloitte, 2020).

At the same time, RPA itself presents a fertile market for startups to serve as automation specialists. Small and medium-sized businesses often lack the resources to build automation infrastructure, creating opportunities for startups to offer consulting services, identify automatable processes, design strategy maps, and provide scalable RPA solutions. Models such as *custom bot development* (e.g., invoice handling, data migration, compliance monitoring) and *Automation-as-a-Service (AaaS)* allow startups to generate recurring revenue while making automation affordable for smaller firms.

As RPA converges with artificial intelligence, machine learning, and natural language processing, startups are positioned to deliver "smart automations"—adaptive solutions that go beyond rule-based tasks to include predictive insights and enhanced user experiences. This positions startups not only as technology adopters but also as innovation drivers in the global automation ecosystem.

Ultimately, RPA empowers emerging businesses to scale efficiently, compete with larger players, and pioneer intelligent automation models. As the demand for digital transformation accelerates, entrepreneurial ventures that leverage RPA will play a pivotal role in shaping future-ready, vibrant businesses across industries.

7 Implementation Challenges and Risk Considerations

According to Deloitte's Global Robotics Survey, 53% of businesses have already implemented RPA, with an additional 19% planning adoption within two years. Similar adoption trends are reported in Forrester's *State of RPA* study (Forrester,

2021) and UiPath's *Automation Now and Next* report (UiPath, 2023), which highlight increasing enterprise-wide scaling of automation solutions.

Despite its potential, 30–50% of initial RPA projects fail, often due to underestimated costs and timelines (EY). To realize its full benefits, organizations must address the following:

- **Operational Risks**

Poorly designed processes and overreliance on automation can centralize failure points. RPA should be business-led with IT support, not the other way around.

- **Financial and Regulatory Risks**

Errors in algorithms can compromise financial reporting and regulatory compliance. Currently, there are no universal standards for RPA governance (Internal Controls, 2018).

- **Organizational and Cultural Impacts**

Automation may initially impact morale. However, training programs and strategic communication can promote acceptance, especially when bots take over monotonous tasks. The shortage of RPA expertise further highlights the need for skill development.

- **Technology Selection**

Choosing the right tool and vendor is critical. Consider server failover, capacity planning, storage needs, and vendor support. Deep evaluation is essential for a robust pilot or PoC (Successful Implementation, 2017).

- **Governance and Accountability**

Review and reinforce control frameworks. Assign clear ownership for bot operations and allocate resources for system maintenance, updates, and audits (Successful Implementation, 2017).

- **Cybersecurity Threats**

As RPA digitizes manual processes, it also creates new cyber vulnerabilities. AI-integrated bots can become targets or be exploited if not secured. Strong cybersecurity measures are vital (Gotthardt et al., 2019).

RPA and AI are transformative technologies with the power to significantly enhance productivity and efficiency. However, organizations must navigate myths, plan for risks, and build the right foundation—technologically and culturally—to ensure long-term success.

8 Benefits and Challenges of RPA in Finance

8.1 Benefits of RPA

Robotic Process Automation offers a wide spectrum of advantages to financial institutions, ranging from operational improvements to strategic market positioning.

1. **Financial Benefits**
   RPA can reduce operational costs by 15–90%, depending on the nature of the automated tasks and the chosen implementation model. Unattended bots, centrally managed, often yield the highest returns. Cost savings are realized not only through labor reduction but also through increased throughput and efficiency.
2. **Operational Efficiency**
   Bots operate 24/7 without fatigue, enabling faster transaction processing and eliminating delays caused by human schedules. This capability allows banks and accounting firms to meet tighter deadlines and process higher transaction volumes without additional headcount.
3. **Accuracy and Compliance**
   By following predefined rules, RPA reduces human error, ensuring greater data integrity in accounting and auditing tasks. Every bot action is logged, creating a robust audit trail for regulatory compliance. This is particularly valuable in meeting standards such as KYC, AML, and SOX.
4. **Scalability and Flexibility**
   RPA can be rapidly scaled to meet fluctuating workloads without the delays and costs associated with hiring and training new staff. Financial institutions can reallocate human resources to strategic, high-value activities.
5. **Strategic and Competitive Advantages**
   Beyond operational improvements, Robotic Process Automation (RPA) provides organizations with strategic advantages that extend across the financial sector. By enabling faster and more accurate processes, RPA supports agility, scalability, and continuous innovation. Integrated with artificial intelligence and analytics, it empowers firms to leverage data-driven insights, create adaptive workflows, and deliver superior customer experiences. These capabilities not only reduce costs but also strengthen market positioning, enhance competitiveness, and allow businesses to respond quickly to evolving regulatory and client demands.

8.2 Challenges and Risks of RPA

While the benefits of RPA are substantial, successful implementation requires navigating several risks and limitations (Eulerich et al., 2024; EY, 2022).

1. **Implementation Risks**
   Poorly designed processes, lack of stakeholder buy-in, and insufficient change management can lead to project failures. EY (2022) reports that 30–50% of initial RPA deployments fail due to underestimated costs and timelines.
2. **Governance and Accountability**
   Without clear ownership of bot operations and maintenance, automation initiatives can suffer from inconsistent performance, compliance lapses, or security vulnerabilities. Organizations must establish robust governance frameworks.
3. **Financial and Regulatory Risks**
   Errors in both algorithms or data inputs can compromise financial reporting and regulatory compliance. Given the absence of universal RPA governance standards, firms must establish their own controls.
4. **Cultural and Workforce Impacts**
   Automation can trigger employee resistance if perceived as a threat to jobs. Effective communication and upskilling programs are essential to promote acceptance and align staff with automation goals.
5. **Cybersecurity Threats**
   Automating manual processes increases exposure to cyberattacks, especially when bots access sensitive financial data. AI-enabled bots can also be exploited if not secured through encryption, access control, and regular monitoring.

By addressing these challenges through strategic planning, stakeholder engagement, and strong governance, organizations can ensure that RPA adoption delivers sustained value while minimizing risks.

9 RPA Implementation Strategy and Organizational Readiness

Implementing Robotic Process Automation (RPA) in an organization, like any emerging technology, requires more than simply installing software. It involves redesigning information processes, restructuring workflows, and aligning organizational culture to support change (Colesca & Dobrin, 2006; Fotache & Păvăloaia, 2015). RPA offers transformative potential to meet evolving business and tax objectives, but successful implementation demands a strategic approach rather than simply "throwing a robot on spreadsheets." The structured roadmap for RPA implementation is shown in **Fig. 3**

Organizations should begin with a structured roadmap. Below are **five key steps** that support a scalable, value-driven automation journey:

Step 1: Identify High-Impact Processes

Start by selecting finance and accounting functions that involve repetitive, rule-based, and high-volume tasks. Suitable processes include accounts payable/ receivable, general accounting, expense management, budgeting, payroll, internal

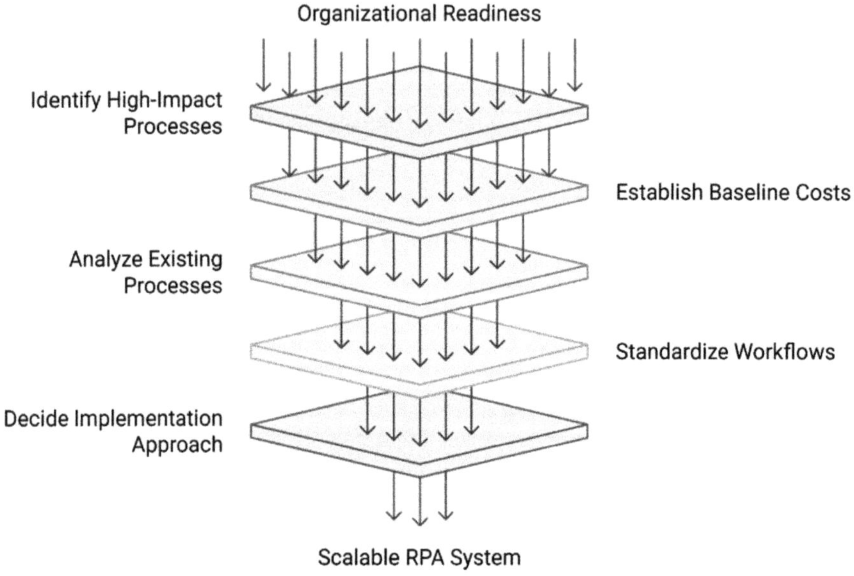

Fig. 3 RPA implementation strategy funnel. *Source* Author's own creation

audit, and compliance. A proof-of-concept or pilot in a focused area reduces risk and validates feasibility.

Step 2: Establish Baseline Operational Costs

Before quantifying automation benefits, companies must understand the current cost of operations. Estimating baseline costs helps communicate the ROI of RPA to stakeholders and gain executive support.

Step 3: Analyze and Document Existing Processes

Conduct a detailed review of current workflows to identify automation candidates. Use standardized modeling formats like **BPMN 2.0**, which enhance clarity and ensure seamless handoffs between business analysts and implementation teams. Lack of process documentation often hampers success.

Step 4: Standardize Workflows

Automation is most effective when processes are consistent and stable. Standardizing procedures ensures that bots can operate efficiently and reduces the likelihood of exceptions or errors. This step often marks the beginning of deeper digital transformation within finance.

Step 5: Decide Between In-House or Vendor-Led Implementation

Organizations can either build RPA capabilities internally using online platforms and training resources or collaborate with specialized vendors. Each option requires investment in learning and change management, but both can be viable depending on available resources and strategic objectives.

Many organizations are scaling RPA enterprise-wide, with expectations that bots could eventually handle up to 20% of full-time equivalent workloads. Although the survey reports a rapid three-month payback period for successful implementations, 63% of respondents noted their timelines were longer than expected, and 37% reported higher-than-anticipated costs—highlighting the importance of realistic planning in RPA strategy.

10 Impact of Robotic Automation on Accounting

As more automation technologies (e.g., Robotic Process Automation (RPA) and Artificial Intelligence (AI)) have been looked at, there has been interest in the accounting function at both the organizational and individual levels of effect. The advent of computers has led to the investigation of the advantages, the challenges, and the actual uses of automation in accounting and auditing since computers appeared.

11 Outlook: Convergence, Disruption, and Human Adaptation

The future of finance is being rapidly reshaped by the convergence of Robotic Process Automation (RPA), Artificial Intelligence (AI), and cognitive technologies. As these tools evolve, their integration across markets, solutions, and processes will redefine how businesses operate. This shift toward intelligent automation represents not just a technological upgrade but a structural transformation. Organizations must prepare for enterprise-scale deployments where solutions are no longer siloed but integrated into holistic digital ecosystems.

Yet, the human dimension remains central. As automation takes over repetitive tasks, the role of professionals—especially in finance and accounting—must evolve toward strategic thinking, innovation, and system oversight. To remain relevant, the workforce must embrace upskilling in data analytics, AI literacy, and process redesign.

12 Recommendations and Policy Implications

To remain competitive in the twenty-first century, finance professionals must build a blend of technical expertise, analytical thinking, and leadership skills that align with future workforce demands (ICAEW, 2022; World Economic Forum, 2023).

This involves embracing interdisciplinary learning, mastering automation tools, and adapting to the shifting boundaries between human-led and technology-enabled work. This chapter identifies strategic and policy-oriented steps for maximizing the impact of Robotic Process Automation (RPA) in the financial sector, while equipping the workforce to thrive in an evolving, technology-driven environment.

1. **Continuous Learning and Upskilling**
   Given the rapid adoption of Artificial Intelligence (AI) and RPA in accounting, professionals must commit to ongoing skill development. Organizations should invest in structured training programs covering automation tools, data analytics, and AI literacy to ensure employees can adapt to technological advancements. Upskilling enhances both operational efficiency and cost-effectiveness.
2. **Interdisciplinary Collaboration**
   Advancing RPA adoption and research requires close collaboration between accounting experts, AI specialists, and policy-makers. Cross-disciplinary partnerships can accelerate innovation and ensure RPA solutions are both technically sound and operationally relevant.
3. **Exploration of Advanced AI Technologies**
   Beyond rule-based RPA, advanced AI techniques—such as expert systems, neural networks, fuzzy logic, and hybrid models—should be integrated to improve accuracy, decision-making, and predictive capabilities in accounting and auditing workflows.
4. **Enhanced Cybersecurity Measures**
   As RPA becomes embedded in financial operations, organizations must prioritize robust cybersecurity frameworks to safeguard data integrity, resilience, and reliability. AI-enabled bots should be designed with secure coding practices, access controls, and continuous monitoring.
5. **Curriculum Reform in Education**
   Academic and professional training bodies should integrate topics on robotics, AI, and automation into accounting and auditing programs, ensuring future graduates enter the workforce with relevant digital skills.
6. **Building Future-Ready Accountants**
   To remain competitive in the 21st century, accountants must develop a blend of technical expertise, strategic insight, and adaptability. They need to maintain high professional competence by staying current with regulations, emerging technologies, and ethical standards. Strong management and leadership skills are essential for leading teams, overseeing automation projects, and driving strategic initiatives. Technological proficiency must extend beyond basic IT literacy to include programming, data analytics, and automation tools. Analytical thinking is equally important, enabling accountants to extract insights from complex data, assess risks, and guide evidence-based decisions. Finally, effective decision-making capabilities—grounded in an understanding of market dynamics, financial risk, and long-term planning—will ensure that accountants contribute meaningfully to organizational strategy. By mastering these competencies, the profession can

transition from operational task execution to strategic value creation, ensuring that human expertise complements automation rather than competes with it.

13 Conclusion

This chapter has discussed how Robotic Process Automation (RPA) and Artificial Intelligence (AI) can revolutionize the field of finance and accounting with regard to operational efficiency, accuracy, and decision-making capabilities. These technologies not only enable automation of monotonous tasks but also represent a paradigm shift in the delivery and management of financial services.

Nevertheless, implementation does not require software alone. It needs an integrated approach, cross-functional teams, investment in people, and a changeable organizational culture. To remain viable in the ever-more automated environment, professionals need to engage in lifelong learning and combine the expertise of data analytics, process design, and new technologies to maintain relevance in the current modern environment.

As RPA continues to converge with AI, machine learning, and cognitive tools, it is poised to transform not only traditional business models such as BPO but also reimagine the future of finance itself. Ultimately, organizations that treat RPA as a catalyst for digital transformation—rather than merely a cost-saving tool—will be best positioned to lead in the automation-driven economy.

References

Accenture. (2022). *Automation and the future of work: Reimagining business processes with AI and RPA*. Accenture Research.

Automation Anywhere. (2023). *Hybrid bots: The next step in RPA evolution*. https://www.automationanywhere.com

Colesca, S. E., & Dobrin, C. (2006). E-government adoption in Romania. *Electronic Journal of e-Government, 4*(2), 67–74.

Dadgar, K. (2024). FinTech process automation. In *Digital project practice for banking and fintech* (1st ed., pp. 24–35). Auerbach Publications. https://doi.org/10.1201/9781003395560-3

Deloitte. (2020). *Automation with intelligence: Pursuing organization-wide reimagination*. https://www2.deloitte.com

Eulerich, M., Waddoups, N., Wagener, M., & Wood, D. A. (2024). The dark side of robotic process automation (RPA): Understanding risks and challenges with RPA. *Accounting Horizons, 38*(2), 143–152. https://doi.org/10.2308/HORIZONS-2022-019

Edlich, A., & Sohoni, V. (2017). *How to start building your next-generation operating model*. McKinsey & Company.

EY. (2022). *Reducing errors and risk in financial operations with RPA*. https://www.ey.com

Forrester. (2021). *The role of RPA in financial services automation*. https://www.forrester.com

Fotache, D., & Păvăloaia, V. D. (2015). RPA—Robotic Process Automation: The next major revolution in business process management. *Informatica Economică, 19*(1), 110–115.

Gartner. (2023). *Navigating legacy systems with RPA in the financial sector*. https://www.gartner.com

Gotthardt, M., Koivulaakso, D., Oksanen, A., & Varjonen, S. (2019). *Current state and challenges of robotic process automation in accounting and auditing*. Aalto University School of Business Working Paper.
Gotthardt, M., Copeland, R., Dehning, B., & Weitzel, T. (2020). Robotic process automation in financial services: Challenges and opportunities. *Journal of Business Research, 116*, 77–91. https://doi.org/10.1016/j.jbusres.2020.04.024
Institute of Chartered Accountants in England and Wales (ICAEW). (2022). *Artificial intelligence and automation in finance*. ICAEW.
Controls, I. (2018). The future of governance in robotic automation. *Internal Control Systems Journal, 12*(3), 45–53.
Jacobus, M., & Schneider, M. (2024). Robotic process automation in financial institutions. In Digital Project Practice for Banking and FinTech (1st ed., pp. 36–42). Auerbach Publications. https://doi.org/10.1201/9781003395560-4
KPMG. (2022). *Regulatory compliance and automation in financial services*. https://home.kpmg
Kumar, V., & Balaramachandran, V. (2018). Intelligent automation in banking: RPA and cognitive systems in financial institutions. *Journal of Financial Transformation, 47*, 108–115.
Lacity, M., & Willcocks, L. (2016). *Robotic process automation: The next transformation lever for shared services*. LSE Outsourcing Unit Working Paper Series.
Le Clair, C. (2017). *The RPA market landscape*. Forrester Research Report.
McKinsey & Company. (2021). *The next normal in operations: RPA at scale in finance and beyond*. https://www.mckinsey.com
McKinsey & Company. (2023). *The impact of RPA on cost reduction in financial services*. https://www.mckinsey.com
PwC. (2023). *The financial sector's journey to automation with RPA*. https://www.pwc.com
Robotic Process Automation. (2018). Digital workforce for the future of finance. *Journal of Accounting Innovation, 9*(2), 112–120.
UiPath. (2021). *Startup support programs and innovation credits*. https://www.uipath.com
UiPath. (2022). *The future of RPA: Attended and unattended automation*. https://www.uipath.com
UiPath. (2023). *The state of robotic process automation 2023*. UiPath Inc.
van der Aalst, W. M. P., Bichler, M., & Heinzl, A. (2018). Robotic process automation. *Business & Information Systems Engineering, 60*(4), 269–272. https://doi.org/10.1007/s12599-018-0542-4
Willcocks, L., Lacity, M., & Craig, D. (2021). *Robotic process automation: The next transformation of work*. SB Publishing.
World Economic Forum. (2023). *The future of jobs report 2023*. World Economic Forum.

Dr. Deepika Dhingra is a seasoned finance academic with over 17 years of experience spanning teaching, research, and industry. She holds a PhD in Finance from FMS, Delhi University, and an MBA in Finance from Indraprastha University. Currently, she serves as Associate Professor and Area Chair at BML Munjal University and is associated with institutions like IMT CDL, Hero Vired, and GRMI. Her research spans ESG, fintech, corporate restructuring, and sustainability, with publications in ABDC-ranked and Scopus-indexed journals. An accomplished case writer, her work is published by Ivey and Harvard Business Publishing. Dr. Dhingra has consulted on fintech and curriculum design for clients in India and the UK. She is proficient in financial modeling and data analysis using tools like E-Views, Stata, and MATLAB. A committed educator and PhD guide, she is a member of the American Finance Association and regularly contributes to academic conferences and institutional development initiatives.

Dr. Jaskiran Arora serves as Professor and Dean of Education Quality at BML Munjal University, where she oversees teaching standards, curriculum design, and educator development across the institution. With more than 25 years of experience spanning academia and the corporate sector, she leads training programs on online pedagogy, curriculum innovation, spreadsheet modelling, risk analysis, and finance literacy for educators and professionals. Dr. Arora earned her PhD from

Maharshi Dayanand University, an MBA in Finance, and postgraduate credentials from Lancaster University and Harvard University. Her scholarly output includes peer-reviewed articles and conference papers in accounting, finance, and education, and she has been recognized for excellence in teaching, case writing, and academic mentoring. She also contributed to strategic partnerships like the ACCA integration with BMU's accounting curriculum, reflecting her commitment to making education both rigorous and industry-relevant.

Beyond Borders: Asian Entrepreneurs Driving the Global Frontier

Pravin Kumar

Abstract This chapter examines how the Asian entrepreneur has become a key player in transforming international business not just through the opportunities of digital innovation but also through what are socio-cultural resources, like diaspora networks. It brings together comparative knowledge and exemplary profiles across a variety of contexts, India, China, Southeast Asia, Korea, Japan, Bangladesh, and the Philippines, in order to explore how entrepreneurial ecosystems relate and deviate throughout the region. Instead of providing detailed case studies, the discussion points out trends of flexibility, technology usage, and cross-border relationships that spur inclusive and sustainable cross-border business. This analysis gives a strong feature of the fact that hybrid models, such as the localization of global competitiveness practiced by China, or the remittance-based enterprises in Bangladesh, the world realizes that entrepreneurial dominance of the Asian region is forward and progressive, and is a model of long-term business of sustainable, inclusive, and culturally oriented global business.

1 Introduction

Entrepreneurial activity has made Asia a central force in the global economy in the twenty-first century (Ahmad & Seymour, 2008). As the twentieth century revealed the Zenith of Asian manufacturing potential, Indian-origin entrepreneurs in Silicon Valley show how transnational connections accelerate global scaling and knowledge transfer. Transnational connections enhance the pace of global scale, and knowledge transfer looks like a typo or leftover of a digitalized corporate and transnational business (Knight & Liesch, 2016). Entrepreneurs now restricted to local markets have gone global with cultural knowledge, digital and technology expertise, and diaspora networks, managing to generate new types of market disruption in the

P. Kumar (✉)
Brainware University, Kolkata, India
e-mail: pvk.mgmt@brainwareuniversity.ac.in

T. Endress and Y. F. Badir (eds.), *Business and Management in Asia: Opportunities and Entrepreneurship*, https://doi.org/10.1007/978-981-95-4909-2_15

world (Chen et al., 2024). This chapter addresses the rapid internationally of innovative entrepreneurs, to show resiliency and flexibility in their business development strategies (Choi & Shepherd, 2004).

Researchers have found networks of entrepreneurs not only connected but also to regional and international markets in cities such as Bengaluru, Shenzhen, Ho Chi Minh City, and Jakarta (Demirbag & Yaprak, 2015). Some of the various disciplines that these ventures are solving issues through adopted technologies include the use of e-commerce platforms, blockchain, and artificial intelligence in financial inclusion and post-pandemic healthcare. Informal cross-border partnerships, diaspora networks, and capital streams are reinforcing the expansion and further development of these enterprises, while they are also accentuated at the same time on cultural sensitivity and local adjustability (Harms & Groen, 2017).

Asian entrepreneurship also stands to disrupt Eurocentric modes of innovation and progression in the world economy. New business models are coming out of the region that balance old values with new global demands and present a new roadmap for the integration of the Orient and the Occident. These trends bring forth other strategies that can be used in growth and inclusion that have been very applicable to the emerging economies today (Darnihamedani et al., 2024).

As a result of this entrepreneurial revolution, the chapter focuses on digitalization, socio-cultural capital, and supportive policies that enable entrepreneurs to transcend the geographical and institutional boundaries. It integrates economic knowledge, sociological understanding, and management orientations to exhibit how Asian business leaders adapt to keep pace with complicated global times in developing unique regional cultures of entrepreneurship.

2 Objectives

This chapter explores the pressure that drives Asian entrepreneurs into going global by looking at technological innovation, diasporic networks, and shifting consumer markets. It measures motivators such as digital advances, policy support, and cultural capital. This discussion focuses on patterns and trends that affect the decision-making of Asian businessmen, in reversing the trends of an industry, and learning about flexible business strategies. It also examines regional economic systems and how Asian entrepreneurship reorganizes the world business dynamics.

3 Literature Review

The rise of global entrepreneurship has evolved radically over the past decades as a result of the shift in global forces, digitalization, and demographic trends (Oviatt & McDougall, 2005). As opposed to dealing with these trends singularly, studies are also focusing more on the interconnectivity of various trends with each other, such that they create systems of a complicated entrepreneurial landscape within Asia as well as other parts of the world (Terjesen et al., 2016). The aspects of innovation, risk-taking, and opportunity recognition have remained the fundamental characteristics of research on Western entrepreneurship, but most recent investigations on entrepreneurship in the Asian context emphasize the aspects of diaspora linkages and institutional background that influence the behavior of entrepreneurship (Al Mamun et al., 2019). An example is diaspora entrepreneurship, which not only allows the inflow of capital but also translates cultural knowledge, which allows allowing the company to enter a market more easily, in its developed and emerging economies (Riddle & Brinkerhoff, 2011). The presence of institutional theory can be used to account for the different effects of similar entrepreneurial strategies in settings such as Singapore, Kazakhstan, and Vietnam because of the levels of state intervention, regulatory sophistication, and informal norms (Spigel, 2017).

Recent publications demonstrate that Asian business people now contend and collaborate with those in Africa and Latin America, inventing South-South chains of innovation (Terjesen et al., 2016). These results provide conflicting effects on an Asian scenario since the investigation through comparative learning about the Kenyan fintech industry and the Brazilian agri-tech start-up shows evidence of the same insights towards digital leapfrogging and diaspora involvement (Sinkovics et al., 2013). To the degree that such parallels exist, the Asian experience does not mark an exception to a broader change in the geography of innovation (Oviatt & McDougall, 2005).

Moreover, the sectoral studies have shown that technological entrepreneurship is an entrepreneurial activity, where the operational focus is on blockchain, artificial intelligence, and platform business models, as well as emerging in the Central and being developed in West Asia in the context of such studies (Al Mamun et al., 2019). As an example, the fintech industry in Kazakhstan has seen cross-border investment by both Russian and Middle Eastern venture capital firms, an indication of how interregional capital flows can be used to diversify the established funding mechanisms (Vahlne & Johanson, 2020). This is consistent with the institutional theory, which says that the existence of favorable policy conditions presents potential to inspire innovation even in comparatively new environments (Spigel, 2017).

Or likewise, diaspora entrepreneurship in Central Asia is now starting to follow similar patterns to earlier experiences in South Asia, where experienced entrepreneurs returning create businesses in new destinations using experiences of existing markets and modifying them to suit local environments (Riddle & Brinkerhoff, 2011). Returning ICT graduates in Uzbekistan are establishing export-based software development firms in the country as part of making it align with international supply chains in Europe (Zucchella & Siano, 2014). These developments can help in the chapter since there is empirical discussion on how cultural capital, together with institutional reforms, can improve the speed of scaling up of entrepreneurs (Fennell, 2021).

Nevertheless, there are still gaps: it is frequently nationally synchronized, and even though sectors such as Central Asia start to be incorporated into global supply chains by their textile entrepreneurs in Kyrgyzstan and IT services providers in Uzbekistan, they have been passed over (Zucchella & Siano, 2014). The synthesis of empirical evidence about the analysis of the digital economy, diaspora studies, and consistency of institutional construction in this chapter fills the gaps as to how entrepreneurs negotiate and work on the transformation of global business opportunities (Sinkovics et al., 2013; Vahlne & Johanson, 2020).

4 Approach and Sources

Asian entrepreneurship can be realized at its finest through various sources that include international databases, policy reports, and industry research. This chapter draws on these materials to build comparative portraits. The comparative portraits and regional descriptions of India, China, Southeast Asia, Korea, Japan, Bangladesh, and the Philippines have been incorporated into the chapter, but with no formal research design. These examples are not exhaustive case studies, but snapshots that reflect the diversity of entrepreneurial practices, and instead are meant to represent a snapshot of the variation that can be expected in entrepreneurial practices across institutional environments and development stages.

Due to the ability to draw inferences based on various sources, the chapter reveals certain patterns in attributes and unique characteristics, and, at the same time, reveals peculiarities that may vary across regions. This strategy emphasizes common forces that lead to success in entrepreneurship, such as digital innovation, diasporic affiliations, and supporting institutions, as well as unique national pathways. The confluence of these comparative typologies has provided a holistic insight into the role of Asian entrepreneurs in the process of globalization and how this has become a practice that is contributing to the incorporation of adaptable forms of entrepreneurship.

5 Comparative Profiles and Discussion

The section is constituted by the comparative profiles that display the description of the entrepreneurial dynamics of Asia. They are not deep case studies, but illustrative snapshots of secondary sources and regional briefs. They emphasize the operation of various entrepreneurial landscapes in the larger framework of global trends, which provides new insight into similarities and differences between countries.

In this comparative frame, the chapter detects some common drivers, including digital innovation, diaspora affiliations, and institutional assistance, as well as admitting distinctive trajectories with the sources of change played out by local circumstances. In this approach, the entire study of the global expansion of Asian entrepreneurs using innovation, policy responsiveness, and socio-cultural capital is given an experiential aspect.

The comparative study brings to the fore comparisons and contrasts among regions. As such, India and China rely on the infrastructure and the state-based approach to scale, whereas Southeast Asia prioritizes the value of frugality and inclusivity. Korea and Japan demonstrate the utility of high-tech R&D and cultural export, and Bangladesh and the Philippines demonstrate the usefulness of remittance-centric entrepreneurship and community-based networks. Collectively, these portraits show how the entrepreneurial ecologies of Asia are playing a role in making the world a diverse and connected economy.

Table 1 gives a summary of the key entrepreneurial characteristics, notable startups, and the enabling factors for selected Asian economies.

Such a view of comparison shows the gap in the entrepreneurial scene of Asia. Whereas India and China illustrate the scale digitally by having infrastructure and state-driven initiatives, respectively, Southeast Asia focuses more on frugal innovation and inclusivity (Chen et al., 2018). Korea and Japan leverage the worth of their cultural exports and richness in technology (Kim, 2024), and Bangladesh and the Philippines are evidence of how the gracious models and remittance-driven capital have become the mechanisms that drive the local and global basis (Dheer, 2018). The difference also underscores the different functions of diaspora networks, where there are more and stronger transnational ties in South Asia than in the most localized but tech-advanced environment of East Asia (Joardar & Wu, 2025).

Table 1 Comparative overview of Asian entrepreneurial ecosystems

Region/country	Key characteristics	Startup examples	Key enablers
India	Digital innovation, diaspora influence, global SaaS scaling	Razorpay, PhonePe, Freshworks, Zoho, Postman	Startup India program, Indian diaspora networks, VC ecosystems
China	Government-backed tech expansion, aggressive acquisition, and global e-commerce	Alibaba, Tencent, ByteDance, Shein, Temu	State support, data-driven platforms, logistics excellence
Southeast Asia	Frugal innovation, youth-driven digital growth, and social inclusion	Gojek, VNG Corporation, MoMo	Mobile-first economy, inclusive regulatory frameworks, ASEAN collaboration
Korea & Japan	High-tech R&D, cultural exports (K-pop, anime), deep-tech entrepreneurship	Samsung, LG, Naver, Weverse, SM Culture & Contents	Strong IP laws, export-driven policies, and entertainment-tech hybridization
Bangladesh and Philippines	Grassroots entrepreneurship, migrant remittance-led innovation, and inclusive tech	BRAC, Grameenphone, PayMaya, Edukasyon.ph	Remittance flows, social enterprises, and resilient community networks

Source Adapted from OECD (2023) and Startup Genome (2023)

Table 2 Startup growth in India, China, and Southeast Asia (2015–2024)

Year	India	China	Southeast Asia
2015	3200	5000	1500
2017	4700	6500	2500
2019	7200	8300	4100
2021	9200	10,000	5800
2023	10,500	12,000	6900
2024	11,800	13,200	7800

Source Data compiled from Statista (2015–2024) and World Bank Entrepreneurship Database (2015–2024)

It is from this comparative angle that one can determine the synthesis of how different regions within Asia develop a specific variety of entrepreneurial approaches and effects.

The figures in Table 2 show that the number of startups has been highly proliferated in India, China, and SEA in roughly a decade (2015–2024). This trend of growth can be explained by the manner in which the local ecosystems have evolved into high-energy incubator centers for start-ups. By including the 2024 statistics, it can be seen that the trend is even more positive: There is an excess of 11,800 startups in India, 13,200 in China, and nearly 7800 in Southeast Asia. This gradual growth explains how Asian markets are increasingly becoming competitive and full of potential in the global business scene.

Table 2 shows the growth in the number of startups for 8 years across three major Asian regions.

Adding the 2024 figures demonstrates a further positive trend: India had more than 11,800 startups, China had more than 13,200, and Southeast Asia had almost 7,800. This confirms that Asian entrepreneur ecosystems are resistant to economic insecurities worldwide.

However, let's first take a close look at the line chart below that indicates the growth trajectory of the startups based in India, China, and the Southeast Asian countries until 2024 to better understand the startup trends in these key Asian regions when it comes to entrepreneurship.

Figure 1 is a visualization of the growth arc of startups over the same time, up to the year 2024. The revised timeline reinforces the claim that the optimistic trends that were witnessed until 2023 have been carried through into 2024, making it clear that economies in Asia are one of the key drivers of entrepreneurial activity in the world.

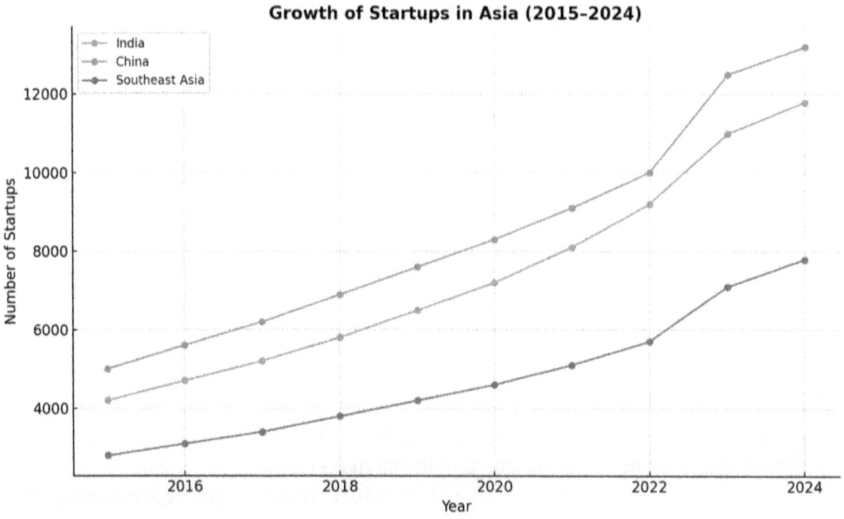

Fig. 1 Growth of startups in Asia (2015–2024). *Source* Author's illustration

5.1 India: Digital Leap and Diasporic Power

This example supports the main contention of this chapter, which is that the use of distinctive socio-cultural capital, digital infrastructures, and diaspora connections helps Asian entrepreneurs to attain fast global access (Dheer, 2018).

The digital ecosystem, alongside a globally dispersed Indian diaspora, particularly in the US and the UK, has become the foundation of India's entrepreneurial growth (Joardar & Wu, 2025). Since its launch in 2016, the Startup India program has increased investment in new businesses through fiscal advantages, together with streamlined regulatory mechanisms and funding channels. The Indian startup landscape centers itself on fintech, along with Software-as-a-Service (SaaS), EdTech, and HealthTech sectors because they serve both Indian domestic requirements and worldwide market potential (Kapoor & Agarwal, 2017).

The Indian fintech startups Razorpay, PhonePe, and Pine Labs led digital payment developments in India and extended their operations into Southeast Asia and the Middle East (Giones & Brem, 2017). Three globally successful SaaS unicorns—Freshworks, Zoho, and Postman demonstrate India's ability to scale the development of world-class software solutions (Kapoor & Agarwal, 2017).

Indian entrepreneurs based in Silicon Valley leverage their diasporic influence to accelerate the global expansion of Indian businesses (Dheer, 2018). Indian-origin venture capitalists have created networks that both enable international scalability and help facilitate cross-border knowledge sharing between members (Joardar & Wu, 2025). A growing number of Indian business founders who studied overseas now bring their international perspective back to India to develop productive business models that integrate Western business approaches and a detailed understanding of Indian markets.

The path of China proves the thesis that state-facilitated ecosystems, once supplemented with a forceful market landscape, can be used to reset the industry world standards (Zhang, 2022).

5.2 China: State Strategy and Cross-Border Scale

Government initiatives combine with financial assistance from government authorities to provide funds for large-scale technological companies and emerging actors (Zhang, 2022).

Chinese businessmen seize this opportunity to build up their e-commerce sites, expand the usage of mobile payment, and invest in AI businesses. The huge success of Alibaba, Tencent, and ByteDance at the global level, as well as the new contemporary businesses like Shein and Temu, shows how data, as well as the expedited delivery system, revolutionize the fast fashion and global e-commerce industry (Giones & Brem, 2017).

China drives its model via large-scale operational strategies and accelerates its expansion by aggressive acquisitions of companies (Ramamurti & Williamson, 2019).

5.3 Southeast Asia: Agility and Inclusive Innovation.

Digital entrepreneurship in Southeast Asia demonstrates mobile-first development and frugal adaptability in Indonesia and Vietnam (Chen et al., 2018). These countries' youthful population with tech literacy and expanding middle class positions them well to support startups across e-commerce, alongside digital payments, ride-hailing, and social commerce.

Starting as an unconventional ride-hailing company in Indonesia, Gojek has now developed into an all-encompassing Super Application, including services of payment solutions and food delivery, along with logistics infrastructure (Kapoor & Agarwal, 2017). Vietnam's entrepreneurial sector wins from gaming and fintech, and EdTech industries, which provide services for domestic and regional spaces by entities including VNG Corporation and MoMo (Giones & Brem, 2017).

These countries have developed their government support through the implementation of regulatory sandboxes alongside digital economy blueprints, which increase their tolerance for experimental activities. Social innovation stands as a central element that simultaneously drives societal development (Chen et al., 2018). A significant number of startup ventures create inclusive products that serve minority market segments, including micro-lending to small business owners and digital healthcare for remote areas.

This incident shows that technology, cultural branding, and strong IP regimes can be an independent way to global competitiveness, as the chapter has argued that hybrid strategies were anchored on local capabilities (Kim, 2024).

Newly established entrepreneurs can now access pan-Asian capital networks and mentorship support through regional startup collaborations and events, including the ASEAN Startup Summit. The ecosystems enable companies to develop quick market adaptation alongside cultural adaptability within diverse geographical areas (Chen et al., 2018).

5.4 *Korea and Japan: High-Tech Innovation and Cultural Exports*

South Korea, along with Japan, demonstrates a distinct entrepreneurial model that includes advanced technological manufacturing alongside effective cultural exports (Kim, 2024). The government's R&D and incubation programs in South Korea led to technological dominance in the semiconductor space, combined with leadership in mobile phones and video games. Smaller startups in South Korea can now explore deep-tech and AI applications thanks to market leaders including Samsung, LG, and Naver (Kapoor & Agarwal, 2017).

Korea's cultural industries' success with K-pop and K-drama and webtoons has generated new startup waves dedicated to entertainment production combined with fan platform services and celebrity brand-driven e-commerce ventures (Kim, 2024). Across four categories, Weverse and SM Culture & Contents have revolutionized the global drive to monetize fans by restructuring fan revenue systems.

This segment is indicative of how the concept of grassroots entrepreneurship, with the power of remittance economic flows and community networks, has served as an inspiration to the argument brought out in this chapter (Dheer, 2018). It is the argument that resiliency and resourcefulness are essential instruments to transnational success.

Japanese startup growth is on the right trajectory to grow because the government has started to change, and more so, the corporate business is starting to accept risk-taking startups. Entrepreneurship is increasingly focused on three emerging fields, which include robotics alongside Greentech and HealthTech (Giones & Brem, 2017). Entrepreneurs across both countries benefit from superior technology and powerful IP regulations and employ them with Western partners to achieve international growth.

The combination of engineering prowess and soft business strategies, with a growing acceptance of failure and a weakening of hierarchical values, drives entrepreneurs from Korea and Japan toward global markets (Kim, 2024).

5.5 *Bangladesh and Philippines: Grassroots Globalism*

The Bangladeshi and the Philippines entrepreneurial practice grows from localized resourceful populations that network through migrant communities and devise collective, genuine business strategies (Dheer, 2018). These two nations both have huge migrant populations whose remittance services can boost the local economy of their home country and foster small businesses (Joardar & Wu, 2025).

Social enterprises Grameenphone and BRAC in Bangladesh created the essential infrastructure for mobile banking services and rural connectivity, and women-oriented microbusiness models. Export-oriented SMEs in Bangladesh's apparel sector began using digital connectivity to build relationships with international buyers (Giones & Brem, 2017).

The Philippines moves forward with digital service startups through its established BPO sector and skilled English-speaking population, which now expands into EdTech, telemedicine, and e-commerce sectors (Chen et al., 2018). Inclusive tech-enabled services gain attraction through platforms like PayMaya and Edukasyon.ph.

The unique "remittance-led entrepreneurship" pattern persists in both nations due to mergers between international money transfers with locally developed innovations, which form scalable social enterprises (Dheer, 2018). Missing robust institutional backing from developed economies leads these entrepreneurs to employ resilience, coupled with their access to community networks and their ability to deliver frugal innovation solutions (Chen et al., 2018).

6 Thematic Comparison Across Cases

However, across these various contexts, several common themes stand out. What unites all three, and most innovation I see around, is the thread running through the fintech, the content platforms, and the inclusive business models (Giones & Brem, 2017). Innovation is adapted to each country's specific socio-economic and cultural context, producing a wide variety of globally significant solutions (Chen et al., 2018).

Resilience is equally important, particularly for entrepreneurs operating in emerging markets who face weak institutions, an uncertain funding environment, and infrastructure gaps (Ramamurti & Williamson, 2019). Adaptability to survival and success is seen at the grassroots level in Bangladesh and rapid scale models in Indonesia.

The decisive role of institutional support, either and regulatory reform, startups' missions, or public-private partnerships in fostering the entrepreneurial ecosystems (Zhang, 2022). Those countries that have proactive policies involving internationalization tend to be the fastest and to have the most confidence of domestic and foreign investors; India, China, and South Korea, for example.

In addition, diaspora networks serve as strategic assets in multiple cases and, beyond capital, they can provide credibility, market access, and mentorship (Joardar & Wu, 2025). Through these transnational ties, cultural divides are bridged and globalization is accelerated (Dheer, 2018).

Taken together, these cases highlight how Asian entrepreneurs are not simply reacting to global trends; they are changing them (Ramamurti & Williamson, 2019). They are leading the way in transnational entrepreneurship through hybrid models, digital fluency, and socio-cultural capital to instill a new blueprint of inclusive and adaptable entrepreneurship embedded deeply in local realities (Chen et al., 2018).

7 Key Insights and Implications

Some of these themes offered by the comparative profiles explain why Asian entrepreneurs have been successful in the global markets. The main enablers of multinational advancement include adaptability, diasporic networks, and digital scaling strategies, as can be seen in Fig. 2. When brought together, these factors depict the process through which the entrepreneurial ecosystems in Asia incorporate cultural intelligence, technology, and transnational connections to establish continental presence.

Adaptability is the key focus of entrepreneurs in dynamic markets. Adapting products and services to meet the new environments and adapting to the changing institutional framework, the entrepreneurs stretch their activities across regions.
Diaspora networks do not just provide financial capital, but also credibility and mentorship, and international modes of access into markets. A good example can be the Indian-origin entrepreneurs of Silicon Valley. Indian-origin entrepreneurs in Silicon Valley are an example of how the speed of global scaling and transfer of knowledge is quickened by transnational relations.
Digital scaling allows an entrepreneur to quickly grow across borders. Whether it is fintech or Software-as-a-Service, digital tools enable Asian companies to satisfy the needs of domestic and global markets simultaneously.

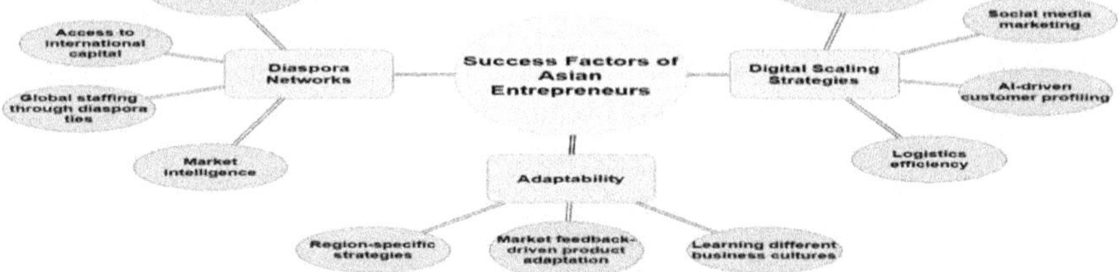

Fig. 2 Success factors of Asian entrepreneurs in global markets. *Source* Author's illustration

More recent 2024 data reinforce this finding, as the velocity of startup scaling has not decelerated, and digital-first business models continue to dominate growth.

These insights have broader implications for different stakeholders:

- The key to being an entrepreneur in the future lies in whether he or she possesses the skills to develop what is dubbed a Global Systems Mindset, one that takes into account cultural sensitivity and diplomacy, as well as developing technological expertise and strategic dexterity.
- Policymakers must launch supportive ecosystems by organizing cross-border start-up exchanges, investment establishments providing support by the diaspora, and less restrictive regulations that reduce the barrier to growth.
- There is a need to expand business and management education beyond Western practices to consider the dynamics of the Asian diaspora, literacy in the digital space, and flexible learning styles.
- Investors and incubators ought to appreciate the role of cultural intelligence and digital capability in their opportunity evaluation, not merely business models, but also the aspects of cross-cultural scaling, as mentors offer.

Cumulatively, those insights indicate that Asian entrepreneurs are not mere observers of world trends, but they actively help in forming them. The hybrid business models, digital fluency, and social-cultural capital are adaptable to change, and their characteristics present a model of global entrepreneurship that harbors inclusivity.

8 Recommendations

The synchronization of policy, business, and institutional levels is needed in order to ensure the sustainability of cross-border entrepreneurship and innovation. Practical ways forward:

8.1 For Policymakers

Governments can make a significant impact as they promote regulatory environments that promote innovation and internationalization. Entrepreneurs can benefit from simplified licensing procedures, single-stop digital platforms where entrepreneurs can register for tax, and cross-border start-up exchanges. Sustainable entrepreneurship would also be stimulated by tax exemptions, grants to green as well as digital ventures.

8.2 *For Entrepreneurs*

Business people have to enhance their cultural intelligence (CQ) to overcome the challenges of multicultural markets and negotiating styles. The flexibility in having a global expansion can be achieved through the construction of a hybrid form of business models that involve local alliances, digital channels, and sustainable approaches. Sustainable, inclusive, and environmentally friendly strategies are gaining relevance in their ability to attract investors and consumers.

8.3 *For Institutions*

Institutions and research bodies need to develop platforms that embrace international teamworking, mentoring, and innovation towards long-term sustainability. Collaboration centers, innovation hubs, and incubators can equip entrepreneurs with a better understanding of how business works across borders. The institutions can assist in shaping entrepreneurial global leaders through management training, followed by cultural studies and the use of technology.

9 Conclusion

Asian entrepreneurs are creating as agents of change to transform markets; they are also creating disruptive innovations that alter established patterns of business success in a long-established format. Such leaders are also regional values, ingenuity, and resilience, with the growing economic strengths of the world merging into a multi-polar world; however, they also possess global aspirations. Their activities demonstrate that entrepreneurial success is competitive and culturally situated in the modern world, and these kinds of approaches create business frames that may be outside a range of contexts.

Asian entrepreneurship is greater than mere capacity building in a local setting; it is an emergent redefinition of global business leadership. Entrepreneurs in Asia are very much on track to establish a new standard and adaptive growth through a combination of digital innovation, diaspora linkages, and inclusive practices. Their narrations exhibit how the entrepreneurial development is not surviving on its toes but rather proactive in the face of forward-looking ideologies based on the hybridization of culture-smart thinking with technological changes.

This increased momentum also registers the need to have better industry-academia ties in producing the next generation of entrepreneurs. Sustainable, innovative, and socially responsible ecosystems will play a crucial role in extending such a trend. These ecosystems are capable of giving skills, knowledge, and institutional backing essential so that entrepreneurs can compete and be successful in an interconnected world.

The latest 2024 statistics confirm that Asian entrepreneurship is growing dynamically, indicating a long-term trend that positions the region as a global leader in the sphere of entrepreneurship.

This chapter shows, with the help of comparative profiles throughout Asia, that the dynamism of all entrepreneurship in the region cannot be attained in the form of isolated studies. Instead, it requires a holistic perspective, which has identified shared enabling mechanisms, flexibility, uptake of digital, diaspora communities, and the distinctive national pathways that bring variety and strength. Taken together, these factors show how far Asian business people are remapping the frontier on the world frontier, in offering not simply to make money but also to a trajectory of inclusive, sustainable, and adaptable avenues to globe-spanning entrepreneurs.

References

Ahmad, N., & Seymour, R. G. (2008). Defining entrepreneurial activity: Definitions supporting frameworks for data collection.

Al Mamun, A., Fazal, S. A., & Muniady, R. (2019). Entrepreneurial knowledge, skills, competencies and performance: A study of micro-enterprises in Kelantan, Malaysia. *Asia Pacific Journal of Innovation and Entrepreneurship, 13*(1), 29–48.

Chen, J., Yin, X., & Mei, L. (2018). Holistic innovation: An emerging innovation paradigm. *International Journal of Innovation Studies, 2*(1), 1–13.

Chen, X., Bandara, D., & Sanford, B. (2024). A literature review on transnational diaspora entrepreneurship: Utilizing a combined approach of traditional and topic modeling. *New England Journal of Entrepreneurship, 27*(2), 136–151.

Choi, Y. R., & Shepherd, D. A. (2004). Entrepreneurs' decisions to exploit opportunities. *Journal of Management, 30*(3), 377–395.

Darnihamedani, P., Block, J. H., & Jansen, J. (2024). Institutional reforms and entrepreneurial growth ambitions. *International Small Business Journal, 42*(7), 805–840.

Demirbag, M., & Yaprak, A. (Eds.). (2015). *Handbook of emerging market multinational corporations.* Edward Elgar Publishing.

Dheer, R. J. (2018). Entrepreneurship by immigrants: A review of existing literature and directions for future research. *International Entrepreneurship and Management Journal, 14*, 555–614.

Fennell, D. A. (Ed.). (2021). *Routledge handbook of ecotourism.* Routledge.

Giones, F., & Brem, A. (2017). Digital technology entrepreneurship: A definition and research agenda. *Technology Innovation Management Review, 7*(5), 44–51.

Harms, R., & Groen, A. (2017). Loosen up? Cultural tightness and national entrepreneurial activity. *Technological Forecasting and Social Change, 121*, 196–204.

Joardar, A., & Wu, S. (2025). An examination of impact of immigrant entrepreneur cultural intelligence on performance during crisis. *International Journal of Cross Cultural Management.* https://doi.org/10.1177/14705958251340545.

Kapoor, R., & Agarwal, S. (2017). Sustaining superior performance in business ecosystems: Evidence from application software developers in the iOS and Android smartphone ecosystems. *Organization Science, 28*(3), 531–551.

Kim, S. (2024). *Korea's platform empire: An emerging power in the global platform sphere.* Routledge.

Knight, G. A., & Liesch, P. W. (2016). Internationalization: From incremental to born global. *Journal of World Business, 51*(1), 93–102.

Oviatt, B. M., & McDougall, P. P. (2005). Defining international entrepreneurship and modeling the speed of internationalization. *Entrepreneurship Theory and Practice, 29*(5), 537–553.

Ramamurti, R., & Williamson, P. J. (2019). Rivalry between emerging-market MNEs and developed-country MNEs: Capability holes and the race to the future. *Business Horizons, 62*(2), 157–169.

Riddle, L., & Brinkerhoff, J. (2011). Diaspora entrepreneurs as institutional change agents: The case of Thamel.com. *International Business Review, 20*(6), 670–680.

Sinkovics, N., Sinkovics, R. R., & "Bryan" Jean, R. J. (2013). The internet as an alternative path to internationalization? *International Marketing Review, 30*(2), 130–155.

Spigel, B. (2017). The relational organization of entrepreneurial ecosystems. *Entrepreneurship Theory and Practice, 41*(1), 49–72.

Terjesen, S., Hessels, J., & Li, D. (2016). Comparative international entrepreneurship: A review and research agenda. *Journal of Management, 42*(1), 299–344.

Vahlne, J. E., & Johanson, J. (2020). The Uppsala model: Networks and micro-foundations. *Journal of International Business Studies, 51*(1), 4–10.

Zhang, C. (2022). Formal and informal institutional legacies and inward foreign direct investment into firms: Evidence from China. *Journal of International Business Studies, 53*(6), 1228–1256.

Zucchella, A., & Siano, A. (2014). Internationalization and innovation as resources for SME growth in foreign markets: A focus on textile and clothing firms in the Campania Region. *International Studies of Management & Organization, 44*(1), 21–41.

Dr. Pravin Kumar is an Assistant Professor at Brainware University, Kolkata, with a teaching experience of more than 12 years in Marketing Management at some of the prestigious Indian institutions. He holds a PhD in Management from T.M. Bhagalpur University and majored in visual merchandising and consumer behavior in branded apparel. Having an MBA in Marketing, he has an interdisciplinary approach to his studies.

Dr. Kumar has published widely in Scopus, UGC-CARE, and peer-reviewed journals on topics including consumer behavior, brand personality, and AI in sales. He has presented at numerous national and international seminars and FDPs on subjects like cross-cultural marketing and leadership.

His industry experience in the automobile and pharmaceutical sectors adds practical value to his teaching. Known for his engaging teaching style and commitment to Universal Design for Learning, Dr. Kumar has also served as a Placement Officer and contributed to initiatives like NSS and Unnat Bharat Abhiyan.

Financing Opportunities in Central Asian Emerging Markets: Lessons from Kazakhstan

Iakov Sadchikov

Abstract Kazakhstan's financial ecosystem offers critical insights into how resource-dependent economies can diversify their financing landscapes while navigating post-Soviet institutional legacies. This chapter analyzes Kazakhstan's multi-layered financing architecture comprising traditional banking controlling the vast majority of financial assets, nascent venture capital growing at 35% compound annual growth rate from 2018 to 2024, and underutilized Islamic finance markets. Through systematic analysis of financing mechanisms ranging from state-led initiatives like QazInnovations' innovation grants to private sector transformations exemplified by Kaspi.kz's 15-billion dollar market capitalization as of December 2025, the chapter identifies three transferable lessons for emerging markets. First, hybrid institutional frameworks play a critical role in attracting foreign investment, with Kazakhstan securing over four hundred billion dollars since 1991. Second, government-private sector coordination proves essential in developing venture ecosystems from nascent stages. Third, financial deepening faces persistent challenges from institutional gaps and market concentration. These findings provide business practitioners with frameworks for navigating similar markets characterized by concentrated banking sectors, evolving regulatory environments, and untapped alternative finance opportunities.

1 Introduction

Kazakhstan represents a unique case for understanding financial development in resource-rich transition economies. With a GDP exceeding 288 billion dollars and GDP per capita approaching 14000 dollars in 2024, the country has achieved significant economic growth since independence. However, this growth masks complex challenges in developing a diversified financial system capable of supporting economic transformation beyond natural resource extraction.

The theoretical importance of studying Kazakhstan's financial evolution stems from its position at the intersection of multiple economic transitions. The country

I. Sadchikov (✉)
KIMEP University, Almaty, Kazakhstan
e-mail: i.sadchikov@kimep.kz

T. Endress and Y. F. Badir (eds.), *Business and Management in Asia: Opportunities and Entrepreneurship*, https://doi.org/10.1007/978-981-95-4909-2_16

simultaneously navigates the post-Soviet institutional transformation, the challenge of escaping resource dependence, and the opportunities of digital financial innovation. These parallel transitions create both unique challenges and opportunities that offer insights for other emerging markets facing similar structural transformations.

Understanding Kazakhstan's financing landscape requires appreciating the fundamental tension between rapid market reforms and persistent institutional legacies. Unlike gradual transitions observed in some post-Soviet states, Kazakhstan embraced aggressive privatization and liberalization, attracting significant foreign investment particularly in its oil and gas sector. This approach created a bifurcated economy where sophisticated, internationally connected energy companies coexist with traditional businesses struggling to access modern financial services.

This chapter employs an institutional analysis framework to examine how formal rules, informal practices, and organizational structures shape financing opportunities and constraints. The analysis draws on established institutional economics literature, particularly North's framework of institutions as "rules of the game" and the concept of path dependency in economic development. This theoretical lens helps explain why certain financial innovations succeed while others fail despite apparent market demand.

The examination proceeds across three analytical levels. At the macro level, the chapter analyzes how Kazakhstan's legal framework, regulatory environment, and political economy create the foundational conditions for financial development. The meso level examines specific financial institutions and intermediaries, including banks, venture funds, and state development agencies. The micro level investigates how individual businesses navigate this complex landscape to secure financing.

Data sources include official statistics from the World Bank, International Monetary Fund, and Kazakhstan government agencies, supplemented by reports from international development organizations and industry analyses.

2 The Evolution of Kazakhstan's Financial Architecture

Kazakhstan's current financial system cannot be understood without examining its Soviet origins and subsequent transformation. The Soviet monobank system, where a single state bank handled all financial intermediation, left no foundation for market-based banking. This complete absence of financial infrastructure, credit assessment capabilities, and risk management systems created both opportunities and challenges for post-independence development.

The rapid privatization of the 1990s established a nominal banking sector almost overnight, but these new institutions lacked the human capital, systems, and governance structures necessary for effective financial intermediation. Early banks often served as treasuries for industrial groups rather than independent financial intermediaries, a pattern that continues to influence ownership structures and lending practices today.

The global financial crisis of 2008 exposed these structural weaknesses dramatically. Several major banks required government support, revealing excessive reliance on foreign borrowing, poor risk management, and inadequate regulatory oversight. The crisis forced a painful but necessary consolidation that strengthened remaining institutions while reducing overall banking sector competition.

These historical experiences created lasting effects on the contemporary financial system. The memory of banking crises makes both regulators and depositors conservative, favoring stability over innovation. The concentration that resulted from post-crisis consolidation creates oligopolistic dynamics that may limit access to finance for smaller businesses. The close relationships between banks and industrial groups persist, potentially affecting capital allocation efficiency.

Today's banking landscape reflects these historical influences through high concentration and conservative lending practices. The top three banks in Kazakhstan control approximately 55% of total banking assets according to World Bank's, 2024 report. This concentration creates a paradox where the banking system appears stable and well-capitalized by international standards, yet many businesses, particularly small and medium enterprises, struggle to access credit.

The dominance of a few large banks affects financing availability in several ways. These institutions naturally focus on larger corporate clients and government-related lending where risks are better understood and transaction costs are lower relative to loan size. Small business lending requires different capabilities in credit assessment and relationship management that concentrated banks may lack incentives to develop. The result is a "missing middle" where businesses too large for microfinance but too small for corporate banking face particular challenges accessing formal credit.

Interest rates for business loans reflect both macroeconomic conditions and structural features of the banking sector. Rates exceeding 20% annually for local currency loans to small businesses incorporate inflation expectations, risk premiums for inadequate collateral or credit history, and the operational costs of serving smaller clients in a concentrated banking system. These high rates create a vicious cycle where only the riskiest borrowers willing to pay such rates seek loans, further justifying banks' conservative lending stance.

Collateral requirements present another structural barrier to credit access. Banks typically require collateral valued at well over 100% of the loan amount, often including personal guarantees from business owners. This practice reflects weak contract enforcement, limited credit information systems, and banks' risk aversion following past crises. For many businesses, particularly those in services or technology without significant physical assets, these collateral requirements effectively exclude them from bank financing.

Kazakhstan's capital markets remain underdeveloped relative to the banking sector, a common pattern in emerging markets. The market capitalization of Kazakhstani companies was approximately seventy-five billion dollars as of December 2025, concentrated in a relatively small number of large companies primarily from extractive industries and banking. This limited depth and breadth constrains capital markets' ability to serve as an alternative financing channel for most businesses.

Several structural factors explain the slow development of capital markets despite various government initiatives to promote them. The small number of institutional investors limits demand for securities, while weak minority shareholder protection reduces companies' willingness to raise public equity. Information disclosure requirements and corporate governance standards, while formally aligned with international practices, face enforcement challenges that undermine investor confidence. The result is thin trading, high volatility, and limited price discovery that make capital markets an unreliable funding source for most companies.

Corporate bond markets show somewhat more promise, with several large companies successfully issuing debt securities at rates below bank loan costs. However, this option remains available only to the largest and most established companies with strong credit profiles and name recognition. Smaller companies face prohibitive issuance costs relative to funding needs, limited investor appetite for lesser-known credits, and regulatory requirements designed for larger issuers.

3 State-Led Financial Innovation

Kazakhstan's government plays an active role in shaping financial development through both direct intervention and institutional innovation. This approach reflects a pragmatic recognition that market forces alone may not generate adequate financing for economic diversification, particularly in sectors deemed strategically important but commercially risky. However, state intervention also raises questions about market distortion, political influence in capital allocation, and the sustainability of subsidized financing programs.

The institutional architecture of state financial support has evolved considerably since independence. Early ad-hoc interventions have given way to more structured programs delivered through specialized agencies. This institutionalization aims to provide more consistent, transparent, and professional management of state financial resources while maintaining strategic government influence over development priorities.

QazInnovations, established as Kazakhstan's National Agency for Technological Development, represents the government's effort to address the specific financing needs of innovative businesses. The agency offers grants of approximately forty thousand dollars for technology commercialization across priority sectors including information technology, fintech, greentech, and biotechnology. These grants target a critical gap in the financing ecosystem where projects have progressed beyond pure research but lack the commercial validation needed to attract private investment.

The design of QazInnovations' programs reflects both international best practices and local constraints. Requiring applicants to have completed acceleration or incubation programs creates a filtering mechanism that should improve project quality while building ecosystem connections. Focusing on specific sectors aligns with national development priorities while concentrating limited resources where government support might have the greatest impact. The relatively modest grant sizes reflect fiscal constraints while still providing meaningful support for early-stage validation.

However, several implementation challenges affect program effectiveness. The requirement for prior program participation may exclude promising innovations from entrepreneurs outside established networks. The focus on particular sectors might miss opportunities in areas not currently prioritized by government planning. The grant sizes, while helpful for software or service innovations, may be insufficient for hardware or deep technology ventures requiring more capital-intensive development.

Baiterek National Managing Holding represents a more comprehensive approach to state financial intervention, encompassing multiple institutions serving different market segments. Baiterek Venture Fund, with ove 80 million dollars deployed across private equity and venture capital funds, focuses on technology and innovation companies. Qazaqstan Investment Corporation targets larger infrastructure and industrial projects with average investments of four and a half million dollars. This multi-tier approach aims to provide appropriate financing across the business development spectrum.

The Baiterek ecosystem's value extends beyond capital provision. Portfolio companies gain access to government networks that can facilitate regulatory approvals, public sector contracts, and partnerships with state-owned enterprises. International connections through Baiterek's partnerships with global development institutions provide pathways to foreign markets and expertise. This "smart capital" approach recognizes that emerging market entrepreneurs often need more than just funding to succeed.

Nevertheless, questions remain about the optimal balance between support and market distortion. State backing might create unfair advantages for selected companies, potentially crowding out private investment or supporting businesses that would not be viable without subsidies. The selection processes, while formally merit-based, operate in an environment where political connections and informal influences remain important. Measuring real economic returns versus political or social objectives presents ongoing challenges for evaluating program effectiveness.

4 Venture Capital Emergence

Kazakhstan's venture capital ecosystem has experienced notable growth, expanding from 12 million dollars in 2018 to 79 million dollars in 2024, representing a compound annual growth rate of 35% according to KPMG's, 2025 report. This growth rate exceeds global averages but starts from such a low base that absolute investment levels remain minimal relative to the economy's size. StartupBlink's, 2025 report ranks Kazakhstan seventieth globally and first in Central Asia for startup ecosystems, with Astana ranking 315th and Almaty 353rd among global cities. The new state fund of funds to invest in venture funds was launched in Kazakhstan in 2025, managed by Qazaqstan Venture Group, secured 115 million dollars in its first closing from Qazaqstan Investment Corporation, which contributed 30 million dollars, Freedom Holding Corp., Astana Hub, and private investors in November 2025.

This growth reflects several positive developments. The emergence of local fund managers with international experience brings professional investment practices and global networks. Success stories, even if limited, demonstrate that high-growth businesses can emerge from Kazakhstan. Government support through Astana Hub and various programs provides essential infrastructure and early-stage capital. International investors, particularly those focused on frontier markets, increasingly include Kazakhstan in their geographic scope.

However, significant structural challenges constrain further development. The small number of investment-ready companies limits deal flow, forcing investors to compete for the few promising opportunities. Limited exit options, with virtually no acquisition market and rare public listings, make it difficult for investors to realize returns and recycle capital into new investments. The shortage of experienced professionals who understand both technology and finance creates capacity constraints throughout the investment process from due diligence to portfolio support.

Astana Hub, established as an international technopark for IT startups, represents the government's most comprehensive effort to build venture ecosystem infrastructure. Offering tax exemptions, simplified visa procedures, and various support programs, Astana Hub aims to position Kazakhstan as Central Asia's technology hub. The announced plan to establish a one-billion-dollar fund-of-funds with Baiterek committing thirty million dollars signals continued government commitment to venture development.

These initiatives have produced tangible results. The number of registered startups has grown significantly, technology events attract international participants, and awareness of entrepreneurship as a career path has increased, particularly among younger Kazakhstanis. The ecosystem shows increasing sophistication with specialized accelerators, angel investor groups, and support services emerging alongside government programs.

Yet fundamental challenges persist in creating a self-sustaining ecosystem. Many registered startups remain at very early stages without clear paths to revenue or growth. The focus on quantity of startups over quality may disperse limited resources too thinly. The emphasis on technology sectors might overlook opportunities in traditional industries where innovation could have immediate impact. Most critically, the ecosystem remains heavily dependent on government support, raising questions about long-term sustainability.

Kaspi.kz stands out as Kazakhstan's most prominent business success story, evolving from a traditional bank to a technology platform and super app with a NASDAQ listing and market capitalization of 15 billion dollars as of December 2025. Processing over 70% of all electronic transactions in Kazakhstan, Kaspi demonstrates the potential for technology-enabled businesses to achieve significant scale in the local market. However, several unique factors limit the generalizability of Kaspi's success.

Kaspi benefited from starting as a licensed bank with access to payment systems and customer funds, advantages unavailable to typical startups. The company's transformation occurred when digital payment adoption was nascent, allowing it to capture first-mover advantages that would be difficult to replicate today. The concentrated nature of Kazakhstan's economy may have facilitated Kaspi's platform strategy in ways that might not apply in more competitive markets. These factors suggest that while Kaspi proves large-scale success is possible, its specific path may not be replicable.

The 1Fit case, achieving 40 million dollars in annual revenue across six countries with less than 2 million dollars in funding, demonstrates a different model based on capital efficiency and international expansion in 2025. The other case is Higgsfield, an over a billion dollar or Unicorn startup achieving 100 million dollars in annual revenue in 2025 by producing AI-generated short-videos with headquarters in Silicon Valley and software engineers in Kazakhstan. This approach, born from necessity given limited local funding availability, may be more relevant for contemporary entrepreneurs. By proving the concept in Kazakhstan before expanding regionally, 1Fit and Higgsfield leveraged the local market as a testing ground while recognizing that real scale required geographic expansion.

5 Alternative Finance Frontiers

Despite Kazakhstan's Muslim-majority population, Islamic finance remains underdeveloped. The AIFC's, 2024 report positions Kazakhstan twenty-second globally in Islamic finance development, but this ranking reflects potential more than actual market presence. The statistic that approximately 80% of potential customers have never engaged with Islamic financial services reveals a significant gap between theoretical demand and practical availability.

Several factors explain this underdevelopment beyond simple lack of awareness. Islamic finance operates on principles of risk-sharing and asset-backing that require different operational models from conventional banking. Developing these capabilities requires significant investment in systems, training, and product development that existing banks may find difficult to justify given uncertain demand. Regulatory frameworks, while formally accommodating Islamic finance, lack detailed guidance on practical implementation issues like taxation of Islamic instruments or dispute resolution for Sharia-compliant contracts.

The absence of a critical mass creates a chicken-and-egg problem where limited supply discourages demand development while uncertain demand deters supply investment. Without local Islamic finance expertise, institutions must rely on expensive foreign consultants. Without established Islamic capital markets, banks cannot easily manage liquidity or risks from Islamic products. Without clear success examples, both institutions and customers remain skeptical about Islamic finance's practical benefits versus conventional alternatives.

Digital payment adoption exceeding 80% of adults represents a genuine transformation in how Kazakhstanis interact with the financial system. This rapid adoption, accelerated by Kaspi's user-friendly platform and the COVID-19 pandemic's push toward contactless transactions, demonstrates that technological leapfrogging is possible even in markets with established traditional infrastructure.

However, widespread payment digitization does not automatically translate into broader financial innovation or inclusion. Most digital adoption represents existing bank customers using new channels rather than previously excluded populations gaining financial access. The dominance of a single platform raises concerns about market concentration, data privacy, and systemic risk. Regulatory frameworks struggle to keep pace with technological change, creating uncertainty for new entrants while potentially entrenching incumbent advantages.

The broader fintech ecosystem remains nascent despite payment success. Peer-to-peer lending platforms face regulatory uncertainty and consumer skepticism following problems in other markets. Insurtech and wealthtech ventures struggle to gain traction in markets with low insurance penetration and limited investable assets. Blockchain and cryptocurrency initiatives, despite government interest in positioning Kazakhstan as a crypto hub, face volatile regulatory attitudes and limited practical applications beyond speculation.

Kazakhstan's commitment to carbon neutrality by 2060 and the establishment of the AIFC Green Finance Centre in 2018 signal recognition of sustainable finance's importance. Several banks now offer green loans with preferential terms, while international development institutions actively support sustainable projects. This emergence reflects both global trends toward environmental, social, and governance considerations and specific opportunities in Kazakhstan's energy transition.

The potential for green finance extends beyond environmental benefits to economic opportunity. Kazakhstan's vast renewable energy resources, particularly wind and solar, could attract significant investment given appropriate financing mechanisms. Energy efficiency improvements in Soviet-era infrastructure offer commercially viable projects with environmental co-benefits. The growing global focus on critical minerals for battery production positions Kazakhstan to benefit from sustainable mining finance initiatives.

Yet several factors constrain green finance development. The definition of "green" remains contested, with concerns about greenwashing undermining market credibility. The additional costs of environmental assessment and monitoring may deter smaller projects. The long-term nature of many sustainable investment conflicts with the short-term focus prevalent in emerging markets. Most fundamentally, the continued dominance of extractive industries in Kazakhstan's economy creates political economy tensions around aggressive green transition policies.

6 Regulatory Framework and Investment Climate

The establishment of the Astana International Financial Centre represents an innovative attempt to create a parallel legal system addressing weaknesses in Kazakhstan's traditional civil law framework. Operating under English common law with its own court system and arbitration center, AIFC aims to provide international investors with familiar legal frameworks and credible dispute resolution mechanisms. This institutional innovation acknowledges that reforming the entire national legal system would take generations, while creating a special zone can provide immediate improvements for financial transactions.

Early evidence suggests AIFC is attracting international interest, with numerous financial institutions establishing operations within its jurisdiction. The AIFC Court's international judges provide expertise and credibility difficult to develop domestically. The regulatory framework, based on Dubai International Financial Centre models, offers familiarity for international financial institutions. These developments demonstrate that institutional grafting—importing proven institutional models—can work under certain conditions.

However, AIFC's impact remains limited to transactions explicitly structured within its jurisdiction. Most domestic businesses and regional investors continue operating under Kazakhstan's traditional legal framework with its associated challenges. The parallel system may create complexity and confusion about applicable law. Questions remain about how AIFC court decisions will be enforced outside its jurisdiction and whether the political commitment to AIFC's independence will persist through changing governments.

Kazakhstan has made measurable progress in improving its business environment according to various international assessments. Company registration can now be completed in one day, tax filing has been digitized, and many licenses can be obtained online. These improvements reflect genuine government commitment to reducing bureaucratic barriers and attracting investment. The Strategic Development Plan until 2025 explicitly prioritizes further business environment reforms.

Nevertheless, implementation gaps persist between formal rules and practical experience. While registration may be quick, obtaining necessary permits and approvals for operations can still take months. Digital systems improve efficiency for routine transactions but may lack flexibility for non-standard situations. Regulatory enforcement remains inconsistent, with some businesses facing excessive scrutiny while others operate with impunity. These implementation challenges reflect deeper institutional issues around bureaucratic culture, capacity constraints, and governance quality that cannot be resolved through technical fixes alone.

The tax environment presents particular complexities for businesses. While headline corporate tax rates of 20% appear competitive, the overall tax burden includes social contributions, property taxes, and various fees that significantly increase total costs. Tax compliance requires navigating complex regulations that change frequently, creating uncertainty and compliance costs particularly burdensome for smaller businesses. The rise in Value Added Tax (VAT) from 12 to 16% in 2026 will further increase the tax burden while potentially improving fiscal sustainability.

7 Strategic Considerations for Market Participants

Businesses operating in Kazakhstan must develop sophisticated strategies for accessing appropriate financing given the fragmented nature of available options. No single source provides optimal financing for all needs, requiring companies to combine multiple sources strategically. Traditional banks may provide working capital but require substantial collateral. Government programs offer subsidized funding but come with restrictions and bureaucratic requirements. Venture capital provides growth funding but expects high returns and eventual exits. Islamic finance could offer alternatives but remains largely theoretical.

Successful financing strategies typically evolve through stages. Early-stage businesses might begin with QazInnovations grants or Astana Hub support to validate concepts. Growing companies could access Baiterek and other venture funding or development bank loans for expansion. Established businesses might tap capital markets or attract foreign investment. This progression requires understanding not just the technical requirements of each funding source but also the informal relationships and expectations that influence access.

The importance of local partnerships cannot be overstated in navigating Kazakhstan's financing landscape. Local partners provide essential understanding of regulatory requirements, government relations, and informal business practices. They can facilitate introductions to decision-makers and help interpret unwritten rules that govern business interactions. However, choosing partners requires careful due diligence given the reputational and operational risks of problematic associations.

Operating in Kazakhstan requires sophisticated risk management across multiple dimensions. Currency risk remains paramount given the tenge's historical volatility, with depreciation exceeding 100% against the dollar since 2015. This volatility affects not just foreign currency borrowings but also input costs, competitive dynamics, and investment returns. Hedging strategies must balance cost against protection while recognizing that perfect hedging may be impossible given market limitations.

Political risk, while difficult to quantify, influences all major business decisions. Kazakhstan has maintained relative stability compared to regional peers, but succession questions, geopolitical tensions, and potential policy shifts create uncertainties that affect long-term planning. Businesses must maintain flexibility to adapt to changing political dynamics while avoiding excessive caution that precludes profitable opportunities.

Operational risks specific to emerging markets require constant attention. These include counterparty risks given limited credit information, regulatory risks from changing or inconsistently enforced rules, and human capital risks from limited specialized expertise. Managing these risks requires not just formal systems but also maintaining diverse information networks and developing institutional knowledge about local market dynamics.

8 Lessons for Other Emerging Markets

Kazakhstan's experience offers several lessons applicable to other emerging markets, though context-specific factors mean these insights require adaptation rather than direct replication. Three categories of countries may find Kazakhstan's experience particularly relevant.

Resource-rich developing countries face similar challenges balancing natural resource exploitation with economic diversification. Kazakhstan demonstrates that resource wealth can provide capital for financial sector development but does not automatically generate diverse financing ecosystems. Success requires deliberate policies to channel resource revenues toward productive investments while avoiding the tendency for resource abundance to crowd out other economic activities.

Post-socialist economies share institutional legacies that affect financial development trajectories. Kazakhstan's experience shows that rapid liberalization can attract foreign investment but may also create fragilities if institutional development does not keep pace. The importance of building regulatory capacity, developing local expertise, and creating market institutions cannot be short-circuited through rapid reform alone.

Frontier markets seeking to develop venture ecosystems can learn from both Kazakhstan's successes and limitations. Government support appears necessary to catalyze ecosystem development, but creating sustainable ecosystems requires developing private sector capabilities and market mechanisms. The challenge lies in providing sufficient support to overcome initial barriers while avoiding dependence that prevents market maturation.

Several factors emerge as critical for financial development based on Kazakhstan's experience. Institutional quality matters more than specific policies or programs. Countries must invest in building regulatory capacity, improving governance, and strengthening rule of law as foundations for financial development. These institutional improvements take time and cannot be substituted with technical fixes or special zones alone.

Balancing stability and innovation presents an ongoing challenge. Kazakhstan's banking sector consolidation improved stability but may have reduced innovation and access. Venture capital development encourages innovation but requires accepting higher failure rates. Countries must consciously manage these tradeoffs rather than expecting simultaneous achievement of all objectives.

The importance of human capital becomes apparent across all aspects of financial development. Limited expertise constrains banking sector sophistication, venture capital effectiveness, and regulatory capacity. Developing local talent requires long-term investment in education and professional development that cannot be fully substituted with foreign expertise.

9 Emerging Opportunities and Challenges

Kazakhstan's financial sector faces several developments that will shape its evolution over the coming decade. The energy transition presents both challenges to traditional revenue sources and opportunities for financing renewable energy and green technology. Digital transformation could enable financial inclusion and innovation but also raises concerns about market concentration and systemic risk. Regional integration through initiatives like the Eurasian Economic Union could expand market opportunities but also increase competitive pressures.

The announced fund-of-funds initiative and continued support for Astana Hub suggest sustained government commitment to developing venture ecosystems. Whether these initiatives can catalyze self-sustaining private sector development remains to be seen. The critical test will be whether successful companies choose to remain and reinvest in Kazakhstan or seek opportunities elsewhere once they achieve scale.

Demographic changes, with a young, increasingly urban, and digitally native population, create conditions favorable for financial innovation. However, realizing this potential requires addressing education system weaknesses, creating professional opportunities that retain talent, and fostering entrepreneurial culture alongside government support programs.

10 Conclusion

Kazakhstan's financial evolution over three decades demonstrates both remarkable achievements and persistent challenges in developing diverse, efficient financing mechanisms. The country has successfully attracted over 400 billion dollars in foreign investment, developed a stable if concentrated banking sector, and begun building venture capital and alternative finance capabilities. These achievements occurred despite starting without market economy foundations and experiencing severe financial crises that could have derailed development entirely.

The current financing landscape reflects these historical experiences through several defining characteristics. Traditional banking dominates financial intermediation but serves primarily larger corporations and government-related entities, leaving significant gaps for smaller businesses and innovative ventures. Government programs partially fill these gaps but raise questions about sustainability and market distortion. Emerging sources like venture capital and Islamic finance show promise but remain subscale relative to economic needs.

Three overarching lessons emerge from Kazakhstan's experience with broader relevance for emerging markets. First, institutional development cannot be short-circuited through rapid reform or special zones alone. Building capable regulators, trustworthy courts, and professional financial institutions requires sustained investment over decades. Second, government intervention can catalyze financial development but must carefully balance support with avoiding dependence and distortion. The challenge lies not in whether governments should intervene but how to design interventions that build rather than substitute for market mechanisms. Third, financial development requires complementary investments in human capital, infrastructure, and supporting institutions that extend well beyond the financial sector itself.

For practitioners engaging with Kazakhstan's market, success requires sophisticated understanding of both formal rules and informal practices. The financing landscape offers multiple options, but accessing them demands strategic thinking about sequencing, relationships, and risk management. Local partnerships provide essential navigation assistance but require careful selection and management. Patient capital and long-term perspective are essential given the market's continued evolution.

Looking forward, Kazakhstan stands at an inflection point in its financial development. The combination of demographic change, technological advancement, and economic pressures for diversification creates conditions for potentially rapid evolution. Whether this potential translates into sustainable financial deepening depends on continued institutional strengthening, effective government policies, and private sector capability development. The trajectory remains uncertain, but Kazakhstan's experience already provides valuable insights for understanding financial development in challenging contexts.

The ultimate measure of success will not be achieving developed country financial metrics but creating a financial system that serves Kazakhstan's specific development needs. This requires financing mechanisms that support economic diversification, enable innovation and entrepreneurship, and provide sustainable livelihoods for the population. Progress toward these goals remains incomplete, but the foundations established over three decades of independence provide a platform for continued evolution. For scholars and practitioners interested in emerging market finance, Kazakhstan remains an important case study in both the possibilities and limitations of financial transformation in the twenty-first century.

References

AIFC. (2024). Islamic finance country report for Kazakhstan. https://aifc.kz/wp-content/uploads/2024/09/ifcr-kazakhstan_2024_eng_print-1.pdf

KPMG. (2025). Venture capital in Central Asia 2024. KPMG Uzbekistan.

StartupBlink. (2025). Global Startup Ecosystem Report 2025. https://www.startupblink.com/startup-ecosystem/kazakhstan

World Bank. (2024). *Republic of Kazakhstan—Financial sector assessment* (Report No. BOSIB13236e6890851bc3c180e1e9066c88). https://documents1.worldbank.org/curated/en/099040524124539810/pdf/BOSIB13236e6890851bc3c180e1e9066c88.pdf

Iakov Sadchikov is a senior lecturer in finance at KIMEP University's Bang College of Business in Almaty, Kazakhstan. He holds a Master's degree in Economics with a major in Financial Economics and is pursuing a PhD in Finance. His research examines the development of venture capital, startups, financial innovation, and economic transformation in emerging markets, with a particular focus on Kazakhstan and other Central Asia economies. Mr. Sadchikov combines academic research with practical experience, having launched, secured venture funding for, and successfully exited two technology ventures in the financial information and search engine sectors. He contributes to Kazakhstan's entrepreneurial finance and startup ecosystem through teaching, research, mentoring, and policy advisory work.

Exploring Entrepreneurial Opportunity in Japan's AI Landscape

Hajer Najeh

Abstract This chapter investigates the novel ways in which Artificial Intelligence (AI) integration shapes the Japanese entrepreneurial ecosystem by fostering new entrepreneurial opportunities. Extending the opportunity-based view of (Shane and Venkataraman, *Academy of Management Review* 25:217–226, 2000), this research uniquely combines the development of the entrepreneurial profile—encompassing digital skills, proactive mindset, and strategic adaptability—with the activation of social networks to explain how AI enhances opportunity recognition and exploitation. Utilizing empirical data from 128 innovative Japanese companies, the study reveals that AI adoption not only transforms individual entrepreneurial capabilities but also expands relational resources, thereby improving market knowledge acquisition. This dual influence advances the understanding of entrepreneurial dynamics in technology-intensive environments and provides actionable insights for entrepreneurs and policymakers aiming to leverage AI for sustained innovation and competitive advantage.

1 Introduction

Classic entrepreneurial theories, notably the opportunity-based view (Shane, 2003; Shane & Venkataraman, 2000), emphasize the entrepreneur's ability to recognize and exploit opportunities under conditions of uncertainty. Yet, recent developments—particularly the integration of artificial intelligence (AI)—have reshaped how opportunities are identified and acted upon. AI technologies facilitate the collection, processing, and interpretation of complex data, enhancing market visibility and enabling more agile decision-making. In this context, AI emerges as both a technological enabler and a strategic resource, transforming traditional entrepreneurial logics (Al-Mamary, 2025; Cockburn et al., 2018; Guetaya et al., 2024; Iansiti & Lakhani, 2020; Li et al., 2025; Nanan-Vallée & Aka, 2024).

H. Najeh (✉)
Higher Institute of Management, University of Gabes, Gabes, Tunisia
e-mail: hajernajah@yahoo.fr

T. Endress and Y. F. Badir (eds.), *Business and Management in Asia: Opportunities and Entrepreneurship*, https://doi.org/10.1007/978-981-95-4909-2_17

However, technology alone is not sufficient. Opportunity recognition is still largely mediated by the entrepreneur's profile, including cognitive style, risk perception, and adaptive behavior. Moreover, social networks play a critical role in disseminating information and facilitating access to key resources (Hoang & Antoncic, 2003). The interplay between these dimensions—entrepreneurial cognition, social capital, and digital tools like AI-raises the following question: *To what extent does the integration of AI stimulate entrepreneurial opportunities by enhancing the entrepreneur's knowledge of the market through social connections and cognitive development?*

By integrating insights from entrepreneurship theory, digital transformation, and cognitive perspectives, this research offers a novel contribution to understanding opportunity-driven entrepreneurship in the AI era.

This chapter explores this question within the Japanese entrepreneurial ecosystem. Japan, known for its strong industrial base and technological innovation, provides a fertile ground to examine how AI adoption affects opportunity creation in both startups and established firms.

The empirical analysis is based on a quantitative study involving 128 innovative Japanese industrial firms.

The chapter is structured as follows: a literature review on entrepreneurial opportunities, AI, and social capital; the research hypotheses and methodology; a presentation of the empirical findings; and a discussion of contributions, limitations, and future research directions.

2 Literature Review

2.1 Entrepreneurship Opportunity Research

The concept of entrepreneurial opportunity is central yet debated in the literature. Opportunities differ from ideas, requiring recognition, evaluation, and exploitation to create value (Borchani et al., 2011; Degeorge et al., 2018; Diandra & Azmy, 2020). This study follows the Opportunity-Based View (Shane, 2003; Shane & Venkataraman, 2000), which sees entrepreneurship as the process of discovering and exploiting opportunities in uncertain contexts (Fig. 1). Two main theories exist: the discovery theory views opportunities as objective and waiting to be found (Shane, 2003), whereas the creation theory argues opportunities arise through entrepreneurs' actions and social interactions (Degeorge et al., 2018). Both emphasize the entrepreneur's cognitive and behavioral skills.

This chapter is grounded in Shane's OBV framework, which emphasizes not only the role of prior knowledge and market alertness but also the entrepreneur's ability to organize resources and act upon opportunities (Shane, 2012). With the rise of Artificial Intelligence (AI), entrepreneurs can now enhance these capabilities, leveraging data-driven insights and automation to identify and exploit opportunities faster and more effectively. For instance, the agricultural technology startup Blue River

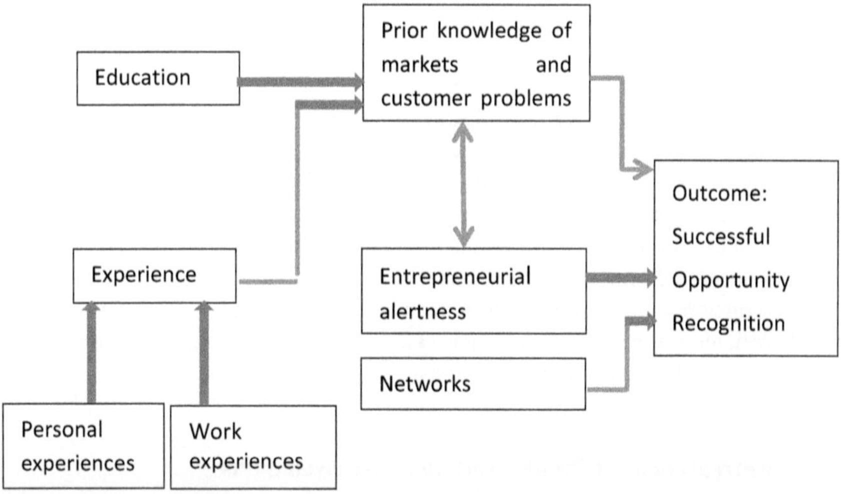

Fig. 1 Opportunity recognition process. *Source* Shane (2003)

Technology developed AI-powered "See & Spray" robots that use computer vision and machine learning to distinguish between crops and weeds, enabling targeted herbicide application that reduces chemical use by up to 90% (Vincent, 2017).

Entrepreneurship, therefore, is not just about having ideas but about transforming those ideas into value-creating actions through opportunity recognition and exploitation.

2.2 *Artificial Intelligence and the Evolution of Opportunity Recognition*

Artificial intelligence (AI) is "a field of computer science that involves designing systems capable of simulating human intelligence in terms of learning, decision-making, and problem-solving based on experience. AI systems are scalable and improvable through adaptation to incoming data" (Lexcellent, 2019). It also refers to software enabling the operationalization of activities such as pattern recognition and problem-solving from multidimensional data, in order to derive insights, conduct analyses, and guide decision-making (Cleantech Group, 2024; Vuarin et al., 2023).

This technology introduces a significant transformation in entrepreneurial opportunity recognition by enhancing cognitive capabilities. Through technologies such as machine learning, natural language processing, and predictive analytics, AI enables entrepreneurs to process large-scale unstructured data, identify weak signals, and detect hidden patterns in volatile environments (Al-Mamary, 2025; Dwivedi et al., 2021; Nanan-Vallée & Aka, 2024). These tools extend entrepreneurial alertness, refining human perception and pattern recognition—two essential elements of opportunity identification (Baron, 2006).

Beyond augmenting opportunity discovery, AI also redefines opportunity creation. Entrepreneurs now simulate markets, test hypotheses, and co-develop value propositions using algorithm-driven insights (Guetaya et al., 2024). This capability blurs the line between externally discovered and internally constructed opportunities, proposing a hybrid model of entrepreneurial cognition (Müller et al., 2018).

This conceptual shift underpins our theoretical model, which integrates AI as a core competency influencing entrepreneurial cognition and behavior. It positions digital proficiency not only as a technical skill but as a strategic enabler of opportunity development in data-intensive ecosystems.

2.2.1 Entrepreneurial Profile: Soft and AI-Driven Skills

In the Opportunity-Based View (OBV), entrepreneurs are active agents who recognize, shape, and exploit opportunities by leveraging their profile, which includes both soft skills and technological competencies (Shane, 2003). A critical component of this profile is market knowledge, encompassing an understanding of market dynamics, consumer needs, and alternative ways to serve the market (Shane, 2003). The advent of artificial intelligence (AI) significantly transforms this entrepreneurial profile by demanding technological literacy, data-driven decision-making, and continuous learning (Brem et al., 2021; Shepherd & Gruber, 2020).

AI tools enable entrepreneurs to collect, analyze, and interpret vast amounts of market information in real time, enhancing their ability to identify emerging trends and unmet needs (Floridi et al., 2021). This technological augmentation improves the accuracy of opportunity recognition by integrating prior knowledge with up-to-date market insights. However, successful entrepreneurship still requires a blend of human intuition, creativity, and ethical awareness, especially given AI's limitations and potential biases (Daugherty & Wilson, 2018).

Thus, AI acts as a catalyst that amplifies the entrepreneur's cognitive and behavioral capacities, strengthening the link between market knowledge and opportunity recognition. Entrepreneurs who effectively combine AI-enhanced data analysis with their experiential and social competencies are better positioned to discover, evaluate, and exploit entrepreneurial opportunities in dynamic markets.

> **H1:** *The profile of the entrepreneur (soft skills and technological compétencies) explains positively the discovery of new knowledge on the market.*

2.2.2 Artificial Intelligence and the Entrepreneur's Social Network

The entrepreneur's social network—comprising relationships with partners, clients, investors, and others—plays a crucial role in accessing resources and identifying opportunities (Hoang & Antoncic, 2003). Drawing from Granovetter (1973), Burt

(2004), and Chollet et al. (2009), prior research highlights how weak ties, structural holes, and heterogeneous networks foster access to diverse information and market knowledge. Empirical studies in the Tunisian context (Omrane, 2013) further confirm that well-structured networks significantly enhance innovation and business growth.

With the rise of artificial intelligence (AI), entrepreneurs now augment these traditional networks with powerful tools that analyze connections, simulate scenarios, and extract insights from unstructured data (Arora & Rahman, 2023; Dwivedi et al., 2021). AI helps map networks, identify influencers, and recommend strategic links, especially among weak or hidden ties. Tools such as natural language processing and machine learning provide real-time feedback on market sentiment and customer behavior, enhancing the entrepreneur's ability to detect opportunities and respond effectively.

This technological augmentation transforms social capital into a dynamic, data-driven asset, reinforcing both the breadth and depth of entrepreneurial networks.

In this dual perspective, the modern entrepreneur leverages both social capital and technological capability to extract, filter, and interpret information from an increasingly complex and data-driven environment. This leads to a refined hypothesis:

H2: *The social network—augmented by the use of artificial intelligence—enhances the entrepreneur's ability to acquire and interpret information about the market, customer preferences, and strategies for market entry.*

Beyond the structure of the network itself, the entrepreneur's personal attributes play a decisive role in how information is interpreted and transformed into actionable insights. As Chollet et al. (2009) argue, not all entrepreneurs extract the same value from their networks; their soft skills, particularly social intelligence, empathy, and strategic vision, shape how they access and leverage external knowledge. Omrane (2013) and Lamine and Fayolle (2014) further emphasize that social skills are essential in the dynamics of network formation and mobilization.

In the age of digital entrepreneurship, this human capacity is increasingly complemented by technological tools—notably Artificial Intelligence. Entrepreneurs can now deploy AI-based systems to map their social networks, detect hidden patterns in communication, and extract meaningful insights from unstructured interactions (Dwivedi et al., 2021). For example, machine learning algorithms can analyze customer sentiment, identify emerging market trends, and simulate scenario-based interactions, thus expanding the entrepreneur's cognitive horizon.

Consequently, the modern entrepreneur combines relational intelligence with algorithmic processing to not only build valuable networks but also interpret their complexity more effectively. This dual capacity supports the following hypothesis:

H3: *The profile of the entrepreneur (soft and technological skills) enhances his ability to perceive, interpret, and act upon valuable information within his social network.*

2.2.3 Artificial Intelligence and Market Knowledge for Entrepreneurial Opportunity Recognition

In the entrepreneurial process, opportunity recognition and exploitation lie at the heart of value creation (Shane & Venkataraman, 2000). While the identification of opportunities often stems from alertness and prior knowledge, the capacity to seize those opportunities requires a deep understanding of market dynamics, as well as the ability to act strategically and decisively.

Market knowledge refers not only to awareness of customer needs or competitor strategies but also to a holistic grasp of evolving trends, structural shifts, and emerging unmet needs (Tang et al., 2012). This form of knowledge is essential for evaluating the timeliness, feasibility, and scalability of an opportunity.

In this regard, Artificial Intelligence (AI) acts as a catalyst. It provides entrepreneurs with the capacity to process vast volumes of data, uncover hidden patterns, and generate real-time insights—capabilities that significantly enhance the recognition and evaluation of opportunities (Arora & Rahman, 2023). For instance, AI-driven analytics can detect nascent market signals that would remain invisible to human observation alone, allowing entrepreneurs to anticipate rather than react to change.

However, AI alone is insufficient. The entrepreneur's profile—particularly the combination of soft and technological skills—plays a pivotal role in translating information into action. Entrepreneurs who are capable of interpreting AI-generated insights through the lens of experience, intuition, and strategic thinking are more likely to transform signals into actionable opportunities (Shane, 2003). Thus, the opportunity is not only perceived but actively constructed and seized, shaped by both external data and internal capacities.

As such, we argue that the integration of AI into market intelligence processes—when combined with an adaptive and skilled entrepreneurial profile—enhances the entrepreneur's ability to seize opportunities in uncertain and complex environments.

H4: *Market knowledge, enriched by artificial intelligence, positively influences the entrepreneur's ability to recognize and exploit entrepreneurial opportunities.*

2.3 Research Model

This research model is presented as follows (Fig. 2).

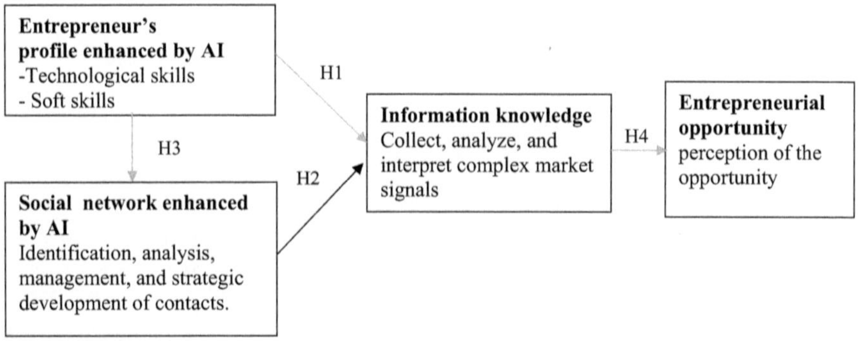

Fig. 2 Research model

3 Methodology

To understand the process of opportunity recognition in the era of artificial intelligence, a quantitative research approach was adopted. This methodology involved the development and administration of a structured questionnaire designed to examine the factors influencing entrepreneurial behavior and key indicators of opportunity recognition. The study followed a hypothetico-deductive reasoning framework, allowing for the empirical testing of predefined hypotheses.

3.1 Sample Description

The empirical investigation targeted Japanese entrepreneurs who had implemented AI-based tools in their innovative business activities over the past 3 years (2022–2024). The sample was specifically selected to capture the intersection between entrepreneurial behavior and the adoption of emerging technologies (Table 1).

3.2 Data Collection

Data were collected using an online questionnaire distributed via email. The questionnaire included items related to behavioral factors, AI usage, and opportunity recognition indicators. Out of the total sample, 130 entrepreneurs responded to the survey, yielding a response rate of 86%. After removing two incomplete responses, the final dataset consisted of 128 valid questionnaires.

Table 1 Description of the Japanese industrial firms sample

Characteristics	Categories	Percentage
Firm size	Small	35.2
	Medium	40.6
	Large	24.2
Sector of activity	Electronics and Robotics	29.7
	Automotive and Machinery	32.0
	Chemicals and Materials	21.1
	Other Industrial Sectors	17.2
Age of the firm	Less than 5 years	14.1
	5–10 years	47.7
	More than 10 years	38.2
Geographic location	Kanto Region	43.0
	Kansai Region	29.7
	Other Regions	27.3

4 Variables and Model Design

4.1 Variables

All variables, except for the dependent variable "opportunity recognition," were measured using five-point Likert scales ranging from 0 ("strongly disagree") to 4 ("strongly agree") (Table 2).

The following variables were operationalized as follow:

- **Entrepreneurial Profile (PRFL)**: This construct includes both technological and soft skills.
  - *Technological skills (TS)* were measured using the MAILS scale (Carolus et al., 2023).
  - *Soft skills (SSKL)* were measured across several dimensions commonly associated with entrepreneurial effectiveness: optimism, social skills, serendipity and synchronicity, and risk propensity.
- **Opportunity Recognition (OPP)**: This is the dependent variable, coded as a binary variable:
  - **0** if the entrepreneur did not identify any new opportunity during the last three years (2022–2024),
  - **1** if one or more opportunities were perceived.
- **Social Network (SONET)**: is measured using the items adapted from Chollet et al. (2009), Arora and Rahman (20230, and Dwivedi et al. (2021)

Table 2 Summary of variable measurement

	Measure		Description	Auteur
Technological skills	AI literacy	Using and applying AI	The ability to understand, evaluate, and effectively interact with artificial intelligence systems	Echelle MAILS créée par Astrid Carolus et ses collègues (2023)
		Knowing and understanding AI		
		detecting AI		
		Ethics of AI		
	Creating with AI		The competence to creatively develop or customize AI-based solutions or tools	
	AI self-efficacy	Problem-solving	Reflects confidence in one's ability to understand and apply artificial intelligence solutions to solve real-world problems	
		learning		
	AI self-management	Persuasion literacy	The capacity to autonomously regulate one's use of AI tools, including setting goals, monitoring AI performance, adapting use strategies, and ensuring ethical and effective application over time	
		Emotion regulation		
	Risk		The ability of an entrepreneur to start and grow a business despite market uncertainties, accepting the possibility of losses in order to seize opportunities for growth or innovation	Developed from Zhao et al., (2005); Caliendo et al. (2009)
	Social skills		The ability to communicate effectively, build and maintain relationships, understand others' perspectives, and navigate social situations in a positive and productive way	Adapted from Chollet et al. (2009), Arora and Rahman (2023) and Dwivedi et al. (2021)

(continued)

Table 2 (continued)

	Measure	Description	Auteur
	Synchronicity	The simultaneous occurrence of events that have no causal relationship	Developed from Chirita et al. (2012)
	Serendipity	The ability to turn unexpected situations into opportunities through creativity	Developed from Chirita et al. (2012)
Perception of the opportunity	To perceive or not perceive an opportunity during the past three years	The entrepreneur's ability to recognize a favorable situation in the market that can be turned into a viable business idea	Adapted from Billings et al. (1980)
Social network	• Identification • Analysis • Management • Strategic development of contacts by using AI	The development of the external network as a source of information	Adapted from Chollet et al. (2009), Arora and Rahman, (2023) and Dwivedi et al. (2021)
Information knowledge	• Collect, analyze, and interpret knowledge • Knowledge about markets • Knowledge of consumer problems • Knowledge of different ways to serve the market	Prior knowledge	adapted from Shane (2003) and Arora and Rahman (2023)

Source The author

- **Market Knowledge (KNOW)**: This mediating variable was measured using items adapted from Shane (2003), capturing the depth and relevance of knowledge related to customer needs, competitor behavior, and market trends.

4.2 *Model Specification*

To test the proposed model, a multiple binary logistic regression analysis was conducted.

The regression model is specified as follows:

$$OPP = \alpha PRFL + \beta SONET + \delta KNOW + \varepsilon$$

- OPP: Dependent variable (opportunity recognition)

Table 3 Characteristics of measurement instruments

	Variance	Cronbach
AI literacy	68.4	0.912
Creating with AI	70.1	0.925
AI self-efficacy	66.7	0.894
AI self-management	65.3	0.882
Risk	73.238	0.687
Social skills	76.027	0.937
Synchronicity	72.749	0.648
Serendipity	85.439	0.633
Social network	62.507	0.789
Information knowledge	85.501	0.941

- PRFL: Independent variable (entrepreneurial profile, combining Technological skills and Soft skills)
- SONET: Independent variable (AI-augmented social network)
- KNOW: Mediating variable (market knowledge)
- ε: Error term

This model enables the examination of both direct and mediated effects of entrepreneurial characteristics and technological usage on opportunity recognition in AI-intensive contexts.

5 Validity and Reliability of the Measurement Instruments

A factor analysis was conducted to improve the measurement instruments. Principal Component Analysis (PCA) was used to remove items with low factor loadings (below 0.60). Then, two additional checks were performed: total variance explained and Cronbach's alpha reliability coefficient, with 0.60 as the acceptable threshold (Table 3). For instance, in the market knowledge scale, only items with strong loadings were retained, explaining 85.5% of the total variance, with a Cronbach's alpha of 0.941.

6 Results and Discussion

We tested our hypotheses using multiple linear regressions and logistic regressions, conducted with SPSS version 20. This section presents the results of the hypothesis testing to assess whether a positive relationship exists between the entrepreneur's profile, social network, and knowledge acquisition on the perception of the opportunity (Table 4).

Regarding Hypothesis 1, which posits that the entrepreneurial profile affects market knowledge, the results support this hypothesis. The analysis of causal relationships shows that the coefficient linking the entrepreneurial profile to market knowledge is positive ($\boldsymbol{\beta} = \mathbf{0.291}$) and statistically significant ($\boldsymbol{t} = \mathbf{2.85}, \boldsymbol{p} = \mathbf{0.005}$). The results support the literature highlighting that an entrepreneur's profile, combining AI skills with traits such as serendipity and risk-taking, positively influences market knowledge acquisition (Arora & Rahman, 2023; Shane & Venkataraman, 2000). We therefore conclude that the entrepreneurial profile positively explains the possession of new market knowledge, validating Hypothesis 1.

Similarly, Hypothesis 2, which suggests that social networks significantly influence market knowledge, is also supported by the data. The analysis reveals that the coefficient associated with the social network variable is positive ($\boldsymbol{\beta} = \mathbf{0.437}$) and statistically significant ($\boldsymbol{t} = \mathbf{5.40}, \boldsymbol{p} = \mathbf{0.000}$). This indicates that an entrepreneur's social network positively affects their ability to access new knowledge about the market environment, thereby confirming Hypothesis 2.

Consistent with prior studies (Burt, 2004; Chollet et al., 2009; Granovetter, 1973), the findings confirm that entrepreneurs' social networks significantly enhance access to diverse market information, which is further strengthened by AI's augmentation capabilities (Arora & Rahman, 2023; Dwivedi et al., 2021).

The results summarized in Table 5 show that the entrepreneurial profile, enhanced by the integration of artificial intelligence, positively influences the entrepreneur's social network ($\boldsymbol{\beta} = \mathbf{0.475}, \boldsymbol{p} < \mathbf{0.000}$). This implies that it becomes easier for entrepreneurs to identify, analyze, manage, and strategically expand their network of contacts. Hypothesis 3 is validated. The results confirm the theoretical assertions in the literature that both entrepreneurs' soft skills and technological abilities shape their social networks (Chollet et al., 2009; Dwivedi et al., 2021; Omrane, 2013).

Regarding Hypothesis 4, which proposes that possessing clear and relevant knowledge about the environment enhances the perception of opportunities, the statistical results support this relationship. Tables 6 and 7 examine this link by

Table 4 Results of the multiple linear regression between entrepreneurial profile, social network, and market knowledge

Model		Unstandardized coefficients		Standardized coefficients	T	Sig
		B	Standard error	Beta		
1	(Constant)	-0.124	0.088		-1.41	0.160
	PRFL	0.291	0.102	0.257	2.85	0.005
	SONET	0.437	0.081	0.494	5.40	0.000

a. Dependent variable: **KNOW**

Table 5 Results of the multiple linear regression between entrepreneurial profile and social network

Model		Unstandardized coefficients		Standardized coefficients	T	Sig
		B	Standard error	Beta		
1	(Constant)	0.159	0.105		1.51	0.134
	PRFL	0.475	0.118	0.386	4.02	0.000

a. Dependent variable: **SONET**

analyzing both the direct effects of the entrepreneurial profile and social network, as well as the mediating effect of market knowledge.

The logistic regression results show that both the entrepreneurial profile (**$\beta = 0.89, p < 0.01$**) and the social network (**$\beta = 1.15, p < 0.001$**) significantly increase the likelihood of opportunity recognition.

Market information knowledge, awareness of consumer problems, and understanding of various ways to serve the market have a positive effect on opportunity recognition (**$p = 0.002$**).

These results align with the established view that possessing clear and comprehensive market knowledge enables entrepreneurs to better perceive and seize opportunities (Omrane, 2013; Shane, 2003).

Table 6 Direct effect of entrepreneurial profile and social network on opportunity recognition (Binary Logistic Regression)

Predictor	B	S.E	Wald	*p*-value	Exp(B)
Constant	-1.12	0.52	4.63	0.031	0.33
Entrepreneurial Profile (PRFL)	0.89	0.32	7.73	0.005	2.43
Social Network (SONET)	1.15	0.28	16.88	0.000	3.16

Note Dependent variable: **Opportunity Recognition** (OPP, binary). Model fit: $\chi^2(2) = 28.3$, $p < 0.001$. Nagelkerke $R^2 = 0.38$. Classification accuracy = 79%

Table 7 Indirect effect of entrepreneurial profile and social network on opportunity recognition via market knowledge (mediation analysis)

Path	B	S.E	Test	*p*-value	Analysis type
PRFL → KNOW	0.26	0.10	2.60	0.011	Linear regression
SONET → KNOW	0.43	0.08	5.38	0.000	Linear regression
KNOW → OPP	0.97	0.31	9.78	0.002	Logistic regression
PRFL → OPP (w/ KNOW)	0.42	0.34	1.53	0.126	Logistic regression
SONET → OPP (w/ KNOW)	0.77	0.29	7.05	0.008	Logistic regression

Note KNOW = Market Knowledge. OPP = Opportunity Recognition. Partial mediation observed for Social Network (SONET), and absence of mediation for entrepreneurial profile (PRFL)

Table 8 Summary of main findings

Research hypotheses	Results
H1. The profile of the entrepreneur (soft and technological skills) explains positively the discovery of new knowledge on the market	Validated
H2. The social network—augmented by the use of artificial intelligence—enhances the entrepreneur's ability to acquire and interpret information about the market, customer preferences, and strategies for market entry	Validated
H3. The profile of the entrepreneur (soft and technological skills) enhances his ability to perceive, interpret, and act upon valuable information within his social network	Validated
H4. Market knowledge, enriched by artificial intelligence, positively influences the entrepreneur's ability to recognize and exploit entrepreneurial opportunities	Validated

Results show that market knowledge significantly mediates the effect of the social network, indicating that stronger social ties enhance access to relevant market information, which in turn improves the perception of opportunities (indirect effect: $\boldsymbol{p < 0.01}$). However, no significant indirect effect is observed for the entrepreneurial profile ($\boldsymbol{p = 0.126}$), suggesting that this trait does not influence opportunity recognition through market knowledge. These findings underscore the selective mediating role of market knowledge in linking social capital to entrepreneurial opportunity identification.

Table 8 summarizes the main findings of the statistical analysis.

7 Conclusion

This research provides significant theoretical and empirical insights into how artificial intelligence (AI) transforms entrepreneurial opportunity recognition. Grounded in the opportunity-based view (Shane & Venkataraman, 2000), the study expands the conceptual framework by integrating AI as a key enabler of entrepreneurial cognition, behavior, and network dynamics. It emphasizes the evolving entrepreneurial profile—characterized by digital fluency, strategic adaptability, creativity, and emotional regulation—as a central construct influenced by AI.

Practically, the study offers actionable implications for entrepreneurs, educators, and policymakers. For entrepreneurs, the study highlights the urgent need to actively develop AI literacy—not only by understanding how AI tools function, but also by learning how to select, evaluate, and apply them in business contexts. This includes using AI for opportunity recognition, customer analysis, and process optimization. In parallel, entrepreneurs must cultivate key soft skills such as synchronicity—being able to align actions with changing market signals—adaptability in the face of technological disruptions, and risk-taking when experimenting with AI-driven business models. These competencies are essential for navigating the uncertainty that often accompanies AI integration, and for seizing the competitive advantages it offers.

Educators are encouraged to redesign entrepreneurship education by embedding experiential learning opportunities and AI-based scenarios that reflect real-world challenges. This approach enables learners to build practical digital competencies while also strengthening critical thinking, collaboration, and innovation capacity. For policymakers, the study calls for the creation of inclusive, AI-enabled entrepreneurial ecosystems. This includes facilitating access to digital infrastructure and data, supporting funding mechanisms for startups, and encouraging public–private partnerships to drive innovation. Moreover, entrepreneurship support programs—often shaped or financed by policy frameworks—should incorporate AI-related training and coaching that address both technological awareness and human-centered capabilities.

However, the research has limitations. It is context-bound to the Japanese innovation ecosystem, which may constrain the transferability of findings to other cultural or institutional settings. The cross-sectional design also limits insight into the temporal evolution of AI's effects on entrepreneurship. Future studies could benefit from longitudinal approaches, multi-country comparisons, and qualitative explorations to refine the causal relationships identified and to capture deeper cognitive and behavioral mechanisms.

8 Summary

The study demonstrates that AI is a transformative enabler in the entrepreneurial process, not only automating tasks but also augmenting the entrepreneur's strategic, social, and cognitive capacities. By embedding AI into the theoretical framework of opportunity recognition, the research offers new insights into how future entrepreneurs can combine human creativity with machine intelligence to navigate complex markets.

References

Al-Mamary, Y. H. (2025). The transformative power of artificial intelligence in entrepreneurship: Exploring AI's capabilities for the success of entrepreneurial ventures. *Futur Bus J, 11*, 104. https://doi.org/10.1186/s43093-025-00533-7

Aldrich, H.E., & Ruef, M. (2018). *Organizations evolving* (3rd ed.). Sage.

Arora, A., & Rahman, Z. (2023). Artificial intelligence and entrepreneurial networking: Challenges and opportunities. *Journal of Business Research, 158*, Article 113614. https://doi.org/10.1016/j.jbusres.2023.113614

Baron, R. A. (2006). Opportunity recognition as pattern recognition: How entrepreneurs "connect the dots" to identify new business opportunities. *Academy of Management Perspectives, 20*, 104–119. https://doi.org/10.5465/amp.2006.19873412

Billings, R. S., Milburn, T. W., & Schaalman, M. L. (1980). A model of crisis perception: A theoretical and empirical analysis. *Administrative Science Quarterly, 25*, 300–316.

Borchani, M., Aloulou, W., & Boujelbene, Y. (2011). *Identifying opportunities by nascent entrepreneurs in Sfax region*. Conference paper AIMS, August.

Brem, A., Giones, F., & Werle, M. (2021). The AI digital revolution in innovation: A conceptual framework of artificial intelligence technologies for the management of innovation. *IEEE Transactions on Engineering Management, 70*(2), 770–776. https://doi.org/10.1109/TEM.2021.3109983

Burt, R. S. (2004). Structural holes and good ideas. *American Journal of Sociology, 110*(2), 349–399.

Carolus, J., Kriegel, M., & Teschner, F. (2023). MAILS: A multidimensional AI literacy scale for entrepreneurs. *Journal of Technological Innovation and Entrepreneurship, 31*(2), 45–67. https://doi.org/10.1108/JTI-03-2022-0005

Caliendo, M., Fossen, F. M., & Kritikos, A. S. (2009). Risk attitudes of nascent entrepreneurs—New evidence from an experimentally validated survey. *Small Business Economics, 32*, 153–167. https://doi.org/10.1007/s11187-008-9159-5

Chirita, M.-G., Masson, M.-A., & Ananou, C. (2012). Construire et développer une opportunité entrepreneuriale par la démarche SynOpp. *Entreprendre & Innover, 15*(3), 66–76. https://doi.org/10.3917/entin.015.0066

Chollet, B., Pirnay, F., & Dhez, F. (2009). Le rôle des réseaux dans la dynamique entrepreneuriale: Une approche par la structuration. *Revue de l'entrepreneuriat, 8*(2), 33–54.

Cleantech Group (2024). *Global Cleantech 100 Report 2024*. Cleantech Group, San Francisco, CA. https://www.cleantech.com/reports/global-cleantech-100

Cockburn, I. M., Henderson, R., & Stern, S. (2018). *The impact of artificial intelligence on innovation*. NBER Working Paper Series, Working Paper 24449. https://doi.org/10.3386/w24449

Daugherty, P. R., & Wilson, H. J. (2018). *Human + machine: Reimagining work in the age of AI*. Harvard Business Review Press.

Degeorge, J.-M., Fayolle, A., & Randerson, K. (2018). L'opportunité entrepreneuriale au cœur d'un processus de réflexion et d'action. *Recherches en Sciences de Gestion, 126*(3), 57–81. https://doi.org/10.3917/resg.126.0057

Diandra, D., & Azmy, A. (2020). Understanding definition of entrepreneurship. *International Journal of Management, Accounting and Economics, 7*(5), 235–241.

Dwivedi, Y. K., Hughes, D. L., Ismagilova, E., Aarts, G., Coombs, C., Crick, T., & Williams, M. D. (2021). Artificial intelligence (AI): Multidisciplinary perspectives on emerging challenges, opportunities, and agenda for research, practice and policy. *International Journal of Information Management, 57*, Article 101994. https://doi.org/10.1016/j.ijinfomgt.2019.08.002

Floridi, L. (2021). *Ethics, governance, and policies in artificial intelligence*. Oxford Internet Institute, University of Oxford.

Goyal, N., & Howerton, E. (2024). The dark side of recommendation systems in entrepreneurial networks. *Journal of Technology and Innovation Management, 39*(1), 55–72.

Granovetter, M. (1973). The strength of weak ties. *American Journal of Sociology, 78*(6), 1360–1380.

Guetaya, L., Addoumi, N., Bougrine, K., & Douari, A. (2024). Innovations disruptives: l'entrepreneuriat dans l'ère de l'intelligence artificielle. *African Scientific Journal, 3*(25), 273–295. https://doi.org/10.5281/zenodo.13173546

Hoang, H., & Antoncic, B. (2003). Network-based research in entrepreneurship: A critical review. *Journal of Business Venturing, 18*(2), 165–187.

Iansiti, M., & Lkhani, K. R. (2020). Competing in the age of AI: Strategy and leadership when algorithms and networks rules. *Harvard Business Review, 1*(98), 60–66.

Lamine, W., & Fayolle, A. (2014). Compétences sociales et réseau entrepreneurial: le cas des créations d'entreprises technologiques. *Entreprendre & Innover*, (1), 95–106. https://doi.org/10.3917/entin.020.0095

Lexcellent, C. (2019). Artificial intelligence according to Laurent Alexandre. In *Artificial intelligence versus human intelligence*. SpringerBriefs in Applied Sciences and Technology (pp. 23–27). Springer. https://doi.org/10.1007/978-3-030-21445-6_3

Lins, K. V., Servaes, H., & Tamayo, A. (2021). Social capital, trust, and firm performance: The value of corporate social responsibility during the financial crisis. *Journal of Finance, 76*(2), 775–818. https://doi.org/10.1111/jofi.13014

Liu, Y., & Singh, P. (2021). Artificial intelligence for entrepreneurial ecosystems: Mapping, prediction, and optimization. *Entrepreneurship Research Journal, 11*(4). https://doi.org/10.1515/erj-2020-0327

Li, Z., Li, Q., & Zhao, X. (2025). Research on enterprises' responses to artificial intelligence from the perspective of opportunity–threat perception. *Journal of Manufacturing Technology Management, 36*(6), 1328–1349. https://doi.org/10.1108/JMTM-09-2024-0539

Müller, J. M., Kiel, D., & Voigt, K. I. (2018). What drives the implementation of industry 4.0? The role of opportunities and challenges in the context of sustainability. *Sustainability, 10*(1), 247. https://doi.org/10.3390/su10010247

Nanan-Vallée, L., & Aka, J.-B. (2024). Intelligence artificielle et entrepreneuriat. *Communication, Technologies et Développement, 16*, 1–12. https://doi.org/10.4000/ctd.12942

Nunnally, J. C., & Bernstein, I. H. (1994). *Psychometric theory* (3rd ed.). McGraw-Hill.

Omrane, A. (2013). Entrepreneurial learning, market orientation, and the role of social networks: A study of Tunisian technology-based firms. *Journal of Small Business and Enterprise Development, 20*(3), 408–430. https://doi.org/10.1108/JSBED-04-2013-0056

Quintejgal, K., & Cherradi, L. (2025). Entrepreneuriat en technologies propres: Opportunités et enjeux à l'ère de l'intelligence artificielle. *African Scientific Journal, 3*(29), 674–697. https://doi.org/10.5281/zenodo.15319284

Shane, S. (2012). The importance of angel investing in financing the growth of entrepreneurial ventures. *Quarterly Journal of Finance, 2*, 901–942. https://doi.org/10.1142/S2010139212500097

Shane, S. (2003). *A general theory of entrepreneurship: The individual-opportunity nexus*. Edward Elgar Publishing.

Shane, S., & Venkataraman, S. (2000). The promise of entrepreneurship as a field of research. *Academy of Management Review, 25*(1), 217–226.

Shepherd, D. A., & Gruber, M. (2020). The role of hope in enterpreneurial process. *Academy of Management Review. 45*(4), 785–812.

Srinivasan, R., Beitelspacher, L., & Teichert, T. (2023). AI-enabled CRM and customer relationships: New opportunities for entrepreneurs. *Journal of Business Research, 152*, Article 112045. https://doi.org/10.1016/j.jbusres.2022.112045

Sun, Y., & Li, X. (2022). Predictive network analysis for entrepreneurial success using machine learning. *Technological Forecasting and Social Change, 179*, Article 121622. https://doi.org/10.1016/j.techfore.2022.121622

Tang, J., Kacmar, K. M. M., & Busenitz, L. (2012). Entrepreneurial alertness in the pursuit of new opportunities. *Journal of Business Venturing, 27*(1), 77–94. https://doi.org/10.1016/j.jbusvent.2010.07.001

Turkle, S. (2023). *The empathy diaries: A memoir*. Penguin Books.

Vincent, J. (2017). John Deere is buying an AI startup to help teach its tractors how to farm. *The Verge*.

Vuarin, L., Lopes, P. G., & Massé, D. (2023). L'intelligence artificielle peut-elle être une innovation responsable ? *Innovations, 72*(3), 103–147.

Zhang, W., Ma, X., & Luo, J. (2022). AI and the social fabric of startups: A review and future directions. *Small Business Economics, 58*(1), 23–45. https://doi.org/10.1007/s11187-021-00470-5

Zhao, H., Seibert, S. E., & Hills, G. E. (2005). The mediating role of self-efficacy in the development of entrepreneurial intentions. *Journal of Applied Psychology, 90*(6), 1265–1272. https://doi.org/10.1037/0021-9010.90.6.1265

Hajer Najeh is a Doctor of Management Sciences and Assistant Master at the Higher Institute of Management in Gabon-Tunisia, whose work focuses on technological innovation, strategic behavior of SMEs and key competences. The basis of her research is mainly inspired by the Japanese model.

Her research and writings focus on technological and behavioral competencies, the link between corporate social responsibility (CSR) and innovation, and entrepreneurial behavior and its impact on the success and failure of entrepreneurs. Her recent work focuses on the resilience of organizations and people in crisis, artificial intelligence, and its impact on the entrepreneurial process.

GPSR Compliance
The European Union's (EU) General Product Safety Regulation (GPSR) is a set of rules that requires consumer products to be safe and our obligations to ensure this.

If you have any concerns about our products, you can contact us on

ProductSafety@springernature.com

In case Publisher is established outside the EU, the EU authorized representative is:

Springer Nature Customer Service Center GmbH
Europaplatz 3
69115 Heidelberg, Germany

www.ingramcontent.com/pod-product-compliance
Ingram Content Group UK Ltd.
Pitfield, Milton Keynes, MK11 3LW, UK
UKHW021838081026
476418UK00002B/41
9789819549085